REVOLUTIONARY PATH

REVOLUTIONARY PATH

KWAME NKRUMAH

INTERNATIONAL PUBLISHERS   New York

*

ISBN (Cloth) 0–7178–0400–3; (Paperback) 0–7178–0401–1
Library of Congress Catalog Card Number 73–78905

Printed in the United States of America

CONTENTS

6

7

PUBLISHER'S NOTE

This book, published posthumously, was compiled during the last two years of the author's life. It was begun in response to many requests for a single volume which would contain key documents, some of them previously unpublished, relating to the development and consistency of Kwame Nkrumah's political thought, and which would at the same time illustrate landmarks in his career as a leading theorist and activist of the African Revolution.

Many of the introductory passages to the documents, specially those in the last half of Part Two, and the general Introduction to Part Three, were written when the illness which finally overcame him was far advanced, and when he was in considerable pain. The Conclusion to the book was dictated by him in October 1971, in a clinic in Bucarest, Romania, where he was receiving medical treatment. Kwame Nkrumah of Africa died in Bucarest six months later, on the 27th of April 1972. He died far from his beloved Africa, and fighting to the last to recover his health so that he might continue to serve the people of Africa and the cause which filled his whole life, the ending of all forms of exploitation and oppression, and the building of a world in which all may live in dignity and peace.

PART ONE

THE STRUGGLE FOR NATIONAL LIBERATION

1

From the Foreword to the 1962 edition of *Towards Colonial Freedom*

'In 1942 when I was a student in the United States of America, I was so revolted by the ruthless colonial exploitation and political oppression of the people of Africa that I knew no peace. The matter exercised my mind to such a degree that I decided to put down my thoughts in writing and to dilate on the results of some of my research concerning the subject of colonialism and imperialism.

My studies at that time, however, left me little time to devote to this work, and it was not until I arrived in London in 1945 and came face to face with the colonial question, experiencing first hand the determination of worker and student bodies fighting and agitating for colonial freedom in the very heart of a country that possessed a vast colonial empire, that I was stimulated to complete this booklet.

It was not really surprising that in spite of much effort on my part, I was unable to find anybody who would undertake to publish my work at that time. I managed to get a few copies printed privately, and these in turn were copied by mimeograph and other means, and distributed to those actively engaged in the freedom movement of Africa.'

But it was not until 1962 that the work was published in London. It was printed exactly as it was originally written. No changes or corrections were made, and nothing was added or taken from it. The views I expressed then are precisely the views I hold today concerning the nature of imperialism and colonialism. Furthermore, most of the points I made then have been borne out to the letter, and confirmed by subsequent developments in Africa and Asia.

There is, however, one matter on which my views have been expanded, and that is regarding African unification. When *Towards Colonial Freedom* was written, my ideas on African unity, important even as I considered them at that time, were limited to West African unity as a first step. Since I have had the opportunity of putting my ideas to work, and in the intensification of neocolonialism, I lay even greater stress on the vital importance to Africa's survival of a political unification of the entire African continent. Regional groupings, specially when based purely on economic co-operation, in areas which are already dominated by neocolonialist interests, retard rather than promote the unification process.

TOWARDS COLONIAL FREEDOM

PREFACE

This essay affirms, and postulates as inevitable, the national solidarity of colonial peoples and their determination to end the political and economic power of colonial governments. The purpose of this pamphlet is to analyse colonial policies, the colonial mode of production and distribution and of imports and exports. It is to serve as a rough blue-print of the processes by which colonial peoples can establish the realization of their complete and unconditional independence.

14

We have read articles, papers, pamphlets and books on the subject and are weary of the platitudes of their authors and distortion of facts. We have written as we see the facts and are indebted to no one but our own conscience quickened by the rich revolutionary heritage of historical epochs.

The point of view maintained in this pamphlet stands in an uncompromising opposition to all colonial policies. It exposes the inherent contradictions between (i) colonial labour and capital investments in the colonies, between (ii) the financial monopolist combines and the imperialist powers in their unquenchable thirst for colonies and the national aspirations of the colonial peoples, and between (iii) the stated policies of the colonial governments and the practical application of these policies in the colonial areas.

Those who formulate the colonial issue in accordance with the false point of view of colonial powers, who are deluded by the futile promises of 'preparing' colonial peoples for 'self-government', who feel that their imperialist oppressors are 'rational' and 'moral' and will relinquish their 'possessions' if only confronted with the truth of the injustice of colonialism are tragically mistaken. Imperialism knows no law beyond its own interests.

Kwame Nkrumah

London,
October, 1947.

INTRODUCTION

Colonial existence under imperialist conditions necessitates a fierce and constant struggle for emancipation from the yoke of colonialism and exploitation. The aim of all colonial governments in Africa and elsewhere has been the struggle for raw materials; and not only this, but the colonies have become the dumping ground, and colonial peoples the false recipients, of manufactured goods of the industrialists and capitalists of Great Britain, France, Belgium and other colonial powers who turn to the dependent territories which feed their industrial plants. This is colonialism in a nutshell.

The basis of colonial territorial dependence is economic, but the basis of the solution of the problem is political. Hence political independence is an indispensable step towards securing economic emancipation. This point of view irrevocably calls for an alliance of all colonial territories and dependencies. All provincial and tribal differences should be broken down completely. By operating on tribal differences and colonial provincialism, the colonial powers' age-long policy of 'divide and rule' has been enhanced, while the colonial national independence movement has been obstructed and bamboozled. The effort of colonial peoples to end colonial exploitation demands the eager and earnest collaboration of all of them. They must bring into its service all their energies, physical, mental, economic and political.

Beneath the 'humanitarian' and 'appeasement' shibboleths of colonial governments, a proper scrutiny leads one to discover nothing but deception, hypocrisy, oppression and exploitation. Such expressions as 'colonial charter', 'trusteeship', 'partnership', 'guardianship', 'international colonial commission', 'dominion status', 'condominium', 'freedom from fear of permanent subjection', 'constitutional reform' and other shabby sham gestures of setting up a fake machinery for 'gradual evolution towards self-government' are means to cover the eyes of colonial peoples with the veil of imperialist chicanery. But the eyes of colonial peoples are beginning to see the light of day and are awakening to the true meaning of colonial policies. China discovered it; India has discovered it; Burma, Netherlands East Indies, French Indo-China, the Caribbean Islands and Africa are awakening to such a discovery.

The idea that Britain, France or any other colonial power is holding colonies under 'trusteeship' until, in their opinion, the colonies become 'capable' of self-government is erroneous and misconceived. Colonial powers cannot afford to expropriate themselves. And then to imagine that these colonial powers will hand freedom and independence to their colonies on a silver platter without compulsion is the height of folly.

Let us take for example, Britain.* In an attempt to reconcile the inherent contradictions within her capitalistic economy, she has two courses only left to keep her home population from starvation; either her population must be dispersed in the colonial territories, or she must guarantee subsistence to them by exploitation of the colonies. The former, if put into action, will ultimately necessitate agitation for dominion status or no less than independence by the white settlers, as was the case in colonial America or in the Union of South Africa. Such a step may also lead to 'race' conflict between the settlers and the aborigines, as is now the case in the Union of South

* I have made constant reference to Britain and her relation to her African colonies not because she is an isolated case but because she is the greatest colonial power of modern times. Although I have concentrated on colonial Africa, the thesis of the pamphlet applies to colonial areas everywhere.

Africa. The latter is 'natural', since Britain or any other colonial power depends on the exports of her manufactured goods and the cheap imports of raw materials.

The colonies are thus a source of raw materials and cheap labour, and a 'dumping ground' for spurious surplus goods to be sold at exorbitant prices. Therefore these colonies become avenues for capital investments, not for the benefit and development of the colonial peoples, but for the benefit of the investors, whose agents are the governments concerned. That is why it is incoherent nonsense to say that Britain or any other colonial power has the 'good intention' of developing her colonies for self-government and independence. The only thing left for the colonial peoples to do is to obtain their freedom and independence from these colonial powers.

Whatever camouflage colonial governments may decide upon, be it in the form of appeasements cloaked in 'constitutional reforms' or the 'Pan Africanism'* of Jan Smuts, there is only one road, the road of the national liberation movement, to colonial independence. It cannot come through delegations, gifts, charity, paternalism, grants, concessions, proclamations, charters or reformism, but only through the complete change of the colonial system, a united effort to unscramble the whole colonial egg of the last hundred years, a complete break of the colonial dependencies from their 'mother countries' and the establishment of their complete independence.

I: COLONIALISM AND IMPERIALISM

The basic driving force today is economic, and economics are at the root of other types of imperialism. However, there have been three fundamental doctrines in the philosophical analysis of imperialism: (a) the doctrine of exploitation; (b) the doctrine of 'trusteeship' or

* This plan proposes to group the various colonial territories of the several powers in Africa into loose geographical regions. Each group of territories would be covered by a central Regional Council on which would sit representatives of the various powers possessing colonies in that respective zone. In addition to these, there will be also representatives of other powers having only strategic commercial interests in that area, sitting in that council.

Behind Jan Smuts' regional plan (condominium) is a conscious drive for wider markets for the output of raw commodity interests which the war had inaugurated and expanded in the colonial areas. It is a subterfuge attempt to give assistance to the annexationist powers to exploit Africa on a wider scale. It offers ample opportunities for colonial annexations for which the anachronistic mandate system has already paved the way.

'partnership' (to use its contemporary counterpart); and (c) the doctrine of 'assimilation'. The exponents of these doctrines believe implicitly and explicitly in the right of stronger peoples to exploit weaker ones to develop world resources, and 'civilize' backward peoples against their will.

In general, imperialism is the policy which aims at creating, organizing and maintaining an empire. In other words, it is a state, vast in size, composed of various distinct national units, and subject to a single, centralized power or authority. This is the conception of empire: divers peoples brought together by force under a common power. It goes back to the idea of Alexander the Great with his Graeco-Asiatic empire. He conquered the then known world, and sat down and wept because he had no more territory to conquer. The imperialism of Julius Caesar needs no comment here. Modern imperialism, however, must be distinguished from that of the ancients exemplified by Caesar and Alexander the Great. Neither the Norman conquest nor the annexations of Frederick the Great, nor the expansions of the American pioneers into the western plains can be called imperialism, but the annexation of one nation or state by another and the application of a superior technological strength by one nation for the subjugation and the economic exploitation of a people or another nation constitutes outright imperialism.

Colonialism is, therefore, the policy by which the 'mother country', the colonial power, binds her colonies to herself by political ties with the primary object of promoting her own economic advantages. Such a system depends on the opportunities offered by the natural resources of the colonies and the uses for them suggested by the dominant economic objectives of the colonial power. Under the influence of national aggressive self-consciousness and the belief that in trade and commerce one nation should gain at the expense of the other, and the further belief that exports must exceed imports in value, each colonial power pursues a policy of strict monopoly of colonial trade, and the building up of national power. The basic notion, that of strict political and economic control, governs the colonial policies of Britain, France, Belgium and other modern colonial powers.

The dominant reasons for the quest for colonies* and particularly

* The term colony originally meant a transplanted organized group of people settling in a foreign land. In the political sense, a colony is either a settlement of the subjects of a nation or state beyond its frontiers, or a territorial unit geographically separated from, but owing allegiance to, it. Thus modern colonial history exhibits two types of colonies: a settlement colony and an exploitation colony. A settlement colony is one in which the

the penetration into Africa by European capitalist powers were stated by Jules Ferry, the master of imperialistic logic, in a statement made by him in 1885 in the Chamber of Deputies while speaking in defence of the colonial policy of the government of France, of which he was then the Premier. Ferry said: 'The nations of Europe desire colonies for the following three purposes: (i) in order that they may have access to the raw materials of the colonies; (ii) in order to have markets for sale of the manufactured goods of the home country; and (iii) as a field for the investment of surplus capital.'

Albert Sarraut, Colonial Secretary of State for France in 1923, at the École Coloniale, Paris, said: 'What is the use of painting the truth? At the start, colonization was not an act of civilization, was not a desire to civilize. It was an act of force motivated by interests. An episode in the vital competition which, from man to man, from group to group, has gone on ever-increasing; the people who set out for taking and making of colonies in distant continents are thinking primarily only of themselves, and are working only for their own power, and conquering for their own profits.' Sarraut concluded his speech with these words, and thus exposed the falsehood of the 'white man's burden', and the 'mission civilisatrice' policy in colonization: 'The origin of colonization is nothing else than enterprise of individual interests, a one-sided and egotistical imposition of the strong upon the weak.' Such is the phenomenon of European capitalist aggressiveness, one which has been rightly termed 'colonial imperialism'.

Our best illustration is the 'scramble for Africa', which began when the economic insufficiency of Great Britain, France, Germany, Spain, Portugal, Belgium and Italy impelled their political leaders to look beyond the seas for markets and storehouses of wealth and resources in order to consolidate their individual states and guarantee their economic security.

In 1881 France extended her colonial sway over Tunis and, the year following, Britain secured control over Egypt. In 1884 the first German colony was established at Angra Pequena Bay in South-West Africa. The occupation of Togoland and Cameroons in West Africa followed. The spectacular advent of Germany as a colonial power provoked the jealousy of France. A French force was

---

geographical and racial environment is not very different from that of the 'mother country', while an exploitation colony consists typically of groups of business men, monopolist combines, cartels, trusts, administrators, soldiers and missionaries – all of which are thrust and dumped into conditions and environment quite different from their home country.

despatched to seize the unoccupied territory between the Cameroons and the Portuguese colony of Angola. This became the French Congo. In 1894 the tricolour was raised over Timbuktu, Dahomey and the Ivory Coast. The whole of the western Sudan was soon under French occupation. In 1885 a protectorate was established over Madagascar.

Then ensued the Anglo-French colonial jealousy which culminated in a crisis in 1898 when the occupation of the Sudanese port of Fashoda threatened to upset Britain's colonial annexations within that area. France withdrew and the Eastern Sudan came under the control of Britain.

France then began to make advance towards the conquest of Morocco. Such action contravened the intention of Germany. A dispute between France and Germany arose which resulted in the calling of a conference of the colonial powers at Algeria, in 1905, which left Morocco open to the penetration of all the other nations. But the right of France and Spain was recognized as a sort of joint protectorate over Morocco. In 1911 Germany raised further colonial claims and succeeded in buying a slice of the French Congo.

Italy felt herself cheated of a possible field of expansion by the moves of Britain and France. This was one of the results of the formation of the Triple Alliance. A colonial rush to secure some parts of Africa now took place. In 1882 Italy occupied Assab, and three years later Massawa was taken. In 1898 Italian Somaliland was formed into a colony. Abyssinians revolted and the battle of Adowa ensued. Italy was defeated.

In 1876 the International African Association was formed under the direction of Leopold II, King of Belgium, for the occupation of the Congo Basin. In 1885 at a conference held in Berlin, Leopold obtained permission of the other colonial powers to erect these Belgian settlements into a 'Congo Free State' under his 'protection'. The cruel treatment meted out by the Belgians to the Africans in the colonies is a common story in colonial exploitation.

Thus Africa became not only the market for European goods but a field for capital investments. As British, German, French and European industry was organized the products were divided between the entrepreneur and the capitalists, who got salaries and dividends at the expense of the African labourer.

The bankers of the European colonial powers had surplus capital to invest in competition with one another. To protect these investments they reduced the colonies to exploited subject status. It was circumstances like this that led to the rebellion of Egypt under Arabi

Pasha. While the French hesitated, Great Britain crushed the revolt and thus Egypt became a British colony. Briefly, then, imperialism in Africa was a direct answer for the capitalists, bankers and financiers of the colonial powers to the problem of how to accrue for themselves super profits from their foreign investments.

The fate of the colonies changes in accordance with the results of European imperialist wars. After the first World War (1914), Great Britain received German East Africa, a quarter of Togoland and a piece of the Cameroons. France took over the remaining three-quarters of Togoland and a greater part of the Cameroons, while Belgium and Portugal got slices of German East Africa. The Union of South Africa received German South-West Africa.

Thus present day partitioning of Africa falls into the following colonial regions:

I. NORTH AFRICA, includes: (1) Rio de Oro (Spanish); (2) Morocco (French); (3) Algeria (French); (4) Tunisia (French); (5) Libya (formerly Italian); (6) Egypt (independent); (7) Anglo-Egyptian Sudan (British).

II. EAST AFRICA, includes: (1) Kenya (British); (2) Uganda (British); (3) Tanganyika (British); (4) Nyasaland (British); (5) Portuguese East Africa; (6) Abyssinia (Independent); (7) The Somalilands (British, French, Italian).

III. SOUTH AFRICA,* includes: (1) The Union of South Africa (European rule) and the mandated territories of South-West Africa.

IV. WEST AFRICA, includes: (1) Senegal (French); (2) Ivory Coast (French); (3) Portuguese Guinea; (4) French Sudan; (5) Liberia (Independent); (6) Dahomey (French); (7) French Equatorial Africa; (8) Belgian Congo; (9) The Cameroons (British and French); (10) Angola (Portuguese); (11) Gambia (British); (12) Sierra Leone (British); (13) The Gold Coast (British); (14) Togoland (French mandate); (15) Nigeria (British).

* Nearly seven million Africans, almost three-fourths of the entire population of the Union of South Africa, possess less than twenty per cent of the total area of the Union. They are by law denied the right of acquiring more land either by purchase or by other means. Regardless of qualification, they are deprived of the right to vote in the regular parliamentary elections and are constitutionally denied the right to become members of the Union Parliament. Further, they are gravely limited in their right to organize, form trade unions, in their right to strike, to move about freely, to buy land to trade, to acquire education, and to aspire to full citizenship in their own country.

Since we feel that mercantilism – as an aspect of imperialism is – the *basis* of colonial economics, a brief history of the term is essential here. Mercantilism is a term applied to the economic policy which had its inception in Europe just at the close of the Middle Ages. In fact, it was the next historical development of feudalism. Its doctrine, in the extreme sense, made wealth and money identical; but as the years rolled on mercantile economists based the definition of the system on money exclusively. Money was therefore regarded as the main object of a community. Thus it was held that the community must confine itself to dealing with other nations on such lines as would attract the most possible precious metals to itself. This method of trade among nations led to what is known in the realm of economics as the 'balance of trade', which meant the relationship of equilibrium between export and import.

Eventually, this system of 'balance of trade' was considered favourable when more money was received into the country than was paid out. To assure a favourable balance of trade, governments of nations resorted to certain economic and political expedients. For instance: (i) high duties on imports; (ii) exports of home manufactured goods; (iii) receiving only raw materials from other countries; (iv) restrictions on the exports of precious metals; (v) exaltation of foreign trade over domestic trade; (vi) organizing of industries and factories at home; (vii) the importance of dense population as an element of national strength to safeguard foreign trade, and last but not least; (viii) the employment of state action in furthering such ends.

Governments took great interest in these mercantile programmes because they needed money and men for the maintenance of the army and for the unification of their national states. Thus statesmen and business aristocracy conjectured that for them to further their political and economic ambitions successfully, industries and the mercantile system must prosper. Eventually, this conception of trade led to the great problem of colonization.

The purpose of founding colonies was mainly to secure raw materials. To safeguard the measures for securing such raw materials the following policies were indirectly put into action: (i) to make the colonies non-manufacturing dependencies; (ii) to prevent the colonial subjects from acquiring the knowledge of modern means and techniques for developing their own industries; (iii) to make colonial 'subjects' simple producers of raw materials through cheap labour; (iv) to prohibit the colonies from trading with other nations except through the 'mother country'. The methods employed by the imperialists today are developments of mercantilism.

Colonial economics may be traced through three main phases corresponding to its history. The mercantile period, the free-trade period and the period of economic imperialism, all being respectively dominated by merchant capital, industrial capital and finance capital. We are here mainly concerned with the last phase, economic imperialism with its dominance of finance capital.

The most searching and penetrating analysis of economic imperialism has been given by Marx and Lenin. According to the Marx-Lenin point of view, economic imperialism is not only the natural stage in the development of the capitalist system, but its highest stage in which the inner contraditions and inconsistencies of the system foreshadow its doom and demolition.

The Marxist-Leninist position may be stated thus: In the capitalist system of production labour is treated as a commodity to be bought and sold in the market like any other commodity. As such, it figures in the capitalist-producer's calculations merely as one production cost among others. But since the system is a competitive system, the capitalist-producer is compelled to keep wages down in order to keep the margin of profit high. Here it becomes obvious that the economic philosophy of high wages, even though it may operate well in special industries whose circumstances favour a combination of high wages with low wage-costs per unit of production, cannot under capitalism be applied to industry as a whole. This means that under the capitalist system of production a point is soon reached where wages appear a necessary evil even to the capitalist-producer, who now realizes that the incomes distributed as wages form the body of the market for what he wants to sell. And since competition and the necessity of profit determine the outlook of capitalism, it cannot raise incomes 'up to the limits of productive capacity'.

The capitalist-producer, in seeking profit by limiting his wage bill, impedes his own effort to find buyers for the increasing volume of his production.

This dilemma becomes even more confounded by the introduction of combines and monopolies due to the fact that these combines and monopolies continue to compete with other combines and monopolies producing similar commodities in other countries. Thus complete elimination of competition from the capitalist system of production is not only a contradiction but an impossibility.

23

To find a way out of this contradiction the capitalist-producer turns his profit-seeking eyes to the colonies and dependent territories. He does so first by killing the arts and crafts in these areas through the competition of his cheaper machine-made goods (exports) and, secondly, by thrusting capital loans upon them for financing the construction of railways, harbours and other means of transportation and communication in so far as these constructions cater to his profits and safeguard his capital. Industrial capital thus fuses with finance capital.

It is when the number of the capitalist countries relying on foreign markets and fields of investment increases and the number of colonizable areas diminishes that rivalries among the colonial powers ensue, rivalries which issue first in minor wars of colonial conquests and later in the great imperialist wars of modern times. Lenin in his *Imperialism the Highest Stage of Capitalism,* summarizes the position thus:

Imperialism is capitalism in that stage of development in which the domination of monopolies and finance capital has taken shape; in which the export of capital has acquired pronounced importance; in which the division of the world by the international trusts has begun, and in which the partition of all the territory of the earth by the greatest capitalist countries has been completed.

The effect of this type of imperialism on colonial peoples is dramatic. The stage opens with the appearance of missionaries and anthropologists, traders and concessionaires, and administrators. While 'missionaries' with 'Christianity' perverted implore the colonial subject to lay up his 'treasures in Heaven where neither moth nor rust doth corrupt', the traders and concessionaires and administrators acquire his mineral and land resources, destroy his arts, crafts and home industries. Since the rise of colonial industry would entail more competition and undercutting, these finance-capital-producers and their imperialist cohorts do everything in their power to prevent its development.

Economic development in the colonial areas is perverted precisely because the monopoly stage, which should come as a logical advanced feature of capitalism, is introduced before even the most primitive manifestation of local capitalist development. Hence the stagnation and decay characteristic of colonial economy.

But the introduction of capitalism into the colonies does not take the 'normal' course it took in western countries. Free competition does not exist, and monopoly control of all resources of the colonies demonstrates the perversion of finance capital. It is canalized to

24

suit the monopolist combines and investors. The finance capitalist and investor find the easiest and richest profits not from establishing industry in the colonies, which would compete with home industries and necessitate a drastic rise in wages and a high standard of living in order to create a purchasing power formidable enough to render increased production possible, but by exhausting the natural and mineral resources of the colonies, and by considering their human resources just as another commodity to be used and thrown away.

This brings us to the question: what is the relationship between the monopolist, non-industrial economy engineered by the colonial powers in the colonies and the migrant labour system? Briefly and precisely, it is this: that the concentration of large bodies of colonial labourers in constant contact with realities of the most repressive and degrading conditions of life, leads to the creation of a class-conscious working class which is in a position to defend itself against its oppressors. At all costs the finance capitalist must prevent the formation of such a class-conscious group in order to prevent his destruction. This is the reason why colonial workers are recruited and forcibly broken up and disbanded every year by their capitalist exploiters, and compelled to retire to their homes and villages where capitalist exploitation is indirectly exercised through corrupted 'warrant' chiefs and a politically sold intelligentsia. Thus, resentment against the foreign capitalist oppressors is arrested, and conditions for mass organization against them aborted.

Take Britain, for instance, and see what she does in her African colonies. She controls exports of raw materials from the colonies by preventing direct shipment by her colonial 'subjects' to foreign markets, in order that, after satisfying the demands of her home industries, she can sell the surplus to other nations, netting huge super-profits for herself.

The colonial farmer-producer has no share in these profits. The question may be raised to the effect that the colonial powers utilize part of these profits for public works, health projects and 'loans'. The fact generally forgotten is that such 'loans' come from taxing the colonial 'subjects', and the profit gotten from their produce and mineral resources, and the greater part of these very loans is used in paying European officials in the colonies.

A recent White Paper* released by the Colonial Office reveals a fabulous profit of £3,676,253 sterling netted by the British Government from exploitation of 800,000 families of West African colonial cocoa farmers. This is how it was done: A Cocoa Control Board was

* Cmd. 6554. H.M. Stationery Office, London.

established by, and was responsible to, the Colonial Office, and acting as 'trustees' for the West African cocoa farmers, it was empowered to purchase the total production of cocoa, and to prescribe the prices to be paid to the farmers; and, not only this, but the board was also responsible for the general disposal of cocoa from the colonies. The Board, during the period from 1939–1943, squeezed out the aforesaid profit – a profit not shared by the colonial farmers. Such profits resulted from the fact that the cocoa for which the African farmer received one and one-fourth pence (two and one-half cents) a pound brought four pence (eight cents) and four and one-half (nine cents) a pound in London and New York, respectively. In short, while the African peasants' cost of living and demands on his labour were increasing, and his income falling, the monopolist chocolate combines were reaping super-profits.

We learned also of a fund called 'Aid for Colonial Development and Welfare', which provides £120,000,000 sterling in grants to the colonies. A little arithmetical reflection, however, shows that when the population of the colonial empire is taken into consideration the amount works out at eighteen pence (thirty-six cents) per inhabitant per year. During the first year and a half after the passage of the said Act the amount spent was two pence (four cents) per inhabitant per year. Nor is this all. The benefits of the Colonial Development Fund are largely illusory, since the £120,000,000 is not in the safe keeping of a Bank of the British Empire as such where any colonial territory can apply for the money it may need for its 'welfare development'. To simplify the issue: supposing, say, Nigeria needs £40,000 for its 'welfare development', the British Government in Nigeria then goes to Barclays Bank, which advances the £40,000 to the people of Nigeria at six per cent interest. On this basis the people of the 'colony' of Nigeria eventually find themselves in perpetual debt to the very agencies which are supposed to be concerned with their 'welfare development'. It is a common economic experience that wherever there is economic dependence there is no freedom.

The policy underlying the economic situation in the colonies is that of monopoly control forcing the farmer and peasant to accept low fixed prices by eliminating open competition, and forcing the same colonial farmer and peasant consumer to buy at high fixed prices. Marketing of produce and manufactured goods in the British West African colonies, for instance, is done by the European merchants, through a 'pool' system.

As a result of the operations of this monopolist combine and the mining companies, with the aid of their agency, the government, gold and money leave the country, and consequently no local capital is left in the colonies. Industrial and commercial aspirations and growth on the part of the colonial subjects is thus arrested; wages drop, and the colonial 'subject' finds it impossible to acquire capital of any sort for any business enterprise; and worse than this, whether as a wage earner or as a peasant, he is always in debt due to the fact that when he buys the manufactured goods he loses, and when he sells his produce he loses; and the colonial government sees that he remains in perpetual debt by further taxing him. The colonial subject is thus economically strangled by his very 'trustees' who are supposed to prepare him for self-government.

Furthermore, the colonial subject cannot go into any form of business and succeed because the wholesale prices charged by the monopolist combines leave him no margin of profits. And this in addition to the secret arrangements between the combines and the manufacturers makes it impossible for him to buy directly from the manufacturers. No matter how large an order he gives them, he is always referred to the local agents, who are members of the powerful monopolist combines.

Since the advent of capitalism into the colonies colonial peoples have been reduced to the level of labourers and contract bondsmen, and are unable to organize effectively due to government and monopolist combine interference. The philosophy of European capitalism in the colonies is that colonial subjects should labour under any foreign government with uncomplaining satisfaction. They are supposedly 'incapable' of developing the resources of their own country, and are taught to labour and appreciate European manufactured goods so as to become 'good' customers. The meagre stipend given to them as a wage by the European capitalists is spent on spurious imported manufactured goods, the only kind they get. Curiously enough, the same coin that is given to the 'native' as a wage by his exploiter eventually returns to the pocket of that wily exploiter.

The slogan 'buy British and trade imperial' is used to stimulate the maintenance of higher prices for British manufactured goods. 'Preferential tariff' (higher customs duties and low quotas) are applied on foreign manufactured goods. However, American goods are given much higher quotas than Japanese manufactured goods. In spite of the preferential duty the Japanese continued to produce cheaper goods and to export them to British colonies. In order to freeze the importation of cheaper-priced Japanese goods, the local governments of the British colonies, agents of British monopolist combines and industrialists, continued to raise the tariff on the Japanese goods and finally froze them out. This underlies the denunciation of the Anglo-Japanese Treaty of 1934.

Tariffs are usually applied to protect domestic economy, but this is not so in the colonies. For there tariffs are applied for the protection of British trade and profits since the colonies do not manufacture their own goods. The same preferential tariff that protects the imports of British manufactured goods also protects the produce and raw materials of the colonies (exports) against shipment to foreign countries except through British agencies. This is done to ensure much higher prices and therefore huge profits for the combines and companies. This is what we term the two-way fixed price system, basic in colonial economics. The object of this system is to buy cheap raw materials and labour from the colonies and to sell high-priced manufactured goods back to the colonies. It is the colonial peasants who suffer most considerably from this evil system. This again goes to prove that as long as colonial powers are able to keep the colonies under this economic system (importing only manufactured goods and exporting only raw materials and produce) colonial subjects will not progress to any notable extent and will always remain poverty stricken with a sub-normal standard of living.

That is one of the reasons why we maintain that the only solution to the colonial problem is the complete eradication of the entire economic system of colonialism, by colonial peoples, through their gaining political independence. Political freedom will open the way for the attainment of economic and social improvement and advancement. It must be otherwise under foreign rule.

THE LAND QUESTION

The alienation to Europeans of enormous tracts of land which were once available for African use, and the consequent rise of an alien absentee land interest, a class of European settlers and concessionaires, intent on raising the money value of their holdings and on acquiring political ascendancy as a means to that end, is the basic trend in the colonial land question.

The African is robbed of most of his lands, through legal extortion and forced concession. In the West African colonies, for example, where there is no personal private ownership of land, for all land belongs to some clan or tribe, the personal ownership of land always develops whenever colonial powers have disregarded the

African land-tenure system in favour of their own. For while agriculture, in its rude and infant stage, is primarily the 'affair' of the African clan or tribe, the mining and large plantations are entirely in the hands of the suzerain power itself or of foreign industrialists and capitalists.

The land question, like any other colonial question, is handled by the colonial powers in such a way as to yield maximum profits for their mining and plantation investments. In order to confiscate the land of colonial subjects certain devices are used. We enumerate the following, using British land confiscating tactics as a typical example.

(1) Britain, by certain 'legal' enactments, has secured direct and indirect ownership, control and possession of the land of colonies and protectorates. The Foreign Jurisdiction Act of 1890 is a good example of these 'legal' enactments. This Act contains the declaration that 'however the powers of the Crown might have been acquired, whether by treaty, grant, usage or other lawful means, its jurisdiction is as ample as if it had been derived from the cession or conquest of territory.' This abrogates her treaty relations with her colonies and gives her sole possession, outright ownership, of the colonies. Hence it becomes a mockery to speak of colonial lands as belonging to the colonial 'subjects', who only possess 'surface rights' when valuable minerals are found on such lands. Other colonial powers have also used similar enactments for the purpose of confiscating the colonial lands under their control.

(2) 'Ordinances' are passed to further the confiscating and exploiting effect. These 'ordinances' cause certain areas to be roped off for afforestation. These areas contain valuable mineral wealth. Thus, afforestation is simply the mask to delude the colonial people. However, the lands that are wanted for urgent profits, mining and plantation, are claimed outright by the 'Land Office' for the Crown. The *onus probandi* of ownership rests upon the rightful owner, the colonial 'subject', who suffers here because his ancestors were not required to register their lands.

(3) Ninety-year leases are drawn up and forced upon the colonial subjects by 'provincial commissioners', agents of the colonial powers. These leases grant concessions to private companies for exploiting the land and the mines. In some instances meagre and inadequate rentals are paid for the concessions of the land. This is an indirect method of the British of seizing land 'legally'. The French method of confiscating land differs from the British in that they make no pretence of seizure through 'legal' means but seize the land outright.

In East and South Africa the other European powers also use the 'outright seizure' method.*

(4) The latest development in the colonial land confiscating programme is the enactment of military defence acts, by which land in the colonies is being confiscated for ultimate use of the colonial and other capitalistic powers concerned.

3: Colonial Policies: Theory and Practice

Within the African continent there are different types of dependent areas: colonies, protectorates and mandates. In the British West African colonies, for example, each colony is under the direct control and administration† of the Colonial Office through its representative, the governor, who is also the Commander-in-Chief and Vice-Admiral of the colony and protectorate.

* In February, 1944, the Governor of Nigeria, in spite of strong opposition, passed a bill through the local legislature giving the British Government in Nigeria the right to take possession of all minerals discovered on land in the possession of Africans. This obnoxious law strikes at the very foundation of the West African land tenure system.

Under the Ashanti Concessions Ordinances of 1903, mineral rights in the Gold Coast remain with African authorities, but negotiations in connection with concessions are supervised by European District Commissioners and the British Government in the Gold Coast has control of all money derived from the sales. The concessions are not worked on a royalty basis, but at a fixed rental, very often as low as £50, and nowhere exceeding £400 per year.

† In the administration and legislation of colonial possession by the colonial powers, three basic principles may be distinguished:

(1) Most of the legislation for the colonies is enacted in the 'Mother Country' through her home legislative organ. Other supplementary legislation is enacted in the legislative councils of the colonies, the head of which is the governor, appointed by the Secretary of State for the Colonies. The governor is endowed with veto powers and is subject to no one but the government of the 'Mother Country'.

(2) Under the second type of colonial administration most of the legislation is supposed to be enacted by the colony itself. However, both the executive and the legislative councils in the colony are under strict and direct control of the all-powerful governor of the colony.

(3) The third system provides creation of a representative legislative body in the colony with official members appointed by the governor and unofficial members supposed to be elected by the people of the colony. The official members are in the majority and represent heads of the various governmental and commercial concerns.

Under these systems it is impossible to vote the 'government' out of office. In reality the legislative power rests basically with the parliaments of the 'Mother Countries'. In Great Britain this is justified by so-called 'royal prerogative', which allows the King to enact legislation for the colonial possessions. These systems also deliberately prevent and curb any aspirations towards independence on the part of the colonial peoples. In fact, such administrative systems are not only the embodiment of colonial chaos and political confusion but definitely nullify the ideas of true democracy.

Although colonial rules have drawn distinction between a colony and a protectorate, there is practically no difference of any legal validity between them in the international position.

The mandates were created after the First World War, when the former German territories in Africa were placed under the League of Nations. The underlying philosophy common to all mandates is the principle that the 'well-being and development of such peoples form a sacred trust of civilization'. The mandate system is a feeble and dangerous compromise between Wilsonian idealism, self-determination and the concept of trusteeship, on the one hand, and annexationists' ambition, political subjugation and economic exploitation, on the other. In other words, it is a cowardly compromise between the principle of self-determination for dependent territories and imperialism. It becomes nothing but a useful tool in the hands of the powers to whom the territories are mandated in order to carry out their intentions and to perpetuate the economic exploitation of these territories by a combination of colonial powers. The same consequences will follow if the newly-proposed international supervision of the dependent territories is carried out.

The doctrine of 'trusteeship' is supposed to be more humanitarian in its significance and approach than that of exploitation. It is the fundamental factor underlying the system of 'dual mandate', exponents of which think that exploitation involves a sacred duty towards the exploited peoples. The colonial subjects must be exploited and 'civilized', but, in doing so, their 'rights' must be 'respected' and 'protected'. The philosophy underlying this doctrine reminds us of an African saying that a mouse biting at the feet of its victim blows cool air from its mouth and nostrils on the spot to mitigate the pain it is inflicting. In other words, exploit the colonial peoples, but be cunning enough not to let them know that you are doing so. There are abundant proofs that the primary motives underlying the quest for colonies and the present administrative and

31

economic policies of the colonial powers are rooted in economic exploitation and not in humanitarianism.

The Conference of Berlin (1890), the Treaty of Versailles, the Covenant of the League of Nations, and the Trusteeship System of UNO, each and every one of these pacts contained provisions 'to protect and guard' colonial peoples. These provisions, however, were adopted to camouflage the economic philosophy of colonial powers so as to exploit with impunity. The material development – railways, roads bridges, schools, hospitals – which are noticeable in the colonies have been merely accidental adjuncts to facilitate economic exploitation of the colonies.

The colonial powers build hospitals because if the health of the colonial subjects is not taken care of it will not only jeopardize their own health but will diminish the productive power of the colonial labourer. They build schools in order to satisfy the demand for clerical activities and occupations for foreign commercial and mercantile concerns. The roads they build lead only to the mining and plantation centres. In short, any humanitarian act of any colonial power towards the 'ward' is merely to enhance its primary objective: economic exploitation. If it were not so, why haven't the West African colonies, for instance, been given the necessary training that provides for complete political and economic independence?

The attitude of Britain, France, Spain, Italy and other colonial powers towards what they call 'participation' by colonial peoples in colonial government and public affairs are half-way measures to keep them complacent and to throttle their aspiration for complete independence.

The principal difference between French and British colonial policies is that the former stands for 'assimilation', a centralized government with uniform policy decided upon in Paris, and considering the French colonies as almost a part of France, emphasizing the use of the French language and drawing a line of distinction between a limited élite (notables évolués) with many privileges, and the teeming ignorant masses in her colonies: the latter, on the other hand, stands for decentralization and disunity in her colonial areas; emphasis is on 'indirect rule', the encouragement of 'Africans to remain Africans'. It pretends to build up African culture, folkways, art and 'civilization' and to adjust the character of government to the special needs of different tribes and groups, systematic application of the 'divide and rule' policy, and the exhibition of scientific exploitation through 'practical anthropology'. Yet, paradoxically

32

enough, the full growth of industry in the colonies is arrested by the British.

Taking into account all of the arguments in favour of these colonial policies and the fact that the actual conditions in the colonies are not in harmony with the stated theories of colonial rule, and because such harmony is impossible, it will not be incorrect to say that democracy, self-determination, independence and self-government are incompatible with the doctrines of 'trusteeship', 'partnership', and 'assimilation'. Indirect rule, 'native administration' policies, social projects, agricultural planning, facilities for 'full participation' in government, condominium, regionalism and dominion status merely serve as means to one end: the perpetuation of foreign rule upon colonial peoples and the economic exploitation of their material resources and manpower for the benefit of the so-called 'mother countries'.

We therefore repeat that only the united movement of the colonial people, determined to assert its right to independence, can compel any colonial power to lay down its 'white man's burden', which rests heavily upon the shoulders of the so-called 'backward' peoples, who have been subjugated, humiliated, robbed and degraded to the level of cattle.

4: APOLOGY FOR APOLOGETICS

In the foregoing pages we have given the picture of the colonial situation as it exists and have demonstrated and exposed the contradictions between theories and practices of colonial rule. But before we make any suggestion as to what must be done for the liberation of the colonies we want to point out briefly the futility in the points of view advanced by some colonial and non-colonial writers in reference to the freedom and independence of the West African colonies. They speak of 'internal self-government' and gradual evolution to membership of the 'British Commonwealth'.

The stubborn fact these people fail to realize is that the imperialist governments stand for political and economic domination, no matter under what mask, 'democracy' or what not, and therefore will never give colonial subjects equal status with other dominions such as the Union of South Africa, Australia, New Zealand and Canada within the British Commonwealth of Nations. They forget that the British dominions are all in league with the financial oligarchy of Great

Britain for the exploitation of the colonies, and utterly fail to see the intimate connections between political domination and economic exploitation. They apparently ignore the fact that such steps as they propose in asking for gradual withdrawal of the political administration are in effect asking the 'mother country' to expropriate herself. Isn't economic exploitation the driving force and basic principle of colonization? Dominion status carries with it certain political as well as economic advantages which the 'mother country' is determined to deny the colonial dependencies. In considering the colonial question it is necessary to have a clear-cut distinction between those colonies of the capitalist countries which have served them as colonizing regions for their surplus population, and which in this way have become a continuation of their capitalist system (e.g. Australia, Canada, New Zealand, South Africa, etc.), and those colonies which are exploited by the imperialists primarily as sources of raw materials and cheap labour, as spheres for export of capital, and as markets for their manufactured goods and commodities. Our colonial apologists and social-democratic reformists, who advocate 'self-government' and 'dominion status' as the solution to the colonial problem, fail to realize that this distinction has not only a historic but also a great economic, social and political significance. They fail to grasp the essential point, that capitalist development reproduces among the population of the imperialist countries the class structure of the metropolis (i.e. the imperial centre or 'Mother Country') while the indigenous native population of the colonial territories are either exploited, subjugated or exterminated. In the dominions, not only do the capitalists present the colonial extension of the capitalism and imperialism of the mother countries, but their colonial interests, directly or indirectly, coincide. That is why the term 'self-government', 'dominion status', or what the French imperialists now call *autonomie*, are nothing but blinds and limitations in the way of the struggle of the national liberation movement in the colonies towards self-determination and complete national independence.

The reasons advanced for becoming members of the British Commonwealth of Nations, and remaining as such, is that if colonial 'subjects' sever connections with their 'mother country' they will not have enough protection to ward off other European aggressor nations. The situation is rather the reverse. For instance, whenever Britain is at war she has to call upon her colonies and dominions and other foreign powers to help defend herself. Not only does England need the help of her colonies, but in every case in the last war her deliberate policy of refusing to permit industrialization of the colonies has made them indefensible against modern mechanized warfare. Needless to call attention here as to how France depends upon her colonial troops for defence. The point of emphasis here is that, if left alone, the colonies are able to forge the weapons of defence which they are prevented from making in order to defend themselves successfully.

Another excuse offered by colonial apologists for their desire to hang on and act like the tail of the kite of the British Empire is that if colonial 'subjects' sever connections with the colonial powers it will hamper their scientific advancement. Britain and other colonial powers have been in Africa for over two centuries yet that continent is almost as technologically backward as when they found it. In fact they have arrested and stultified its growth. If Liberia and Abyssinia are still backward in technological advancement it is chiefly because European and other powers have wilfully limited their advancement through their financial and economic machinations.

The political and economic predicament of Liberia demonstrates the fact that unless there is a complete national unity of all the West African colonies it will be practically impossible for any one West African colony to throw off her foreign yoke. Russia and the United States of America are a conglomeration of different peoples and cultures, yet each has achieved political unity. Cultural and linguistic diversities are by no means inconsistent with political unity.

We are aware of the fact that blind nationalism is one of the weapons of aggression, of cut-throat competition, of imperialism and warfare, but we disagree with those who advocate no nationalism, 'the state of being a nation, a political unity'. The West African colonies, for example, must first unite and become a national entity, absolutely free from the encumbrances of foreign rule, before they can assume the aspect of international co-operation on a grand scale; for the wish to co-operate internationally presupposes independent political status. The Dumbarton Oaks Security Conference, the Bretton Woods Financial Conference, the San Francisco World Security Organization and the United Nations Organization support this contention. They all exclude any consideration of the colonies for independence now, and implicitly point out that the majority of mankind who form the inhabitants of the colonies are not entitled to human equality, except through the generosity of the colonial powers whose interest lies in preserving their power and income by means of exploitation of the colonies.

Such American organizations as the Council on African Affairs, the Committee on Africa, the War and Peace Aims, the Committee on African Studies, and the Special Research Council of the National Association for the Advancement of Coloured Peoples on Colonies and Peace, advocate the 'gradual evolution towards self-government' policy for colonial peoples through some sort of international colonial commission. The reason given is that the colonial peoples are 'unprepared' for independence now, as if the European monopoly interests, which, incidentally, rule the colonial powers as well as the colonies, can be persuaded to move out and give the colonies' natural wealth back to their peoples. Do these organizations expect these monopoly interests and their agents, the colonial governments, to expropriate themselves ? The answer to this question is as self-evident as the ignorance with which most of these organizations claim that the 'gradual evolution towards self-government' policy is the solution to the colonial problem. Nevertheless, we understand their point of view, to the extent that they reject the colonial system and favour internal self-government, but we feel that they do not go far enough and express the fundamental aspirations of the masses of colonial peoples.

Let us remind our apologists of this occurrence: speaking in the United States of America, Colonel Oliver Stanley, Britain's erstwhile Secretary of State for the Colonies, declared that Britain's objective in colonial policy was the achievement of the fullest possible measure of self-government within the British Empire at some unknown future date, and added that it was 'British presence' alone which prevented 'disastrous disintegration in her colonies'. We grant Colonel Stanley this fact in a way. But it is the same supposedly altruistic 'British presence' that in 1929 mowed down by machine-gun fire poor defenceless Nigerian women for peacefully and harmlessly protesting against excessive taxation, the counterpart of India's Amritsar. Indeed, it is 'British presence' that has compelled poor African workers to toil day in and day out in mines and on plantations for a mere pittance of ninepence (18 cents) a day of over 10 working hours. It is 'British presence' that has persecuted and jailed and deported colonial labour leaders, only for having dared to organize labour in the colonies. It is 'British presence' that has brought war, oppression, poverty and disease and perpetuated mass illiteracy upon colonial peoples. It is 'British presence' that bleeds them white by brutal exploitation in order to feed the 'British lion' with red meat. These are the achievements of 'British presence' in the colonies. This is the 'disintegration' which 'British presence' is nobly preventing in the colonies.

When this same Oliver Stanley visited Nigeria, a British West

36

African colony, he told the Nigerian Press that Britain desires 'economic independence' for colonies before 'political independence'. The way to achieve this economic independence, according to his thinking, is for the Nigerian people to produce more cocoa, more palm oil, more cotton, more rubber, and more and more raw materials for the British manufacturers and industrialists, who, incidentally, pay for these raw materials at their own prices.

The practical demonstration of the way to hasten this 'economic independence' was a Bill presented to the British-dominated Legislative Council of Nigeria when it met on 5 March. The Bill provides for the British 'Crown' the ownership of all minerals in Nigeria, an eye-opener for those who advocate the 'gradual evolution towards self-government' policy, and wax so eloquently about the 'unpreparedness' of colonial peoples to govern themselves.

A 'Charter for Coloured Peoples' recommending uniform rights for colonial peoples, and submitted to the governments of the United Nations, has been rejected by the British Colonial Office on the ground that the British Government is directed to guiding and assisting the social, economic and political development of each territory according to its particular needs and capacities. What an astonishing hypocrisy! Of course, 'uniform rights' does not suit the British or 'Anglo-Saxon' taste of inferior status for colonial peoples.

It is often alleged that colonial peoples are not 'ripe' for independence. The facts of history not only contradict this allegation but repudiate it. The imperialist contention of 'unreadiness' for self-government is a blind, because the British imperialists are *not* taking serious steps to prepare the colonies for self-government; the direction is not towards self-government but towards Britain's economic self-aggrandizement. Under the colonial powers' 'tutelage' the colonies will *never* be 'ripe' for self-government. The reason is quite obvious.

The English, for instance, were living in a state of semi-barbarism when the Romans left them. But today it is a different story altogether. The Russians, thirty years ago, were almost as backward in modern western technology as colonial peoples, and had ninety-five per cent illiteracy, but are now one of the most powerful people of Europe. The Latin American Republics have considerable illiteracy and are not as economically advanced as other nations, but are governing themselves. In colonial West Africa, there is a sufficiently informed leadership to direct public affairs without the supervision of Europeans. What right has any colonial power to expect Africans to become 'Europeans' or to have 100 per cent literacy before it considers

37

them 'ripe' for self-government? Wasn't the African who is now considered 'unprepared' to govern himself 'governing' himself before the advent of Europeans? In fact, the African's way of living even today is more democratic than the much vaunted 'democratic' manner of life and government of the 'West'.

5: WHAT MUST BE DONE

We have demonstrated that the imperialist powers will never give up their political and economic dominance over their colonies until they are compelled to do so. Therefore, we suggest the following general plan, theory and method, leaving the details to be filled in by the truly enlightened leadership that will carry out the colonial liberation.

The growth of the national liberation movement in the colonies reveals:

(1) The contradictions among the various foreign groups and the colonial imperialist powers in their struggle for sources of raw materials and for territories. In this sense imperialism and colonialism become the export of capital to sources of raw materials, the frenzied and heartless struggle for monopolist possession of these sources, the struggle for a re-division of the already divided world, a struggle waged with particular fury by new financial groups and powers seeking newer territories and colonies against the old groups and powers which cling tightly to that which they have grabbed.

(2) The contradictions between the handful of ruling 'civilized' nations and the millions of colonial peoples of the world. In this sense imperialism is the most degrading exploitation and the most inhuman oppression of the millions of peoples living in the colonies. The purpose of this exploitation and oppression is to squeeze out super-profits. The inevitable results of imperialism thus are: (a) the emergence of a colonial intelligentsia; (b) the awakening of national consciousness among colonial peoples; (c) the emergence of a working class movement; and (d) the growth of a national liberation movement.

In present-day historical development, West Africa represents the focus of all these contradictions of imperialism.

Theoretical Basis:

The theory of the national liberation movement in colonial countries proceeds from three fundamental theses:

(1) The dominance of finance capital in the advanced capitalist countries; the export of capital to the sources of raw materials (imperialism) and the omnipotence of a financial oligarchy (finance capital), reveal the character of monopolist capital which quickens the revolt of the intelligentsia and the working class elements of the colonies against imperialism, and brings them to the national liberation movement as their only salvation.

(2) The increase in the export of capital to the colonies; the extension of 'spheres of influence' and colonial possessions until they embrace the whole world; the transformation of capitalism into a world system of financial enslavement and colonial oppression and exploitation of a vast majority of the population of the earth by a handful of the so-called 'civilized' nations.

(3) The monopolistic possession of 'spheres of influence' and colonies; the uneven development of the different capitalist countries leading to a frenzied struggle between the countries which 'have' and the countries which 'have not'. Thus war becomes the only method of restoring the disturbed equilibrium. This leads to aggravation of a third front, the inter-capitalist alliance front (e.g. Anglo-American imperialism), which weakens imperialism and facilitates the amalgamation of the first two fronts against imperialism, namely, the front of the working class of the capitalist countries and the front of the toiling masses of the colonies for colonial emancipation. Hence these conclusions:

(a) Intensification of the crisis within the imperialist-colonial powers in the colonies.

(b) Intensification of the crisis in the colonies and the growth of the liberation movement against local colonial governments on the colonial front.

(c) That under imperialism war cannot be averted and that a coalition between the proletarian movement in the capitalist countries and the colonial liberation movement, against the world front of imperialism becomes inevitable.

It is, therefore, in this alone that the hope of freedom and independence for the colonies lies. But how to achieve this? First and foremost, Organization of the Colonial Masses.

The duty of any worthwhile colonial movement for national liberation, however, must be the organization of labour and of youth; and the abolition of political illiteracy. This should be accomplished through mass political education which keeps in constant contact with the masses of colonial peoples. This type of education should do away with that kind of intelligentsia who have become the very architects of colonial enslavement.

Then, the organizations must prepare the agents of progress, must find the ablest among its youth and train their special interests (technological, scientific and political) and establish an education fund to help and to encourage students of the colonies to study at home and abroad, and must found schools of its own for the dissemination of political education. The main purpose of the organization is to bring about the final death of colonialism and the discontinuance of foreign imperialist domination. The organization must root itself and secure its basis and strength in the labour movement, the farmers (the workers and peasantry) and the youth. This national liberation movement must struggle for its own principles and to win its aims.

It must have its own press. It cannot live separately from, nor deviate from the aims and aspirations of the masses, the organized force of labour, the organized farmers, and the responsible and cogent organization of youth. These form the motive force of the colonial liberation movement and as they develop and gain political consciousness, so the drive for liberation leaves the sphere of mere ideas and becomes more real.

The peoples of the colonies know precisely what they want. They wish to be free and independent, to be able to feel themselves on an equal with all other peoples, and to work out their own destiny without outside interference, and to be unrestricted to attain an advancement that will put them on a par with other technically advanced nations of the world. Outside interference does not help to develop their country. It impedes and stifles and crushes not only economic progress, but the spirit and indigenous enterprise of the peoples themselves.

The future development of the people of West Africa and of other colonial peoples can only take place under conditions of political freedom that will assure ample latitude for the formation and execution of economic plans and social legislation, as are now imperative for any truly civilized country, that will be truly beneficial to the people and that will be supported and approved by the people themselves. Such conditions cannot exist under alien governments and the people will certainly not prosper under colonialism and imperialism.

We therefore advance the following programme, confident that it will meet with the enthusiastic support and approval of the great masses of colonial peoples because it puts into concrete form what are their already expressed or instinctive desires:

(1) *Political Freedom,* i.e. complete and absolute independence from the control of any foreign government.

(2) *Democratic Freedom,* i.e. freedom from political tyranny and the establishment of a democracy in which sovereignty is vested in the broad masses of the people.

(3) *Social Reconstruction,* i.e. freedom from poverty and economic exploitation and the improvement of social and economic conditions of the people so that they will be able to find better means of achieving livelihood and asserting their right to human life and happiness.

Thus the goal of the national liberation movement is the realization of complete and unconditional independence, and the building of a society of peoples in which the free development of each is the condition for the free development of all.

PEOPLES OF THE COLONIES, UNITE: The working men of all countries are behind you.

2

When I arrived in England in 1945, after ten years of work and study in the USA, the first person I met was George Padmore, a West Indian journalist. He was then busily engaged, together with T. R. Makonnen and Peter Abrahams, in preparing for the Pan-African Congress due to be held in Manchester in October of that year. Within a week I had become joint secretary with Padmore of the Organization Committee. We worked long hours making arrangements for the Congress, and sending letters to various organizations throughout the world, explaining its purpose.

There had been four previous Pan-African Congresses. These were attended mainly by intellectual and other bourgeois elements of African descent living either in the USA or the Caribbean. The First Pan-African Congress was held in Paris in 1919. The Second and Third were held in London in 1921 and 1923 respectively. The Fourth took place in New York in 1927.

The Fifth Pan-African Congress was different. For the first time, there was strong worker and student participation, and most of the over two hundred delegates who attended came from Africa. They represented re-awakening African political consciousness; and it was no surprise when the Congress adopted socialism as its political philosophy.

The Congress was held under the joint chairmanship of Dr W. E. DuBois, an Afro-American scholar and one of the founders of the National Association for the Advancement of Coloured Peoples, and Dr Peter Milliard, a doctor of medicine from Guyana.

Two Declarations were addressed to the imperial powers, one written by DuBois, and the other by myself. Both asserted the right and the determination of colonial peoples to be free, and condemned capitalism. Colonial peoples were urged to organize into political parties, trade unions, co-operatives, and so on, in order to achieve their political freedom, and thereby to make possible economic improvement for the masses.

After the Congress, a working committee was set up with DuBois as chairman and myself as general secretary, to organize the implementation of the programme agreed in Manchester. The Congress headquarters was to be in London.

Soon, colonial liberation movements were under way in Africa. But it was not until after Ghana's Independence in 1957 that Pan-Africanism moved to Africa, its real home, and Pan-African Conferences were held for the first time on the soil of a liberated African state.

DECLARATION TO THE COLONIAL PEOPLES OF THE WORLD

Approved and adopted by the Pan-African Congress held in Manchester, England, 15–21st October, 1945. Written by Kwame Nkrumah:

We believe in the rights of all peoples to govern themselves. We affirm the right of all colonial peoples to control their own destiny. All colonies must be free from foreign imperialist control, whether political or economic. The peoples of the colonies must have the right to elect their own government, a government without restrictions from a foreign power. We say to the peoples of the colonies that they must strive for these ends by all means at their disposal.

The object of imperialist powers is to exploit. By granting the right to the colonial peoples to govern themselves, they are defeating that objective. Therefore, the struggle for political power by colonial and subject peoples is the first step towards, and the necessary pre-requisite to, complete social, economic and political emancipation.

The Fifth Pan-African Congress, therefore, calls on the workers and farmers of the colonies to organize effectively. Colonial workers must be in the front lines of the battle against imperialism.

This Fifth Pan-African Congress calls on the intellectuals and professional classes of the colonies to awaken to their responsibilities. The long, long night is over. By fighting for trade union rights, the right to form co-operatives, freedom of the press, assembly, demonstration and strike; freedom to print and read the literature which is necessary for the education of the masses, you will be using the only means by which your liberties will be won and maintained. Today there is only one road to effective action – the organization of the masses.

COLONIAL AND SUBJECT PEOPLES OF THE WORLD – UNITE.

3

It was one thing to meet in open Congress, and to make Declarations and to pass resolutions. But if the Fifth Pan-African Congress of 1945 was to have any more meaning than the previous four, it had to be followed up by practical measures to implement the policies and decisions agreed upon. Already it was clear from the discussions and speeches of African delegates representing working class interests in Africa that there was a new militancy among colonial peoples, and an impatience to get on with the practical business of national liberation.

The next step was to set up organizational machinery as a basis for mass participation in the national liberation struggle; and equally important, to train cadres for a vanguard political party.

We formed in London, a West African National Secretariat. Its purpose was to organize and direct the programme for Independence for the British and French colonies in West Africa. I became secretary, and soon our small office in 94 Gray's Inn Road became the centre of African and West Indian anti-imperialist activity. During this period I travelled to France to talk with various African members of the French National Assembly, in an effort to draw them into a unified liberation struggle in West Africa. I remember some lively discussions with Sourous Apithy, Leopold Senghor and Houphouet-Boigny among others. We discussed the possibility of setting up a Union of African Socialist Republics, though it was clear to me, even then, that men such as Senghor and Houphouet-Boigny, when they spoke of socialism, meant something very different from the scientific socialism to which I was committed. However, as a result of our talks it was agreed that a West African National Congress should be held in Lagos in October 1948 to which all political organizations and people's movements throughout Africa should be invited. I was made responsible for convening the conference, and as soon as I returned to London began the preparations. But the Congress never in fact took place.

It was one of the busiest periods of my life. Apart from the work of the West African National Secretariat, I was running a monthly paper called *The New African*. The first issue appeared in March 1946 with the sub-title: 'The Voice of the Awakened African', and with the motto: 'For Unity and Absolute Independence'. The aim was to publicize our campaign for national liberation, and to call for unified effort. But the paper, though each edition was quickly sold out almost as soon as it appeared, had to close down for lack of funds.

Perhaps a more effective practical step was the setting up of an organization known as 'The Circle'. This came about as a result of the regular meetings of groups of students and others who supported the West African National Secretariat. The need was felt for a vanguard group – a political cadre – to train for revolutionary work in any part of the African continent. I was made chairman of the Circle.

One of our first tasks was to draw up a document known as 'The Circle', which stated our aims and prescribed conduct. Membership cost seven guineas, and only those who were ideologically sound, and were

46

dedicated to the liberation struggle were admitted. We met regularly, and organized and planned. Always, in our discussions there were two points of emphasis. First, the imperative need to organize, and to organize through a vanguard party pursuing principles of scientific socialism and based on mass worker and peasant participation. Second, the necessity for unification. We were at that time concerned mainly with West African unity, as the unification of British and French colonial peoples in West Africa seemed then the only practical possibility. But we always regarded West African unity as merely a first step leading eventually to the unification of the entire African continent.

Although we did not rule out the use of armed force to achieve our Circle objectives (see item 4), we clearly stated that it was to be used only as a last resort. Clearly, non-violent methods such as strikes, boycotts, civil disobedience and so on, would be employed, and it would only be after all such methods had failed to bring results that violence would be considered. One thing was very clear to us, that the colonial powers would never restore our freedom voluntarily. Independence had to be won, and by our own efforts.

The Circle was very active for a time, but disintegrated at the end of 1947 when I returned to the Gold Coast to become general secretary of the United Gold Coast Convention.

THE DOCUMENT KNOWN AS THE CIRCLE

Name: THE CIRCLE
Motto: The Three S's—Service, Sacrifice, Suffering

Aims: 1. To maintain ourselves and the Circle as the Revolutionary Vanguard of the struggle for West African Unity and National Independence.

2. To support the idea and claims of the All West African National Congress in its struggle to create and maintain a Union of African Socialist Republics.

INTRODUCTION

Since no movement can endure unless there is a stable organization of trained, selected and trusted men to maintain continuity and carry its programme forward to successful conclusion.

And since the more widely the masses of the African peoples are drawn into the struggle for freedom and national independence of their country, the more necessary it is to have an organization such as THE CIRCLE to establish stability and thereby making it impossible and difficult for demagogues, quislings, traitors, cowards and self-seekers to lead astray any section of the masses of the African peoples.

And since, in a country like West Africa with foreign, despotic and imperialist governments the more necessary it is to restrict THE CIRCLE to persons who are trained and engaged in political revolution as a profession, and who have also been trained in the art of combating all manner of political intrigues and persecutions thereby making it difficult for any one to disrupt the national liberation movement.

I therefore accept and abide by the laws of THE CIRCLE which are as follows:—

1. I will irrevocably obey and act upon the orders, commands, instructions and directions of the Grand Council of THE CIRCLE.

2. I will always serve, sacrifice and suffer anything for the cause for which THE CIRCLE stands, and will at all times be ready to go on any mission that I may be called upon to perform.

3. I will always and in all circumstances help a member brother of THE CIRCLE in all things and in all difficulties.

4. I will, except as a last resort, avoid the use of violence.

5. I will make it my aim and duty to foster the cause for which THE CIRCLE stands in any organization that I may become a member.

6. I will on the 21st day of each month fast from sunrise to sunset and will meditate daily on the cause THE CIRCLE stands for.

7. I accept the Leadership of Kwame Nkrumah.

Oath of Allegiance

On my life, honour and fortunes, I solemnly pledge and swear that I shall always live up to the aims and aspirations of THE CIRCLE, and shall never under any circumstances divulge any secrets, plans or movements of THE CIRCLE, nor betray a member brother of the circle; and that if I dare to divulge any secrets, plans and movements of THE CIRCLE, or betray a member brother or the cause, or use the influence of THE CIRCLE for my own personal interests or advertisements, I do so at my own risk and peril.

Duties of Circle Members

Each circle member should join an organization and should adopt two methods of approach:

(*a*) Advocate and work for the demands and needs of that Organization.

(*b*) Infuse that Organization with the spirit of national unity and the national independence of West Africa, and the creation and maintenance of the Union of African Socialist Republics.

Circle Fund

Members of each branch of THE CIRCLE shall maintain a fund by voluntary contributions, such fund to be used for furthering the cause of THE CIRCLE only.

Circle Meetings

The Grand Council of THE CIRCLE shall meet at least once a year and shall decide general policy and give directions to territorial and local branches of THE CIRCLE. Members of each branch of THE CIRCLE shall meet on the 21st day of each month, and at such other times as members may deem advisable.

Circle Communication

A close liaison shall at all times be maintained between the Grand Council and the individual territorial and local branches of THE CIRCLE. As far as possible all communications should be done by personal contact, couriers and messengers. Letters, telegrams, telephones and cables should be used only for making appointments. Discussion of CIRCLE matters in public places is forbidden.

Circle Member Recognition

Ordinary handshake with thumb pressure.

CIRCLE GOAL

At such time as may be deemed advisable THE CIRCLE will come out openly as a political party embracing the whole of West Africa, whose policy then shall be to maintain the Union of African Socialist Republics.

4

The promoters of the United Gold Coast Convention (UGCC) came from the middle class. They were lawyers, doctors, academics, and indigenous business men, with little or no contact with the masses. When they invited me to become general secretary of the UGCC they hoped that I would help them to bridge this gap, and to draw into their movement the growing anti-colonial, nationalist elements, particularly among the youth, which were at that time beginning to make their voices heard throughout the country.

I did not immediately accept the invitation from the UGCC, knowing that it was a movement sponsored by bourgeois reactionaries, whose objectives stopped short at national liberation, and who had no plans to bring about fundamental economic and social change. But I agreed to accept the position after consultation with the West African National Secretariat. The time had come to get to grips with imperialism on the soil of Africa, and by working for the UGCC I would at least be actively engaged in the national liberation struggle to end colonial rule. I knew, however, that it might not be long before the basic differences between our long term objectives might make it impossible for me to continue to work for them.

On the journey home I visited Sierra Leone and Liberia, and tried to arouse interest in a West African Conference. But already my thoughts were concentrating more and more on the development of the political struggle within the Gold Coast. I was convinced that before there could be any meaningful economic and social progress, there must be a successful political revolution. For without political freedom and an end to colonial rule, we should not be in a position to plan our future, and the work of building socialism could not proceed. Colonialism and capitalism are part and parcel of the same oppressive and exploitive processes, and an attack on one of them is synonymous with an attack on the other.

During the Governorship of Sir Alan Burns (1941–47), various political reforms had been introduced as a result of pressure from the growing political consciousness of the Gold Coast intelligentsia. In October 1944, a new constitution, known as the Burns Constitution, was approved by the Legislative Council and the Colonial Office, and Africans were appointed to the Executive Council. But the Burns Constitution did not satisfy the critics of the government, and on 29th December 1947, the UGCC was officially launched at Saltpond to oppose the Burns Constitution, and to press for self-government 'in the shortest possible time'.

On my arrival in the Gold Coast to take up my appointment, one of my first tasks, after organizing an office, was to draw up a programme of action. This I laid before the Working Committee of the Convention on 20th January, 1948. It included the following items:

Shadow Cabinet

The formation of a Shadow Cabinet should engage the serious attention of the Working Committee as early as possible. Membership is to be composed of individuals selected *ad hoc* to study the jobs of the various ministries that would be decided upon in advance for the country when we achieve our independence. This Cabinet will forestall any unpreparedness on our part in the exigency of Self-Government being thrust upon us before the expected time.

Organizational Work

The organizational work of implementing the platform of the Convention will fall into three periods:

First Period:

(a) Co-ordination of all the various organizations under the United Gold Coast Convention: *i.e.* apart from individual Membership, the various Political, Social, Educational, Farmers' and Women's Organizations as well as Native Societies, Trade Unions, Co-operative Societies, etc., should be asked to affiliate to the Convention.

(b) The consolidation of branches already formed and the establishment of branches in every town and village of the country will form another major field of action during the first period.

(c) Convention Branches should be set up in each town and village throughout the Colony, Ashanti, the Northern Territories and Togoland. The chief or Odikro of each town or village should be persuaded to become the Patron of the Branch.

(d) Vigorous Convention weekend schools should be opened wherever there is a branch of the Convention. The political mass education of the country for Self-Government should begin at these weekend schools.

Second Period:

To be marked by constant demonstrations throughout the country to test our organizational strength, making use of political crises.

Third Period:

(a) The convening of a Constitutional Assembly of the Gold Coast people to draw up the Constitution for Self-Government or National Independence.

(b) Organized demonstration, boycott and strike – our only weapons to support our pressure for Self-Government.

The programme was approved in principle, though there was a later denial by members of the UGCC who appeared before the Watson Commission, and I was asked to get the organization going with all speed.

I began the task of organizing branches of the UGCC throughout the country. This involved almost continuous travel, endless meetings and rallies, and the delivery of hundreds of speeches. Within six months, well over five hundred branches of the UGCC had been established. I usually travelled in the old car bought by the UGCC, but frequently had to hitch lifts on lorries, or had to trek on foot when the car broke down and there was no other means of transport. In most of the places I visited I was given food and accommodation in the homes of supporters of the movement. But there were many nights when I and my companions slept in the open by the roadside, when it had not been possible for some reason or other to reach our destination by nightfall.

It was during this time that I became acutely aware of the already deep-seated feeling of frustration and discontent among the people, and began to become confident that all this latent unrest could be organized into a genuine grass roots movement for self-government as a necessary preliminary for basic economic improvement.

A countrywide boycott of European and Syrian merchants had been called by a sub-chief of the Ga State, Nii Kwabena Bonne, in an attempt to force foreign shopkeepers to reduce the high prices of their goods. The boycott spread quickly and lasted about a month. On 28th February, the very day the boycott was called off, two ex-servicemen were killed and five other Africans wounded in the course of a demonstration by the Ex-Servicemen's Union in Accra. As a result there was widespread rioting and looting in Accra for several days, during which some twenty people were killed and 237 injured.

The Governor declared a state of emergency. In the meantime, I had called a meeting of the Executive Committee of the UGCC, and we had sent telegrams to A. Creech Jones, Secretary of State for the Colonies, calling for the sending of a special commissioner to be sent to the Gold Coast to hand over the administration to an interim government of chiefs and people, and to witness the immediate calling of a constituent assembly.

Shortly afterwards, the colonial authorities arrested the 'Big Six' of the UGCC, as we had come to be called; Danquah, Ofori Atta, Akufu Addo, Ako Adjei, Obetsebi Lamptey, and myself. We were flown to Kumasi and imprisoned there for three days. During those days we drew up plans for a future constitution of the Gold Coast. But already it was clear to me that I was the odd man out. Practically everything I suggested was opposed by the other five; and they began to blame me for their predicament. When it was rumoured that the youth of Ashanti planned to attack the prison to release us, we were transferred to the Northern Territories where I was imprisoned in a small hut in conditions of more or less solitary confinement. After six weeks we were all flown back to Accra to appear before the Commission of Enquiry which had been set up by the Governor under the chairmanship of Aiken Watson KC, to enquire into the disturbances.

After lengthy sessions during which we were closely interrogated, the Commission recommended that the Burns Constitution be replaced by a more democratic

55

constitution, and that a working committee should be set up to draft it. In its published Report, the Commission stated that:

> 'It is significant that, although from his evidence, it must be plain that Mr Nkrumah has not really departed one jot from his avowed aim for a Union of West African Soviet Socialist Republics, the Convention has not so far taken any steps to dissociate themselves from him.
>
> Mr Kwame Nkrumah has never abandoned his aims for a Union of West African Soviet Socialist Republics and has not abandoned his foreign affiliations connected with these aims.'

It is of interest to note that the word 'Soviet' was inserted by the Commissioners, and was not included in the Circle document.

In December 1948, as a result of the Watson Commission, a committee known as the Coussey Constitutional Committee was set up under the chairmanship of Mr Justice Coussey to draw up a new constitution. There were forty members, all nominated by the Governor, and among them not one member of the working people of the country.

It was evident to me that further effort was necessary if the true aspirations of the people were to be satisfied. Returning to my work as general secretary of the UGCC relations between myself and the working committee worsened. The committee objected to my founding the Ghana College to accommodate those students from various colleges and secondary schools who had gone on strike and had been expelled when we were arrested and banished to the Northern Territories. They also objected to the formation of the Youth Study Group, which was later embodied in a nationalist youth movement with the Ashanti Youth Association and the Ghana Youth Association of Sekondi, and known as the Committee on Youth Organization (CYO). They further objected to the steps I was taking to establish a newspaper in order to publicize our policies to the rank and file of the people.

The inevitable split was imminent. Early in June 1949, during a special conference in Tarkwa of the CYO, it was decided that we should break away from the UGCC and form our own political party quite separate from it, and that the party should be called the Convention People's Party (CPP). It was to be a mass-based, disciplined party pursuing policies of scientific socialism. Its immediate task was to obtain 'Self-Government *NOW*'. There was to be no tribalism or racialism within the CPP. Everyone would be free to express their views, but once a majority decision was taken, such a decision had to be loyally executed, even by those who might have opposed the decision. This we considered and proclaimed to be the truest form of democratic centralism – decisions freely arrived at, and loyally executed.

The CPP was launched in Accra on Sunday, 12th June 1949, before a crowd of about 60,000 people. In my speech I declared:

'The time has arrived when a definite line of action must be taken if we are going to save our country from continued imperialist exploitation and oppression. In order to prevent further wrangling between the CYO, who are ready for action, and the Working Committee of the UGCC, who are out to suppress this progressive youth organization, the CYO has decided on a line of action that will be consistent with the political aspirations of the chiefs and the people of the country ... I am happy to be able to tell you that the CYO, owing to the present political tension, has decided to transform itself

57

into a fully-fledged political party with the object of promoting the fight for full self-government now.'

After my speech, and still standing on the platform, I asked for pen and paper, and using somebody's back as a support, I wrote out my official resignation from the UGCC and then read it to the people.

CONSTITUTION OF THE CONVENTION PEOPLE'S PARTY
(C.P.P.)
Motto: Forward ever-Backward never

*

PART ONE

NAME
The name of the Party shall be the *Convention People's Party* (*C.P.P.*)

AIMS AND OBJECTS
NATIONAL

(I) To fight relentlessly to achieve and maintain independence for the people of Ghana (Gold Coast) and their chiefs.

(II) To serve as the vigorous conscious political vanguard for removing all forms of oppression and for the establishment of a democratic government.

(III) To secure and maintain the complete unity of the people of the Colony, Ashanti, Northern Territories and Trans-Volta/Togoland regions.

(IV) To work with and in the interest of the Trade Union Movement, and other kindred organizations, in joint political or other action in harmony with the constitution and Standing Orders of the Party.

(V) To work for a speedy reconstruction of a better Ghana (Gold Coast) in which the people and their Chiefs shall have the right to live and govern themselves as free people.

(VI) To promote the Political, Social and Economic emancipation of the people, more particularly of those who depend directly upon their own exertions by hand or by brain for the means of life.

INTERNATIONAL

(I) To work with other nationalist democratic and socialist movements in Africa and other continents, with a view to abolishing imperialism, colonialism, racialism, tribalism and all forms of national and racial oppression and economic inequality among nations, races and peoples and to support all action for World Peace.

(II) To support the demand for a West African Federation and of Pan-Africanism by promoting unity of action among the peoples of Africa and of African descent.

MEMBERSHIP

There shall be two classes of membership:

(I) Individual.
(II) Affiliated.

(I) *Individual Membership.* Any person who is of the age of 18 or above and who accepts the objects, policy, programme and discipline of the Party shall be eligible for membership provided that:

(a) He or she does not support Imperialism, Colonialism, Tribalism and Racialism.

(b) He or she is not a member of any other political party or of any organization whose policy is inconsistent with that of the Party.

(c) He or she is not a member of a Trade Union, Farmers' Organization or other *bona fide* organization proscribed by the Party.

Application for individual membership normally shall be made on a duly prescribed form which shall be completed by the applicant and passed to a Branch Secretary for consideration by his committee as to acceptance or otherwise. On enrolment every member shall be supplied with a membership and dues card.

Admission Fee: Each individual member of the Party shall be requested to pay on enrolment an Admission Fee of two shillings.

Membership Dues. Each individual member of the Party shall

59

pay membership dues of three shillings (3s.) a year to his Branch, or as otherwise determined by the Party at any particular time.

(II) *Affiliated Members* shall consist of the following:

    (i) Trade Unions.
    (ii) Ex-Servicemen's Union.
    (iii) Farmers' Organizations.
    (iv) Co-operative Societies, Unions, Associations.
    (v) Organizations of professionals, artisans and technicians.
    (vi) Youth and Sports Organizations.
    (vii) Cultural Organizations.
    (viii) Women's Organizations.
    (ix) Other organizations approved by the National Executive of the Party.

(*a*) All such organizations must accept the aims and objects, policy and programme of the Party.

(*b*) They must in the opinion of the National Executive be *bona fide* democratic organizations.

(*c*) An organization wishing to affiliate shall forward a resolution to that effect duly passed by that organization and signed by its President and Secretary, to the General Secretary of the Convention People's Party, who shall in turn bring it before the National Executive Committee of the Party for acceptance or otherwise.

(*d*) Each organization upon being accepted for affiliation shall pay an Affiliation Fee of one pound one shilling.

(*e*) Affiliated organizations shall pay an annual fee as determined by the Party.

Note. Affiliations are apt to cause divided loyalties; so as much as possible only individual membership should be encouraged, though the Party should be on the closest of terms with the various organizations.

FUNDS OF THE PARTY

The general funds of the Party shall be derived from proceeds of functions (dances, football matches, etc.), voluntary subscriptions, appeals, donations, bequests, sale of Party literature, badges, admission fees of individual members and organizations, membership dues and other sources approved by the Party.

Except in the case of authorized imprest accounts all funds shall be deposited in a Bank, and applications for withdrawals must be signed by the Chairman and either the Secretary or the Treasurer.

N.B. All remittances to National Headquarters should be sent to the Treasurer, National Headquarters, Convention People's Party, P.O. Box 821, Accra. Cheques, Postal and Money Orders should be made payable to the Convention People's Party and crossed.

PARTY FLAG

The official colours of the Party shall be: RED, WHITE AND GREEN. The Party tricolour flag shall be in horizontal form with red at the top.

NATIONAL ANNUAL CONFERENCE

The National Annual Conference of the Party shall be convened annually in August at such date and place as may be fixed by the National Executive. A special emergency national conference may be convened by the National Executive whenever deemed necessary, provided that at least two weeks notice is given. As regards the former, notices must go out at least two months before the Conference.

COMPOSITION OF ANNUAL CONFERENCE

The National Annual Conference shall be constituted as follows:

(i) Six delegates duly elected by each constituency.
(ii) Six delegates elected by the C.P.P. Women's section.
(iii) Six delegates elected by the C.P.P. Youth League.
(iv) Delegates duly elected and mandated by each affiliated organization to the number of two delegates for each five thousand or part thereof.
(v) *Ex-officio* Members. *Ex-officio* members of the Party Conference shall be the following:
    (*a*) All National officers of the Party.
    (*b*) Members of the National Executive of the Party.
    (*c*) Members of the Central Committee.
    (*d*) Members of the Legislative Assembly.

Note. The *ex-officio* delegates shall not be entitled to vote unless they are also duly elected as representatives by their constituencies, Women's Section, Youth League or an affiliated organization.

ELECTION OF DELEGATES TO THE PARTY CONFERENCE

Qualifications and disqualifications of delegates:

(i) Every delegate must individually accept and conform to the constitution, programme, principles and policy of the Party.

(ii) Delegates must be *bona fide* members or officials of the organization electing them.

(iii) No person shall act as a delegate for more than one organization.

(iv) No person shall act as a delegate who has not paid his or her dues up to date, or who has not paid the political levy of his or her Trade Union or other affiliated organization.

FUNCTIONS AND POWERS OF THE NATIONAL ANNUAL DELEGATES' CONFERENCE

The National Annual Delegates' Conference shall have the power:

(i) To lay down the broad basic policy and programme of the Party for the ensuing year. The decisions of the Annual Delegates' Conference shall be binding on all members of the Party and affiliated organizations.

(ii) To consider the reports and audited accounts presented by National Officers on behalf of the National Executive Committee.

(iii) To deal with other matters affecting the Party and the Country.

AMENDMENTS TO CONSTITUTION

The existing Constitution, or any part thereof, may be amended, rescinded, altered, additions made thereto by Resolution carried by a majority vote at an Annual Delegates' Conference.

Proposals regarding any amendment of the Constitution must be sent to the General Secretary at least two months before the Conference for inclusion in the Agenda. Notice of such Resolutions and the Conference Agenda shall be communicated in writing to all Constituencies at least one month before the Delegates' Conference.

Only Party organizations—Branch, Constituency, Regional or Affiliated Organizations—and *not individual members* shall send resolutions for determination at the Annual Delegates' Conference.

NATIONAL EXECUTIVE COMMITTEE

Composition: The National Executive Committee shall be composed of:

(i) Chairman.

(ii) National Officers.

(iii) Chairman of Standing, Finance and Staff Committee.

(iv) Secretary of Standing, Finance and Staff Committee.

(v) Members of Central Committee.

(vi) One Representative elected by each Constituency at the Annual Constituency Conference.

All members of the National Executive Committee have voting rights.

The Chairman (and in his absence the Deputy Chairman) shall preside at meetings of the National Executive Committee. In the absence of both a member shall be elected at the meeting to preside.

Duties of the National Executive Committee

(i) To carry out the policy and programme of the Party as laid down by the Annual Delegates' Conference.

(ii) To help organize Regional Councils, Constituencies and Branches and to guide and supervise their work.

(iii) To enforce the Constitution, Rules, Regulations, Standing Orders and Bye-laws of the Party and to take any action it deems necessary for such purpose whether by way of dis-affiliation of an affiliated organization, dissolution or suspension of a branch of the Party, suspension or expulsion of an individual member of the Party. Any such action taken by the National Executive Committee shall be reported to the next Annual Delegates' Conference of the Party, to which appeals shall lie from the organization, branches and members concerned.

(iv) To maintain Party Finance and submit a report and a statement of account to the Annual Delegates' Conference of the Party.

(v) To initiate and undertake all such activities as may further the aims and objects of the Party.

(vi) To approve candidates for Central and Local Government Elections from lists prepared and submitted by the regional and Constituency Executive Committees or other body duly empowered by the Committee.

(vii) The National Executive Committee shall delegate powers to the Central Committee to set up specialized departments and other advisory bodies at the National Secretariat to carry out the aims and objects of the Party.

(viii) Any vacancy occurring in the National Executive Committee during the course of the year shall be filled as provided in the Constitution.

(ix) The National Executive Committee shall be in plenary session at least once every six months to hear reports on the state of the Party and the work of the Central Committee.

(x) Emergency meetings of the National Executive Committee shall be convened as thought fit by the Life Chairman or on a resolution endorsed by twelve Constituency Executives.

Quorum. At least one-third of the Constituency Representatives must be present.

CENTRAL COMMITTEE OF THE NATIONAL EXECUTIVE

Composition

The Central Committee of the National Executive shall consist of:

(i) The Party Leader.

(ii) Eight other members selected by him and approved by the National Executive Committee.

(iii) Other special members also approved by the National Executive Committee.

Functions

(i) The Central Committee shall act as the 'Directorate' of the National Executive in seeing that the decisions and policies of the National Executive are duly executed.

(ii) To supervise the administrative machinery of the Party at all levels—national, regional and branch executives—and to take such measures as it deems necessary to enforce decisions and the programme of the Party as laid down by the National Executive.

(iii) The members of the Central Committee shall normally reside in Accra the capital and shall meet in permanent session at least once a week or if emergency arises from day to day to review major trends, formulate tactics and strategy for the guidance of the National Executive, and in the event of emergency to assume full responsibility of safeguarding the basic programme of the Party, its security and defence, and report to National Executive.

(iv) The Leader of the Party shall appoint from among the members of the Central Committee a Secretary who shall be held responsible for summoning the meetings of the Central Committee, keeping its records, and preparing necessary reports to the National Executive Committee.

(v) The Central Committee shall work in closest collaboration with all members of the Party in the National Legislative Assembly and see especially to the proper working of the Parliamentary Committee.

(vi) As the main 'Directorate' of the National Executive Committee, all actions taken by the Central Committee shall be reported to the next half-yearly meeting of the National Executive Committee plenary session for ratification.

Discipline

There shall be a Tribunal of Justice consisting of three or more members appointed by the National Executive Committee.

Its decision shall be reported to the National Executive Committee at its next session for ratification or otherwise. Appeals lie to the Annual Delegates' Conference. Members of the Tribunal of Justice are appointed annually, but members can be re-appointed.

Only the National Executive Committee can expel a member and submit this to the Annual Delegates' Conference for ratification. Branches, Constituencies, Regions and the Central Committee can only suspend defaulting members and report to the National Executive Committee for action.

Any member acting as candidate or supporting a candidate in opposition to the Party's official candidate in any Central or Local Government Election as duly announced shall be expelled from the Party.

REGIONAL PARTY ORGANIZATION

REGIONAL CONFERENCE

A Regional Conference shall be convened annually by the Regional Committee or on the instructions of the National Secretariat. A special Regional Conference shall be convened by the Regional Committee on the instructions of the National Executive Committee through the Secretariat at National Headquarters, Accra, or on the demand of at least one-third of the Constituencies of the Party in the Region. The Regional Conference shall consist of two representatives from each Constituency within the Region.

REGIONAL OFFICERS

The Regional Officers shall be as follows:
  (i) Regional Chairman, elected at the Annual Conference.
 (ii) Regional Vice-Chairman, elected at the Annual Conference.
(iii) Regional Treasurer, elected at the Annual Conference.
      These officers are elected for one year, but can be re-elected.
 (iv) Regional Propaganda Secretary.
  (v) Regional Secretary.
 (vi) Other Regional Officers.
      These officers are appointed by the National Executive Committee as full-time officers.

The members of the National Executive from the Region concerned shall be *ex officio* delegates to the Regional Conference with full rights.

Powers of Regional Conference

The Regional Conference shall have the power:

(a) To lay down Regional policy and programme for the ensuing year providing that such policies and programmes are in conformity with the basic policy and programme laid down by the Annual National Delegates' Conference.

(b) To consider the political and organizational reports and statements of account presented by the Regional Secretary on behalf of the Regional Organization.

(c) To do things calculated to promote the Party in the respective. regions.

Composition of Regional Committees

The Regional Committee shall consist of the following:

(i) All the National Executive members in the Region.

(ii) All the Assemblymen in the Region.

(iii) Six members appointed by the National Executive Committee.

(iv) The Regional Secretary.

(v) The Regional Propaganda Secretary.

(vi) Other regional officers appointed from time to time by the National Executive Committee.

(vii) Regional Chairman, Vice-Chairman and Treasurer.

Duties of Regional Committees

The duties of the Regional Committees shall be:

(a) To help organize constituencies and branches in the cities, towns and villages within the Region and to co-ordinate their activities and work.

(b) To help carry out the policy and programme of the Party and instructions and directives received from the National Headquarters Secretariat. The Regional Committees shall be entitled to make recommendations to the National Secretariat on matters of dis-affiliation, dissolutions or expulsions of affiliated organizations, branches and members of the Party within the Region.

(c) To submit reports and statements of accounts to the Regional Conference, as well as to the National Secretariat for transmission to the National Executive Committee.

(d) To help manage, control and guide the work of the Party in Local Government affairs as well as the work in educational and cultural organizations under the general supervision of the National Headquarters Secretariat.

(e) To undertake all such activities as may further the work of the Party in the Regions concerned.

66

REGIONAL FUNDS

Any funds for the region shall be properly kept as determined by the National Executive Committee.

CONSTITUENCY PARTY ORGANIZATION

ANNUAL CONFERENCE

A Conference of the Constituency shall be held at least once a year to which every branch in the Constituency possessing a Charter shall send two delegates. The place of the Conference shall be determined by the Constituency Executive. Special Emergency Constituency Conferences shall be held at the discretion of the Constituency Executive Committee or at the instance of a resolution endorsed by one-third of the Branches in the Constituency.

COMPOSITION OF CONSTITUENCY EXECUTIVES

The Constituency Executive Committee shall consist of:

Chairman
Vice-Chairman
Financial Secretary
Treasurer
Eight Committee Members elected
at the Annual Delegates' Conference
Retiring members may be re-elected
Constituency Secretary
Constituency Propaganda Secretary appointed by
the National Executive Committee

The Secretary and Propaganda Secretary for the Constituency shall be full-time officials appointed by the National Executive. Other paid officers may be appointed from time to time.

The Quorum for a meeting of the Constituency Executive Committee shall be eight.

FUNCTIONS OF THE CONSTITUENCY EXECUTIVE COMMITTEE

The Constituency Executive Committee shall carry out the policy and decision of the Annual Constituency Conference which must be in keeping with the basic policy and programme of the Party as laid down by the Annual Delegates' Conference and in the Constitution, Rules and Regulations of the Party.

BASIC PARTY ORGANIZATION

The Branch is the basic organization of the Party. The Party shall establish branches in all towns and villages. Each branch shall be governed by a Branch Executive Committee which shall be elected annually at a General Meeting of the Branch. The Branch may appoint full-time paid officers where funds permit.

In big towns which have been divided into wards for local elections, there shall be Party Wards corresponding with these wards. ALL PARTY WARDS shall function within their respective branches in the towns, but each Party Ward shall have a Party Ward Executive, and representatives of the various wards shall be members of the Branch Executive. Where towns are considered too large they could be divided up into Wards as in the Municipalities.

Branches in the rural constituencies shall deal direct with their respective constituency Headquarters.

Kumasi, Accra, Sekondi/Takoradi, Cape Coast, being constituencies in themselves shall deal direct with National Headquarters.

BRANCH GENERAL MEETINGS

There shall be a general meeting of each branch once a month.

BRANCH EXECUTIVE COMMITTEE

There shall be a Branch Executive Committee consisting of the following officers: Chairman, Vice-Chairman, Secretary, Assistant Secretary, Treasurer, Financial Secretary, Propaganda Secretary, 5 Executive Members.

DUTIES OF BRANCH EXECUTIVES

The duties of the Branch Executives shall be:

(i) To carry on propaganda and organizational work among the masses of the people in order to realize the stand point advocated by the Party.

(ii) To pay constant attention to the sentiments and remarks of the masses of the people, and report same to the National Headquarters Secretariat, Accra.

(iii) To pay heed to the political, economic and cultural life of the people and to take the lead to organize the people in the locality in which the branch operates in order to solve their own problems by encouraging the spirit of initiative among the masses.

(iv) To recruit new members, and to collect Party membership dues.

(v) To check and verify the record for Party membership and to report to the National Headquarters Secretariat, Accra, any act of indiscipline and other offences which might bring the Party into dishonour and disrepute.

(vi) To foster the political and general education of Party members and especially Party Cadres.

The Branch Executive Committee has no mandatory powers to expel any member. In cases of indiscipline, the Branch can suspend the members so concerned and report the matter to the General Secretary for action.

PARLIAMENTARY COMMITTEE ON THE PARTY

(i) The Parliamentary Committee of the Party shall consist of
  (a) all Party members in the Legislative Assembly,
  (b) members appointed by the National Executive Committee.

(ii) The Parliamentary Committee shall be under the direct supervision and control of the Party Leader who will report to the National Executive and the Central Committee of the work, activities and general behaviour of all members of the Party in the Assembly.

(iii) The Party Leader shall appoint the Chairman of the Parliamentary Committee. The Parliamentary Committee Chairman shall maintain daily contact with the Party Leader or his deputy.

Quorum. The quorum of every organization of the Party shall consist of one-third of the membership of Party Branch Executive, Constituency Executive, Regional Committee or the National Executive.

PART TWO

INNER PARTY ORGANIZATION
NATIONAL SECRETARIAT

(i) The Central Administrative machinery of the Party shall be known as the National Secretariat and shall consist of the Deputy Chairman, General Secretary, Assistant General Secretary, National Treasurer, and National Propaganda Secretary. They shall be appointed by the National Executive Committee. The National Executive Committee shall also have power to appoint such other officers as the work of the Party may necessitate.

(ii) The National Secretariat shall be under the direct supervision and control of the Central Committee of the National Executive Committee of the Party.

(iii) The Secretary of the Central Committee shall serve as a liaison between the National Secretariat and the National Executive Committee of the Party. He shall be responsible to report to the plenary meetings of the National Executive Committee on the work and activities of the Central Committee.

(iv) The chief function of the National Secretariat is to transmit decisions of the National Executive Committee and the Central Committee to the Regional Committees, Constituency Executives and the Party branches, and to perform such other duties connected with Party administration. The National Secretariat shall maintain close contact with Branch Secretaries as well as Constituency and Regional Secretaries.

C.P.P. WOMEN'S LEAGUE

Individual women members of the Party shall be organized into women's sections. Women's sections may be organized on Branch and Ward basis. A General Council of Women's Sections shall be established to co-ordinate the activities of the women in the Party. Leaders appointed by each Women's Branch or Ward shall be responsible for the co-ordination of work amongst women in the Branch or Ward.

There shall be no separate status of women in the Party. A woman who becomes an individual member of the Party becomes thereby a member of the Women's Section of her Branch. Women may join the Party through the Women's Sections.

The Women's Section shall hold rallies, dances, picnics and other social functions throughout the year. A special Ghana Women's Day shall be observed once a year at Easter.

Each Party Branch shall have a Women's Section to cater for the special interests of women, but the Women's Section shall be part and parcel of the Branch. There shall be only one Executive Committee for each Branch, including the Women's Section.

C.P.P. YOUTH LEAGUE

The Youth of the country (aged 15 to 30 years) shall be organized into the C.P.P. Youth League. The Central Committee shall appoint a member to serve on the Party Youth League Executive, and each Branch of the Party shall also appoint a member of the Local Branch to serve on the Branch Youth League Executive.

PUBLICATIONS

The Party shall publish its own literature, periodicals, magazines, pamphlets, books, etc., as and when they shall be deemed desirable.

PARTY MANIFESTO

The National Executive Committee of the Party shall decide which items from the Party Programme shall be included in the Manifesto which shall be issued by the National Executive Committee prior to every General or Local Government Election.

PARTY NATIONAL HOLIDAYS

1 Independence Day   January 8
2 Youth Day   February 21
3 Women's Day   Easter Sunday
4 Anti-Imperialist Day   May 24
5 Party Anniversary   June 12
6 Annual Conference   August Bank Holiday
7 Life Chairman's Birthday September 18

5

In 1948 I bought by instalments a Cropper printing machine which an Accra printer allowed me to install in his printing office. With the help of an assistant editor and four men to operate the machine, the first edition of my paper, the *Accra Evening News*, appeared on 3rd September, 1948 – the same day that the UGCC Working Committee relieved me of my post of general secretary.

The *Accra Evening News* always carried the three slogans:

- We prefer self-government with danger to servitude in tranquillity
- We have the right to live as men
- We have the right to govern ourselves

It was a vanguard paper, publicizing CPP objectives, exposing the exploitation and injustices of imperialism, and giving practical guidance on how best to promote the Independence struggle.

Through daily editorials, I constantly exhorted the people to organize, and condemned the dishonest, delaying tactics of the colonial government which claimed to be 'preparing' us for self-government. My central theme was always 'Self-government *NOW*', unlike the UGCC which campaigned for self-government in the shortest possible time. But it was made clear that national independence was but the first step in the revolutionary struggle. It would be only when both political and economic independence had been won that we could call ourselves truly free, and could establish a society in Ghana in which each would give according to his ability and receive according to his needs.

Because of lack of funds, the paper was for some time a single sheet. The editorial usually occupied the centre of the front page. Perhaps the second most important column was the one headed 'Accra Diary' and signed 'Rambler'. This column reported on actual examples of corruption, inefficiency, and injustice brought to the notice of the paper by the many 'scouts' whose task it was to ferret out the facts. The following Accra Diary extracts are typical:

Children's Hospital

The mill of Imperialism grinds on and it knows no stopping until it is forced to. That is why we have entered into the age of POSITIVE ACTION in order to uproot it from this Ghana.

My scouts were at a Press Conference held yesterday with the Director of Medical Service. One of the questions which attracted my scouts was: Is there a full time, qualified doctor in charge of the Children's Hospital, Accra? If no, what steps are being taken to secure one?

Answer: No. Really we do not consider it necessary to provide these clinics with medical officers.

I wonder! Does the Director of Medical Service mean to say that he did not consider the lives of the tiny tots, the future mothers and fathers of this country, precious enough to place them in the hands of qualified medical practitioners?

The reply is vague and I should have thought that the D.M.S. would have given good reasons for thus denying the children the service of doctors.

I do not think the Director of Medical Service considered this question seriously giving the reply he did, for if it was not 'necessary' to provide these clinics with medical officers, why did they consider it necessary to provide the Kumasi clinic with a Medical Officer?

The people who pay for the upkeep of these clinics demand that the present lady in charge not being a qualified doctor should be made to give way to a qualified doctor. We demand this with every seriousness. Public disapproval alone should have given the lady in charge the inkling that the people of this country do not want her to take charge of this clinic. She will do well to resign.

(*Accra Evening News*, 10th March, 1949)

The Manager, Airways Corporation
My scouts have just brought the information that you dismissed one of your drivers last week for alleged attempt to give a lift to another workman.

I am informed that the truck was not even in motion before you took up the charge of dismissal against him. Anyway, I understand the Airways Workers Union has taken up the matter seriously and has lodged preliminary protests against this arbitrary step. So better get your old chappie back so that he can go back to work. These lapses do call for understanding between workers and employers.

(*Accra Evening News*, 9th November, 1949)

There was no person, business or organization too powerful to escape the attention of Rambler and his scouts. The identity of Rambler remained a close-kept secret, but I, as editor of the paper, became involved in many libel actions brought by discredited and angry victims of Rambler. At one time, claims against me amounted to around £10,000. All the claimants were civil servants, and included the Commissioner of Police. Supporters managed to collect enough money to settle the claim of the Commissioner of Police and a few others who insisted on immediate payment. The rest were paid off over a period of time. I learnt later, that some of the people who had filed libel actions had been urged to do so by certain government officials who hoped to put an end to my political work, and to force the *Accra Evening News* to close. At a later stage, Danquah sued the paper for libel for an article written about the Kibi ritual murder case. He was awarded damages, and not content with this, bought the rights of the paper. But we had

74

anticipated him. The Head Press, as it then was, was immediately taken over by the Heal Press, which continued to publish the same newspaper under a new name – The *Ghana Evening News*. Right from the start I had always used the name 'Ghana' instead of the Gold Coast, and so by the time we gained our Independence the people already thought of themselves as Ghanaians.

The *Accra Evening News* carried no commercial advertisements. Although always hard pressed for money we refused to accept them in order to preserve the paper's independence. The only advertisements were for CPP meetings and rallies, and other functions connected with the liberation struggle. Owing to lack of space, the paper contained mainly local news. There was a daily CPP Newsletter, and public announcements, prominence being given to Party business.

The paper proved to be such a success that in January 1949 I established the *Morning Telegraph* in Sekondi; and in December the same year the *Daily Mail* in Cape Coast.

After the reactionary seizure of power in Ghana by a clique of army and police officers on 24th February, 1966, the *Evening News*, which I had founded, and which had since 1948 expressed African revolutionary aspirations, was closed down as part of the senseless campaign to try to obliterate all trace of my work.

EDITORIALS FROM THE
ACCRA EVENING NEWS

Editorial 13th January 1949

BULLETS OR NO BULLETS

It is interesting to note the number of British troops being poured into this country as if a pitched battle is soon to be expected here,

75

or as if the Third World War is in the offing. Apart from the movements of troops, our scouts have reported the nocturnal comings and goings of planes under suspicious circumstances.

Moreover, frequent reports have it that arms are being distributed to the European element in this country. Further, the other day there was news about some illegal parcel containing pistols which a European gentleman had ordered through the post. How amusing these reports!

With the present political upsurge among the masses of the people for full Self-government, the British Government is manoeuvring feverishly to delay what must eventually come to pass. Moreover, the military preparations in this country apparently imply that the Government cannot fool the people any longer and is therefore prepared to use force to quell the people's legitimate demand for political Freedom. But this will fail; for more than ever before the Gold Coast is determined to get Self-government this year. We have no arms, but we have tremendous weapons at our disposal which neither steel nor bullets can vanquish. We are giving the British Government here every opportunity to live up to that sense of democratic fairplay which they have been preaching to the world. Nothing can prevent us from restoring our political freedom this year.

The amazing thing about the disposition of British troops in this country is that all the world knows that Britain is in financial and economic difficulties unparalleled in her history, and instead of keeping her youth at home to work in the factories, in the mines and on the land to produce more food and wealth for her needs, Imperialist Britain is rather sending out the flower of her youth to waste away their lives in indolence and useless parades just to keep a watch on Africans whose only sin consists in their demand to govern themselves in their own land!

'Britain never shall be slaves,' yet Imperialist Britain wants to enslave others. Colonization is nothing but slavery, and 'no nation that oppresses another nation can itself be free'.

Bullets or no bullets, British troops or no British troops, there is nothing that can deter us from our determined march towards the goal of complete Self-government and Independence.

ORGANIZE! ORGANIZE!! ORGANIZE!!!

What the people of this country demand now more than anything else is full Self-government. We have every right to 'manage or mismanage' our own affairs in this country. In order to restore Self-government, we must unite, and in order to unite, we must organize. We must organize as never before, for organization decides everything.

Time and again, we have preached unity and organization, and, we shall not be tired of preaching these until Self-government has been fully realized. We must organize in order to make an effective demand for the Control of our own affairs, so that we can be in a position to remedy the innumerable economic and social ills which mar life in this country and reduce us to miserable specimens of humanity.

We must organize in order to be able to break down the chains of Imperialism. The agents of our so-called trustees are busy; their DCs and PROs are working to upset our indigenous democratic system of Government and to delay the fruition of our legitimate political aspiration.

Since unity is the vital issue in our present political struggle, we must be organized consciously to attain that goal. Let individuals, men and women, join any of the Political Organizations, farmers' unions, trade unions, co-operative societies, youth movements. No section of the people of this country should be left unorganized. No individual person should be without membership in some organization.

Do not be worried about the Chiefs. As Kwame Nkrumah has been saying, if we are well organized and strong, our Chiefs shall know where to stand. Do not be unduly concerned about them; they are with us. They all know what we are suffering.

Do not be worried too by the presence of the vicious pro-foreign Government activities of some of our own Africans – the quislings, the stooges and their fellow travellers; they are few and will eventually bow to the organizational strength of the people of this country. There is nothing which Imperialist Governments respect more than this. The strength of the organized masses is invincible.

Fellow Ghanaians, the issue is clear: we demand Self-government now or never. FLOREAT GHANA

THE SPIRIT OF A NATION

When a people who have smarted under a foreign rule suddenly wake up to the indignities of such a rule and begin to assert their national and inherent right to be free then they have reached that stage of their political development when no amount of oppressive laws and intimidation can keep them down. Invariably, it is through a prolonged and sometimes bitter struggle that they gain their freedom. History is replete with instances of the struggle for freedom of oppressed peoples the world over.

Those who by design or chance find themselves the 'masters' of other people either of their own race or not, and use an oppressive hand over their 'subjects' may as well look into history to find out what has been the lessons and verdicts of history; what sooner or later happened to their overlordship. When the spirit of the oppressed people revolts against its oppressors that revolt continues until freedom is achieved. It carries in its wake a force which it is dangerous to suppress.

When the American colonies smarted under the domination of their British cousins and were unable by peaceful and constitutional methods to convince them that they too were men and had the right to be free and govern themselves the American War of Independence was declared.

When India found her continuance under British rule an indignity that belittled her nationality, and was unable by peaceful and constitutional means to obtain her freedom, Ghandhi appeared on the scene with the weapons of non-co-operation and civil disobedience movement.

When Burma was unable any longer to endure British domination after she had only a few short years previously at the risk of national life fought and defeated a worse enemy, she, under the youthful leaders of Burma, evolved the new method of youth organization and dynamic activity that led to her freedom and independence. Today, we the people of Ghana, find ourselves following in the wake of these erstwhile oppressed peoples and demanding to be set free. The more we demand to be free, the more the oppressors seem to be tightening their hold on us.

The day of deliverance is now at hand; we tarry but awhile. We have not the arms with which to fight as the Americans did, but we have moral and spiritual forces at our disposal which out-number all physical weapons and with those forces which no arms can conquer nor gold can buy, we shall succeed in removing all oppressive rule from this country of ours.

Editorial 10th March 1949

THE DAWN OF POSITIVE ACTION

On Sunday, March 6th 1949, this country, pursuing her relentless and adamant struggle for Self-government was ushered into a new political era – the era of POSITIVE ACTION.

It had become evident that after a year of intense platform agitation, unless we organized our potential strength into a monstrous and gigantic force capable of dealing a knockout blow to the forces of Imperialism, all the evil machinations of which Imperialists are capable would be used by them to entrench themselves for an indefinite period of more disgraceful exploitation of this country of ours. It is clear that unless this is done platform talks would avail us but little. The Committee of Youth Organization, the Youth Movement within the Convention, has laid down a programme, which they are passing on to the anxiously waiting people of this country. The Coussey Constitutional Committee has given abundant evidence by their dilatory and delaying tactics that we cannot completely rely on them to produce the Constitution the people of this country demand.

When the Watson Commission was here, they held sittings from 8 a.m. to 12 and from 3 to 6 p.m. and finished work within 'the shortest possible time'. Why cannot the Coussey Committee do the same?

It would therefore be folly on the part of the people of this country to relax their efforts at organizing. We must adopt a definite political action programme, whilst the Committee continues to sit.

We would recommend, making generous allowance for all the delaying, the following time-table:

By May, the Committee's recommendations should be ready for handing in at Christiansborg Castle. They would have had four months to make it.

By July, it should be in Downing Street or Whitehall, London. By September, it should be back in Accra for the Chiefs and the People of this country to accept or reject.

Whilst we are waiting for the Committee to produce their

79

recommendations, we shall not allow ourselves to be caught napping, or we cannot wisely continue to be talking all the time. We must get ready for action if action becomes necessary for procuring the Self-government we uncompromisingly demand. We must organize and plan to uproot Imperialism this year from our midst if it will not respect our demand and hand over honourably.

The period of politics of words is getting to its end; we enter into a new period of political struggle – the period of POSITIVE ACTION.

Editorial 18th May 1949

NEVER RELAX YOUR EFFORTS

Yes, we must continue to blame the Imperialists and indict them before the bar of public and world opinion, as we pointed out in the Editorial of yesterday's issue, because the imperialists are the prime cause of all our troubles, political, social and economic. The pity is that our own people allow themselves to be used as imperialist agents to suppress, exploit and dominate us to the ruin of the whole country. It is in this respect that we can echo the words of Shakespeare:

'The fault, dear Brutus, is not in our stars,
But in ourselves that we are underlings.'

As long as we continue to live under a foreign power, this power will always use the means at its disposal to 'Divide and Rule' us. A favoured group has been created with a vested interest in the present order of things, and therefore look on the national liberation movement with contempt and annoyance. Subtly and viciously, the imperialists try to set people against Chiefs, Chiefs against people, people against people, and leaders against leaders!

Another serious setback to the national liberation movement is the wicked and diabolical tactic of the imperialists in getting our leaders busy – working for them! Some may call it 'learning the art of government', but it is really getting these leaders occupied so as to deprive them of the time for organizing and educating their own people for the art of government and satisfying their wants.

The history of colonial liberation movement shows that the first essential thing is ORGANIZATION. Some may say 'unity', but unity presupposes organization. At least, there must be an organization to unify the country; one person cannot do it; a few leaders cannot do it; but when the masses and the leaders share common ideals and purposes, they can come together in an organization, regardless of tribal and other differences, to fight for a cause.

Leaders may come and go; they may rise and fall; but the people live on for ever, and they can only be joined together by an organization that is active and virile and doing the things for which it was established. The role of an organization, especially in the colonial struggle, is of paramount importance; for victimization, bribery and corruption, defaulting of leaders and other vicissitudes are strewn in the way of such movements. These test the stamina of leaders; these test the preparedness of the people for emancipation from age-long imperialist bondage, and both leaders and followers are to be wary of the imperialists 'even when they offer gifts'.

One thing we must bear in mind is that imperialism never gives way until it cannot help it; even when imperialism appears to give way, it tries to sabotage it by the back door. What is happening in the Gold Coast today is an ample justification of this point.

Therefore, Countrymen, don't live on promises and don't live on rumours about something good turning up, for the enemy is sly and vicious and always waiting for an opportunity to disintegrate our efforts to attain our SG this year. Let us therefore never relax our efforts until we have ACTUALLY secured our Self-government.

Editorial 5th September 1949

THE STRUGGLE GOES ON

The struggle moves on inexorably and relentlessly to its inevitable and logical conclusion, and the next few months will decide the fate of Ghana for generations to come. This is the time for mighty decisions and brave deeds. The greater the danger, the greater share of honour; and with the backing and support of the masses and Chiefs who share the same ideals and aspirations as we do, we shall not fight in vain.

THE GREATEST IS SG

Three weighty decisions await us: Firstly, the increase in wages of government employees at this time when an inflation is already on; secondly, the Government prohibition on Civil Servants from taking part in politics and, finally, the acceptance or rejection of the Coussey Report by the Chiefs and People of this country.

The announcement that the Finance Committee (consisting of Africans with a European Chairman) has sanctioned the pay increase should cause no despondency. It is one of the evils we are fighting against – this accursed system of nominations; it does not matter who is on such a Committee; as long as we remain under the Crown Colony System, such Committees will always produce such shameful and unreasonable results.

With regard to Civil Servants and politics, the show-down will come very speedily. The Government has set October 1st next as the dateline after which no Civil Servant can be a member of a Political Party! We hope the Government will have the courage to check up and enforce such a measure! Isn't it fine for the top-ranking Civil Servants to play high politics and at the same time prevent others from doing so! 'It is hypocrisy to preach virtue and practise vice.'

MONEY CAN'T BUY US

Today, the Police are joining or forming Unions to safeguard their rights or promote their professional interests; tomorrow they are granted pay increases. Today, Civil Servants are prevented from joining political parties, tomorrow they are granted pay increases. But, let the imperialists make no mistake, they cannot be saved by these clever manoeuvres; their end shall surely come, and that very speedily.

The publication of the Coussey Report will decide the whole issue between us and our foreign oppressive overlords. The imperialists can give us all the money in the world, but we must have back our freedom. Therefore, whatever we do, we must bear in mind that it is Self-government we are after and we must subordinate every other thing to getting it.

'SIN PI PREKO'

Let every flouting of the will of the public be an incentive to redouble our efforts to liquidate imperialism from Ghana with all speed. Let us organize solidly to act effectively against imperialist attempts to prolong our enslavement. Let us decide, once and for all to rid ourselves from the shackles of imperialism.

'Long live the forward march of the people of Ghana towards their true and just inheritance.'

Editorial 10th November 1949

WE SHALL PROTEST AND DEMONSTRATE
TO THE WORLD

All over the world, Colonial peoples at the height of their struggle for emancipation from slavery, political, social or economic, find it expedient to uphold the philosophy that 'to sit mute and inarticulate when circumstances demand protest is sinful cowardice'. Today, the Gold Coast people have reached the same stage and they will continue to protest and demonstrate to the world against an iniquitous system of government that has, for the past 100 years and over exploited, oppressed and misgoverned them.

We have kept mute for too long over our miseries, we have been kept too long away from light, and we can no longer afford to condone slavery or toy with the destiny of our nation. Grave though the problems political, social and economic that confront us today, we are resolved to accept no longer any system that savours of imperialism. We believe in the equal rights of all nations; we believe in democracy and freedom and the right of all peoples to govern themselves. We are marching forward indomitably to the glorious end.

Twice in our generation have the Youth of this nation been sacrificed on the altar of freedom for the sake of other people, and twice in our time have those who served to maintain the freedom of others been denied the very freedom and equality for which they fought; but we have now awakened to the realization of our inherent liberty and we shall not rest until we have achieved our hearts' desire.

Self-government is our inherent right and no nation has the right to take it away from us under the pretext of 'Protection and Trusteeship'. Just as Britain will not tolerate America or any other nation to come and lord it over her in her own country, so also, we in our own land will no more kowtow with hat in hand to imperialist dictates. That age when we were babes and swallowed sweet promises that Self-government would be offered us on a silver platter when we were 'ripe' is past and gone forever; the age when others promised us Self-government from their pockets is also dead and buried. We are now living in an age of realities when sweet-sounding offers and promises are not just sufficient; we do not want any promises; we want freedom.

We are too far gone to be disillusioned by the shadows of a substance and no amount of fanning us will make us sleep again. SG is the slogan of our day. Therefore, we shall forge ahead to protest and demonstrate to the world against the evils and oppression of an out-dated system of government under which we are still labouring and languishing.

Forward, therefore, gallant sons and daughters of Ghana towards our just inheritance; forward, brave youth, to the new Ghana of freedom and opportunity; forward sweet Ghanaians to our goal of Self-government. Long live Ghana.

6

At the launching of the Convention People's Party in June 1949, I used the term Positive Action to describe the tactics which would be employed if the government continued to disregard the people's demand for self-government. I did not then specifically define the term, but I had used the expression frequently in the columns of the *Evening News*, and it was generally understood that I referred to non-violent struggle, involving strikes, boycotts, and other forms of non-cooperation.

There was rapidly mounting unrest, particularly in Accra, and I was summoned to appear before the Ga State Council, the traditional local authority, to discuss 'the unfortunate lawless elements in the country and any possible solution'. I went along with two comrades, and was confronted with not only the Ga State Council but with the ex-members of the Working Committee of the UGCC. They demanded an explanation of what I meant by Positive Action, and without waiting to hear me, accused me of advocating violence. I explained the term to them at some length, and then agreed at their request to call a meeting to give the same explanation to Party members.

On leaving the meeting with the Ga State Council, I decided that the explanation must be made immediately, and that it should take the form of a carefully considered, written statement. Working through the night, therefore, kneeling on the floor and using my bed as a table, I wrote: WHAT I MEAN BY POSITIVE ACTION. As soon as the draft was ready, the rest of the night was spent printing off some five thousand copies on the *Evening News* Cropper printing machine. By nine o'clock in the morning all was finished. I then read the statement to a mass meeting of supporters, and afterwards reported my actions to the Ga State Council..

The statement had been written in great haste, but it was not a hastily conceived document. I had given the whole question of Positive Action prolonged and intensive thought over many months.

At the time I wrote it, the people of the Gold Coast were still awaiting the publication of the Coussey Report, and it was possible that Positive Action might never become necessary if the Report proved acceptable. But I felt that unless plans were made to declare Positive Action in the event of the Report proving unsatisfactory, we would be unprepared to continue our freedom struggle. It would have been fatal to have relaxed our efforts in any way. The keeping of the initiative in revolution is vital. It is only by sustained, relentless pressure, and meticulous attention to detailed organization that success can be achieved.

In *What I Mean by Positive Action*, I called for non-violent methods of struggle. We had no guns. But even if we had, the circumstances were such that non-violent alternatives were open to us, and it was necessary to try them before resorting to other means.

In those days, when we talked of tactics of non-violence we meant the kind of tactics employed by Ghandhi in India. 'Violence' was to pick up the gun. 'Non-violence' implied practically any other means short of actually picking up a gun. In recent times, revolutionaries refer to 'violence' in rather different terms, though the issues are still much the same. They see it in more general terms, as any kind of exploitation or oppression. For example, when a peasant in Africa or elsewhere dies of starvation in a world of plenty, they call it violence. It is violence when a whole class of people suffers indignity, deprivation and exploitation at the hands of a selfish, privileged minority. Reactionary violence must be met with revolutionary violence. The latter is employed every time the oppressed take action to end their oppression, whether or not they actually resort to armed struggle. Looked at in these terms, our campaign of Positive Action was far from non-violent. But at the time when it was carried out, it was considered to be a peaceful form of revolutionary struggle.

The Coussey Report was published in October 1949. It recommended that the new Legislative Assembly should consist of a Speaker, to be elected by the Assembly from among its members or outside it, and eighty-four elected members. Five seats were to be allocated to the municipalities, two for Accra, one each for Cape Coast, Sekondi-Takoradi and Kumasi; thirty-three rural members were to be elected in two stages, first by direct primary voting and secondly through electoral colleges; nineteen inhabitants of the Northern Territories were to be elected by the Territorial Councils of the Colony, Ashanti and Trans-Volta/Togoland; six special members were to be elected in equal proportion by the Chamber of Commerce and the Chamber of Mines and three ex-officio members were to be nominated by the Governor. They were the Minister of Defence and External Affairs, the Minister of Finance and the Minister of Justice.

We considered the Report unsatisfactory. On 20th November, 1949, therefore, I called together the Ghana People's Representative Assembly, with the purpose of organizing effective action against the Report. It was the first time that such an Assembly had been called in the Gold Coast; and the only organizations which did not send representatives, though they were invited to do so, were the UGCC and the Aborigines Rights Protection Society.

The Assembly resolved 'that the Coussey Report and His Majesty's Government's statement thereto are unacceptable to the country as a whole', and declared 'that the people of the Gold Coast be granted immediate self-government'. We demanded the calling of a Constituent Assembly and a general election so that the people could decide for themselves whether to adopt or reject the Coussey Report. In addition, a Memorandum was drawn up outlining the structure of central and local government which should form the basis for the new constitution.

The Chiefs at Dodowah did not accept the views of the Assembly. However, I called a meeting of the executive committee of the CPP, and it was agreed that I should inform the Governor, in a letter, that if the administration ignored the legitimate aspirations of the people embodied in the amendments to the Coussey Committee's Report by the People's Representative Assembly, then the CPP would embark on a campaign of Positive Action. At a rally in Accra I proclaimed a time limit of two weeks for the British Government to call a Constituent Assembly, after which if nothing happened there would be a call for Positive Action.

There followed the arrest of editors of newspapers which I had founded, and I was summoned to appear in court on a charge of contempt for an article which appeared in the *Sekondi Morning Telegraph*. I was faced with a fine of £300 or four months' imprisonment. The fine was paid by the people of Accra and various Party members, and I was able to continue my work. I toured the country, addressing rallies, organizing and preparing the people for Positive Action. On my return to Accra I was invited to meet the Colonial Secretary. He warned me against calling for Positive Action, saying that it would bring chaos and disorder, and that if anyone was killed or hurt I would be held personally responsible. During the next few days there were further exchanges between the Executive Committee and the Colonial Secretary, but no progress was made. In an attempt to confuse the people, it was announced over the radio that Positive Action had been abandoned, and I had quickly to correct this mis-information by calling a mass meeting in the Accra Arena.

On 8th January, 1950, after a further request by the Colonial Secretary to postpone Positive Action, I called another meeting at the Arena, and it was then that I proclaimed the start of Positive Action. I called for a general strike to begin at midnight. Only hospital workers, the police, and those employed on maintaining essential public services such as water conservancy, were to be exempt.

I immediately travelled to Cape Coast, Sekondi and Tarkwa, and in each of these places called for Positive Action. On my return to Accra on 10th January, some of the initial enthusiasm for Positive Action seemed to have evaporated, probably as a result of the intensive efforts made over the radio by the administration encouraging people to go back to work. A few of the stores were beginning to open. The following day, therefore, at one of the biggest rallies ever to be held in the Arena, I spoke for about two hours, and afterwards the atmosphere was so tense in Accra that the Governor declared a state of emergency and imposed a curfew. Public meetings were forbidden. The *Evening News* office was raided and closed down, and the same action was taken against my other newspapers. Party leaders in Sekondi and Kumasi were arrested.

At the height of the Positive Action campaign, when the whole of the economic life of the country had been brought to a standstill, I together with leaders of the ex-servicemen and the Trade Unions were invited to appear before the Joint Provincial Council of Chiefs, to try to work out a peaceful settlement with the Government. The ex-servicemen were arrested before they arrived at Dodowah. The TUC representatives were forewarned and did not go. But I and three comrades managed to get through to attend the meeting. Once again, I put before the Council the findings of the Ghana People's Representative Assembly and declared that Positive Action would continue unless the demands were met. It was quite obvious that the Joint Provisional Council of Chiefs and the Government were in league in attempting to deny the people's legitimate demands.

One by one, Party leaders were arrested, and homes and offices ransacked by the police. On the night of 21st January our Party headquarters were raided again, and most of my comrades arrested. If I had been present at the time I also would have been taken, but I had left to visit a Party member in Labadi, where I stayed the night. The following day, when I returned to Party headquarters I found the police waiting for me, and I was arrested and taken to James Fort Prison.

I was in due course charged with inciting people to take part in an illegal strike under the terms of Positive Action, in an attempt to coerce the Government of the Gold Coast. I was sentenced to two years' imprisonment, and condemned to another year's imprisonment, making three years in all, for publishing a so-called seditious article in the *Cape Coast Daily Mail*.

The campaign for Positive Action had not succeeded in bringing down the Government, but it had shaken it to its very foundations, and it never recovered. The hitherto omnipotent colonial administration had been confronted for the first time by organized people's power, and its rottenness and inherent weaknesses had been exposed.

There is no surer way to learn the art of revolution than to practise it. The experience of shared effort and suffering engenders a political awareness that no amount of armchair theorizing can evolve. The people had seen with their own eyes the economic life of the Gold Coast brought to a halt by unified people's effort in the form of a general strike. Never again would they accept that it was hopeless to attempt to attack a seemingly mighty power structure as that represented by the colonial administration. The 'paper tiger' had been exposed, and this was the essential first step in its destruction. The political revolution in the Gold Coast had begun in earnest, and it was only a question of time before the decisive confrontation would take place.

WHAT I MEAN BY POSITIVE ACTION*

Preamble: Party Members, Friends and Supporters

In our present vigorous struggle for self-government, nothing strikes so much terror into the hearts of the imperialists and their agents than the term *Positive Action*. This is especially so because of their fear of the masses responding to the call to apply this final form of resistance in case the British Government failed to grant us our freedom consequent on the publication of the Coussey Committee Report.

The term *Positive Action* has been erroneously and maliciously publicized, no doubt, by the imperialists and their concealed agents – provocateurs and stooges. These political renegades, enemies of the Convention People's Party for that matter of Ghana's freedom, have diabolically publicized that the CPP's programme of positive action

* Written in 1949.

means riot, looting and disturbances, in a word violence. Accordingly, some citizens of Accra, including myself, were invited to a meeting of the Ga Native Authority and the Ga State Council on Thursday, October 20th, at 1 p.m. 'to discuss', as the invitation stated, 'the unfortunate lawless elements in the country and any possible solution'.

At that meeting, I had the unique opportunity of explaining what *Positive Action* means to the satisfaction of the Ga Native Authority and the Ga State Council, and the meeting concluded with a recommendation by them that I should call a meeting to explain to the members of the Convention People's Party as I did to them, what I mean by *Positive Action* in order to disabuse the minds of those who are going about misinterpreting the Positive Action Programme of the Convention People's Party.

Before I proceed to my proper topic, I must take this opportunity to dispel the wild rumour, that the Ga Manche said at the meeting that the Convention People's Party should be suppressed and that I should be deported from Accra. Nothing of the sort was ever suggested by the Ga Manche even though some of the speakers tried to convey such idea but the Ga Manche promptly overruled that.

And at this point allow me to protest vehemently against the diabolically false Reuter's news which no doubt must have been sent by their correspondent in this country. I read to you the text of the Reuters' news:—

'Local African Chiefs have sent ultimatum to Extremist Home-Rule Leader Kwame Nkrumah demanding undertaking by next Wednesday not to cause trouble when Coussey Report on Constitutional Advancement of Gold Coast is published next week. He has also been told to promise Loyal co-operation of his Convention People's Party. If he refuses African Authority will "Forcibly Eject" him from Accra to his Native Village of Nzima about 250 miles inland. All Political Leaders Promised co-operation in keeping peace except Dr. Nkrumah who said he had "No Guns to Fight" but would resort to Boycott, Strikes and Spiritual Force to carry on struggle. Coussey Commission was set up last January to examine Proposals for Constitutional and Political Reforms in Gold Coast.'

Party members, imagine the wicked misrepresentation, chicanery falsehood, the untruths, the lies and deception, in such news. This is the way our struggle is being misrepresented to the outside world; but the truth shall ultimately prevail.

Why Positive Action?

It is a comforting fact to observe that we have cleared the major obstacle to the realization of our national goal in that ideologically the people of this country and their Chiefs have accepted the idea of self-government even now. With that major ideological victory achieved, what is left now is chiefly a question of strategy and the intensity and earnestness of our demand. The British Government and the people of Britain, with the exception of die-hard imperialists, acknowledge the legitimacy of our demand for self-government. However, it is and must be by our own exertion and pressure that the British Government can relinquish its authority and hand over the control of affairs, that is, the Government to the people of this country and their chiefs.

There are two Ways to Achieve Self-government

There are two ways to achieve self-government: either by armed revolution and violent overthrow of the existing regime, or by constitutional and legitimate non-violent, methods. In other words, either by armed might or by moral pressure. For instance, Britain prevented the two German attempts to enslave her by armed might, while India liquidated British Imperialism there by moral pressure. We believe that we can achieve self-government even now by constitutional means without resort to any violence.

We live by experience and by intelligent adaptation to our environment. From our knowledge of the history of man, from our knowledge of colonial liberation movements, Freedom or Self-government has never been handed over to any colonial country on a silver platter. The United States, India, Burma, Ceylon and other erstwhile Colonial territories have had to wage a bitter and vigorous struggle to attain their freedom. Hence the decision by the Convention People's Party to adopt a programme of non-violent Positive Action to attain Self-government for the people of this country and their Chiefs.

We have talked too much and pined too long over our disabilities – political, social and economic; and it is now time that we embarked on constitutional positive steps to achieve positive results. We must remember that because of the educational backwardness of the Colonial countries, the majority of the people of this country cannot read. There is only one thing they can understand and that is Action.

What is Positive Action?

By Positive Action we mean the adoption of all legitimate and

93

constitutional means by which we can cripple the forces of imperialism in this country. The weapons of Positive Action are:

(1) Legitimate political agitation;
(2) Newspaper and educational campaigns and
(3) as a last resort, the constitutional application of strikes, boycotts, and non-co-operation based on the principle of absolute non-violence.

How is Positive Action to be Applied?

We have been unduly criticized by our political opponents, that it is wrong for us to tell the imperialists that we shall resort to non-violent strikes and boycotts as a last resort, if need be, to attain our freedom. Their contention is that we should have kept this secret and spring a surprise on the Government. As for us, our faith in justice and fair play forbids us to adopt such sneaky methods.

We like to use open methods and to be fair and above board in our dealings. We have nothing to hide from the British Government. Secondly, and what is more important if the CPP is a democratic organization, then the members must be taken into confidence and their approval secured for such an important policy, and they must be given the opportunity to prepare for any eventuality. Even, in the case of declaration of war, notice is first given.

Mr. C. V. H. Rao in his book entitled *Civil Disobedience Movement in India* has this to say.

'Constitutional agitation without effective sanction behind it of organized national determination to win freedom is generally lost on a country like Britain, which can appreciate only force or its moral equivalent ... An important contributory factor to the satisfactory settlement of a disputed issue is the extent and the nature of the moral force and public sympathy generated by the righteousness of the cause for which the suffering is undergone and the extent of the moral reaction it has produced on the party against which it is directed.'

The passive sympathy of the masses must be converted into active participation in the struggle for freedom; there must also be created a widespread political consciousness and a sense of national self-respect. These can only be achieved when the mass of the people understand the issue. These are not the days when people follow leaders blindly.

When To Call Positive Action into Play

As already explained, Positive Action has already begun by our political education, by our newspapers agitation and platform speeches and also by the establishment of the Ghana Schools and Colleges as well as the fearless and legitimate activities of the CPP.

But as regards the final stage of Positive Action, *namely Nation-wide Non-violent Sit-down-at-home Strikes, Boycotts and Non-co-operation,* we shall not call them into play until all the avenues of our political endeavours of attaining self-government have been closed. They will constitute the last resort. Accordingly, we shall first carefully study the Report of the Coussey Committee. If we find it favourable, we shall accept it and sing alleluya. But if we find it otherwise, we shall first put forward our own suggestions and proposals and upon refusal to comply with them, we shall invoke Positive Action straight away on the lines indicated above.

What we all want is self-government so that we can govern ourselves in our own country. We have the natural, legitimate and inalienable right to decide for ourselves the sort of government we want and we cannot be forced against our will in accepting or perpetuating anything that will be detrimental to the true interests of the people of this country and their Chiefs.

Therefore, whilst we are anxiously awaiting the Report of the Coussey Constitution Committee, I implore you all in the name of the Party to be calm but resolute. Let us advance fearlessly and courageously armed with the Party's programme of Positive Action based on the principle of absolute non-violence.

Long live the Convention People's Party. Long live the forward march of the people of this country. Long live the new Ghana that is to be .

KWAME NKRUMAH

7

Suffering and sacrifice are inevitable in revolutionary struggle, since no reactionary regime makes a voluntary surrender of its power. It may, in the initial stages of a revolutionary struggle, try by velvet glove treatment, to block revolutionary progress. But when direct confrontation occurs, and vital pillars of the reactionary power structure are threatened by revolutionary forces, it resorts to the most brutal and repressive action to suppress them. It is at this stage that the heaviest casualties of revolution occur. Sometimes there is open armed conflict; in which case there are casualties in the physical sense, and loss of life. Other times, the confrontation is non-violent and the casualties of the revolution are those who suffer arrest and imprisonment, victimization, persecution, and all the many other forms of repression employed by reactionaries when their backs are against a wall.

With the call for Positive Action in the Gold Coast in 1950, a point of open and direct confrontation between the CPP and the colonial administration had been reached. The response of the Government was immediate. A state of emergency was declared, a curfew imposed, public meetings banned, and progressive newspapers closed down. Most of the CPP leadership was arrested and thrown into prison.

During my imprisonment in James Fort, I was able to keep in touch with the Party by writing messages on sheets of toilet paper. These were smuggled out to Party headquarters by a friendly warder, who also brought me in news of the political situation. I used to write the messages at night in the small patches of light made on the floor and wall by a street lamp which shone into our cell. On one night, having scrounged as much toilet paper as possible from other prisoners, I remember writing over fifty sheets.

Conditions in the prison were very bad. There were eleven of us crowded into one small cell, and for sanitation a single bucket in the corner. The food was scanty and poor. But our morale was high. Before long, we had organized committees of Party members in the prison; and unknown to the prison authorities, we met regularly. There were plans to be made and policies to be decided upon so that the Party could participate in the General Election due to take place on the 8th of February 1951. The CPP had to win a majority in the new Legislative Assembly, and it was vital that every seat should be contested. I insisted that my name be registered on the electoral roll for Accra Central, and arranged for Party members to pay my deposit and to sign the necessary papers on my behalf. I then set to work to write the Party manifesto. This was soon completed and smuggled out to Party headquarters.

It was in the early hours of the morning of 9th February that I was told that I had been elected for Accra Central, and that I had received the largest individual poll ever recorded in the country – 22,780 votes out of a possible 23,122. The following day, the Executive Committee of the CPP were permitted by the Governor of the prison to discuss with him the question of my release, since it was likely that as leader of the CPP I would be asked to form a government.

On the morning of the 12th of February, 1951, after having served fourteen months of my three year sentence, I was released from prison and driven through immense, cheering crowds first to the Arena for an expiation ceremony, and then to Party headquarters. The next day the Governor invited me to form a government, for the CPP had won 34 out of a possible 38 elected seats in the municipal and rural areas, and the Party had also a majority in the Assembly over the nominated candidates. A meeting of the Central Committee was convened, and a Government was formed. As leader of the majority Party in the Assembly, I became Leader of Government Business.

It was going to be difficult to work under the conditions of the Coussey Constitution, but I at once made it clear that we intended to go ahead with our campaign for full self government. Our sweeping victory at the polls was our mandate; and nothing would stand in our way. We did not rule out the possibility of further Positive Action if colonial officialdom obstructed our purpose. 'The die is cast', I said in an Address to CPP members of the Assembly, 'the exploited and oppressed people of colonial Africa and elsewhere are looking up to us for hope and inspiration. Progressive people in Britain and elsewhere are also solidly behind us. The torch of the Liberation Movement has been lifted up in Ghana for the whole of West Africa, and it will blaze a trail of freedom for other oppressed territories.'

The decision to continue the struggle for national liberation by constitutional means was taken simply because it was considered to be the method most likely to succeed in the circumstances of the time. For the sole criterion in deciding upon what form a revolutionary struggle should take at a particular time is the revolutionary objective, and how best to achieve it. If the CPP had contracted out of the procedure of parliamentary government which the colonial power had foisted upon us, the progress towards national liberation could not have gone ahead at that time, and the political revolution would have been immeasurably delayed. By participating in the general election of 1951, and winning it, the Party was able to demand my release from prison before even half my sentence had been served, and the CPP was able to form a government and proceed with the practical business of carrying out its revolutionary objectives. We therefore decided for as long as it suited our purpose, to make use of the parliamentary procedures which the colonial administration had always practised and which it could not therefore condemn or refuse to recognize.

On the 5th of March 1952, the Governor told the Assembly that the Colonial Secretary of State had announced in the British House of Commons a change in the Coussey Constitution, removing the office of Leader of Government Business, and providing for the establishment of the office of Prime Minister. Henceforth, the Governor was to consult the Prime Minister before submitting to the Assembly the names of persons he proposed for appointment as representative members of the Executive Council and before allocating them portfolios. Some two weeks later, on the 21st of March the Assembly approved my appointment as Prime Minister.

Clearly further constitutional changes were necessary, and I began to initiate steps for the replacement of the three ex-officio ministers by representative ministers, and to plan the reform of the Legislative Assembly, the latter contained three ex-officio members, six special members, and 75 other members. Of the 56 members representing the Colony, Ashanti and Southern Togoland, eighteen, or one third, represented the chiefs and traditional authorities, and were elected not by universal adult suffrage, but by the Joint Provincial Council, the Asanteman Council, and the Trans Volta Southern Togoland Electoral College. Obviously, this state of affairs could be tolerated no longer.

After exhaustive discussions and consultations throughout the country, a Government White Paper on constitutional reform was published. Shortly afterwards, I called an emergency delegate's conference of the CPP, and told them that the Party National Executive had decided to call on the delegate's conference to recommend that the Government of the Gold Coast make representations to the Queen in Council, through the Secretary of State for the Colonies, that the chiefs and people of the Gold Coast demand immediate self government, and that an Act of Independence be simultaneously passed by the United Kingdom Parliament and the Gold Coast Legislative Assembly declaring the Gold Coast to be, under the new name of Ghana, a sovereign and independent state. A Motion on constitutional reform was moved in the Legislative Assembly on 10 July 1953. It is this Motion which has become popularly known as the Motion of Destiny. The Motion was passed unanimously. The Coussey Constitution had been amended, but it was still necessary to call a general election to give effect to the changes, and by a further CPP victory at the polls to bring the final pressure to bear on the British Government to force the ending of colonial rule in the Gold Coast. Our employment of the colonial power's own parliamentary procedures was bringing results, and justifying the Party's constitutional tactics at that stage of the revolutionary struggle.

THE MOTION OF DESTINY

10th July, 1953

'Mr. Speaker, I beg to move that this Assembly in adopting the Government's White Paper on constitutional reform do authorize the Government to request that Her Majesty's Government as soon as the necessary constitutional and administrative arrangements for independence are made, should introduce an Act of Independence into the United Kingdom Parliament declaring the Gold Coast a sovereign and independent State within the Commonwealth; and further, that this Assembly do authorize the Government to ask Her Majesty's Government, without prejudice to the above request, to amend as a matter of urgency the Gold Coast (Constitution) Order in Council 1950, in such a way as to provide *inter alia* that the Legislative Assembly shall be composed of members directly elected by secret ballot, and that all Members of the Cabinet shall be Members of the Assembly and directly responsible to it.

Mr. Speaker, it is with great humility that I stand before my countrymen and before the representatives of Britain, to ask this House to give assent to this Motion. In this solemn hour, I am deeply conscious of the grave implications of what we are about to consider and, as the great honour of proposing this Motion has fallen to my lot, I pray God to grant me the wisdom, strength and endurance to do my duty as it should be done.

We are called upon to exercise statesmanship of a high order, and I would repeat, if I may, my warning of October, that 'every idle or ill-considered word – will militate against the cause which we all have at heart'. It is, as Edmund Burke said (and I am quoting him here):

> 'our business carefully to cultivate in our minds, to rear to the most perfect vigour and maturity, every sort of generous and honest feeling that belongs to our nature. To bring the dispositions that are lovely in private life into the service and conduct of the commonwealth, so to be patriots as not to forget we are gentlemen.'

At the outset, I would like to remind Honourable Members of a passage in the White Paper, that 'only after the Legislative Assembly debate will the proposals of this Government take their final shape and be communicated to the United Kingdom Government'. Therefore, let your arguments be cogent and constructive. The range of this debate must be national, not regional; patriotic, not partisan; and I now ask that a spirit of co-operation and goodwill pervade this debate. It was Aristotle, the master who knows, who said:

> 'In practical matters the end is not mere speculative knowledge of what is to be done, but rather the doing of it. It is not

IOI

enough to know about virtue, then, but we must endeavour to possess it, and to use it . . .'

As with virtue, so with self-government: we must endeavour to possess it, and to use it. And the Motion which I have prepared is the means to possess it.

In seeking your mandate, I am asking you to give my Government the power to bring to fruition the longing hopes, the ardent dreams, the fervent aspirations of the chiefs and people of our country. Throughout a century of alien rule our people have, with ever increasing tendency, looked forward to that bright and glorious day when they shall regain their ancient heritage, and once more take their place rightly as free men in the world.

Mr. Speaker, we have frequent examples to show that there comes a time in the history of all colonial peoples when they must, because of their will to throw off the hampering shackles of colonialism, boldly assert their God-given right to be free of a foreign ruler. Today we are here to claim this right to our independence.

Mr. Speaker, the Motion is in two parts. The first part not merely states our aim, but poses the question to Her Majesty's Government which is more fully set out in the White Paper. There is a general demand in the Gold Coast for self-government within the Commonwealth, and the United Kingdom Government should be informed of this demand, and be requested to make a declaration recognizing the existence of this demand, and expressing Her Majesty's Government's readiness to introduce an Act of Independence. This is the question which we are asking Her Majesty's Government in terms which clearly require an answer. That is the first thing we want: a declaration. But, even more important, we want to possess our self-government; we want an Act of Independence.

The second half of the Motion sets out in a straightforward manner to obtain the authority of the House for the presentation to Her Majesty's Government of the detailed proposals which we have made for immediate constitutional reform. We ask that these proposals may be considered on their merits and without prejudice to the request which has been made in the first half of the Motion. We request that the composition of our Assembly may be so amended that all its members shall be directly elected by secret ballot. Similarly, we have gone forward to request that the whole Cabinet may be composed of representative ministers. We have also made other proposals of immediate and striking importance, and I am confident that this Assembly will give the Motion before it its unanimous endorsement and support.

Last year, I brought this House changes in the constitution which were, at the time, regarded as of minor importance. I was accused, indeed, of personal ambition in seeking the title of Prime Minister. We can now, Mr Speaker, see the result for ourselves. Certainly nobody outside the Gold Coast has regarded my position as anything but what the name implies. The prestige of the Gold Coast Government overseas has, in fact, been enhanced by this change. Even the co-ordination of the functions of my own colleagues has been made more successful by the increase in status. I believe that there is more decision in our activities as a Cabinet than there was before, and that we are better equipped to get things done. The freedom we demand is for our children, for the generations yet unborn, that they may see the light of day and live as men and women with the right to work out the destiny of their own country.

Mr Speaker, our demand for self-government is a just demand. It is a demand admitting of no compromise. The right of a people to govern themselves is a fundamental principle, and to compromise on this principle is to betray it. To quote you a great social and political scientist –

> 'To negotiate with forces that are hostile on matters of principle means to sacrifice principle itself. Principle is indivisible. It is either wholly kept or wholly sacrificed. The slightest concession on matters of principle implies the abandonment of principle.'

The right of a people to decide their own destiny, to make their way in freedom, is not to be measured by the yardstick of colour or degree of social development. It is an inalienable right of peoples which they are powerless to exercise when forces, stronger than they themselves, by whatever means, for whatever reasons, take this right away from them. If there is to be a criterion of a people's preparedness for self-government, then I say it is their readiness to assume the responsibilities of ruling themselves. For who but a people themselves can say when they are prepared? How can others judge when that moment has arrived in the destiny of a subject people? What other gauge can there be?

Mr Speaker, never in the history of the world has an alien ruler granted self-rule to a people on a silver platter. Therefore, Mr Speaker, I say that a people's readiness and willingness to assume the responsibilities of self-rule is the single criterion of their preparedness to undertake those responsibilities.

I have described on a previous occasion in this House what were the considerations which led me to agree to the participation of my party in the General Election of 1951, and hence in the Government of the Gold Coast under the terms of the 1950 Constitution Order in Council. In making that decision, I took on the task of proving to the world that we were prepared to perform our duties with responsibility, to set in motion the many reforms which our people needed, and to work from within the Government and within the Assembly, that is, by constitutional means, for the immediate aim of self-government. We have only been in office, Mr Speaker, for two and a half years, and we have kept these objectives constantly in mind. Let there be no doubt that we are equally determined not to rest until we have gained them. We are encouraged in our efforts by the thought that in so acting we are showing that we are able to govern ourselves and thereby we are putting an end to the myth that Africans are unable to manage their own affairs, even when given the opportunity. We can never rest satisfied with what we have so far achieved. The Government certainly is not of that mind. Our country has proved that it is more than ready. For despite the legacies of a century of colonial rule, in the short space of time since your Representative Ministers assumed the responsibilities of office, we have addressed ourselves boldly to the task of laying sound economic and social foundations on which this beloved country of ours can raise a solid democratic society. The spirit of responsibility and enterprise which has animated our actions in the past two years will continue to guide us in the future, for we shall always act in the spirit of our Party's motto: 'Forward ever, backward never'. For we know notwithstanding that the essence of politics is the realization of what is possible.

Mr Speaker, we have now come to the most important stage of our constitutional development; we can look back on these stages through which we have passed during these last few years: first, our discussions with the Secretary of State leading to the changes of last year; then the questions posed in the October statement, which were to be answered by all parties, groups and councils interested in this great issue; the consultations with the Territorial Councils, with the political parties, with the Trades Union Congress. We have proceeded logically and carefully, and as I view it, the country has responded fully to my call. Every representation which we received – and there were many – has received my careful consideration. The talks which I had with the political parties and the Trades Union Congress, and the committees of the Asanteman and Joint Provincial Councils, were frank and cordial.

I had also received a special invitation to attend a meeting in Tamale with the Territorial Council, the Traditional Rulers and the Members of the Legislative Assembly. Naturally I accepted the invitation, because it was clear that if I had not held discussions with the Northern Territories, the unity of the Gold Coast might have been endangered and our progress towards self-government might have been delayed. The reverse has been the case. We have adapted some of our proposals to meet Northern Territories wishes, and have been able to set their minds at rest on several issues of the greatest importance to them and to the Gold Coast as a whole. Mr Speaker, sir, the days of forgetting about our brothers in the North, and in the Trust Territory, are over.

Criticisms have been levelled against the Government for the secrecy with which these talks were surrounded, and I should like to tell the country why this was necessary. When we went to the talks, of course, the Government members had some idea of the way their collective views on the representations were being formulated. We carefully explained, however, that our views were not finally decided and they would not be until we had had an opportunity of hearing any further views which these bodies might care to express in addition to their memoranda submitted. Having heard these views, we also sought an expression of opinion on specific problems which had occurred to us. But in order that our discussions could be of true value, frank and unreserved, I stated at an early stage that I should be grateful if the conversations could be regarded as strictly confidential. I am glad to place on record the value of the discussions which we held and the extent to which the undertaking which I was given was honoured. I hope that the bodies which were consulted also feel that the discussions were worthwhile.

Mr Speaker, knowing full well, therefore, the will of the chiefs and people whom we represent, I am confident that with the support of this House, Her Majesty's Government will freely accede to our legitimate and righteous demand to become a self-governing unit within the Commonwealth.

I put my confidence in the willing acceptance of this demand by Her Majesty's Government, because it is consistent with the declared policy of successive United Kingdom Governments. Indeed, the final transition from the stage of responsible government as a colony to the independence of a sovereign state guiding its own policies, is the apotheosis of this same British policy in relation to its dependencies.

Mr Speaker, pray allow me to quote from Britain's own Ministers. Mr Creech Jones, as Colonial Secretary in the first post-war Labour

Government, stated that 'The central purpose of British Colonial policy is simple. It is to guide the Colonial Territories to responsible self-government within the Commonwealth in conditions that ensure to the people concerned both a fair standard of living and freedom from oppression from any quarter.'

Again, on 12th July, 1950, in the House of Commons, Mr James Griffiths, Mr Creech Jones' successor, reiterated this principle: 'The aim and purpose,' he said 'is to guide the Colonial Territories to responsible self-government within the Commonwealth and, to that end, to assist them to the utmost of our capacity and resources to establish those economic and social conditions upon which alone self-government can be soundly based.'

Last, I give you the words of Mr Oliver Lyttleton, Colonial Secretary in Her Majesty's Conservative Government of today: 'We all aim at helping the Colonial Territories to attain self-government within the Commonwealth.'

Nor is this policy anything new in British Colonial history. The right to self-government of Colonial Dependencies has its origin in the British North American Act of 1867, which conceded to the provinces of Canada, complete self-rule. The independence of the other white Dominions of Australia and New Zealand was followed by freedom for South Africa. And since the end of the Second World War, our coloured brothers in Asia have achieved independence, and we are now proud to be able to acknowledge the sovereign States of India, Pakistan, Ceylon and Burma.

There is no conflict that I can see between our claim and the professed policy of all parties and governments of the United Kingdom. We have here in our country a stable society. Our economy is healthy, as good as any for a country of our size. In many respects, we are very much better off than many sovereign states. And our potentialities are large. Our people are fundamentally homogeneous, nor are we plagued with religious and tribal problems. And, above all, we have hardly any colour bar. In fact, the whole democratic tradition of our society precludes the *herrenvolk* doctrine. The remnants of this doctrine are now an anachronism in our midst, and their days are numbered.

Mr Speaker, we have travelled long distances from the days when our fathers came under alien subjugation to the present time. We stand now at the threshold of self-government and do not waver. The paths have been tortuous, and fraught with peril, but the positive and tactical action we have adopted is leading us to the New Jerusalem, the golden city of our hearts' desire! I am confident, therefore, that I express the wishes and feelings of the chiefs and people of this country in hoping that the final transfer of power to your Representative Ministers may be done in a spirit of amity and friendship, so that, having peacefully achieved our freedom, the peoples of both countries – Britain and the Gold Coast – may form a new relationship based on mutual respect, trust and friendship. Thus may the new partnership implicit in the Statute of Westminster be clothed in a new meaning. For then shall we be one of the 'autonomous communities within the British Empire, equal in status, in no way subordinate one to another in any aspect of their domestic or external affairs, though united by a common allegiance to the Crown, freely associated as members of the British Commonwealth of Nations', in accordance with the Balfour Declaration of 1926 which was embodied in the Statute of Westminster in 1931.

Today, more than ever before, Britain needs more 'autonomous communities freely associated'. For freely associated communities make better friends than those associated by subjection. We see today, Mr Speaker, how much easier and friendlier are the bonds between Great Britain and her former dependencies of India, Pakistan and Ceylon. So much of the bitterness that poisoned the relations between these former colonies and the United Kingdom has been absolved by the healing power of a better feeling that a new friendship has been cemented in the free association of autonomous communities.

These, and other weighty reasons, allied with the avowed aim of British colonial policy, will, I am confident, inspire Britain to make manifest once more to a sick and weary world her duty to stand by her professed aim. A free and independent Gold Coast, taking its rightful place in peace and amity by the side of the other Dominions, will provide a valid and effective sign that freedom can be achieved in a climate of good will and thereby accrue to the intrinsic strength of the Commonwealth. The old concepts of Empire, of conquest, domination and exploitation are fast dying in an awakening world. Among the colonial peoples, there is a vast, untapped reservoir of peace and goodwill towards Britain, would she but divest herself of the outmoded, moth-eaten trappings of two centuries ago, and present herself to her colonial peoples in a new and shining vestment and hand us the olive branch of peace and love, and give us a guiding hand in working out our own destinies.

In the very early days of the Christian era, long before England had assumed any importance, long even before her people had united into a nation, our ancestors had attained a great empire, which lasted until the eleventh century, when it fell before the attacks of the Moors of the North. At its height that empire stretched from Timbuktu to Bamako, and even as far as to the Atlantic. It is said that lawyers and scholars were much respected in that empire and that the inhabitants of Ghana wore garments of wool, cotton, silk and velvet. There was trade in copper, gold and textile fabrics, and jewels and weapons of gold and silver were carried.

Thus may we take pride in the name of Ghana, not out of romanticism, but as an inspiration for the future. It is right and proper that we should know about our past. For just as the future moves from the present so the present has emerged from the past. Nor need we be ashamed of our past. There was much in it of glory. What our ancestors achieved in the context of their contemporary society gives us confidence that we can create, out of that past, a glorious future, not in terms of war and military pomp, but in terms of social progress and of peace. For we repudiate war and violence. Our battles shall be against the old ideas that keep men trammelled in their own greed; against the crass stupidities that breed hatred, fear and inhumanity. The heroes of our future will be those who can lead our people out of the stifling fog of disintegration through serfdom, into the valley of light where purpose, endeavour and determination will create that brotherhood which Christ proclaimed two thousand years ago, and about which so much is said, but so little done.

Mr Speaker, in calling up our past, it is meet, on an historic occasion such as this, to pay tribute to those ancestors of ours who laid our national traditions, and those others who opened the path which made it possible to reach today the great moment at which we stand. As with our enslaved brothers dragged from these shores to the United States and to the West Indies, throughout our tortuous history, we have not been docile under the heel of the conqueror. Having known by our own traditions and experience the essentiality of unity and of government, we constantly formed ourselves into cohesive blocs as a means of resistance against the alien forces within our borders. And so today we recall the birth of the Ashanti nation through Okomfo Anokye and Osei Tutu and the symbolism entrenched in the Golden Stool; the valiant wars against the British, the banishment of Nana Prempeh the First to the Seychelle Islands; the temporary disintegration of the nation and its subsequent reunification. And so we come to the Bond of 1884. Following trade with the early merchant adventurers who came to the Gold Coast, the first formal association of Britain with our country was effected by the famous Bond of 1844, which accorded Britain trading rights in the country. But from these humble beginnings of trade and friendship, Britain assumed political control of this country. But our inalienable right still remains, as my friend, George Padmore, puts it in his recent book, *The Gold Coast Revolution*, and I quote – 'When the Gold Coast Africans demand self-government today they are, in consequence, merely asserting their birthright which they never really surrendered to the British who, disregarding their treaty obligations of 1844, gradually usurped full sovereignty over the country.'

Then the Fanti Confederation – the earliest manifestation of Gold Coast nationalism occurred in 1868 when Fanti Chiefs attempted to form the Fanti Confederation in order to defend themselves against the might of Ashanti and the incipient political encroachments of British merchants. It was also a union of the coastal states for mutual economic and social development. This was declared a dangerous conspiracy with the consequent arrest of its leaders.

Then the Aborigines Rights Protection Society was the next nationalist movement to be formed with its excellent aims and objects, and by putting up their titanic fight for which we cannot be sufficiently grateful, they formed an unforgettable bastion for the defence of our God-given land and thus preserved our inherent right to freedom. Such men as Mensah-Sarbah, Atta Ahuma, Sey and Wood have played their role in this great fight.

Next came the National Congress of British West Africa. The end of the first Great War brought its strain sand stresses and the echoes of the allied slogan, 'We fight for freedom' did not pass unheeded in the ears of Casely-Hayford, Hutton-Mills and other national stalwarts who were some of the moving spirits of the National Congress of British West Africa. The machinations of imperialism did not take long to smother the dreams of the people concerned, but today their aims and objects are being more than gratified with the appointment of African judges and other improvements in our national life.

As with the case of the National Congress of British West Africa, the United Gold Coast Convention was organized at the end of the Second World War to give expression to the people's desire for better conditions. The British Government, seeing the threat to its security here, arrested six members of the Convention and detained them for several weeks until the Watson Commission came. The stand taken by the Trades Union Congress, the farmers, students and women of the country, provides one of the most epic stories in our national struggle.

In June, 1949, the Convention People's Party with its uncompromising principles led the awakened masses to effectively demand their long lost heritage. And today, the country moves steadily forward to its proud goal.

Going back over the years to the establishment of constitutional development, we find that the first Legislative Council to govern the country was established in 1850; thirty-eight years later the first African, in the person of John Sarbah, was admitted to that council. It was not until 1916 that the Clifford Constitution increased the number of Africans, which was four in 1910, to six. But these were mainly councils of officials.

The Guggisberg Constitution of 1925 increased the unofficial representation in the council almost to par with the officials. This position was reversed by the Burns Constitution of 1946 which created an unofficial majority. The abortive Colony-Ashanti Collaboration of 1944 was the prelude to this change.

The Coussey Constitution of 1951 further democratized the basis of representation; and now, for the first time in our history, this Government is proposing the establishment of a fully elected Assembly with Ministers directly responsible to it.

We have experienced Indirect Rule, we have had to labour under the yoke of our own disunity, caused by the puffed-up pride of those who were lucky to enjoy better opportunities in life than their less fortunate brothers; we have experienced the slow and painful progress of constitutional changes by which, from councils on which Africans were either absent or merely nominated, this august House has evolved through the exercise by the enfranchized people of their democratic right to a voice in their own affairs and in so doing they have shown their confidence in their own countrymen by placing on us the responsibility for our country's affairs.

And so through the years, many have been laid to final rest from the stresses and dangers of the national struggle and many, like our illustrious friends of the Opposition, notwithstanding the fact that we may differ on many points, have also contributed a share to the totality of our struggle. And we hope that whatever our differences, we shall today become united in the demand for our country's freedom.

As I said earlier, what we ask is not for ourselves on this side of the House, but for all the chiefs and people of this country – the right to live as free men in the comity of nations. Were not our ancestors ruling themselves before the white man came to these our shores? I have earlier made reference to the ancient history of our more distant forebears in Ghana. To assert that certain people are capable of ruling themselves while others are not 'ready', as the saying goes, smacks to me more of imperialism than of reason. Biologists of repute maintain that there is no such thing as a 'superior' race. Men and women are as much products of their environment – geographic, climatic, ethnic, cultural, social – as of instincts and physical heredity. We are determined to change our environment, and we shall advance in like manner.

According to the motto of the valiant *Accra Evening News* – 'We prefer self-government with danger to servitude in tranquillity.' Doubtless we shall make mistakes as have all other nations. We are human beings and hence fallible. But we can try also to learn from the mistakes of others so that we may avoid the deepest pitfalls into which they have fallen. Moreover, the mistakes we may make will be our own mistakes, and it will be our responsibility to put them right. As long as we are ruled by others we shall lay our mistakes at their door, and our sense of responsibility will remain dulled. Freedom brings responsibilities and our experience can be enriched only by the acceptance of these responsibilities.

In the two years of our representative Government, we have become most deeply conscious of the tasks which will devolve upon us with self-rule. But we do not shrink from them; rather are we more than ever anxious to take on the reins of full self-government. And this, Mr Speaker, is the mood of the chiefs and people of this country at this time. On the fundamental choice between colonial status and self-government, we are unanimous. And the vote that will be taken on the motion before this Assembly will proclaim this to the world.

Honourable Members, you are called, here and now, as a result of the relentless tide of history, by Nemesis as it were, to a sacred charge, for you hold the destiny of our country in your hands. The eyes and ears of the world are upon you; yea, our oppressed brothers throughout this vast continent of Africa and the New World are looking to you with desperate hope, as an inspiration to continue their grim fight against cruelties which we in this corner of Africa have never known – cruelties which are a disgrace to humanity, and to the civilization which the white man has set himself to teach us. At this time, history is being made; a colonial people in Africa has put forward the first definite claim for independence. An African

III

colonial people proclaim that they are ready to assume the stature of free men and to prove to the world that they are worthy of the trust.

I know that you will not fail those who are listening for the mandate that you will give to your Representative Ministers. For we are ripe for freedom, and our people will not be denied. They are conscious that the right is theirs, and they know that freedom is not something that one people can bestow on another as a gift. They claim it as their own and none can keep it from them.

And while yet we are making our claim for self-government I want to emphasize, Mr Speaker, that self-government is not an end in itself. It is a means to an end, to the building of the good life to the benefit of all, regardless of tribe, creed, colour or station in life. Our aim is to make this country a worthy place for all its citizens, a country that will be a shining light throughout the whole continent of Africa, giving inspiration far beyond its frontiers. And this we can do by dedicating ourselves to unselfish service to humanity. We must learn from the mistakes of others so that we may, in so far as we can, avoid a repetition of those tragedies which have overtaken other human societies.

We must not follow blindly, but must endeavour to create. We must aspire to lead in the arts of peace. The foreign policy of our country must be dedicated to the service of peace and fellowship. We repudiate the evil doctrines of tribal chauvinism, racial prejudice and national hatred. We repudiate these evil ideas because in creating that brotherhood to which we aspire, we hope to make a reality, within the bounds of our small country, of all the grandiose ideologies which are supposed to form the intangible bonds holding together the British Commonwealth of Nations in which we hope to remain. We repudiate racial prejudice and national hatred, because we do not wish to be a disgrace to these high ideals.

Her Majesty, Queen Elizabeth the Second has just been crowned – barely one month ago – the memory is still fresh in our minds; the Queen herself has not forgotten the emotions called forth as she first felt the weight of the Crown upon her head; the decorations in London streets are hardly down; the millions of words written about the Coronation and its meaning will endure for centuries; the prayers from millions of lips are still fresh; the vows of dedication to duty which the Queen made are a symbol of the duties devolving on the Commonwealth. And so, we repudiate the evil doctrines which we know are promulgated and accepted elsewhere as the truth.

To Britain this is the supreme testing moment in her African relations. When we turn our eyes to the sorry events in South,

Central and East Africa, when we hear the dismal news about Kenya and Central African Federation, we are cheered by the more cordial relationship that exists between us and Britain. We are now asking her to allow that relationship to ripen into golden bonds of freedom, equality and fraternity, by complying without delay to our request for self-government. We are sure that the British Government will demonstrate its goodwill towards the people of the Gold Coast by granting us the self-government which we now so earnestly desire. We enjoin the people of Britain and all political parties to give our request their ardent support.

The self-government which we demand, therefore, is the means by which we shall create the climate in which our people can develop their attributes and express their potentialities to the full. As long as we remain subject to an alien power, too much of our energy is diverted from constructive enterprise. Oppressive forces breed frustration. Imperialism and colonialism are a two-fold evil. This theme is expressed in the truism that 'no nation which oppresses another can itself be free'. Thus we see that this evil not only wounds the people which is subject, but the dominant nation pays the price in a warping of their finer sensibilities through arrogance and greed. Imperialism and colonialism are a barrier to true friendship. For the short time since we Africans have had a bigger say in our affairs, the improved relations between us and the British have been most remarkable. Today there exists the basis of real friendship between us and His Excellency the Governor, Sir Charles Arden-Clarke, and the *ex-officio* Ministers of Defence and External Affairs, of Finance and of Justice. I want to pay tribute to these men for their valuable co-operation in helping us to make a success of our political advance. I feel that they have done this, firstly because as officers in the British Colonial Service, it is their duty to guide the subject territory in the attainment of self-government in accordance with the expressed aim of British colonial policy and, secondly, because we have, by our efforts in managing our own affairs, gained their respect, and they are conscious of the justice of our aspirations.

Let me recall the words of the great Casely-Hayford which he spoke in 1925:

'It must be recognized that co-operation is the greatest word of the century. With co-operation we can command peace, goodwill and concord. Without: chaos, confusion and ruin. But there can really be no co-operation between inferiors and superiors. Try as they may, there must come a time when the elements of superiority will seek to dictate, and the inferior ones will resent such dictation. It logically follows, therefore, that unless an honest effort is made to raise the inferior up to the prestige of the superior, and the latter can suffer it, all our talk of co-operation is so much empty gas ...'

Unless, therefore, our claim to independence is met now, the amicable relations which at present exist between us and the British may become strained. Our chiefs and people will brook no delay. But I feel confident that our claim, because of the reasons I have already given, will be accepted and our amity towards Britain will be deepened by our new association.

The strands of history have brought our two countries together. We have provided much material benefit to the British people, and they in turn have taught us many good things. We want to continue to learn from them the best they can give us and we hope that they will find in us qualities worthy of emulation. In our daily lives, we may lack those material comforts regarded as essential by the standards of the modern world, because so much of our wealth is still locked up in our land; but we have the gifts of laughter and joy, a love of music, a lack of malice, an absence of the desire for vengeance for our wrongs, all things of intrinsic worth in a world sick of injustice, revenge, fear and want.

We feel that there is much the world can learn from those of us who belong to what we might term the pretechnological societies. These are values which we must not sacrifice unheedingly in pursuit of material progress. That is why we say that self-government is not an end in itself.

We have to work hard to evolve new patterns, new social customs, new attitudes to life, so that while we seek the material, cultural and economic advancement of our country, while we raise their standards of life, we shall not sacrifice their fundamental happiness. That, I should say, Mr Speaker, has been the greatest tragedy of Western society since the industrial revolution.

In harnessing the forces of nature, man has become the slave of the machine, and of his own greed. If we repeat these mistakes and suffer the consequences which have overtaken those that made them, we shall have no excuse. This is a field of exploration for the young men and women now in our schools and colleges, for our sociologists and economists, for our doctors and our social welfare workers, for our engineers and town planners, for our scientists and our philosophers.

Mr Speaker, when we politicians have long passed away and been forgotten, it is upon their shoulders that will fall the responsibility of evolving new forms of social institutions, new economic instruments to help build in our rich and fertile country a society where men and women may live in peace, where hate, strife, envy and greed, shall have no place.

Mr Speaker, we can only meet the challenge of our age as a free people. Hence our demand for our freedom, for only free men can shape the destinies of their future.

Mr Speaker, Honourable Members, we have great tasks before us. I say, with all seriousness, that it is rarely that human beings have such an opportunity for service to their fellows.

Mr Speaker, for my part, I can only re-echo the words of a great man: 'Man's dearest possession is life, and since it is given him to live but once, he must so live as not to be besmeared with the shame of a cowardly existence and trivial past, so live that dying he might say: all my life and all my strength were given to the finest cause in the world – the liberation of mankind.'

Mr Speaker, 'Now God be thank'd, Who has match'd us with His hour!'

8

Before the general election of 1st June 1954 took place, electoral and representational reforms were made to increase the membership of the Legislative Assembly and to make it more representative. The country was divided into 104 constituencies, and the CPP resolved to contest every seat.

During the election campaign, it was necessary to expel 81 members from the Party for putting themselves up as candidates against the official Party candidates. Largely as a result of this, a new Party, the Northern People's Party (NPP) was formed in the Northern Territories, and NPP candidates opposed CPP candidates in each of the constituencies of the North. Yet in spite of this, the CPP won 72 out of the 104 seats in the Assembly, including 9 of the 21 seats for the Northern Territories. The remaining 20 seats were held by Independents, though within two years, seven Independents joined the CPP, giving us a voting strength of 79 out of 104.

The day after the election, I was invited to form a government. The leader of the NPP tried to establish himself as the official Opposition Leader, but I objected on the grounds that the NPP could not form an alternative government if called upon to do so; and furthermore, only represented one region of the country.

The CPP government was prepared to recognize the NPP as an unofficial Opposition, but within a few months the NPP and the remnants of various other Parties which had at one time or another opposed the CPP, merged to form the National Liberation Movement (NLM). The NLM at once began to campaign for a federal form of government. The Asanteman Council, headed by the Asantehene, joined forces with the NLM, and drew support from certain sections of the Ashanti people opposed to the Cocoa Duty and Development Funds (Amendment) Bill which was passed in August 1954. This Bill fixed and guaranteed the price paid to cocoa farmers, and provided for the use of the funds from cocoa sales to expand the economy of the country as a whole. In general, the cocoa farmers welcomed the Bill, but anti-CPP elements made use of it to attack the government by stirring up regional animosities. In particular, it was alleged that the government was spending too much on developing the coastal or Colony region, and neglecting Ashanti, the main cocoa-producing region. Outbreaks of violence occured in Ashanti. Hundreds of Ashanti CPP members were compelled to leave the region, and certain CPP chiefs were destooled. It was during this period of unrest that an attempt was made to assassinate me. A bomb exploded at my house in Accra, shaking it severely and shattering all the windows. I was at home at the time, and although the house was filled with people fortunately no-one was injured.

Meantime, the Opposition continued to agitate for another election, basing their campaign on the federation issue. Three times the NLM turned down invitations to discuss the matter, and NLM members walked out of the Assembly every time constitutional issues were raised. I therefore introduced a Motion in the Assembly on 5th April, 1955 for the setting up of a Select Committee to examine the question of a federal system of government.

But Opposition members once more left the House, and would not participate in the work of the Select Committee.

The Select Committee, after exhaustive examination of the pros and cons of federation, issued its Report on 26th July, 1955, in which it declared against a federal form of government, and recommended the establishment of Regional Councils to which the central government would delegate certain powers and functions. Two months later, in September 1955, the British government sent Sir Frederick Bourne to the Gold Coast to help in the drafting of a constitution. He visited all the regions, and invited all Parties and organizations to express their views to him. The NLM, however, refused to see him on the grounds that the State Councils (Ashanti) Amendment Bill, passed in November 1955 to permit Chiefs who had been destooled because of their opposition to the federal idea the right of appeal to the Governor, had made it impossible for them to take part in any discussions on constitutional matters.

On 17th December, 1955, Sir Frederick Bourne issued his Report recommending the devolution of certain consultative and deliberative powers and functions to Regional Assemblies, but leaving the actual business of legislation in the hands of the central legislature.

- The British government still insisted that no firm date could be given for Independence until a substantial majority of the people of the Gold Coast had shown that they wanted independence in the very near future, and had agreed upon a workable constitution. It was in order to satisfy these two conditions that I called a conference in February 1956 of all the principal organizations in the country to discuss Sir Frederick Bourne's Report and the whole constitutional question. Once again, the NLM refused to participate, and although the conference agreed to most of the recommendations contained in the

Report, it was necessary for the government to draw up its own constitutional proposals for Independence.

The CPP victory in the 1954 election had given us a clear mandate to negotiate 'self government now', and there was no justification for calling another general election before Independence. But the British government insisted that a general election must be held, and a Motion calling for Independence be passed by 'a reasonable majority' in the newly-elected Legislature, before a firm date could be agreed for Independence.

In May 1956 I presented to the Assembly the Government's White Paper containing the constitutional proposals for a sovereign and independent Gold Coast, to be known in future as Ghana. The Motion was debated and passed on the 5th of June, whereupon the Governor dissolved the National Assembly and declared that a general election would take place in July.

In the introduction to the CPP election manifesto I said that there were only two questions which the elector need consider: 'Do I want independence in my life time? or 'Do I want to revert to feudalism and imperialism?' The red-herring of federalism could not be allowed to confuse the issue.

As a result of the election, the CPP won 71 seats, increased later by the support of one of the Independents, to give a CPP majority of 40 in the Assembly of 104 members, a 'reasonable majority' acceptable to the British government, specially since our support came from every region of the country. Even in Ashanti, where the NLM boasted strong support, the CPP gained 43 per cent of the total votes cast. The NLM leadership, however, refused to accept the verdict of the people, declared once more in favour of a federal form of government, and announced that Opposition members would not attend the Assembly when the Independence Motion came before the House.

After the Independence Motion was passed, by 72

votes to none, Dr Busia, official leader of the Opposition, actually travelled to London to appeal to the British government not to grant Independence. But on 17th September I was informed by the Governor that the British government had at last, in response to our formal request for a firm date for Independence, fixed on the 6th of March, 1957.

At midnight on 5/6th March, 1957, a crowd estimated at 100,000 assembled on the Polo Ground in Accra to hear the official pronouncement of Independence. The Union Jack was lowered, and the red, green and gold flag of Ghana raised in its place to the cries of FREEDOM, FREEDOM, FREEDOM.

By employing the oppressor's own methods of parliamentary procedure, and through the tactics of Positive Action, we had been able to exert sufficient pressure on the colonial power to force a negotiated independence. The political, or nationalist revolution had been won, and without the necessity to resort to armed struggle. But the struggle for true freedom in the wider context of the African Revolution and the world socialist revolution was only just beginning. In order to liberate and unify Africa under an All-African Union Government, and to defeat the forces of imperialism and neocolonialism, and construct socialism, it would be necessary in future to employ all forms of political action, including armed struggle.

EXTRACT FROM THE MIDNIGHT PRONOUNCEMENT OF INDEPENDENCE

5th–6th March, 1957

At long last the battle has ended. And thus Ghana, your beloved country is free for ever. And here again, I want to take the opportunity to thank the chiefs and people of this country, the youth, the farmers, the women, who have so nobly fought and won this battle. Also I want to thank the valiant ex-servicemen who have so co-operated with me in this mighty task of freeing our country from foreign rule and imperialism. And as I pointed out at our Party conference at Saltpond, I made it quite clear that from now on, today, we must change our attitudes and our minds. We must realize that from now on we are no more a colonial but a free and independent people. But also, as I pointed out, that entails hard work. I am depending upon the millions of the country, the chiefs and people to help me to reshape the destiny of this country . . .

We are going to see that we create our own African personality and identity; . . . We again re-dedicate ourselves in the struggle to emancipate other countries in Africa., *for our independence is meaningless unless it is linked up with the total liberation of the African continent.*

130d Costume of an aristocratic Livonian lady
Pen drawing on paper with watercolour washes/
18.7 × 19.7/1521
Paris, Louvre (E. de Rothschild Collection)

131d Folk dress in Livonia
Pen drawing on paper with watercolour washes/
19.1 × 20.1/1521
Paris, Louvre (E. de Rothschild Collection)

132d Rich Livonian lady
Pen drawing on paper with watercolour washes/
27.5 × 18.5/1521
Paris, Louvre (E. de Rothschild Collection)

130

131

132

Virgin and Child (No. 107)
Dürer depicted the Virgin
Mary throughout his life.
Small painted pictures were
intended for personal devotion.
The human bond between
Mother and Child augments the
composition of the picture.

PART TWO

SOCIALIST CONSTRUCTION, and the STRUGGLE FOR THE LIBERATION and UNIFICATION OF AFRICA

9

Three alternatives are open to African states; first, to unite and to save our continent; secondly, to continue in disunity and to disintegrate; or thirdly, to sell out and capitulate before the forces of imperialism and neocolonialism. As each year passes, our failure to unite strengthens our enemies and delays the fulfilment of the aspirations of our people.

Long before 1957, I made it clear that the two major tasks to be undertaken after the ending of colonial rule in Ghana would be the vigorous prosecution of a Pan-African policy to advance the African Revolution, and at the same time the adoption of measures to construct socialism in Ghana. For political freedom is only the first step in the path towards full independence. It is a necessary pre-requisite for economic and social progress in Africa, but is meaningless while any part of the continent remains unliberated, and while the masses are exploited by the forces, both domestic and foreign, of international monopoly finance.

Pan-Africanism had to be reactivated on the soil of Africa, and it seemed that this could best be begun by the calling of a Conference of Independent African States, to be followed closely by an All-African People's

Conference to discuss common problems and to organize tactics and strategy.

Among the most pressing of common problems was the fact that by far the larger part of Africa was still unliberated. There were in fact only eight independent African States in 1958 when I called the Conference of Independent African States. They were Ghana, Ethiopia, Libya, Tunisia, Morocco, Egypt, Liberia and Sudan. Each of them was represented at the Accra Conference.

The countries participating in the Conference of Independent African States, held in Accra in April 1958, agreed to co-ordinate their economic planning to take measures to develop and encourage trade among their countries; to exchange educational, cultural and scientific information; to improve communications between the African States; to assist people still under colonial rule in their struggle to be free, and to provide training and educational facilities for them. It was decided that the 15th of April should be named Africa Freedom Day, to mark each year the onward progress of the liberation movement, and to symbolize the determination of the people of Africa to free themselves from foreign domination and exploitation.

The Accra Conference of Independent African States was the first conference of its kind ever to be held, and it paved the way for a succession of other Pan-African conferences of various kinds. A process was begun of direct consultation between African states, a process which has continued ever since, and which was marked by the setting up of the Organization Of African Unity (OAU) in 1963.

But probably the most important single achievement of the Conference was the adoption of the formula of one man, one vote, as an objective of the African Revolution. This gave the liberation movement direction and cohesion, and an impetus which was expressed shortly after the

Conference ended, in riots in the Congo and risings in Nyasaland (Malawi).

As a follow-up operation to the Conference I led a 15-man delegation to each of the countries which had taken part. The purpose was to cement contacts and to exchange views on African and international developments which had taken place since the Accra Conference. I was particularly anxious to discuss the question of how to speed up the actual process of liberation throughout Africa. For the independent states have a great responsibility to see to it that they consolidate their own states so that they become safe and strong base areas for the support of those fighting against colonialism, imperialism and racial oppression.

We travelled over 20,000 miles, going first to Ethiopia, then to Sudan, Libya, Tunisia, Morocco, Egypt, and returning to Ghana via Kano and Monrovia. At all the discussions I stressed that the struggle against imperialism, neocolonialism and racial oppression, and the task of building socialism, meant coming to grips with the forces of exploitation both at home and abroad. For Pan-Africanism and socialism are organically complementary; one cannot be achieved without the other.

EXTRACTS FROM SPEECH OF WELCOME TO REPRESENTATIVES OF INDEPENDENT AFRICAN STATES, ACCRA 15 APRIL 1958

This is a memorable gathering. It is the first time in history that representatives of independent sovereign states in Africa are meeting together with the aim of forging closer links of friendship, brotherhood, co-operation and solidarity between them.

As we look back into the history of our continent, we cannot escape the fact that we have for too long been the victims of foreign domination. For too long we have had no say in the management of our own affairs or in deciding our own destinies. Now times have changed, and today we are the masters of our own fate. This fact is evidenced in our meeting together here as independent sovereign states out of our own free will to speak our minds openly, to argue and discuss, to share our experiences, our aspirations, our dreams and our hopes in the interests of Mother Africa.

What is the purpose of this historic conference? We are here to know ourselves and to exchange views on matters of common interest; to explore ways and means of consolidating and safeguarding our hard-won independence; to strengthen the economic and cultural ties between our countries; to find workable arrangements for helping our brothers still languishing under colonial rule; to examine the central problem which dominates the world today, namely, the problem of how to secure peace.

We have learnt much about the old forms of colonialism. Some of them still exist, but I am confident they will all disappear from the face of our continent. It is not only the old forms of colonialism that we are determined to see abolished, but we are equally determined that the new forms of colonialism which are now appearing in the world, with their potential threat to our precious independence, will not succeed.

Similarly with racialism. Many of the advocates of colonialism claimed in the past – as some of them do now – they were racially superior and had a special mission to colonize and rule other people. This we reject. We repudiate and condemn all forms of racialism, for racialism not only injures those against whom it is used but warps and perverts the very people who preach and protect it; and when it becomes a guiding principle in the life of any nation, as it has become in some parts of Africa, then that nation digs its own grave. It is inconceivable that a racial minority will be able for ever to maintain its totalitarian domination over an awakened majority.

Africa is the last remaining stronghold of colonialism. Unlike Asia, there are on the continent of Africa more dependent territories than independent sovereign nations. Therefore we, the free independent states of Africa, have a responsibility to hasten the total liberation of Africa. I believe that there are lessons from the past which will help us in discharging this sacred duty.

If I have spoken of racialism and colonialism it is not, as I have said, because I want to indulge in recrimination with any country by listing a catalogue of wrongs which have been perpetrated upon our continent in the past. My only purpose in doing so is to illustrate the different forms which colonialism and imperialism old and new can take, so that we can be on our guard in adopting measures to safeguard our hard-won independence and national sovereignty. The imperialists of today endeavour to achieve their ends not merely by military means, but by economic penetration, cultural assimilation, ideological domination, psychological infiltration, and subversive activities even to the point of inspiring and promoting assassination and civil strife. Very often these methods are adopted in order to influence the foreign policies of small and uncommitted countries in a particular direction. Therefore we, the leaders of resurgent Africa, must be alert and vigilant.

We must leave no stone unturned in our endeavours to lessen tensions in Africa no less than elsewhere, as every success which we are able to achieve in resolving issues like frontier disputes, tribal quarrels and racial and religious antagonisms, will be a step forward in the bringing about of world peace. To the extent that we are able by our own exertion and example, to maintain peace and friendship within our own states and on our continent will we be in a position to exert moral pressures elsewhere and help to quench the flames of war which could destroy us all.

Today we are one. If in the past the Sahara divided us, now it unites us. And an injury to one is an injury to all of us. From this Conference must go out a new message: 'Hands off Africa! Africa must be free!'

10

By the end of 1958 there were clear indications that foreign powers, far from withdrawing from Africa, were in fact increasing their exploitation of the continent. In many of the so-called independent states, neocolonialism replaced the old-style colonialism; while in the States still under colonial rule, or suffering government by racist minorities, imperialist aggression took the form of increased repression. The process could not be seriously challenged until collective imperialism was confronted with unified African effort in political, economic and military spheres.

In 1958, there were already in existence throughout Africa well developed trade union and co-operative movements, and also progressive movements of youth, women and others concerned with the freedom struggle. Delegates from 62 nationalist organizations attended the All-African People's Conference in Accra in December 1958.

The primary aim of the Conference was to encourage nationalist political movements in colonial areas as a means towards continental unity and a socialist transformation of society. In my Address inaugurating the Conference I spoke of the four main stages of Pan-Africanism:

(i) national independence
(ii) national consolidation
(iii) transnational unity and community
(iv) economic and social reconstruction on the principles of scientific socialism

After long discussion during which political and trade union leaders from all over Africa expressed their views and shared their experiences, it was agreed to:

(i) work actively for a final assault on colonialism and imperialism
(ii) use non-violent means to achieve political freedom, but to be prepared to resist violence if the colonial powers resorted to force
(iii) set up a Permanent Secretariat to co-ordinate the efforts of all nationalist movements in Africa for the achievement of freedom
(iv) condemn racialism and tribalism wherever they exist and work for their eradication, and in particular to condemn the apartheid policy of the South African government
(v) work for the ultimate achievement of a Union or Commonwealth of African States

These have remained the basic objectives of African freedom fighter organizations, though equally important is their determination to end all forms of exploitation.

While in 1958 some progressive leaders of Africa still hoped to achieve their aims by non-violent methods, it has since become generally accepted that all methods of struggle, including armed struggle, must be employed in the face of the increasingly violent and aggressive onslaught of imperialist and neocolonialist forces and their indigenous agents.

Further All-African People's Conferences were held in Tunis in 1960, and in Cairo in 1961. About two hundred delegates attended the latter, and it was at this Conference that the dangers of neocolonialism were thoroughly examined. Among the resolutions passed were ones calling for the expulsion of South Africa from the United Nations Organization, and the dissolution of the Central African Federation.

PROVISIONAL AGENDA OF THE ALL AFRICAN PEOPLE'S CONFERENCE

AIMS AND OBJECTS

The main purpose of the All-African People's Conference to be held in Accra, Ghana, in December, 1958, will be to formulate concrete plans and work out the Gandhian tactics and strategy of the African Non-Violent Revolution in relation to:—

1. **Colonialism and Imperialism.**
2. **Racialism and Discriminatory Laws and Practices.**
3. **Tribalism and Religious Separatism.**
4. **The position of Chieftaincy under:**
   (*a*) Colonial Rule
   (*b*) A Free Democratic Society

The time has come for an open exposure of, and an onslaught upon, the propagators of Tribalism, who are today the most dangerous black agents of the Imperialists, for it is their poisonous policy of inciting Africans against Africans, brothers against brothers, tribes against tribes, which constitutes the greatest obstacle to the achievement of **United Freedom Fighters Fronts**, which alone can bring about a speedy end to foreign domination.

Not until we expose and unmask the anti-patriotic role of those African political careerists whose activities only help the Imperialists to maintain their traditional policy of **"divide and rule"**—the last bulwark of Colonialism—will Africa regain her lost freedom and take her rightful place among the comity of nations on an equal footing with others.

This problem of "divide and rule" along tribal lines is an ever-pressing danger in the so-called multi-racial territories of East and Central Africa, where our uncompromising demands must be:

1. **Land to the Africans.**
2. **Equal voting rights for all, regardless of race, tribe, colour or creed.**
3. **Implementation of the Universal Declaration of Human Rights of the United Nations.**

THE CONFERENCE will also examine the question of Irredentism and discuss plans for the regrouping of Independent African States on the basis of:

1. **Adjustment of existing artificial frontiers.**
2. **Amalgamation or federation of territories on a regional basis.**
3. **The progressive federation or confederation of geographical regional State Groupings into an ultimate Pan-African Commonwealth of Free, Independent United States of Africa.**

ALL AFRICAN PEOPLE'S CONFERENCE

A CALL TO INDEPENDENCE

Attention, all Africans!
Have you heard the clarion call to action?—**HANDS OFF AFRICA!**

AFRICA MUST BE FREE!
Now in order to translate this call into action and thereby enable the oppressed and exploited masses of Africa to achieve their

legitimate human rights and political aspirations of self-government, independence and self-determination, we the representatives of the sponsoring organizations have taken the initiative in convening an All African People's Conference as the rallying centre of Emergent African Nationalism.

THIS CONFERENCE will take place in Accra, the capital of the new progressive State of Ghana, in December, 1958.

THIS CONFERENCE, unlike the recent Conference of Independent African States, will be on a non-governmental level and will be attended by hundreds of representatives of progressive political, nationalist, trade union, co-operative, youth, women's and other organizations of the people from every country throughout Africa committed to the struggle for complete Independence.

PEOPLE OF AFRICAN DESCENT, as well as representatives from non-African organizations which endorse the aims and objects of the Conference will also be invited as fraternal delegates and unofficial observers.

THIS CONFERENCE will be the greatest gathering of its kind ever to be brought together on African soil. It will demonstrate the solidarity and fraternity which bind the awakening peoples of Africa, cutting across race, tribe and the artificial frontiers which the imperialists have contrived in order to divide us and so maintain their evil system of Colonialism, Racial Domination and Tribal Separatism.

THIS CONFERENCE will formulate and proclaim our African Personality based on the philosophy of Pan-African Socialism as the ideology of the African Non-Violent Revolution.

HENCEFORTH OUR SLOGAN SHALL BE:

  PEOPLES OF AFRICA, UNITE! YOU HAVE NOTHING TO LOSE BUT YOUR CHAINS! YOU HAVE A CONTINENT TO REGAIN! YOU HAVE FREEDOM AND HUMAN DIGNITY TO ATTAIN!

And to the Colonialists we say!
HANDS OFF AFRICA! AFRICA MUST BE FREE!!

11

A first step towards the political unification of Africa was taken on November the 23rd, 1958, when Ghana and the Republic of Guinea united to form a nucleus for a Union of African States. It was arranged for resident ministers to be exchanged, who were recognized as members of both the governments of Ghana and Guinea, and it was their task to provide the practical day to day co-operation between the two countries.

The Ghana-Guinea Union was an expression of the determination of President Sékou Touré and myself to start the unification process by setting up an embryo organization which other States could join as and when they wished.

The following year, in July 1959, President Tubman of Liberia, President Sékou Touré and I met in Sanniquellie to discuss the whole question of African liberation and unity. At the end of our talks we issued a Declaration of Principles explaining the nature of the organization we agreed to form which was to be known as the Community of Independent African States. The Community was not a political union of states, but an economic, cultural and social organization designed to promote African unity by building up a 'free and prosperous African Community for the benefit of its peoples and the peoples of the world, and in the interest of international peace and security'. However, Item 6 clause (c) of the Declaration stated that a main objective of the Community was to help accelerate the liberation of African states still subjected to 'domination'.

We agreed to submit the Declaration to a conference of independent states and states which had fixed dates for their independence. The conference would discuss and work out a charter which would achieve the ultimate goal of unity between independent African states.

The conference opened in Addis Ababa on the 14th of June 1960. Members confirmed the decisions of the Accra Conference of Independent African States, and adopted resolutions calling for greater co-operation between the states in the assistance being given to the liberation movement.

But already it was becoming very clear that there were wide differences in the policies of the various independent states on the methods to be adopted in order to achieve the ultimate objective of a totally liberated and unified Africa. Some advocated a gradualist approach, emphasising economic co-operation and regional and sub-regional organizations as a prelude to political association. The more progressive states, however, argued that imperialist and neocolonialist aggression made speedier progress essential, and that African unification based on an All-African Union Government was the only possible framework within which the fullest development of Africa could be achieved.

In December 1960, when I met Sékou Touré and Modibo Keita in Conakry, we decided that a special committee should meet in Accra from 13–18 January to draw up proposals for a Ghana-Guinea-Mali Union. The groundwork having been prepared, the three of us met again in Accra from 27–29 April and agreed upon a Charter for the Union of African States (UAS). As in the case of the Ghana-Guinea Union the organization was to form a nucleus for a Union of African States, and provision was made for the admission of other African states which might join at a later date.

The following Article 3 of the Charter states the aims of the Union:

The aims of the Union of African States (UAS) are as follows:
to strengthen and develop ties of friendship and fraternal co-operation between the Member States politically, diplomatically, economically and culturally; to pool their resources in order to consolidate their independence and safeguard their territorial integrity; to work jointly to achieve the complete liquidation of imperialism, colonialism and neo-colonialism in Africa and the building up of African Unity;
to harmonize the domestic and foreign policy of its Members, so that their activities may prove more effective and contribute more worthily to safeguarding the peace of the world.

The Charter provided for the holding of quarterly summit conferences in Accra, Bamako and Conakry respectively. At the second conference of the UAS held in Bamako in June 1961, we issued a joint communiqué reaffirming our determination to continue to support the liberation struggle of the African people, particularly in Algeria, the Congo and Angola.

The Charter formally bringing into being the Union of African States formed by Ghana, Guinea and Mali was published simultaneously in the three capitals, Accra, Conakry and Bamako, on the first of July 1961.

In each of the early attempts at unification, in the Ghana – Guinea Union, at Sanniquellie, and again in the

137

Ghana – Guinea – Mali Union, emphasis was placed on the need to give practical support to the liberation struggle. Our unity of purpose was absolutely clear on this point and it was the liberation issue above all others which led to the calling of the Casablanca Conference when the so-called radical grouping of African states comprising Ghana, Guinea, Mali, Libya, Egypt, Morocco and the Algerian FLN met in Casablanca from 3–7 January 1961 to discuss the situation in the Congo, the war in Algeria, and apartheid in South Africa. In the African Charter of Casablanca, published at the end of the Conference we stated:

> We, the Heads of African States, convened in Casablanca from the 3rd January to the 7th January, 1961, reaffirm our faith in the Conference of Independent African States, held in Accra in 1958, and in Addis Ababa in 1960, and appeal to all Independent African States to associate themselves with our common action for the consolidation of liberty in Africa and the building up of its unity and security.

In the speech I made at the closing session of the Conference, I again stressed the urgent need for Africa to unite:

> I can see no security for African States unless African leaders, like ourselves, have realized beyond all doubt that salvation for Africa lies in unity ... for in unity lies strength, and as I see it, African States must unite or sell themselves out to imperialist and colonialist exploiters for a mess of pottage, or disintegrate individually

The French-speaking independent African states who had at the Addis Ababa Conference in 1960 advanced the theory that economic co-operation should precede political integration, did not attend the Casablanca Conference. The governments of Tunisia, Nigeria and Liberia also refused to send representatives.

We agreed at Casablanca to set up an African Consultative Assembly 'as soon as conditions permit'; a Heads of State Committee; economic and cultural committees; and a Joint African High Command. A protocol was signed in Cairo on the 5th of May 1961 by the Foreign Ministers of the Casablanca Powers putting into effect the organization provided for in the Charter. Parallel meetings of the Heads of State and the Foreign Ministers were also held in Cairo in August 1961. It was announced at the conclusion of the meetings that a Secretary-General had been appointed for the group's permanent Secretariat with headquarters in Bamako; and a Commander of the Joint African High Command with headquarters in Accra.

The group's Economic Committee later signed agreements on the following joint organizations:

(i) an Economic and Customs Union and an Economic Council
(ii) an African Common Market in which customs barriers and import quotas would be progressively ended within a five year period.
(iii) an African Economic Development Bank with a capital of 30,000,000 dollars
(iv) an African Payments Union to facilitate the settling of accounts between member States
(v) a postal and telecommunications union
(vi) a joint shipping company

It was also decided that an agreement on economic and technical co-operation should be concluded between member states; that labour legislation in member countries should be gradually co-ordinated; and that members should conduct a joint foreign policy.

The group's Cultural Committee reached agreement designed to 'safeguard African values' and to promote wider knowledge of the contribution of the African continent to human civilization. It decided that an Institute of African Studies be set up for this purpose.

I do not think that I have ever attended a single meeting or conference between African states where I have not warned against the dangers of delaying unification. It is not practical politics in Africa today to work for any other goal. There is not an African state which is secure, or which is free to develop its resources to the full for the benefit of its own people. All are economically weak, and all are politically unstable. Unless we unite there can be no progress, and the suffering of the African masses will continue.

DECLARATION OF PRINCIPLES
SANNIQUELLIE CONFERENCE

July 1959

1. The name of the organization shall be the Community of Independent African States.
2. Africans, like all other peoples have the inherent right to independence and self-determination and to decide the form of government under which they wish to live.
3. Each state or federation, which is a member of the Community, shall maintain its own national identity and constitutional structure. The Community is being formed with a view to achieving unity among independent African states. It is not designed to prejudice the present or future international policies, relations and obligations of the states involved.

4. Each member of the Community accepts the principle that it shall not interfere in the internal affairs of any other member.

5. (a) The acts of states or federations which are members of the Community, shall be determined in relation to the essential objectives which are Freedom, Independence, Unity, the African Personality, as well as the interest of the African peoples. (b) Each member-state or federation shall, in its acts or policies, do nothing contrary to the spirit and objectives of the Community.

6. (a) The general policy of the Community shall be to build up a free and prosperous African Community for the benefit of its peoples and the peoples of the world and in the interest of international peace and security. (b) This policy shall be based essentially on the maintenance of diplomatic, economic and cultural relations, on the basis of equality and reciprocity, with all the states of the world which adopt a position compatible with African interests and African dignity. (c) Its main objective will be to help other African territories, subjected to domination, with a view to accelerating the end of their non-independent status.

7. The Community shall set up an Economic Council, a Cultural Council and a Scientific and Research Council.

8. Membership of the Community shall be open to all independent African states and federations, and any non-independent country of Africa shall have the right to join the Community upon its attainment of independence.

9. The Community shall have a flag and an anthem to be agreed upon at a later date.

10. The motto of the Community shall be: INDEPENDENCE AND UNITY.

> *Signed:* W. V. S. Tubman, President of the
> Republic of Liberia
> Sékou Touré, President of the
> Republic of Guinea
> Kwame Nkrumah, Prime Minister
> of Ghana

12

On the first of July 1960, Ghana became a republic under a new constitution approved by the Ghanaian people in a plebiscite held in April 1960. Two original provisions were of basic importance in the constitution:

(i) the proclaiming of the principle of one man, one vote
(ii) the conferring of powers providing for the surrender of Ghana's sovereignty, in whole or in part, if at any time Ghana joined a Union of African States.

I was elected President in the same plebiscite. Here again, our republican constitution was unique in that, unlike other republican constitutions, it provided that the President should be the executive head of government, and should represent the majority party in the National Assembly. In the event of disagreement between the President and the Assembly, the issue was to be decided by a general election. In the first instance the President was to be elected by the will of the people expressed in the April plebiscite, but subsequently he was to be elected by the Assembly after each general election. Thus, full legislative power was vested in the Assembly, and the President had no power to make laws or provisions having the force of law except under the authority of the Assembly.

The provision concerning the possible surrender of Ghana's sovereignty on joining a Union of African States caused quite a stir since no constitution had ever before contained such a provision. It did not mean that Ghana was not a sovereign state when the republican constitution came into operation in July 1960, but it did mean that the Assembly had the power to surrender sovereignty as soon as a Union of African States became practicable. As in the case of the Ghana-Guinea Union, it was intended to set a precedent which other states might follow.

When darkness fell on the evening of the first of July 1960, Republic Day, a symbolic ceremony was performed before an immense crowd on the race course at Accra where a large circular bowl of concrete had been erected to contain a perpetually burning flame. It was my task to light the flame, and by that symbolic gesture to proclaim the opening of the next phase of the African Revolution and to commit the Republic of Ghana to the continuing struggle for African liberation.

In lighting the flame I reminded the people of Ghana that our struggle was by no means over, but had merely moved into a new phase. We had started a movement which would set the whole of Africa ablaze to eliminate the last bastions of colonialism, imperialism and racialism from the face of the African continent.

SPEECH AT THE CEREMONIAL LIGHTING OF THE FLAME OF AFRICAN FREEDOM

1st July, 1960

We have come here tonight to light the torch of African freedom. This flame which we are about to light will not only enshrine the spirit of the Republic of Ghana, but will also provide a symbol for the African freedom fighters of today and tomorrow. We shall draw inspiration from this perpetual flame for the struggle of African emancipation.

Day after day and year after year this flame will reflect the burning desire of the African people to be free – totally free and independent – fettered by no shackles of any nature whatsoever, and will signify their ability to manage and direct their own affairs in the best interest of themselves.

I light this flame not only in the name of the people of Ghana but also in sacred duty to millions of Africans elsewhere now crying out for freedom. And I charge all of us here present to remember that this great struggle of African emancipation is a holy crusade to which we must constantly stand dedicated and which must be prosecuted to a successful end.

Your Excellencies, Ladies and Gentlemen: I now light this flame and may it burn perpetually and constitute a symbol of victory for our cause.

*

13

The year 1960 has come to be known as 'Africa Year' because in that year so many African states obtained their freedom from direct colonial rule. The Congo was one of them. In fact, the Congo declared its independence on the 30th of June, 1960, the day before the Republic of Ghana was proclaimed.

I have written in detail in my book CHALLENGE OF THE CONGO of the events which preceded and followed the declaration of the Congo's independence. In brief, the country had not been prepared for the ending of colonial rule. There were hardly any experienced Congolese political leaders or administrators, and the country was torn by political dissension. Patrice Lumumba was the only man who could claim support from all the provinces of the Congo. His party, the Congo National Movement (MNC) gained 33 of the 137 seats in the National Assembly, while the People's National Party, the party of his nearest rival, Joseph Kasavubu, won only 19. Yet Lumumba managed to organize a working majority in the Assembly and became the first prime minister of the Congo. Almost immediately trouble began with a rising among the Force Publique at Thysville. This was followed on the 11th of July, by the secession, under Moise Tshombe of the rich mining province of Katanga from the Republic of the Congo.

On the 12th of July, Lumumba appealed to the United Nations for aid to prevent the secession and the attempt to destroy the territorial integrity of the Congo. I immediately sent a mission to the Congo to offer Lumumba's government 'all possible aid, including, if it is desired by the Government of the Congo, military assistance'. Though Ghana was prepared to act either alone or jointly with the United Nations I made it clear that Ghana considered the Congo crisis was a matter which should be solved if possible by the efforts of the independent African states.

Tshombe's action posed a threat to the whole of independent Africa, for if Katanga succeeded in its secession, the independent Republic of the Congo could not hope to survive. Katanga contains some of the world's most valuable mineral resources, and it was essential that the Congo's richest province should form part of a unified state. But Katanga's economic strength was precisely the reason for imperialist and neocolonialist interest in directing Tshombe's traitorous moves. The powerful Union Minière du Haut Katanga, which exploited Katanga's mines and which produced at least 45% of the Congo's exports, did not wish to see the province come under the control of Lumumba's government. Tshombe therefore, and other indigenous bourgeois groups throughout the Congo, were used as tools by foreign exploiters and oppressors so that they might continue to rob the Congo of its wealth, and to deprive the impoverished majority of the Congolese people of their birthright.

Ghana's offer of military help was immediately accepted by Lumumba, and on the 15th of July Ghanaian troops were flown to the Congo in planes made available by the UN. It was hoped that with the arrival of troops in the Congo under UN direction, the struggle would soon be over. But Tshombe's imperialist and neocolonialist

146

support was strong, and soon it became clear that a protracted struggle was inevitable.

United Nations intervention in the Congo resulted in the fall of Lumumba's government in September 1960, and in his ultimate murder. But UN intervention would never have been necessary if there had been a Pan-African force to answer Lumumba's call for military assistance, and to provide early and prompt action. Even if there had been in existence rudimentary political machinery through which independent African states could consult together and organize joint action, most of the disorganization and disorder which followed the Congo's independence might have been avoided.

On the 8th of August 1960, I addressed the Ghana National Assembly about the continuing struggle in the Congo:

The evil of balkanization, disunity and secessions, is that the new balkan states of Africa will not have the independence to shake off the economic shackles which result in Africa being a source of riches to the outside world, while grinding poverty continues at home.

There is real danger that the colonial powers will grant a nominal type of political independence to individual small units so as to ensure that the same old colonial type of economic organization continues long after independence has been achieved.

I concluded:

This is a turning point in the history of Africa. If we allow the independence of the Congo to be compromised in any way by the imperialist and capitalist forces, we shall expose the sovereignty and independence of all Africa to grave risk. The struggle of the Congo is therefore our struggle. It is incumbent on us to take our stand by our brothers in the Congo in the full knowledge that only Africa can fight for its destiny. In this struggle we shall not reject the assistance and support of our friends, but we will yield to no enemy, however strong.

On the 7th of August, 1960, Patrice Lumumba arrived in Accra after visiting the USA and various African countries to explain the desperate situation in the Congo, and to appeal for sufficient help to end Katanga's secession. The UN force in the Congo seemed to be ineffective, and although the Security Council had called on Belgium to withdraw its forces from the country this had not been done.

Lumumba spent the 7th and the 8th of August in Ghana at my invitation. It was his first visit to Ghana since 1958 when, as a leader of the national liberation struggle in the Congo, he attended the All-African People's Conference in Accra. At the end of our talks we issued the following Joint Communique:

> On his return from a visit to the United States of America, His excellency Mr Patrice Lumumba, Prime Minister of the Congo, made a brief stop in Accra from the 7th to the 8th of August 1960 at the invitation of Osagyefo Dr Kwame Nkrumah, President of the Republic of Ghana.
>
> In the course of the discussions President Dr Kwame Nkrumah and Prime Minister Lumumba re-affirmed their determination to work in the closest possible association with the other Independent African States for the establishment of a Union of African States, with a view to liberating the whole continent of Africa from colonialism and imperialism. The two Heads of Government:
>
> (a) Condemned unreservedly the refusal of the

Belgian Government to withdraw their troops from the Congo, contrary to the decision of the Security Council of the United Nations. They agreed, in conjunction with other Independent African States, that in the event of the United Nations failing to effect a total and unconditional withdrawal of Belgian troops from the Congo as a whole, they will establish a Combined High Command of military forces to bring about a speedy withdrawal of these foreign troops from the Congo. They will also enlist the support of any other nation prepared to assist them in the achievement of the following objectives:

(i) withdrawal of Belgian troops from Katanga and all other parts of the Republic of Congo;
(ii) recognition of the sovereignty and territorial integrity of the Republic of the Congo;
(iii) total and complete evacuation of the military bases in Kitona and Kamina.

(b) They agreed to issue invitations to an African Summit Conference of the Independent African States to be held in Leopoldville from the 25th to the 30th August, 1960.

The Secret Agreement which follows, was signed the same day 8th August, 1960. It was never implemented, due to the breakdown of Lumumba's government in September, and his subsequent tragic murder at the hands of the puppets of imperialism and neocolonialism.

SECRET AGREEMENT
BETWEEN
GHANA AND THE CONGO

Signed in Accra, 8th August, 1960

The President of the Republic of Ghana and the Prime Minister of the Republic of Congo have given serious thought to the idea of African Unity and have decided to establish with the approval of the Governments and peoples of their respective states, among themselves a UNION OF AFRICAN STATES. The Union would have a Republican Constitution within a federal framework. The Federal Government would be responsible for:

(*a*) Foreign Affairs
(*b*) Defence
(*c*) The issue of a common currency
(*d*) Economic Planning and Development

There would be no customs barriers between any parts of the Federation. There would be a Federal Parliament and a Federal Head of State. The Capital of the Union should be Leopoldville. Any State or Territory in Africa is free to join this Union. The above Union presupposes Ghana's abandonment of the Commonwealth.

Dated at Accra this 8th day of August 1960

KWAME NKRUMAH   PATRICE LUMUMBA
President of the   Prime Minister of the
Republic of Ghana   Republic of the Congo

14

The political revolution ending direct colonial rule is the essential pre-requisite for the revolution to bring about a radical transformation of society. With the national liberation struggle over it is then possible to come to grips with the class struggle expressed in the continuing exploitation and oppression of imperialists and neo-colonialists and the indigenous bourgeoisie.

In this more difficult and protracted struggle, where the enemy is less obvious and is supported by the giant complexes of international monopoly finance capital, it is more than ever necessary to have a well-disciplined progressive party pursuing socialist revolutionary policies. The broad base on which it was necessary to construct the party while the struggle for national liberation was being waged, meant that it contained many who had strong reservations about the kind of society they wished to see constructed after independence. Indigenous bourgeois and petty bourgeois elements, deeply committed to capitalism, aspired to replace the foreigner and not to see power pass to the masses. The extent of their commitment to capitalism has been seen clearly in the many reactionary military coups which have taken place throughout Africa to block the advance of the African Revolution. After independence, therefore, party organization and discipline must be tightened and strengthened, and ideological education of the masses pursued with the utmost vigour.

Unlike the bourgeoisie of 'developed' countries, which may be termed a business bourgeoisie, the African bourgeoisie is mainly bureaucratic and professional. It is in general not engaged in production, nor does it control production. For its survival it depends on producers, and their production is controlled by imperialism. It is this small, but powerful section of our population which is particularly affected by the disease of the mind which is the legacy of colonialism, and which has been aptly named the 'colonial mentality'. The disease is apparent in the minds of those who, at independence, wish to step into the shoes of their old colonial masters, and to run the state machinery and the armed forces as their masters did before them, in their own interests, and to keep the masses in permanent subjection. This indigenous bourgeoisie, with their imperialist and neocolonialist allies, sabotage any moves by the newly-independent government which threaten the main pillars of their positions of power and privilege. If all else fails, they engineer a coup to remove a progressive government by force.

The revolution to end social and economic exploitation and oppression involves confrontation not simply with a single foreign colonial power, but with the powerful international empires of monopoly finance and with an indigenous fifth column prepared to sell out for money and position. In the national liberation struggle the enemy is visible and easily isolated. But in the socialist revolutionary struggle the enemy is all around and within, exercising insidious, under-cover pressures of all kinds aimed at blocking any measures which threaten the basic pillars supporting capitalist growth. Such an enemy is difficult to attack because it is dispersed and deeply entrenched both in the fabric of our society and within the minds of the people.

My broadcast to the people of Ghana early in the morning of 8 April 1961, and known as the Dawn Broadcast, was a call to action to revitalize the CPP, to end self-seeking, to energize the efforts of the people towards socialism; in short to stir up the people to fight the battle of the mind with greater determination.

EXTRACTS FROM DAWN BROADCAST

8th April, 1961

In accordance with the cherished customs of our fathers, whereby advice is sought or given at early dawn, I have come to the microphone this early morning to share some thoughts with you in a homely chat.

Four years ago we achieved independence and set out on a new road to nationhood. On the 1st of July, 1960, we consolidated this political achievement by setting up the Republic as an expression of our sovereign will. That day marked the real beginning of the life of our nation and settled upon us responsibility not only for the development and reconstruction of Ghana, but also for the faithful duty of assisting other African territories to achieve their freedom and independence.

This responsibility casts upon all Ghanaians an obligation to protect the national stability we have so ably created and to guard ever jealously the solidarity of our nation. For this reason I have been rather unhappy about reports which I have received since my return from the United Kingdom; and this has led me to speak to you this morning, to examine the matters forming the subject of these reports, and to discuss them openly and sincerely.

When I was away certain matters arose concerning the Trades Union Congress, the National Assembly, the Co-operative Movement and the United Ghana Farmers Council. These matters created misunderstandings and led to some regrettable demonstrations.

I do not think that at this stage of our national life, when all our efforts should be concentrated upon building a first-class nation, we should allow petty misunderstandings and squabbles to divert our attention from our great and worthy aims and objectives.

What was the cause of these unfortunate circumstances? Some Parliamentarians criticized the Trades Union Congress and the other wing organizations of the Convention People's Party. The officials of these organizations objected to the criticism and made counter-criticisms against certain Parliamentarians and this started a vicious circle of criminations and recriminations. This is clearly unfortunate. I have taken certain steps, and I hope that no occasion will arise to cause a recurrence of a similar situation.

The Convention People's Party is a great brotherhood. Its strength is embedded in the unity of its membership and since both sides to this unfortunate dispute are members of the Convention People's Party, I wish to examine the situation and look deeper for the causes of this incident.

I have stated over and over, that members of the Convention People's Party must not use their party membership or official position for personal gain or for the amassing of wealth. Such tendencies directly contradict our party constitution, which makes it clear that the aims and objects of the party, among other things, are the building of a socialist pattern of society in which the free development of each is the condition for the free development of all – a pattern or society consonant with African situations, circumstances and conditions.

I have explained very clearly this socialist structure and have on many occasions elaborated the five sectors into which our economy may be divided. These sectors are: first, the state sector, in which all enterprises are entirely state-owned; second, the joint state-private sector, which will incorporate enterprises owned jointly by Government and foreign private capital; third, the co-operative sector, in which all enterprises will be undertaken by co-operative organizations affiliated with the National Co-operative Council; fourth, the private enterprise sector, which will incorporate those industries which are open freely to foreign private enterprise; and fifth, the workers' enterprise sector.

I have had occasions to emphasize the part which private enterprise will continue to play in our economic and industrial life. A different situation arises with Ghanaian businessmen who attempt to combine business with political life. Being a party Member of the Assembly – and much more, being a Ministerial Secretary or a

Minister – means that the persons who take up these positions owe a duty to those who have elected them or who have given them their positions with confidence. To be able to maintain this confidence, therefore, they should not enter into any type of industrial or commercial undertaking. Any party Member of Parliament who wishes to be a businessman can do so, but he should give up his seat in Parliament. In other words, no Minister, Ministerial Secretary or party Member of Parliament should own a business or be involved in anyone else's business, Ghanaian or foreign.

In spite of my constant clarifications and explanations of our aims and objectives, some party Members in Parliament pursue a course of conduct in direct contradiction of our party aims. They are tending, by virtue of their functions and positions, to become a separate social group aiming to become a new ruling class of self-seekers and careerists. This tendency is working to alienate the support of the masses and to bring the National Assembly into isolation.

Members of Parliament must remember at all times that they are representatives of their constituencies only by reason of their party membership and that on no account should they regard constituency representation as belonging to them in their own right. In other words, constituencies are not the property of Members of Parliament. It is the party that sends them there and fights for them to become Members of Parliament. I am sure that from now on all Parliamentarians will be guided accordingly in their conduct of representing the party in Parliament.

When I look at the other side of the picture, I must say that some Trades Union officials have now and again indulged in loose talk and reprehensible statements which do no good either to the party, to the Government or to the nation. This is not the time for unbridled militant trade unionism in our country. Trade union officials must shed their colonial character and their colonial thinking. The approach of the Trades Union Congress to our national issues should be reasoned and constructive in accordance with our present circumstances.

Let me now turn to some other causes which I consider plague Ghanaian society generally and militate against undisturbed progress. A great deal of rumour-mongering goes on all over the country.

'Berko said that the Odikro informed Asamani that the Ohene said he paid a sum of money to a party official to become a paramount chief.'

'Kojo said that Mensah told him that Kweku took a bribe.'

'Abina stated that Ekua said that Esi uses her relations with Kweku to get contracts through the District Commissioner with the support of the Regional Commissioner and the blessing of a minister in Accra.'

So, day after day, night after night, all types and manner of wild allegations and rumours are circulated and they are always well sprinkled with: *They say, They say, wo see, wo see, akee, akee!*

Many members of the party and of the public are guilty of this conduct. I have directed that in future, any allegations or rumours so made or circulated against any person must immediately be brought before the central committee of the party for investigation.

One of the most degrading aspects of party conduct is the tendency on the part of some comrades to go round using the names of persons in prominent positions to collect money for themselves. Equally degrading is the tendency on the part of some persons in prominent positions to create agents for collecting money. This is a shameful and highly criminal tendency which must be crushed in the most ruthless manner.

May I take this opportunity to stress an essential point. Statements which may be regarded as Government policy statements are those which I make myself, personally, and those which are clearly stated in the text to be the official policy of the Government.

In recent months people in Ghana and abroad have frequently been confused and the Government's policies made uncertain as a result of unauthorized statements which have been made by persons employed by the Government, or quasi-Government bodies. Often these statements have conflicted with the Government's policies, and although they have been corrected subsequently by the Government, much harm has been done, and confusion and suspicion have resulted.

In spite of the freedom of speech which can reasonably be allowed in such cases, I consider that firm action should, in the national interest, be taken. From now on, therefore, no public statement affecting Government policy will be made by any Minister, Ministerial Secretary, member of a Government corporation or institution, Government official or any other person employed by the Government, unless that statement has first had Presidential or Cabinet approval. It is my intention to take strong disciplinary action against any individual who infringes this procedure.

I am aware that the evil of patronage finds a good deal of place in our society. I consider that it is entirely wrong for persons placed in positions of eminence or authority to use the influence of office in patronizing others, in many cases wrong persons, for immoral favours. I am seeing to it that this evil shall be uprooted, no matter whose ox is gored. The same thing goes for nepotism, which is, so to speak, a twin brother of the evil of patronage.

At this point, I would like to make a little divergence and touch upon Civil Service red tape. It amazes me that up to the present many civil servants do not realize that we are living in a revolutionary era. This Ghana, which has lost so much time serving colonial masters, cannot afford to be tied down to archaic snail-pace methods of work which obstruct expeditious progress. We have lost so much time that we need to do in ten years what has taken others a hundred years to accomplish. Civil servants, therefore, must develop a new orientation, a sense of mission and urgency to enable them to eliminate all tendencies towards red tape-ism, bureaucracy and waste. Civil servants must use their initiative to make the Civil Service an effective instrument in the rapid development of Ghana. . .

I have recently been alarmed at the amount of travelling abroad which is undertaken by Ministers, Ambassadors, Ministerial Secretaries and civil servants of all ranks. In many cases it is clear that approval is sought from no one before the journeys concerned are made. In future, travelling abroad, unless approved by the Cabinet, will not be paid for by the Government. The cost of any journeys which are undertaken without this approval will be sur-charged to the persons concerned. I have also directed that instructions should be given to the heads of all public boards and corporations, to ensure that no officers of these boards and corporations travel outside Ghana at Government expense without my specific approval or that of the Cabinet.

Ghanaian Ambassadors take their children with them when they proceed to their stations, at the expense of the Government. I am taking steps to discourage this practice, for it seems to me that on psychological and other grounds, it is better for these young children to begin their education at home.

At any rate this practice cannot be justified on financial grounds. In future, Ambassadors and foreign service officers will not be allowed to take their children abroad unless such children are below the age of five years. The procedure will apply equally to civil servants and other Ghanaian public functionaries serving abroad.

Let me now come back to the party.

It is most important to remember that the strength of the Convention People's Party derives from the masses of the people. These men and women include those whom I have constantly referred to

157

as the unknown warriors – dedicated men and women who serve the party loyally and selflessly without hoping for reward. It is therefore natural for the masses to feel some resentment when they see comrades whom they have put into power and given the mandate to serve the country on their behalf, begin to forget themselves and indulge in ostentatious living. High party officials, Ministers, Ministerial Secretaries, chairmen of statutory boards and corporations must forever bear this in mind. Some of us very easily forget that we ourselves have risen from amongst the masses. We must avoid any conduct that will breed antagonism and uneasy relations. Let us always keep in mind the fact that constant examination and correction are necessary for maintaining the solidarity of the party. The aim of all correction, however, must be to build and not to destroy. The central committee proposes to issue instructions shortly on the duties and rights of party members.

Coming to the integral organizations of the party, I consider it essential to emphasize once more that the Trades Union Congress, the United Ghana Farmers' Council, the National Co-operative Council and the National Council of Ghana Women, are integral parts of the Convention People's Party, and in order to correct certain existing anomalies, the central committee has decided that separate membership cards of the integral organizations shall be abolished forthwith. The membership card of the party will be the only qualification for membership within these organizations, namely, the Trades Union Congress, the United Ghana Farmers' Council, the National Co-operative Council and the National Council of Ghana Women, and no other membership card other than that of the Convention People's Party shall be recognized by these bodies. In all regional headquarters, provision will be made for the central party and these integral organizations to be housed in one building. This is necessary for effective co-ordination and control. Also the separate flags used by these organizations will be abolished and replaced by the flag of the Convention People's Party.

At this stage, I wish to take the opportunity to refer to an internal matter of the Trades Union Congress. It has come to my notice that dues of 4s. per month are being paid by some unions, whereas others pay 2s. monthly as membership dues. I understand that this position is causing some irritation. I have therefore instructed, after consultation with the Trades Union Congress officials, that union dues shall remain at 2s. per month.

Finally, I wish to state that in considering remedial measures, I have found it necessary to direct that a limit be imposed on property acquisition by Ministers, party officials and Ministerial Secretaries in order to enable them to conform to the modest and simple way of life demanded by the ideals and principles of the Convention People's Party.

Countrymen: Our mission to Ghana and to Africa and the unique personality of our party as a vanguard of the African liberation movement impose upon us increasing responsibility, not only to set our own house in order, but also to set very high standards from which all who seek to emulate us shall draw devotion and inspiration in their own struggles.

15

During a struggle for national liberation where the colonial power is compelled to surrender as a result of sustained, overwhelming pressures of a non-violent kind, and not because of military defeat, it is generally not possible to organize intensive ideological education of the masses while the struggle is actually in progress. This is because until the very day of surrender the colonial power governs the country and controls the information media and the educational system. The position is different in countries where armed struggle is the method adopted by the national liberation movement. For as areas are liberated, the liberation forces are able to administer the freed territory and to set up schools and colleges where party cadres can get down to the great task of ideological education.

In Ghana, we were able to end colonial rule by employing mainly non-violent methods of struggle. This meant that although the masses learned much about our Party's aims during the years of confrontation with the colonial power, their ideological education was largely obtained through practical experience of the national liberation struggle, and in general did not go much beyond the anti-colonial effort.

The broad base on which it was necessary to construct

the Party for the national liberation struggle was a further reason why it was impractical to embark on large scale ideological education before independence. It was essential to include bourgeois nationalists in the national liberation movement, and in the interests of unity in the fight against the colonial power, ideological differences which might bring division within our ranks had to be avoided. All had to be concentrated on the winning of independence, and questions of ideology and the kind of society to be constructed after we had ended colonial rule were matters which could not be brought out into the open until after the political revolution had been won.

As soon as independence had been achieved, however, it was necessary to get quickly down to the task of training cadres to educate the masses so that our socialist policies could be understood, and socialist instruction taken to the people.

We aimed in Ghana to create a socialist society in which each would give according to his ability, and receive according to his needs. Party members called 'vanguard activists', drawn from the most politically educated section of the Party, were recruited. They were to live and work among the people and to instruct them in the work and objectives of the Party as the political and social expressions of the people.

In order to provide a steady flow of ideologically sound cadres to carry on the work of politicization of the masses it became necessary to establish an institution where training and instruction could be given. In addition such an institution was needed as a centre where party members from the Central Committee to local official level could undergo courses of study, and hold discussions on party organization and objectives.

The Ideological Institute at Winneba was founded in February 1961 to provide ideological education for party members and for all from Africa and the world who wished to equip themselves with knowledge for the great freedom fight against colonialism, imperialism and neocolonialism. The Institute provided not only theoretical education but also practical instruction in a Positive Action training centre.

Between its foundation in 1961, and 1966 when it was closed down by the traitors who seized power in Ghana on 24th February 1966, hundreds of men and women from most parts of Africa and the world received ideological education at Winneba. It is a measure of its effectiveness that it was one of the first objects of attack by the February 1966 traitors and their neocolonialist agents. But just as it is impossible to kill a revolutionary movement by killing its leaders, so also is it ridiculous to suppose that the work of Winneba ended with the closing of the Institute.

ADDRESS
AT THE LAYING OF THE FOUNDATION STONE OF THE KWAME NKRUMAH INSTITUTE AND THE INAUGURATION OF THE FIRST COURSE OF THE IDEOLOGICAL SECTION OF THE INSTITUTE AT WINNEBA

18th February 1961

COMRADES AND FRIENDS:
   This day is historic. It is historic because it is the positive beginning of the end of reaction in Ghana through conscious ideological education. It is also historic for another reason. At this meeting of our party today, we have with us a distinguished visitor – one of the illustrious sons of the Union of Soviet Socialist Republics, Mr Leonid Ilyich Brezhnev, President of the Praesidium of the Union of Soviet Socialist Republics. The President accepted an invitation

from me to visit Ghana at the end of his visit to Guinea. I feel sure that the friendship between our two countries will be strengthened by this visit.

As many of you do know, the circumstances of the Convention People's Party, the victorious party of Gold Coast revolution, made it practically impossible to organize any consistent party ideological education. Our party was in death-grips with imperialism and colonialism, and it was a grim fight every inch of the way. The objective of independence was so precious that everything else, including party ideological education, had to be pushed aside in the interim. Thus it has been, that apart from some patch-up nationalist political education, no serious effort for ideological education has previously been undertaken by the Convention People's Party.

The great political struggle which the party started in 1949 formally ended in 1957, when independence was achieved. To the leadership of the party this great struggle did not end until the 1st of July, 1960, when the people of Ghana appointed for themselves the means of government by drawing up a constitution of their own.

For twelve years, twelve long years therefore, no conscious, consistent effort had been made to provide party members with the requisite education in the party's ideology of socialism – socialism based on the conditions, circumstances and peculiarities of our African life.

Today, this unsatisfactory state of affairs comes to an end by the establishment of this institute, which the Central Committee names the Kwame Nkrumah Institute, here at Winneba, to give to the membership of our dynamic party not only the necessary education which should prepare it for the successful prosecution of the difficult task of our social, economic, industrial and technological reconstruction, but also the victorious pursuit of the struggle for African freedom and unity and the complete and total liquidation of colonialism.

At this moment, my mind is thrown back to the day – the remarkable 9th of December, 1947 – when I again set foot on the soil of the land of my birth after my wanderings abroad in search of the Golden Fleece.

It is unnecessary to repeat here in detail what I have already set down in writing in my autobiography. Nevertheless it is right, in my opinion, to recapitulate some of the basic signposts marking the land which the Convention People's Party has covered in victory and in defeat during these twelve years of active national struggle.

As you all know I arrived at the instance of the Working

163

Committee of the United Gold Coast Convention and immediately plunged into organizational work – work absolutely essential for mobilizing our people against the weight of British imperial might in the Gold Coast.

Then followed rapidly the 1948 boycott of goods, the cowardly shooting of ex-servicemen at Osu cross-roads, the disturbances and the detention of the men, including myself, who were supposed to have planned these national disorders.

Comrades, these reminiscences are like tonic to my soul; I cast my eyes back across the field of struggle and see the historic landmarks telling the story of progress which has covered the trail of the Convention People's Party.

I see myself before the Watson Commissioners. I see again the slackening in effort of the leaders of the United Gold Coast Convention. I form the Committee on Youth Organization to ginger up activities of the United Gold Coast Convention. It evokes jealousies and misunderstandings. I am dismissed from my post. The masses rebel against the leadership of the Convention. I stand at the reconciliation meeting at Saltpond. Our ideas are poles apart. I resign. The youth breaks away from the movement. I form the Convention People's Party, on June 12th, 1949.

The Convention People's Party took up the struggle in real earnest. Then came the Coussey Committee and their half-hearted recommendations for constitutional reform with which the Convention People's Party violently disagreed.

The Party demanded Self-Government Now, with the slogan 'We prefer self-government with danger to servitude in tranquillity', and pushed the backs of the imperialists against the wall.

Persecution started and libel suits were filed against me for claims running into thousands of pounds. This was September, 1949. On January 8th, 1950, I declared Positive Action, and was arrested on the 20th of January, 1950, tied, and thrown into prison, in accordance with the super-excellent tenets of colonial justice which colonialists invariably mete out to their colonial subjects who dare to question their right to oppress other people.

Comrades, we have come a long way up the road since then.

I can hear once again the singing of the masses in the evenings outside the prison walls. I can feel once more the violent throbbing of my heart as the blood of inspiration runs through my veins and steels my nerves for the tough struggle ahead. I can see how the party comrades toiled day and night to keep the party flag flying in those days of severe trial.

Then followed the series of our party election victories, my release from prison on the 12th February, 1951, and the formation of the first Government of the Convention People's Party in 1951.

Why do I recount these matters? Why am I re-living the past? Why have I to remind the country of these historical facts?

Comrades, I do so because we have reached a point in the life of our nation when it is absolutely necessary to recapture the lofty spirit of our past and bring home vividly to all members of the Convention People's Party that the end results of the national task is not individual gain and personal prosperity but service to the country and the masses for the cultivation of popular prosperity. The free development of each should be the condition for the free development of all.

The road of the struggle led on and on. The party convened the Gold Coast Representative Assembly. We threw our historic challenge to our opponents to join us in declaring another positive action. They recoiled into their conspiratorial dens. We went forward from one sign-post to another until the 10th of July, 1953, when I tabled the 'Motion of Destiny' in the Legislative Assembly and called on Britain to hand over power to the people themselves.

The sweeping victory of our party in the 1954 general elections followed. We were seated firmly in the saddle, moving steadily on to our goal.

But the imperialists and colonialists were not sleeping. They worked fast with our opponents, and produced the National Liberation Movement, which exerted itself to wreck everything the nation had gained so far and bring back colonialism again upon the people. They attempted exactly what they are now enacting in the Congo, and very soon possibly in Angola. Thanks to the solidarity and strength of our dynamic party, we pulled through what would otherwise have spelled national disaster and engendered despair and failure.

We moved forward again to 1956, obtained another resounding victory over the forces of reaction and sabotage in the imposed general elections, and finally cleared the way for the ushering in of independence and sovereignty on the 6th of March, 1957.

The Convention People's Party moved on, always living up to its motto: 'Forward ever, backward never'. So on we went to the national plebiscite, and the presidential elections, to give to ourselves a Constitution of our own making, creating Ghana a Republic on the 1st of July, 1960.

Comrades, I have looked back a little, looked over the period scanning the last twelve years, to see our performance in a nutshell, and I say 'Well done' to the Convention People's Party.

The struggle still continues, but it continues on a different plane.

Now the Convention People's Party and the people of Ghana grapple with a different problem – the problem of social, cultural, scientific, economic, industrial and technological reconstruction, which must be solved expeditiously, thus repairing the damage done to our country by the imperialist and colonialist despoilers.

But is that the only remaining problem? Not by any means!

There is also the major problem of the total liberation of Africa and the Union of African States.

From my days in London up to the present, I have never once stopped shouting to all Africa about African unity. The sad episode in the Congo more than justifies my fears about the unwisdom to stand alone, each by itself, in the face of this fierce onslaught by the new colonialists, who are equally if not more dangerous and merciless in their come-back endeavours.

When, therefore, I have come to this town of Winneba to lay the foundation stone of the Kwame Nkrumah Institute and to inaugurate the first course in ideological training accommodated in temporary premises, I see a beam of hope shooting across our continent, for the things which will be taught in this institute will strengthen African youth and manhood and inspire it to scale great heights; and the men and women who will pass through this institute will go out not only armed with analytical knowledge to wage the battle of African socialism but will also be fortified with a keen spirit of dedication and service to our motherland.

This institute will comprise two sections, namely the Ideological Education Training Centre and the Positive Action Training Centre.

Everyone of us, from members of the Central Committee, Ministers and high party officials, to the lowest propagandist in the field, will pass through a course in this institute for proper orientation and adjustment. Furthermore, the institute will provide training for non-violent positive actionists, Party Vanguard activists, farmers, co-operators, trade unionists and women organizers, giving particular care to leadership training and making sure that a forum is provided for members of public corporations, the civil service and other governmental bodies for the discussion of the party's programmes, aims, and policies.

Hitherto, the Central Committee and I have viewed with leniency the mistakes of party comrades on the ground that the party had given them no ideological education. From now on, that excuse will not avail anyone who has passed through this institute and gone through the necessary course.

Hitherto, it has been true to say that many members of the Convention People's Party have not understood the significance and value of their membership. This will be corrected when they have passed through the Kwame Nkrumah Institute.

To any Ghanaian, membership of our party should rightly form the dearest possession. The Convention People's Party has been built with great sacrifice and endeavour, iron determination and outstanding patriotism, overwhelming nationalist zeal and selfless comradely service. It is the people's own party, rigidly dedicated to the cause and welfare of the whole people of Ghana, and uncompromisingly devoted to a relentless fight against imperialism and colonialism found anywhere on the continent of Africa, or in the world, for that matter. No one can deny that the Convention People's Party is thus pitchforked by historical circumstances into the spearhead and vanguard of the gigantic struggle for the total liberation of Africa and the independence and unity of African states.

Comrades, as you yourselves have seen, it is a great honour to belong to the fold of the Convention People's Party. But it is right to remind ourselves that this membership carries also a serious responsibility.

Members of the party must be the first to set an example of all the highest qualities in the nation. We must excel in our field of work by working really hard. We must produce unimpeachable evidence of integrity, honesty, selflessness and faithfulness in the positions in which we are placed by the party in service to the nation. We must eschew ridiculous ostentation and vanity when the party has charged us with eminent offices of state, and remember constantly that we hold such offices not in our own right, but in the right of the total membership of the Convention People's Party, the masses of the people who really matter.

I must thus personally warn all members of the Central Committee, all party functionaries, all Ministers of State and Ministerial Secretaries, and chairmen of public boards and corporations and other key public officials, that they owe a great duty to the people, a duty which must be discharged with the highest sense of responsibility.

They must at all times feel conscious of the truth that in ourselves, all of us are nothing except what the party has made us – namely, agents for the execution of the party's programme. It is a travesty of trust, therefore, for anyone of us to consider that we are privileged to install ourselves as masters of the people instead of servants of the masses. The leaders of the party must forge a consistent band of brotherhood with the rank and file of the party, and build a living solidarity for the protection of the people's welfare and the realization of our party objectives.

No comrade should pass through this institute and fail to go out with a proclamation on his lips saying: I live not for myself but for the good of the whole people. The socialist ideals which we pursue must imbue all who pass through this institute with a spirit of selfless devotion to the cause of the nation, to the cause of Africa, and to the cause of the world.

All members of the Convention People's Party who pass through this institute will have a great opportunity for broadening their political knowledge and ideological understanding. They will strengthen their qualities of loyalty and discipline, thereby increasing the overall discipline of the party and the deep affection and loyalty of the general membership.

The structure of the Convention People's Party has been built up from our own experiences, conditions, environments and concepts, entirely Ghanaian and African in outlook, and based on the Marxist socialist philosophy and worldview.

Our party is likened to a tree – a huge and mighty tree with great branches sticking out everywhere. The trunk and the branches form the tree. It is a single unit, living a single life, and when it dies, it dies a single death.

It would appear that many people are under the impression that the four great branches of the Convention People's Party, namely the Trade Union Congress, the United Ghana Farmers' Council, the National Co-operative Council and the National Council of Ghana Women, are mere affiliates of the Convention People's Party. They are not.

These four great wings of the party are not affiliates. They are a composite part of the Convention People's Party. That is to say they are integral elements of the party, living with it and dying with it, as a single entity.

It would be a good idea to qualify them for internal purposes as the Party Industrial Organization, the Party Agricultural Organization, the Party Co-operative Organization and the Party Women's Organization. Members of these organizations must bear this position in mind in all their activities, and so must all other party members.

In addition to these four branch organizations there operates the

National African Socialist Students Organization – the Nasso.

This is the custodian body of the party's ideology and is composed of the most advanced ideological comrades, torchbearers of the party's ideals and principles. The Nasso forms the bark of this mighty tree, and cements the physical and organizational unity of the Convention People's Party.

This institute is, primarily, their school of action. They must be here day and night, imparting knowledge to their less favoured comrades who have not graduated to the Nassoist level.

They must make sure that the whole country is sprinkled with party study groups – yes, in the factories, workshops, departments and Ministries of Government, corporations, boards, and in every nook and corner of Ghana, there must exist a party study group, studying African socialism, party decisions and programmes, explaining Government actions and policies and actively pursuing the 'Cipipification' of the national life.

The Kwame Nkrumah Institute will not cater for Ghana alone. Its doors will be opened to all from Africa and the world both who seek knowledge to fit themselves for the great freedom fight against imperialism and colonialism old or new, and the consolidation of peace throughout the world for the progress of mankind.

I can envisage the future possibilities of this arrangement. When African freedom fighters from all over Africa have come into this institute and quenched their thirst for ideological knowledge, they will go back fortified in the same principles and beliefs, pursue the same objectives and aims, appreciate the same values and advocate the same themes. I see before my mind's eye a great monolithic party growing up out of this process, united and strong, spreading its protective wings over the whole of Africa – from Algiers in the north to Cape Town in the south; from Cape Guardafui in the east to Dakar in the west.

Comrades and friends, at this very moment Ghana mourns the death by brutal murder of Patrice Lumumba, late Prime Minister of the Congo, and his two associates Mpolo and Okito.

We at this gathering should do honour to their memory. But before I call for the observance of a two-minute silence, I wish to say this: Up to today, the murderers of Premier Lumumba and his two associates Mpolo and Okito, have been clouded in mystery.

The childish story of villagers killing these stalwart freedom fighters is the most absurd fabrication, that could emanate only from the diseased brains of Belgian colonialists and their puppet agents.

But just this very afternoon, it has been revealed to me by a reliable source that the murder of Patrice Lumumba, of Maurice Mpolo and of Joseph Okito took place on January 18th.

The information reveals that the men were sent for, one by one, and commanded to kneel and pray. Then, as he prayed, each was shot in the back by the order of a Belgian officer.

When Patrice Lumumba knelt to pray, the African soldier who was ordered to shoot him refused to do so, whereupon the Belgian officer took his revolver and shot Lumumba himself.

I have narrated these facts, not in any desire further to hurt your already wounded hearts. On the contrary, I have done so in order that you who pass through this institute, which I am proud to say bears my name, and which will stand forever for the principles and ideals for which I have always stood and eternally stand, may know the diabolical depths of degradation to which these twin-monsters of imperialism and colonialism can descend. You will then be able to assess the magnitude of the task still ahead and offer yourselves in sacrificial dedication to the cause of African freedom and unity.

Let us all stand up in silence for two minutes for our murdered brothers and comrades in arms.

And now, comrades and friends, it is my most pleasant duty to declare the foundation stone of the Kwame Nkrumah Institute well and truly laid. I feel happy to declare also the first course of the ideological training centre of the institute duly inaugurated.

ADDRESS
AT THE FIRST SEMINAR AT THE
WINNEBA IDEOLOGICAL SCHOOL

3rd February, 1962

COMRADES,

This is the first Party Seminar of its kind to be held here since this Institute was opened. For this reason, I thought I would open it myself and take an active part in its deliberations.

We have reached a stage in the life of our Party and the Nation when we cannot expect to move forward on mere sentiment and emotion. If we expect to move forward, we have to face fact and reality.

You have gathered here as members of the Central Committee, as members of our great Party, as Ministers of State, as Regional Commissioners, as Deputy Ministers, Party officials and District Commissioners. In short, the Party and the Government are fully represented here today. We represent the Party, we represent the Government, we represent the Nation and we represent the people. As such, this meeting is no ordinary meeting, and we must emerge from it fortified and determined to carry through the task and programme before us.

As I have already stated, our Party cannot afford to go forward from the stage it now finds itself, in ignorance. It must equip itself with the requisite knowledge that should make it capable not only of giving the political direction it must give to the people, but also to give the necessary expert guidance in our task of socialist reconstruction of our country. The main theme for our discussion here should centre around Party education, Party organization and Party ideology, and the relation of these to the State and the Government.

Less than a fortnight ago, the Central Committee announced the delimitation of the Party Study Groups. No doubt this announcement must have caused some surprise since we have been talking about the intensification of Party educational work. The Central Committee's decision, Comrades, was taken after a most careful consideration and in the best interest of Party education. If you would look back a little, you would surely find that the work of Party education was formerly undertaken by the NASSO. This was a body of socialist students in the Party devoted to the ideals of socialism and engaged in the study of Party affairs, including the Party Constitution. The NASSO was most useful, but when the time came and it was considered that its work was done, the Central Committee transformed it into the Party Study Groups. You will note that these metamorphoses and transformations are not concerned with aims and principles, but with tactics. Let us not forget that Marxism is not a dogma but a guide to action.

Other things being equal, the Central Committee considers that the NASSO and the Party Study Groups have done their work and done it very well. They have stirred up great enthusiasm in the field of Party education and their activities have led to the general raising of the standard of enlightenment among the rank and file of the Party. Nevertheless, the time has come when Party education should be carried forward to its final stage – the stage of mass Party education. General Party education must reach the masses at the base.

We must now go to the masses and give them help to understand the affairs of our great Party and the Nation by providing them with the necessary knowledge for thought and action.

The Party has defined a social purpose and it is committed to socialism and to the ideology of Nkrumaism. And I take it to mean that when you talk of Nkrumaism, you mean the name or term given to the consistent ideological policies followed and taught by Kwame Nkrumah. These are contained in his speeches, in his theoretical writings and stated ideas and principles. You also mean that Nkrumaism, in order to be Nkruma-istic, must be related to scientific socialism. To be successful, however, this ideology must:

(a) Be all-pervading, and while its theories in full can only be developed in and around the Party leadership, it must influence in some form all education and, indeed, all thinking and action;

(b) Be not only a statement of aims and principles, but must also provide the intellectual tools by which these aims are achieved, and must concentrate on all constructive thinking around achieving those aims; and,

(c) Offer the ordinary man and woman some concrete tangible and realizable hope of better life within his or her lifetime.

With this ideology there should be a full-scale intellectual, educational and organizational attack on all aspects of colonialism, neo-colonialism and imperialism. These are not just mere words. They are concrete manifestations of a world outlook. Colonialism is that aspect of imperialism which in a territory with an alien government, that government controls the social, economic and political life of the people it governs. Neo-colonialism is the granting of political independence minus economic independence, that is to say, independence that makes a State politically free but dependent upon the colonial power economically. Imperialism is nothing but finance capital run wild in countries other than its own.

Of these three, neo-colonialism is the most dangerous not only to the African Liberation Movement as a whole, but also to the independence and unity of Africa. Without going into its philosophy, here are some of its techniques:

(a) To produce a small educated African 'elite' as prospective rulers, whether or not they have the support of the masses.

(b) To educate this 'elite' so that they would automatically accept, as part of the natural order of things, the colonial relationship,

172

and defend it in the name of 'justice', 'political liberty' and 'democracy'.

(c) To prevent by organizational and ideological means, any concentration of power, without which change is impossible.

(d) While paying lip service to democracy, to exclude by organizational and ideological methods, the representatives of the mass of the people for any real control over the State.

(e) To exclude, by all possible means, any teaching which might lead to the advancement and practice of revolutionary ideas.

These are the political techniques which neo-colonialism is employing in order to tighten its economic control of the territory through a puppet 'elite'.

The economics of neo-colonialism is obvious. It gives fake aid to the newly independent country which makes that country virtually dependent economically on the colonial power. Thus it becomes a client state of the colonial power, serving as the producer of raw material, the price of which is determined by the colonial power.

How do we proceed then? I would like to suggest this approach: the Secretariat of the Bureau of Party Education must now go to the people; it must go to the ward, town and village branches as well as to the special branches created in the offices, shops, factories, state farms, corporations and other places of employment, carrying its work to our general membership. It must go to the primary schools through the Young Pioneers; it must go to the secondary schools, colleges and universities. And here it is proper that we confine Party Study Groups to secondary schools, colleges and universities. In this connection, I suggest that Education Secretaries should be appointed wherever a Party branch is established, and these should undertake Party educational work in addition to their normal duties.

Branch Education Secretaries must be taken in hand in a most serious manner by the Bureau of Party Education, so as to ensure that they understand thoroughly the tenets and basic principles of the Party ideology.

A proper plan of work and timetable should be formulated for this work, and tuition and discussion should be carried on both in the local languages and in English.

Periodically a meeting of all Branch Secretaries and Branch Education Secretaries should be held at Flagstaff House, or at such other place as may be decided, in order that they may be addressed by leading members in ideological education on appropriate subjects.

This periodical meeting should take the place of the Party Study Groups meetings at Flagstaff House. In addition to the Branch Secretary and the Branch Education Secretary, party wards, branches and special branches should be allowed to send to such meetings not more than five chosen Party members. This will give opportunity to all members of a branch to be present, at one time or another, at these periodical educational meetings which can conveniently be called the Party Educational Conference.

The Party Educational Conference should be held at three levels: National – which will invariably take place in Accra; Regional – which will take place at Regional Headquarters; and District – which should be held at District Headquarters. These Party Educational Conferences should not be confused with the Party National, Regional and District Conferences.

Similarly, there should be appointed Regional and District Educational Party Secretaries whose responsibilities will be the proper co-ordination and supervision of all Party education work in a given Region or District. It is my hope that these steps, when taken, will go a long way towards facilitating the work of mass Party education.

Let me now turn to other matters. The future of Ghana depends upon the youth, and if the Party is to achieve any worthwhile results by making sure of the future national trend, then it must take positive steps to inculcate in the minds of the nation's youth the ideology of the Party. Only by this way can we envisage the continuity of our line of thought and action long after many of us are gone.

The youth must be imbued not only with a keen spirit of patriotism, but also with a sense of lofty socialist ideals which will enable them to think and act in the best interests of the community as a whole and not in the interest of themselves as individuals.

Another subject of importance is the Party Rally. Hitherto, Party Rallies have been held without proper preparation. The Propaganda Unit does very useful work in drawing the crowds and organizing them into a good audience, but this apart, no plan appears to be made in regard to speakers or their subjects. The result is that quite often persons have spoken on subjects on which neither the Party nor the Government have given any line, and which has resulted as a shock not only to the Party or Government authority, but also to the audience. Such a state of affairs must be corrected.

In future, all Party Rallies should be covered by proper agenda approved by the Regional or District Secretaries, whose-ever responsibility this may be. Party functionaries responsible for organizing rallies will have to arrange for speakers to be properly briefed on the subjects of their address. Where it is not possible to get a local speaker on a particular subject, arrangements must be made with Party Headquarters to provide speakers in respect of that subject. Regional Commissioners and Regional Secretaries of the Party will bear a special responsibility for directing the activities of the Party in regard to rallies.

In any case, the old time 'say anything' sort of attitude, which has long characterized the speeches of Comrades at Party Rallies, must have a new orientation. The masses nowadays have no applause for demagogues. They want to hear something useful and sensible; something to help them along in their daily life. They want to be told the actual facts of a situation.

I now come to general Party organization. We often talk of the integral parts of our great Party, but not many of us find time to examine the real position as regards these various organizations comprising the Party. The integral organizations which primarily combine to form the Convention People's Party consist of:

(1) The Trades Union Congress;
(2) The United Ghana Farmers' Council;
(3) The National Council of Ghana Women;
(4) The Ghana Young Pioneers; and
(5) The Co-operative Movement.

All these bodies have their various functions in the particular aspect of our national life in which they operate, but there is one strain running through all of them, which is basic and fundamental, namely, the membership of the Convention People's Party. Whatever they do, the character of the Convention People's Party must be clearly manifested for all to see. They all have a single guiding light, the guiding light of our Party ideology. This light must constantly be kept bright and full of lustre and must on no account be allowed to dim, for, as soon as this happens, we are bound to find ourselves in difficulties.

Let all Comrades remember, whether we be Trade Unionists, whether we be Farmers, whether we be members of the Women's Council or of the Young Pioneers, that the dominant character which should take precedence in all that we do is the character of the membership of the Convention People's Party. This character is the guiding force of our Ghanaian life and existence and constitutes the bulwark against national treachery, intrigue, subversion and other un-Ghanaian activities.

175

The next category of Party organization includes the Workers' Brigade and the State Construction Workers, which also, indirectly but nonetheless effectively, bolster the Party structure. Why shouldn't the workers of the State, who are composed mainly of the labourer group, be put into uniform? This would give them an added incentive to serve the State, a reason to feel proud of their service and a sense of belonging. They can be employed on various national jobs by the State Construction Corporations. This will eliminate the present element of idleness which takes place when a particular job is completed and the workers await the assignment of another job.

The Asafu Companies also, the members of which are almost all members of the Party individually, will come within this category. They should be properly uniformed and perform their traditional role in a modern manner.

Another group of workers whom we now call 'Watchmen' will have a new orientation and come under this category. And why shouldn't they also be dressed in a smart uniform and be renamed 'Civil Guards'?

All this will lead to one useful result – discipline. The whole nation from the President downwards will form one regiment of disciplined citizens. In this way, we shall move forward with great confidence, stepping ahead ever firmly with a keen sense of purpose and direction.

All these organizations must form a solid forward movement with a new outlook, which must keep constant vigilance to make it impossible for anyone, whether from inside or from without, to compromise the independence of our country.

I would now like to draw your attention to some matters to which I have had occasion to refer from time to time, namely: rumour-mongering, anonymous letter writing, deliberate manufacture of destructive stories about Comrades, invidious whispering campaigns, loose talk and character assassination. All these tend to obstruct the steady progress of our Party and the Nation.

Day in and day out, my desk is literally flooded with hundreds of letters – mostly anonymous – sent in a spiteful campaign aimed at discrediting this or that individual. Those who do this sort of thing, if they are Party members, are not worthy to hold Party cards. Party members should not indulge in this practice.

Sometimes the Police have been able to unearth some of these enemies of the Nation and have brought them to book, but by and large, this useless, demoralizing and unprofitable activity continues, and I wish to appeal to all Comrades to keep their eyes and ears open wide so that we may effectively check this wicked practice. If a Party member – or any other citizen, for that matter – discovers some malpractice or other wrong deeds being committed, then he should report on this in the proper manner and bring the matter to the notice of the proper authority. If you believe that what you write is the truth, then you should have no fear to sign your name. All anonymous correspondence which comes my way goes immediately into the wastepaper basket, which is the only place for the work of such cowards, mischief-makers or crack-pots.

Again, take the practice of using other people's names for the purpose of collecting money. Some Comrades make it their habit to go around the country in a bid to get rich quick by threatening people and collecting money from them in the names of Party Comrades. This is a most vicious and shameful practice and one that must be ruthlessly and severely punished when discovered. It is your responsibility to see that this is checked.

Another malpractice which undermines the efficiency of our Party work, is the manufacture of lying propaganda against men in key positions. This has the result of undermining the confidence of such persons in themselves and therefore of impairing their ability and efficiency, since they constantly live in fear. Conversely, some Party members in high positions use their position to threaten and intimidate those whom they are trying to influence.

These are very dangerous practices and make the Party and the Nation lose ground.

Personally, I do not see why Comrades in key positions should allow themselves to be affected by such talk; and equally, I do not understand why others should allow themselves to be threatened and intimidated by a lot of bragging and boasting. If a Comrade's hands are clean, then surely he must have nothing to fear, no matter how many stories of dismissal and demotion are invented about him, or how frightening may be the threats hurled at him. A Party member protects himself with his own integrity and honesty and by his efficiency. By doing so, and provided his hands are clean, he will maintain his confidence and carry on, knowing that his actions are above suspicion and that his character is unassailable.

It is not necessary for me to dwell at length on the importance of honesty and service. The abuse of power through dishonesty is an abomination. The misuse of office for selfish ends is a crime against the Party and the State, and therefore a greater abomination. The Convention People's Party is the servant of the people, and therefore the men whom it puts into office and power must use that opportunity to serve the people, remembering at all times that selfless and loyal service is a reward in itself.

I do not know of any greater satisfaction than honest and efficient service rendered to the people in the best interest of all the people. I should think that that is enough reward for the gratification of our inner self, but when we forget ourselves and think of office, wealth and power as personal instruments meant to be used for the glorification of self and for the attainment of our individual purposes, then we falter in our charge and fail the Party and the people.

I think the life of our community must be organized right at its base, that is to say, at the village level. It is true that Local Government has been organized at the village level, but only by grouping a number of villages to form an administrative unit. The internal life of particular villages, therefore, remains substantially unadministered, and I believe the time has now come for us to tackle this problem in a forthright manner.

A solution can be found in the formation of village committees which will be granted governmental authority for the administration of the village. In this respect a village committee can be made of the Chairman of the village Party branch, the Secretary and five other appointed members. The Odikro of a particular village will become the President of the village committee in the same way as higher Chiefs occupy the office of President of City and other Councils for ceremonial purposes only.

The real responsibility for the administration of a village will remain with the other members of the committee who, as I have said, will comprise the Party representatives of the village. The Party and the Government will then be able to rest content that State administration goes down right to the town and village levels and makes the ordinary worker, farmer and peasant a participant in the government of the country.

The value of all the organizational wings of the Party and the National Assembly is that they broaden the basis of support for the leadership. The Party naturally must be the main basis from which the leadership draws its strength, and it is therefore important that support is mobilized from as many quarters as possible. The need for central leadership must permeate all the activities of the State. This involves not only those conducted through the classical apparatus, that is, the civil service, the judiciary, the armed forces and the police, but also those conducted through the central banks, government boards and corporations and, indeed, by the Party itself.

This seminar also gives me the opportunity to lay emphasis on the importance of human relations, and in this respect, I am addressing myself particularly to Ministers, Deputy Ministers and all others in authority. It is vital that your relationship with those who serve under you is of the most harmonious kind. It is not enough to see that their official work is properly done. You must also take an interest in their personal lives, show sympathy for their difficulties and, where possible, offer help. The colonialist attitude of 'lording it' over subordinates pays no dividends at all. The way to get results is to keep a man in the picture, take an interest in the job he is doing, correct him if he is wrong, praise him if he excels himself, let him feel that he is a vital part of the machinery, so that his self-respect and dignity are upheld. If, however, this personal approach fails on account of an arrogant or unco-operative attitude of the person concerned, then exercise no mercy.

Ministers, Regional and District Commissioners and all others in responsible positions, should keep contact with their staff by visiting their offices as often as possible, having homely chats with them and making them appreciate the fact that no matter the difference in official status, a Minister and a Messenger are both Ghanaians and both Human beings. I am not advocating negative familiarity: that only spells ruin. What I am advocating is the cultivation of a sincere interest in one another as fellow beings and, arising from that, a mutual interest in the welfare of the State.

Nothing can be more disastrous both to the individual and to the State than a man who becomes so discouraged in his work and so negative in his attitude to life, that he carries out his duties like an automaton – disinterested. He acts like an automaton because he is treated like one. So little interest is taken in the work he turns out that he shrugs his shoulders and says: 'Why should I bother? I get paid for it.' After all, he is human.

Ministers and all those holding responsible positions, should hold regular discussions with their secretaries and those working with them, and acquaint them with the problems of their Ministries and with national problems, so that they become interested in the affairs of State, proud to be taken into the confidence of their superiors and keen to prove their worth.

One subject which should occupy your attention during these discussions is the subject of the Ghanaian attitude to State property. Under the colonial regime, the people were made to feel so remote from the Government and so divorced from it, that they grew up with the idea that the Government and the people were two different entities. In those days, Government property was treated with deliberate negligence, scant attention or dishonesty. Unhappily, this attitude has, to a great extent, remained, and it is causing a good deal of harm to our society today.

It must be clearly understood by everyone that the people and the Government are one, and that property acquired by Government is State property, that is to say, property belonging to the people and property for which the people are responsible. So if a person is put in charge of a particular property that belongs to the State, that is, to the people, he is guarding that property on behalf of himself and the people, who each have a stake in it. It is in his interest, therefore, to guard and preserve it with the greatest care and attention.

This point cannot be too strongly emphasized and I wish all of you here to do your utmost to instil into the minds of the people that State property belongs to all of us individually and collectively, and that it is therefore incumbent upon us to do everything in our power to protect such property from unscrupulous persons who may wish to misuse State property for their personal ends.

Now that we are establishing State farms, State factories, State corporations and other organizations of State, in order to secure our economic future, neglect towards State property could spell disaster for the national economy.

I hope that during your group discussions you will be able to formulate plans and programmes which will strengthen the forward move of our Party, avoiding any conflict between the Party and the people.

Let us always remember that the strength of the Government depends upon the unity and solidarity of the Party and its faithful and unflinching support of the masses, and that in the final analysis, the strength of the Party depends upon the honesty, sincerity and loyalty of the individual members who compose it.

And now, Comrades, I consider that I have spoken long enough to give you some idea of the work and task that this Seminar hopes to achieve at this Institute, and I must conclude to allow you to give active thought to the various subjects which I have spoken to you about.

16

The Party's programme of Work and Happiness, which was adopted in 1962, was designed to define clearly the lines of national development which were to be implemented by the Seven Year Development Plan to be launched in March 1964. These, when completed, were to achieve the basic objectives of our policy, the building of a socialist state devoted to the welfare of the masses, and the turning of Ghana into a power house of the African Revolution.

The First and Second Five Year Development Plans (1951–1956 and 1959–1964); and the Consolidation Plan (1957–1959) provided the basis for the modernization of agriculture and industrial development. Details of the Plans and how they were implemented appear later in this book.*

Immediately after Independence, while wishing to proceed on a socialist path of economic and social development, it was considered advisable, in view of the circumstances operating at the time, to pursue a 'shopping list' approach, estimating how much we could afford, and allocating it to projects drawn up into a list according to priority. But it soon became clear that this approach was not producing results quickly enough, and it was

* See *The Big Lie* (Chapter 5 of *Dark Days in Ghana*).

decided to speed up our socialist programme by comprehensive economic plans which would utilize all the economic and extra-economic resources of the nation. Projects were then not viewed separately, but as part of a totality, and were selected accordingly.

It would not have been possible, given the political and economic conditions of the pre-1960 period, to have embarked on full-scale socialist programmes earlier. Socialism cannot be built without socialists. Ideological education was being given top priority, but had still not reached a satisfactory level. Bourgeois economic interests were too entrenched to be removed entirely, or overnight. Ghana inherited, at Independence, almost total trade dependence on the West. Our economy was almost completely foreign or local capitalist owned. The colonial mentality permeated the professions, and particularly the army, police and civil service. The bureaucratic bourgeoisie whenever it could acted as a brake on our socialist policies. We were determined to remove these reactionary elements as soon as possible as the new ideologically-sound, trained personnel emerged from our schools and colleges.

The strategy was for the public sector, which controlled key areas of the economy, gradually to overtake the private sector until eventually the private sector was entirely eliminated. During this phasing out period, joint projects involving state and private enterprise were embarked upon. It was considered, in the circumstances of the time, that the undertaking of joint projects with already operating capitalist concerns was better than the alternative of economic blockade by the West and consequent lack of development until the assistance of socialist states could be procured and become operational. The most successful joint project completed during this interim period was the Volta River Project, completed one year ahead of schedule, with no misappropriations.

As I said at the time: 'I regard this great scheme as an example of the way in which careful and proper planning together with foreign investment, public control and participation, and the devoted labours of the people, can revolutionize the economic base of society.'

To raise living standards for the people as a whole meant building a new economy. The old could not be adapted to our socialist objectives. This necessitated investment on a very large scale as almost everything had to be imported. Deficits were inevitable. Their size was a measure of our development.

The other major problem facing development, the really crucial one, was the problem of economic scale. Ghana, like the majority of independent African states, is too small an economic unit in terms of population and resources. The optimum zone of development for the African people is the entire continent of Africa. Until there is an All-African Union Government pursuing socialist policies, and planning the economic development of Africa as a whole, the standard of living of the African masses will remain low, and they will continue to suffer from neocolonialist exploitation and the oppression of the indigenous bourgeoisie.

The so-called prestige expenditure of which my government has sometimes been accused, notably the building of a Conference Hall for the OAU Summit in Accra in 1965, was designed to hasten the unification of Africa, without which there can be only very limited economic growth. Haste was dictated by the continually worsening terms of trade between the industrialized countries (IC) and the less developed countries (LDC). The longer the delay, the more difficult the task becomes.

A dash for growth in the case of Ghana was halted by the February 1966 coup almost immediately after the Volta River Project was inaugurated and the infrastructure completed for rapid industrialization. After the coup, the object of policy was to pay overseas creditors by the short term stupidity of liquidating assets and cutting back all forms of development on the grounds that they created more debts. Instead of continuing with the Seven Year Development Plan, to revolutionize agriculture and industry through social and economic development based on the use of science and technology, the clock was put back to colonial times. Ghana quickly degenerated into a beggar state at the mercy of imperialism and neocolonialism.

Bourgeois theorists too often make the mistake of applying capitalist valuations to socialist planning, and of applying IC economics to LDC issues, which require their own science and terminology. The irrelevance of conventional Western discussion to the Ghanaian or LDC situation is epitomized in the importance placed upon a nation's balance of payments. For provided Ghana had low living standards, and practically no investment involving imports to develop and diversify the economy, there would be a reasonable balance of payments as there was prior to Independence. Virtual stagnation of the economy was the price of maintaining the reserves held at Independence. The same critics point to the unprofitability of certain state industries, and even infra-structural services. Infra-structural projects are slow developers, and the profit/loss position, the yardstick of capitalist thinking, does not indicate the social and political or long term value.

Time and truth are inseparable, and the people of Ghana are the best judges of the economic and social progress they experienced between 1957 and 1966. As for the wider impact of our economic growth on the Pan-African struggle the assessment will be made by the masses of Africa as they gradually emerge to claim their just inheritance.

BROADCAST ON GHANA'S SEVEN-YEAR DEVELOPMENT PLAN

5th May, 1962

Organization presupposes planning, and planning demands a programme for its basis. The Government proposes to launch a Seven-Year Development Plan in January, 1963. The Party, therefore, has a pressing obligation to provide a programme upon which this plan could be formulated.

We must develop Ghana economically, socially, culturally, spiritually, educationally, technologically and otherwise, and produce it as a finished product of a fully integrated life, both exemplary and inspiring.

This programme, which we call a programme for 'Work and Happiness', has been drawn up in regard to all our circumstances and conditions, our hopes and aspirations, our advantages and disadvantages and our opportunities or lack of them. Indeed, the programme is drawn up with an eye on reality and provides the building ground for our immediate scientific, technical and industrial progress.

We have embarked upon an intensive socialist reconstruction of our country. Ghana inherited a colonial economy and similar disabilities in most other directions. We cannot rest content until we have demolished this miserable structure and raised in its place an edifice of economic stability, thus creating for ourselves a veritable paradise of abundance and satisfaction. Despite the ideological bankruptcy and moral collapse of a civilization in despair, we must go forward with our preparations for planned economic growth to supplant the poverty, ignorance, disease, illiteracy and degradation left in their wake by discredited colonialism and decaying imperialism.

In the programme which I am today introducing to the country through this broadcast, the Party has put forward many proposals. I want all of you to get copies of this programme, to read and discuss it and to send us any observations or suggestions you may have about it.

Tomorrow, the National Executive Committee of the Party will meet to discuss the Party programme and officially present it to the nation. I feel sure that it will decide in favour of an immediate release of this programme to the people. The Party, however, will take no action on the programme until the masses of the people have had the fullest opportunity of reviewing it. Remember that it is at the moment merely a draft programme and only your approval will finalize it.

At this present moment, all over Africa, dark clouds of neo-colonialism are fast gathering. African States are becoming debtor-nations, and client States day in and day out, owing to their adoption of unreal attitudes to world problems, saying 'no' when they should have said 'yes', and 'yes' when they should have said 'no'. They are seeking economic shelter under colonialist wings, instead of accepting the truth – that their survival lies in the political unification of Africa.

Countrymen, we must draw up a programme of action and later plan details of this programme for the benefit of the whole people. Such a programme is the one that the Party now brings to you, the people of Ghana, in the hope that you will approve it critically and help to make it a success.

We have a rich heritage. Our natural resources are abundant and varied. We have mineral and agricultural wealth and, above all, we have the will to find the means whereby these possessions can be put to the greatest use and advantage. The Party's programme for work and happiness is a pointer to the way ahead, the way leading to a healthier, happier and more prosperous life for us all. When you have examined and accepted this programme, the Government and the people will base on it and initiate our Seven-Year Development Plan, which will guide our action to prosperity.

This programme constitutes for us a vigorous reminder that we must eschew complacency and push forward more determined than ever before to achieve our goal and, through work and enterprise, to create progress, prosperity and happiness for our people.

The Eleventh Congress of the Party is scheduled to take place on the 10th of June. This Congress will give its final approval to the new Party programme.

Countrymen, we have carried out an important work of consolidation. We have stabilized the national structure and established solid security. We have done all this and more within the past ten years and we now prepare to move forward to the next stage.

We do so in the confident expectation that every one of us will do his duty and do it well. The national cause of socialist reconstruction demands sacrifice from us all. Each one of us must sacrifice a little for the total good of the whole people.

This programme for 'Work and Happiness' is an expression of the evidence of the nation's creative ability, the certainty of the correctness of our Party line and action and the greatest single piece of testimony of our national confidence in the future.

Ghana is our country which we must all help to build. This programme gives us the opportunity to make our contribution towards the fulfilment of our national purposes.

As I look at the content of the programme and the matters it covers, such as Tax Reform, Animal Husbandry and Poultry Production, Forest Husbandry, Industrialization, Handicrafts, Banking and Insurance, Foreign Enterprise, Culture and Leisure, I am convinced beyond all doubt that Ghana and Ghanaians will travel full steam ahead, conscious of their great responsibilities and fully aware that the materialization of this bright picture of the future is entirely dependent on their active and energetic industry.

We cannot afford to fail. We cannot afford even to think of failure. But if there is one thing we in this great Party have learnt, it is that nothing has been achieved or will ever be achieved without unstinted effort and the determination to succeed. Nothing succeeds like success. So all of us must tighten our belts and plunge head first into the fight for the urgent socialist reconstruction about which we have talked so much.

It is my sincere hope that each one of you will take an interest in this national exercise and make the Party programme for work and happiness a great success.

And now, Countrymen, I have been speaking to you about our Party programme. From this I turn to a subject of almost equal moment, because it affects what is to me of the greatest importance, namely, the maintenance of the Republic as by law established and the achievement of those aims which under our Constitution I have pledged myself as President to strive for.

An emergent country which attempts to follow a policy of socialism at home and a policy abroad of positive non-alignment, is challenging many vested interests. It would have been the most criminal folly for us not to take note of the lessons of contemporary history.

When you chose me as your President, I took an oath in which I swore that I would preserve and defend the Constitution and that I would do right to all manner of people according to law, without fear or favour, affection or ill will.

I should have been false to my oath had I allowed the Constitution to be overthrown by force, but I consider that the obligations which the Constitution imposes upon me not only call upon me to do justice, but also, wherever possible, to temper justice with mercy.

We have by no means passed through all our difficulties. The need for a Preventive Detention Act still remains, but I believe that the time has come when the security situation has improved sufficiently to allow a number of detainees to be released.

I have therefore ordered the immediate release of many of those at present under detention.

The Government had originally considered that anyone who had been previously detained and released, and who then again engages in subversive activities, should be liable to a maximum imprisonment of twenty years. On this matter, too, I consider that a gesture of reconciliation can be made. The maximum period of five years detention as provided in the existing law will be retained, but the Preventive Detention Act will be so amended as to provide that anyone released from detention who again indulges in subversion, shall be detained again up to the present maximum of five years, and may, in addition, lose all rights as a citizen.

There remains also the question of those few citizens who have fled abroad. In one or two cases detention orders have been made against subversive individuals who have since fled the country, and in the event of such people returning to Ghana, these orders would be reviewed. But in most cases, those who have fled from Ghana have done so because they had a bad conscience or else were frightened by some unscrupulous rumour-monger.

A general amnesty will be extended to all such persons. I call upon them to return and to put their energies into useful purposes for the good of the country. I give them the assurance that they will not be victimized in any way or subjected to any disability for any past act; so long as they remain loyal and law-abiding they will not only have nothing to fear, but will also be assured of the protection which the machinery of the law provides and to which everyone in this country is entitled.

Countrymen, now is the time for reconstruction. We have a gigantic task before us. In solving our problems even those who in the past believed that they could gain their ends by subversion can now, if only they give up illegal methods, find their way back into useful and fruitful work.

SPEECH TO LAUNCH THE SEVEN-YEAR DEVELOPMENT PLAN
WEDNESDAY, 11 MARCH 1964

Mr Speaker, Members of the National Assembly:
I have come here today to present to you, and to the people

of Ghana, our Seven-Year Development Plan which, when completed, will bring Ghana to the threshold of a modern State based on a highly organized and efficient agricultural and industrial programme.

The main tasks of the Plan are: firstly, to speed up the rate of growth of our national economy. Secondly, it is to enable us to embark upon the socialist transformation of our economy through the rapid development of the State and co-operative sectors. Thirdly, it is our aim, by this Plan, to eradicate completely the colonial structure of our economy.

On this occasion, let me take the opportunity here and now to thank all those experienced men and women, Ghanaians and non-Ghanaians, who have contributed so much to the preparation of this Plan.

Mr Speaker, when the Convention People's Party came to power in 1951, the pace of development was so slow and confused that we decided to speed it up by attempting to implement in five years the programme of reconstruction which was designed by the colonial administration to take place over a period of ten years. That programme was not a development plan. It was a collection of various individual petty projects that had to be built in preparation for future planning.

At the conclusion of this programme, it became necessary to pause for two years in order to consolidate our position. By the time we reached the stage of implementing the next phase of our programme, it had already become quite clear to us that the only real solution to the reconstruction of Ghana lay, in the long run, in the adoption of a socialist and co-operative programme for industry, and the mechanization and diversification of our agriculture. Our hopes in this regard lay in the Volta River Project, about which I will have more to say later on.

Mr Speaker, this Seven-Year Development Plan which I now lay before you is therefore the first really integrated and comprehensive economic plan ever drawn up for Ghana's development after a thorough examination of our needs and resources. The Plan is designed to give effect to the Party's Programme of Work and Happiness which has already been accepted by the country. It also embodies a long view of the path which should lead to a self-sustaining economy, based on socialist production and distribution. An economy balanced between industry and agriculture, providing a sufficiency of food for the people, and supporting secondary industries based on the products of our agriculture. In other words, an economy founded securely on the basis of socialist production and distribution.

Our aim, under this Plan, is to build in Ghana a socialist State which accepts full responsibility for promoting the well-being of the masses. Our national wealth must be built up and used in such a way that economic power shall not be allowed to exploit the worker in town or village, but be used for the supreme welfare and happiness of our people. The people, through the State, should have an effective share in the economy of the country and an effective control over it.

A socialist Ghana must also secure for every citizen, at the earliest possible date, an adequate level of education and nutrition and a satisfactory standard of clothing, housing and leisure.

The Party has always proclaimed socialism as the objective of our social, industrial and economic programmes. Socialism, however, will continue to remain a slogan until industrialization is achieved. Socialism demands a very different kind of planning and economic structure from the type that was evolved by the colonial administration. This is why in 1961 we set up a Planning Commission and charged it with the responsibility for drawing up this Development Plan which I present to you today as an instalment in the process by which we hope to turn Ghana into the sort of country we envisage.

A socialist State cannot come by itself, nor can it be established by the formulation of plans. Socialism has to be worked for and even sacrificed for. Socialism, which is aimed at the emancipation of the people from exploitation, has to be built by the people. It is the expression of the people whose Government accepts responsibility for promoting their welfare to the fullest possible extent.

Our youth from the primary schools, through the secondary schools to the universities and higher institutions of learning, should and must be taught and trained in the socialist philosophy. They must be taught to know the workings of neo-colonialism and trained to recognize it wherever it may rear its head. They must not only know the trappings of colonialism and imperialism, but they must also be able to smell out the hide-outs of neo-colonialism.

In this endeavour, we shall expect from each citizen a maximum contribution to the national economy according to his ability and training. It is only in proportion to the contribution which each of us makes to the work of the Nation that we can expect to share in the material gains which the socialist development of the economy will make possible.

Mr Speaker, in order to accomplish our objectives, we have decided that the economy of Ghana will, for some time to come, remain a mixed economy in which a vigorous public and co-operative sector will operate along with the private sector. Let me make it clear that our socialist objectives demand that the public and co-operative sector of the productive economy should expand at the maximum possible rate, especially in those strategic areas of production upon which the economy of the country essentially depends.

We are determined that the economic independence of Ghana shall be achieved and maintained so as to avoid the social antagonisms resulting from the unequal distribution of economic power. We are equally determined to ensure that the operation of a mixed economy leads to the socialist transformation we envisage, and not to the defeat of our socialist aims. It is essential, therefore, that we should remind ourselves at all times of the necessity

firstly, to promote to the maximum the development of the State and co-operative sectors;

secondly, to regulate the pattern of State investment in order to give the highest priority to productive investment, and

thirdly, to determine and direct the forms and conditions of foreign investment, in order to safeguard our socialist policy and national independence.

In this way, we shall ensure that the growth rate of the public and co-operative sector of our economy will exceed the growth rate of the private sector, particularly in industry and agriculture.

Mr Speaker, as you know, we have already established many industrial projects and enterprises, as a means of securing our economic independence and assisting in the national control of the economy. I must make it clear that these State Enterprises were not set up to lose money at the expense of the tax payers. Like all business undertakings, they are expected to maintain themselves efficiently, and to show profits. Such profits should be sufficient to build up capital for further investment as well as to finance a large proportion of the public services which it is the responsibility of the State to provide.

In every socialist country, State enterprises provide the bulk of State revenues, and we intend to follow the same pattern here. Our State enterprises will be set yearly financial and production targets so that they may work towards definite objectives and goals and thereby given every stimulus to operate efficiently and profitably. Hence, the managers of our State enterprises, and those in charge of our State organizations and apparatus should be men trained in management; honest and dedicated men; men with integrity; men who are incorruptible.

When we have succeeded in establishing these principles, Government will then be in a position to lower taxes progressively, to lessen steadily the burden of taxation on the people and eventually to abolish many of them, if not all of them.

I have set up a State Management Committee to bring these ideas to life and to help in building up strong, well managed, efficient and profitable State enterprises.

I intend, however, that the State Management Committee shall do more than that. I want to ensure that the people of this country are fully informed of Government's intentions and plans, particularly with regard to industrialization and agriculture. The people have every right to be fully informed in order that they may know what our objectives are, what progress we are making and how Government funds are being spent in the interest of this country's economic development.

I am convinced that with this knowledge will come that understanding which will give our people the necessary impetus to do all they can to help achieve our objectives for work and happiness and accelerated development.

Mr Speaker, foreign investment as the private sector of our industrial development can play an important role in our economy. It has a valuable contribution to make to our economy and to the attainment of certain specific objectives. Among these will be production of consumer goods, the local processing of Ghanaian raw material and the utilization of Ghana's natural resources in those lines of economic activity where a large volume of investment is required.

We expect, however, that such investments will not be operated so as to exploit our people. On the contrary, we expect such enterprises to assist in the expansion of the economy of the country in line with our general objectives. Foreign investment enterprises will contribute personal initiative, managerial ability and technical skills towards the development of the country. They will also further the growth of similar initiative, ability, technical skills and habits of saving among Ghanaians.

We welcome foreign investors in a spirit of partnership. They can earn their profits here, provided they leave us an agreed portion for promoting the welfare and happiness of our people as a whole as against the greedy ambitions of the few. From what we get out of this partnership, we hope to be able to expand the health services for our people, to feed and house them well, to give them more and better educational institutions and to see to it that they have a rising standard of living. This in a nutshell is what we expect from our socialist objectives.

Mr Speaker, in pursuing these objectives, we shall exert our efforts towards the maximum extension of the public sector within the productive economy. As I have said, within this framework we do not intend or desire to limit private investment.

Our Government has always insisted that the operations of all economic enterprises in Ghana should conform to the national economic objectives and be subject to the rules and regulations which are made in pursuance of our socialist policies. Our experience has been that foreign investors have been willing to invest in Ghana so long as the limits within which they can work are fair and clearly defined, and we shall continue to consult with them in order to ensure that co-operation is as full as possible.

Ghana's economy, particularly at the present stage, has room for all the investment capital which is likely to be provided by foreign investors, by the Central and Local Governments and by individual Ghanaians. In this respect, I believe that there are a considerable number of individual Ghanaians who are in a position materially to assist in finding the necessary capital for the Seven-Year Development Plan.

One of the worst features of colonialism was that it produced an unbalanced economy in which there was little room for investment of the profits which were made by expatriate firms. In colonial days it was natural that profits made in Ghana should be invested abroad. Today the situation is entirely different. An investor who lays out his money wisely in Ghana is likely to make a larger profit than if he invested it in a more developed country. Nevertheless, old habits of investment persist and there are a considerable number of Ghanaians who still maintain their savings in foreign investments and in property outside Ghana.

Under our Exchange Control laws it is, of course, illegal for Ghanaians to have property abroad without having declared this to the appropriate authorities. This aspect of our law is not always understood. The Government has therefore decided, not to penalize any Ghanaian firm or individual who, within the next three months, repatriates foreign holdings of money to Ghana, or who declares ownership of foreign property. A thorough investigation is afoot to discover the extent of holdings of foreign exchange and properties by Ghanaians, and those who do not take advantage of this offer but continue to conceal their foreign assets, must expect, after the three-month period of grace, to be subject to the full rigours of the law.

Mr Speaker, The Seven-Year Development Plan makes provisions for a maximum volume of investment from all sources.

We intend that the State should retain control of the strategic branches of the economy, including public utilities, raw materials and heavy industry. The State will also participate in light and consumer goods industries in which the rates of return on capital should be highest. We intend also that those industries which provide the basic living needs of the people shall be State-owned, in order to prevent any exploitation.

Mr Speaker, Members of the National Assembly, let me now turn to the specific proposals of the Seven-Year Plan.

In the next seven years, it is proposed that there will be a total expenditure of one-thousand-and-sixteen million pounds, that is, over a billion pounds sterling, on development projects in the Plan. Of this total, it is intended that four-hundred-and-seventy-six million pounds should be provided by the Central Government. Foreign investors, individual Ghanaians, Local Authorities and the Co-operative sector are expected to invest about four-hundred-and-forty million pounds. We also hope that individual Ghanaians will contribute nearly one-hundred million pounds' worth of direct labour in the construction of buildings, in community development and in the extension of their farms.

The total government investment will be four-hundred-and-seventy-six million pounds.

Investment throughout the Seven-Year Plan period will average one-hundred-and-thirty million pounds a year. Of this, approximately one half, or sixty-eight million pounds a year, will be invested by Government, and the rest by private investors.

We continue to look to the outside world to contribute to our national development. We expect the more advanced and industrialized countries to facilitate our trade in primary commodities and manufactured goods so that we can finance the bulk of our development out of our own resources and earnings.

We hope that where necessary, the Government of Ghana will be able to borrow money on reasonable terms for essential and productive projects. Let me say again that we welcome foreign investors to come and invest in Ghana's progress. We offer them every assistance, substantial material benefits, and the advantages of a coherent long-term economic strategy which will give them plenty of scope for planning and development. At the same time, we expect them to re-invest an adequate share of their profits in the further progress, both of Ghana and of themselves.

In order to be able to manage these new investments as well as our existing capital with the maximum of efficiency, the country needs a well-trained labour force under competent management. In this sense, the educational programme under the Plan is crucial to the success of the whole Plan. It is directed towards giving education in Ghana a new and more practical orientation and making it available to all who can profit by it. In order to make real economic progress, Ghana must adopt an improved technology in all lines of production. We look to the educational system and educational institutions to equip our people with the latest advancements in industrial and agricultural technology. We expect our Academy of Sciences and our research organizations to adapt this technology to the conditions of Ghana. And we look to the Managers of our enterprises to adopt the technology which is developed, and to foster skills by a maximum programme of 'on the job' training.

The development of Ghana has hitherto not been sufficiently balanced between different parts of the country. It is the deliberate policy of this Plan to correct this imbalance. Naturally we must develop in each part of the country the type of economic activity to which it is best suited by reason of natural resources and geographical location. But a special effort has to be made in order to ensure that the rate of progress in the less favoured parts of the country is even greater than the rate of progress in those sections which have hitherto been more favoured. It is only by this means that we can achieve a more harmonious national development.

In the present Plan period it is proposed to pay special attention to the modernizing of agriculture in the savannah areas of the Northern and Upper Regions. It is hoped through secondary industries based on agricultural raw materials, to turn the Northern areas into major sources of food supplies for the whole country. In this regard, the Government has recognized the importance of irrigation and water conservation in the country, and has already initiated far-reaching plans for major schemes of irrigation and water conservation.

Mr Speaker, the backbone of Ghana's agriculture has always been its farmers who, particularly in recent years, have made a fine contribution to the economy and expressed their patriotism in a number of unselfish ways. The developments the Government is proposing in the areas of State and co-operative farming will bring them a share of the local facilities they have so long been denied. More than this: they will have the opportunity also to share in the up-to-date techniques of farming that must be employed if greater yields and diversity of crops are to be attained.

I want our farmers to understand that the State Farms and Co-operative enterprises are not being encouraged as alternatives to peasant farming. The interests of individual peasant farmers will not be made subservient to those of the State Farms and Co-operatives. We need the efforts of our individual Farmers more than ever, along with our State Farms and Co-operatives, if we are to achieve, at an increased pace, the agricultural targets we have set ourselves. We look to our individual peasant farmers for the enlargement of investment in our agriculture.

Mr Speaker, as I have stressed time and again, the revolution taking place in Ghana is chiefly a revolution of the workers and the tillers of the land. A vital phase of this revolution is the implementation of the Seven-Year Development Plan which aims at the total expansion of all sections of our economy to raise the standard of living of the people of Ghana. I am happy that the workers have demonstrated their complete dedication to our revolutionary cause.

Upon the attainment of independence, the Party, as the conscious political vanguard of the Trade Union Movement, worked with the Trade Unions and created a new and more effective structure of the Trades Union Congress. Government supported the desire of the workers for this new Trade Union structure.

Thus, we were able to create in our labour and industrial laws conditions for resolving quickly and expeditiously the problems of our working population. Thus, also, the workers accepted the responsibility to contribute to the economic and social reconstruction of our economy.

In the State sector of our economy, the workers employed in our State Corporations will be afforded full and equal opportunities for participating in the planning and execution of our industrial projects. It is only in this way that the workers will closely identify themselves with the attainment of the economic and social objectives of our new society and will thus equate their own welfare with the prosperity of our country. Such new working relationships will enable the workers to acquire the sense of complete belonging and full participation and they will no longer consider themselves as working for colonialist exploiters. I have given instructions that some of our State enterprises be handed over completely to the workers who will manage them for themselves on behalf of the State.

The success of this Seven-Year Development Plan will only be attained if the enthusiasm of our workers is mobilized and they know the part they ought to play and are drawn into full consultation in the execution of our Plan.

I therefore call upon all workers, farmers, fishermen and peasants of our country to accept this challenge and fulfil the hopes and aspirations of our people.

Mr Speaker, when I spoke at the opening of the Unilever Soap Factory at Tema on the 24th August, 1963, I said, among other things, that in order to pay tribute to the importance of labour in the development of Ghana, the Government has decided to institute a special Order to be known as the 'Order of the Black Star of Labour'. Details of this Order, which will rank among the highest honours of the State, have now been worked out and all classes of labour will qualify for this Order. It is my confident expectation that this award will provide an ample incentive to all workers, and that every worker of the nation will make it his ambition to qualify for the title of Worker of the Year and to become heroes and heroines of Labour.

Mr Speaker, Members of the National Assembly, I am happy to inform the House that on present estimates, it is confidently expected that the Volta River Project will begin to generate electrical power by September, 1965. On that date, we shall come to the end of one phase of our cherished goal and usher in the beginning of a new and more exciting endeavour to utilize the vast electric power which will be at the country's disposal for the enrichment of our economy and our people.

Completion of the Volta Project will enable us to develop the industrial potential of Ghana. Indeed, the possibilities for our agriculture and industry will be completely revolutionized. First and foremost the Volta Project will increase by nearly 500 per cent the installed electrical capacity of the country. Nearly one half of this new capacity will be taken up by the aluminium smelter in Tema. But there will be an ample reserve of power for other users, and Ghana will have liberated herself decisively from the possibility of power shortage becoming again a brake on the rate of economic progress.

I would like in this context to point out the degree to which the Volta Scheme fits into our chosen combination of a mixed economy with socialist and co-operative goals. A major part of the scheme is being financed by the Ghana Government; but the American and British Governments have joined in the financing of it, together with the World Bank, and we have had the most helpful and fruitful collaboration with American enterprise in the shape of the Kaiser group of industries.

Meanwhile, our Italian contractors, Impregilo, have achieved the remarkable feat of taking one year off the time of construction of the dam. Throughout the scheme, we have worked together in the greatest harmony. I regard this great scheme as an example of the way in which careful and proper planning together with foreign investment, public control and participation, and the devoted labours of the people can revolutionize the economic base of society.

Such an achievement can have a significance far beyond Ghana's frontiers. It is only by strengthening our economy in this way that we can make an effective contribution to our brothers in Africa and the political unification of our continent. In this endeavour, the Seven-Year Plan makes provision for the undertaking of joint enterprises in individual fields of industry and also for the harmonization of our total programme of economic development with that of other African countries.

The Plan we are launching today relates to projects and developments which we wish to see take place in Ghana. It grieves me that we in Ghana, who so strongly advocate the unity of the African Continent, should be forced to take so narrow a view of planning. I have advocated for closer union of Africa times without number. I have emphasized the need for a continental union Government for Africa as the only solution to Africa's ills and problems. Since the Addis Ababa Conference, it has been made abundantly clear that artificial borders which we inherited from the colonial powers should be made obsolete and unnecessary. While we wait for the setting up of a Union Government for Africa, we must begin immediately to harmonize our plans for Africa's total development. For example, I see no reason why the independent African States should not, with advantage to each other, join together in an economic union and draw up together a joint Development Plan which will give us greater scope and flexibility to our mutual advantage. By the same token, I see no reason why the independent African States should not have common shipping and air lines in the interest of improved services and economy. With such rationalization of our economic policies, we could have common objectives and thus eliminate unnecessary competition and frontier barriers and disputes.

As every day passes, it is becoming clearer and clearer that it is only the establishment of a Union Government of Africa which can save our separate States not only from neo-colonialism, but from imperialism itself. We in Ghana are determined to make our whole-hearted contribution toward this objective. We are prepared to make whatever further provisions may be required to enable us to play our part in the achievement and consolidation of African Unity. Recent events in East Africa and in other parts of Africa have shown how urgent is the need for the establishment of a central machinery for dealing with the serious political and economic questions confronting us in Africa today.

Mr Speaker, Members of the National Assembly, the object of the Seven-Year Development Plan which I have outlined to you is. to modernize our agriculture and develop our industry as a basis of our socialist society. I, for my part, am determined that the Plan shall succeed. Its success must rest on the support of each and every one of you and on the devotion and hard work of the officials, Heads of Corporations and Enterprises, whose duty it will be to translate the Plan into action. In the seven years ahead, all our energies must be concentrated on its implementation.

It has long been apparent that the administrative machinery which we inherited was not designed for a country working within the framework of an overall plan, and in which the activities of individual agencies of the nation are directed to clearly defined goals of development. An effective reform of the governmental machinery is therefore needed if the Seven-Year Plan is not to falter on the inadequacies of administration. The first task in this regard will be to attune more closely the policies and actions of every agency or organ of Government to the overall national policy as defined in the Seven-Year Development Plan.

I have caused to be published with the Seven-Year Plan a guide to its implementation. This guide should be studied most carefully by Members of this House, by the Party and Government officials, Managers of State Enterprises, the farmers' organization, the Trades Union Congress and all those who will be concerned with the implementation of the Plan.

I have, earlier this month, established several organizations whose responsibility it will be to see to the rapid execution of the Plan. These are, firstly, the *National Planning Commission,* through which the people will be associated with the Plan, and which will be enlarged to include Ministers, Regional Commissioners, representatives of Corporations and organizations and integral wings of the Party.

Secondly, the *State Planning Committee* which, under my Chairmanship, will be the key body for co-ordinating action and policy on the Plan, and for giving directions on its execution and implementation.

Thirdly, there is the *Budget Committee*, which will make recommendations for the policy of the annual budget.

Fourthly, the *Foreign Exchange Committee*, which will make recommendations regarding the size of yearly imports and exports.

And lastly – though by no means the least – there is the *State Management Committee* which will direct the operations and activities of State Corporations and State Enterprises in order to ensure their efficient and profitable management.

I am sure that if these five bodies carry out their duties honestly and energetically, we shall achieve and even exceed our goals under this Plan. We might even complete the Plan ahead of schedule, that is to say in less than seven years.

Mr Speaker, all our efforts should henceforth be directed to ensuring that everything is done to make this Plan a success. I am sure that all the people of this country are determined in their efforts to ensure that we achieve all our Plan objectives and make our country a happy, progressive, prosperous and advanced nation. We must therefore ensure that State funds and resources are not frittered away uselessly or wastefully or that they find their way into private pockets.

We shall, in order to implement the Plan, be awarding a number of contracts to organizations both here and abroad; we shall also be entering into sales agreements as well as acquiring goods locally. I intend that all contracts, whether for the construction of factories or offices, or for any purchase or sale, should be so safeguarded that our funds will be properly husbanded and utilized for Ghana's advancement and for the welfare and happiness of the people.

In order that our resources are not wasted by corrupt practices and in order to prevent any attempts at personal greed and aggrandisement at the expense of the people and the State, steps will be taken to ensure that no contractor shall offer or give or agree to give to any person in the service of the Government of Ghana any gift or consideration of any kind as an inducement or reward for doing, or forbearing to do, or for having done any act in relation to the obtaining or execution of any contract for the Government of Ghana, or for showing favour or disfavour to any person in relation to any other contract for the Government of Ghana.

We shall also see to it that no contractor shall enter into any contract with the Government of Ghana in connection with which a commission has been paid or agreed to be paid by him or on his behalf, or to his knowledge, unless before the contract is made, particulars of any such commission and of the terms and conditions of any agreement for the payment thereof have been disclosed in writing to a special committee to be appointed by me to represent the Government of Ghana.

Any breach of these conditions shall entitle the Government to determine any contract, and recover from the contractor the amount of any loss which may have resulted from such determination and the amount or value of any such gifts, consideration or commission.

I have therefore directed that every contract for the supply of goods and services or for the execution of any Government project shall embody clauses to give effect to this decision. These conditions are being made in the interest of the tax payer who ultimately has to find the money to pay for these gifts and bribes.

I want the world to know that we shall do everything to set our own house in order. I want all of us here in Ghana also to realize that nothing must be allowed to hamper our efforts to achieve our Plan objectives and that no individuals will be permitted to hamper that effort, to retard our advancement in any way or to grow rich by corrupt practices. Those who have ears to hear, let them hear. The progress, welfare and happiness of the masses is our supreme concern.

Mr Speaker, we know that the desire of people is to have enough to eat without spending too great a part of their income upon food. They want a reasonably comfortable place to sleep; they want light, a ready supply of water, education for the growing children and future generation, adequate medical care and welfare services. Our present plan will go a long way to fulfilling these very legitimate desires of the people. The Volta project will provide us with abundant light and water. In addition, a whole programme of irrigation and water development is engaging our attention very seriously.

Housing, too, is one of our main preoccupations. We are at this moment in the last stages of formulating large-scale housing projects, which we hope to have ready soon. A factory for prefabricated concrete units is now under construction and will come into production sometime this year. When these plans are completed, we shall be able to put up low-cost housing to meet the needs of our working people at the rate of about two hundred houses a month. This should go a long way to offset the pressing housing problem.

In transforming the many centres of over-crowded and insanitary housing that at present exist in some areas, we shall look carefully into the traditional community customs of our people and will, wherever it is feasible and possible, try to maintain such communities in their traditional locations, but with a newer, better and more pleasant look.

Mr Speaker, we would be hampering our advance to socialism if we were to encourage the growth of Ghanaian private capitalism in our midst. This would, of course, be in antipathy to our economic and social objectives. There are some few among us who are seeking outlets for small enterprises. Such people we appreciate have initiative which it would be well to employ suitably in our socialist undertakings. There are some who have small capital savings which they consider they can profitably employ in business that will provide goods and services which are in public demand. Such small businessmen will be encouraged to operate enterprises provided they accept certain limitations as the Government will find it necessary to impose as to the size of the enterprise and the number of persons to be employed in their undertakings.

In this connection it is necessary to distinguish between two types of business which have grown up within recent years. The first is the type which it is the Government's intention to encourage, that of the small businessman who employs his capital in an industry or trade with which he is familiar, and in so doing, fulfils a public need.

The second type is very different. It consists of that class of Ghanaian businesses which are modelled on the old type of colonial exploitation. Individuals who can command capital use their money not in productive endeavour, but by the purchase and re-sale, at high prices, of such commodities as fish, salt and other items of food and consumer goods which are in demand by the people. This type of business serves no social purpose and steps will be taken to see that our banking resources are not used to provide credit for this type of business.

Even more harmful to the economy is yet another type of enterprise in which some Ghanaians have been participating. This consists of setting up bogus agencies for foreign companies which are in fact nothing but organizations for distributing bribes and exerting improper pressures on behalf of foreign companies. It is the intention of the Government to carry out a wholesale investigation into the activities of these firms. They can do incalculable harm to our economy and they must be ruthlessly suppressed.

The initiative of Ghanaian businessmen will not be cramped, but we must take steps to see that it is channelled towards desirable social ends and is not expended in the exploitation of the community.

The Government will encourage Ghanaian businessmen to join with each other in co-operative forms of organization. In this way Ghanaian businessmen will be able to contribute actively in broadening the vitality of our economy and co-operation, and will provide a stronger form of organization than can be achieved through individual small businesses.

We must also discourage anything that can threaten our socialist construction. For this reason, no Ghanaian will be allowed to take up shares in any enterprise under foreign investment. On the contrary, we shall encourage our people with savings to invest in the State sector and co-operative undertakings. I know that among our Ghanaian businessmen, there are some who are ready and willing to turn their businesses into co-operative undertakings. Where well-run private enterprises are offered to and taken over by the State or co-operative undertakings, we hope that businessmen will offer themselves as managers and administrators.

In the same way, Mr Speaker, I want to refer to money-lending which, along with other problems, has been left to us by colonialism. I know that many of those who are carrying on this business of lending money at criminal rates of interest are non-Ghanaians. But, unhappily, not a few of our own people have joined the ranks of those who make quick and easy money out of the difficulties and misery of others. Money-lending and usury are intolerable and inconsistent with the ideals of a socialist state. We should see to it that this practice is eliminated from our society.

Mr Speaker, Members of the National Assembly, I am sure that imbued with the spirit of the Party's programme of Work and Happiness, all those who are responsible for the interpretation and implementation of this Plan will do their work honestly and devotedly. It may be that in the course of the next seven years some of us will from time to time attempt to change the choice of emphasis that we have made and try to direct proportionately more of our national resources into immediate welfare services and proportionately less into agriculture and industry. It will be the duty of those who are charged with the implementation of the Plan to ensure that these pressures are resisted. Otherwise we shall end up in the long run with an economy weak in its productive base and backward in its level of technology.

This Seven-Year Development Plan can only be accounted a success if by 1970 – the year in which we conclude the Plan and the year in which we celebrate the Tenth Anniversary of our Republic – we can truly say that the productive base of the economy has been revolutionized and that the level of technology and productivity in Ghana is approaching modern standards over an adequate area of the national economy.

Mr Speaker, Members of the National Assembly, 1964, the year in which we launch the Seven-Year Development Plan, will be hailed as the turning point in the history of Ghana. In a little over a year from now, we shall be generating electricity from the Volta River Project to feed our expanding factories throughout the country. The Kwame Nkrumah Steel Works in Tema will soon be completed. Tema Harbour itself is already being extended to meet the needs of our expanding economy, and in Tema a growing number of industrial projects are already in production and more are being established. In this connection I want to mention, particularly, the Aluminium Smelter which will produce aluminium for domestic consumption and export, the Dry Dock and Ship Repair Yard – which will be one of the finest and biggest in Africa – and the Accra-Tema Freeway, which will provide fast and safe travelling between the capital and the port of Tema.

I can already see, in my mind's eye, a picture of Ghana as it will be by the end of the Plan period. I see a State with a strong and virile economy, its agriculture and industry buoyant and prosperous, an industrialized nation serving the needs of its people.

Let us therefore, as from today, move forward together, united in devotion and determination, to give of our best in the execution and implementation of this Seven-Year Plan.

Mr Speaker, Members of the National Assembly, it gives me a great pleasure on this historic occasion, and in this House, to launch our Seven-Year Development Plan.

17

An important aspect of Pan-Africanism is the revival and development of the 'African Personality', temporarily submerged during the colonial period. It finds expression in a re-awakening consciousness among Africans and peoples of African descent of the bonds which unite us – our historical past, our culture, our common experience, and our aspirations.

The myth that Africa's history began with the arrival of the European, and that Africans had achieved nothing and had no culture before then, serves the purpose of imperialists who find it necessary to fabricate some kind of justification for capitalist exploitation. It is a part of the more insidious myth of racial inferiority which seeks to provide an excuse for master-servant relationships, and the domination of one race by another.

I was determined, soon after Independence had been achieved in Ghana, to take practical steps to revive the cultural and spiritual unity of the African people, and to promote research into every aspect of our heritage, so that the African Personality would become a strong driving force within the African Revolution, and would at the same time become a factor to be reckoned with in international affairs. Africanist scholars from many parts of Africa and the world were invited to assemble in Accra in December 1962 in the First Africanist Conference, to discuss how best to set about this great task of promoting scholarship and research into Africa's history, culture, thought and resources.

As part of this great enterprise work was begun on the compilation of an Encyclopaedia Africana to contain full and up-to-date information about Africa and the African people. Two brilliant African scholars, Dr W. Alphaeus Hunton and Dr W. E. B. Du Bois came to live in Ghana to work on the project. If it had not been for the reactionary coup of February 1966, the first volumes might have been already providing information and inspiration to those studying Africa.

The spirit of a people can only flourish in freedom. When the liberation and unification of Africa is completed, the African Personality will find full expression and be meaningfully projected in the international community. In the meantime, while Africa remains divided, oppressed and exploited, the African Personality is merely a term expressing cultural and social bonds which unite Africans and people of African descent. It is a concept of the African nation, and is not associated with a particular state, language, religion, political system, or colour of the skin. For those who project it, it expresses identification not only with Africa's historical past, but with the struggle of the African people in the African Revolution to liberate and unify the continent and to build a just society.

SPEECH AT THE CONGRESS OF AFRICANISTS

12th December, 1962

Distinguished Scholars, it is an honour and privilege for me to welcome you to Ghana and to this First Africanist Conference. Your meeting here, within the ramparts of an African university, is a reflection of Africa's recovery and re-awakening. It is also a recognition of the new spirit which now animates the people of this great continent. It is even edifying that this Congress is taking place on African soil. I know that you who have gathered here represent various fields and branches of learning; in fact I see familiar faces of professors of universities and academies. What has impelled you, Distinguished Scholars, to gather here at such a time as this? You are here and are united by the fact that you want to find out the truth about Africa and, when you have found out, to proclaim it to the world.

Scholarly and academic interest in Africa is not a new venture. The desire to know more about Africa has been expressed from the very earliest times, because Africa has been the question-mark of history. To a Roman pro-consul: *Semper aliquid novi ex Africa.*

From the imaginings of the ancient geographers, an inaccurate and distorted picture of Africa often emerged. South of the Atlas ranges, a sandy desert was believed to extend indefinitely, with here and there a providential oasis, a rivulet, which nibbling and corroding its way through the sandy wastes, dripped into the sea. Even so, the ancients had some genuine knowledge of the African Continent, for they had a scientific curiosity about it. Thus Eratosthenes and Aristotle knew that the cranes migrated as far as the lakes where the Nile had its source. And both of them thought that it was there that the pygmies dwelt. Among the travellers of the ancient world who tried to explore Africa, we may recall men like Strabo and Hanno of Carthage.

After these early travels, foreign knowledge of Africa became static until a new impetus was given to it by the Arabs and the Chinese.

The Arabs and the Chinese discovered and chronicled a succession of powerful African kingdoms. One of these kingdoms was that of Ghana, the pomp of whose court was the admiration of that age – and also of ours. It bred and developed within its borders the instruments of civilization and art; its palaces were of solid architectural construction, complete with glass windows, murals and sculpture, and the thrones within the palaces were bedecked with gold. There were other kingdoms, such as those of Songhay, Sala, Berissa, the renowned empires of Bornu, Wangara, Melli. The historians tell us that these empires and kingdoms were maintained with remarkable efficiency and administrative competence. Their splendour was proverbial in mediaeval times.

The Chinese, too, during the T'ang dynasty (AD. 618–907), published their earliest major records of Africa. In the 18th century, scholarship connected Egypt with China; but Chinese acquaintance with Africa was not confined to knowledge of Egypt only. They had detailed knowledge of Somaliland, Madagascar and Zanzibar and made extensive visits to other parts of Africa.

The European exploration of Africa reached its height in the 19th century. What is unfortunate, however, is the fact that much of the discovery was given a subjective instead of an objective interpretation. In the regeneration of learning which is taking place in our universities and in other institutions of higher learning, we are treated as subjects and not objects. They forget that we are a historic people responsible for our unique forms of language, culture and society. It is therefore proper and fitting that a Congress of Africanists should take place in Africa and that the concept of Africanism should devolve from and be animated by that Congress.

Between ancient times and the 16th century, some European scholars forgot what their predecessors in African Studies had known. This amnesia, this regrettable loss of interest in the power of the African mind, deepened with growth of interest in the economic exploitation of Africa. It is no wonder that the Portuguese were erroneously credited with having erected the stone fortress of Mashonaland which, even when Barbossa, cousin of Magellan, first visited them, were ruins of long standing.

I have said that the pursuit of African Studies is not a new experience. But the motives which have led various scholars to undertake these studies have been diverse.

We can distinguish first a true scientific curiosity. Most of the Persian, Greek and Roman travellers exhibited this motive. Even when, as in the case of the Romans, they had a primary military purpose, they still tried and often succeeded in preserving some sense of objectivity.

Arab explorers were also often unbiased in their accounts of Africa, and indeed we are grateful to them for what they wrote concerning our past.

By the time the early European writings on Africa got under way, a new motive had begun to inform African Studies. Those early European works exchanged the scientific motive for one that was purely economic. There was the unbalanced trade in ivory and gold, and there was the illegitimate trafficking in men for which these writings needed to find some sort of excuse.

The point I wish to make at this stage is that much of European and American writing on Africa was at that time apologetic. It was devoted to an attempt to justify slavery and the continued exploitation of African labour and resources. African Studies in Europe and America were thus at their lowest ebb scientifically.

With the abolition of the slave trade, African Studies could no longer be inspired by the economic motive. The experts in African Studies therefore changed the content and direction of their writings; they began to give accounts of African society which were used to justify colonialism as a duty of civilization. Even the most flattering of these writings fell short of objectivity and truth. This explains, I believe, the popularity and success of anthropology as the main segment of African Studies.

The stage was then set for the economic and political subjugation of Africa. Africa, therefore, was unable to look forward or backward.

The central myth in the mythology surrounding Africa is that of the denial that we are a historical people. It is said that whereas other continents have shaped history and determined its course, Africa has stood still, held down by inertia. Africa, it is said, entered history only as a result of European contact. Its history, therefore, is widely felt to be an extension of European history. Hegel's authority was lent to this a-historical hypothesis concerning Africa. And apologists of colonialism and imperialism lost little time in seizing upon it and writing wildly about it to their heart's content.

To those who say that there is no documentary source for that period of African history which pre-dates the European contact, modern research has a crushing answer. We know that we were not without a tradition of historiography, and, that this is so, is now the verdict of true Africanists. African historians, by the end of the 15th century, had a tradition of recorded history, and certainly by the time when Mohamud al-Kati wrote Ta'rikh al-Fattash. This tradition was incidentally much, much wider than that of the Timbuktu school of historians, and our own Institute of African Studies here at this University, is bringing to light several chronicles relating to the history of Northern Ghana.

Of these chronicles, the most exciting traced down to date, appears to be the Isnad al-Shuyukh Wa il-ulama, written around 1751 by al-Hajj Muhama ben Mustafa who lived in Western Gonja in Ghana. It gives details of the conversion of the Dynasty in 1585.

A great deal of interesting work has been done and continues to be done in learned centres in Africa. In Nigeria, for example, Dr Dike has worked on Politics and Trade in the Niger Delta. Here, he reflects, like other Africanist scholars, a new African-centred approach to the study of the relations between the Delta states and Europe in the 19th century. In this connection, the collaboration of archaeologists, historians and anthropologists, studying different aspects of the history, institutions and culture of pre-colonial Africa, has produced beneficial results.

A large collection of manuscripts and other evidence helping this adventure has now been made in many African centres of learning. At the University of Dakar, for example, I understand that a great deal has been collected in the way of documentary material relating to the history of the Western Sudan. In Mali, also, considerable work is being done on pre-colonial history and the Museum at Bamako has gathered a great deal of material both useful and fascinating.

In Guinea, too, the story of the contact between Europe and Africa is being written as an African experience and not as a European adventure. Similar work is being successfully undertaken in the Ivory Coast. In Upper Volta, there is the important work of Professor Ki-Zerbo on the Moshi Kingdom, and he has for some months now been working happily and successfully in our Institute of African Studies as an expression of the cultural unity of Africa.

In the East, a great deal of progressive work continues to be done. Documents and inscriptions in Eg'ez and Amharic, in Swahili and Arabic, in Old Nubian and Meroitic, are being collected in order to make possible our authentic reinterpretation of our past.

In Sudan, in Ethiopia, in Tanganyika, in Somalia, Kenya, Uganda, everywhere in Africa, there is purposeful effort to bring to light those means which alone will enable us to present our history as the history of the African people, the history of our actions and of the ideology and principles behind them, the history of our sufferings and our triumphs. This Congress, among other things, is an attempt to share experience in this common endeavour.

Many of these sources are documents, and documents written in African languages are coming to light. Thus, apart from Hausa, there are vast collections written in Fufulde, Kanuri, Nupe, and Dagbani. These are mainly 18th century documents, but they reflect a tradition of learning which goes back to the mediaeval times.

But our historical records do not consist alone in the facts which we committed in the Arabic script. Every society has methods of preserving facts about its past. And where a society has no literate traditions, it devises rigorous methods of oral recording. Scholars who have studied this phenomenon know this well. Historical recording in Africa therefore rightly comprises the documents in Arabic and African languages on the one hand, and, on the other, the well-preserved and authentic records of oral tradition. Our inheritance of oral literature, of epic and lyric poetry of stories and legends, praise songs and the chronicles of states, Kings and dynasties preserved by palace officials, is of intrinsic interest and merit, as it is of historical importance.

The history of a nation is, unfortunately, too easily written as the history of its dominant class. If the history of a nation, of a people, cannot be found in the history of a class, how much less can the history of a continent be found in what is not even a part of it – Europe. And yet, this is precisely what many a European historian has done in the past. The history of Africa has with them been European centred. Africa was only the space in which Europe swelled up. The African past was ignored and dismissed in these tendentious works as not contributing to, or affecting the European expansion and presence in Africa.

If Africa's history is interpreted in terms of the interests of European merchandise and capital, missionaries and administrators, it is no wonder that African nationalism is regarded as a perversion and colonialism as a virtue.

You who are meeting here today in the First Congress of Africanists, are all representatives of various disciplines, and are determined to pool your immense knowledge of Africa for the progress of the African. Your efforts mark a renascence of scientific [curiosity in the study of Africa and should be directed at an objective, impartial scrutiny and assessment of things African. While some of us are engaged with the political unification of Africa, Africanists everywhere must also help in building the spiritual and cultural foundations for the Unity of our Continent.

In East Africa, in the Sudan, in Egypt, in Nigeria, here in Ghana and elsewhere, the earth is being dug up apace – this time, not for gold or diamonds only, or for bauxite and other mineral riches, but also for its rich information about our past, its testimony to our achievements and its refutation of the sombre prophets of African History. Valuable pieces have already been unearthed, including evidence of the origin of man in Africa.

We have made our contribution to the fund of human knowledge by extending the frontiers of art, culture and spiritual values.

Democracy, for instance, has always been for us not a matter of technique, but more important than technique – a matter of socialist goals and aims. It was, however, not only our socialist aims that were democratically inspired, but also the methods of their pursuit were socialist.

If we have lost touch with what our forefathers discovered and knew, this has been due to the system of education to which we were introduced. This system of education prepared us for a subservient role to Europe and things European. It was directed at estranging us from our own cultures in order the more effectively to serve a new and alien interest.

In rediscovering and revitalizing our cultural and spiritual heritage and values, African Studies must help to redirect this new endeavour. The educational system which we devise today must equip us with the resources of a personality and a force strong enough to meet the intensities of the African presence and situation.

Education must enable us to understand correctly the strains and stresses to which Africa is subjected, to appreciate objectively the changes taking place, and enable us to contribute fully in a truly African spirit for the benefit of all, and for the peace and progress of the world.

African Studies is not a kind of academic hermitage. It has warm connections with similar studies in other countries of the world. It should change its course from anthropology to sociology, for it is the latter which more than any other aspect creates the firmest basis for social policy.

Your meeting here today as Africanists from various countries of the world, is truly historic. It emphasizes the idea that knowledge transcends political and national boundaries. It is incumbent upon all Africanist scholars, all over the world, to work for a complete emancipation of the mind from all forms of domination, control and enslavement.

I cannot leave you today without referring to the distinction achieved by a Zulu student – Isaka Seme – when he won the first prize of the Curtis Medal Orations at Columbia University on the 5th of April, 1906. Distinguished Scholars, let me confess, with humility, that it is not my usual practice to quote others. On this occasion, however, I feel that I have a duty to place on record at this first Africanist Congress taking place here in Africa, the oration of Isaka Seme which, although made some fifty years ago, is still relevant to the postulates of our present situation in Africa.

With your indulgence, Distinguished Scholars, please bear with me while I quote his oration in full.

This is what he said:

"I have chosen to speak to you on this occasion upon 'The Regeneration of Africa'. I am an African, and I set my pride in my race over against a hostile public opinion. Men have tried to compare races on the basis of some equality. In all the works of nature, equality, if by it we mean identity, is an impossible dream! Search the universe! You will find no two units alike. The scientists tell us there are no two cells, no two atoms, identical. Nature has bestowed upon each a peculiar individuality, and exclusive patent – from the great giants of the forest to the tenderest blade. Catch in your hand, if you please, the gentle flakes of snow. Each is a perfect gem, a new creation; it shines in its own glory – a work of art different from all of its aerial companions. Man, the crowning achievement of nature, defies analysis. He is a mystery through all ages and for all time. The races of mankind are composed of free and unique individuals. An attempt to compare them on the basis of equality can never be finally satisfactory. Each is self. My thesis stands on this truth; time has proved it. In all races genius is like a spark, which, concealed in the bosom of a flint, bursts forth at the summoning stroke. It may arise anywhere and in any race.

I would ask you not to compare Africa to Europe or to any other continent. I make this request not from any fear that such comparison might bring humiliation upon Africa. The reason I have stated – a common standard is impossible! Come with me to the ancient capital of Egypt, Thebes, the city of one hundred gates. The grandeur of its venerable ruins and the gigantic proportions of its architecture reduce to insignificance the boasted monuments of other nations. The pyramids of Egypt are structures to which the world presents nothing comparable. The mighty monuments seem to look with disdain on every other work of human art and to vie with nature herself. All the glory of Egypt belongs to Africa and her people. These monuments are the indestructible memorials of their great and original genius. It is not through Egypt alone that Africa claims such unrivalled historic achievements. I could have spoken of the pyramids of Ethiopia, which, though inferior in size to those of Egypt, far surpass them in architectural beauty; their sepulchres which evince the highest purity of taste, and of many prehistoric ruins in other parts of Africa. In such ruins Africa is like the golden sun, that, having sunk beneath the western horizon, still plays upon the world which he sustained and enlightened in his career.

213

Justly, the world now demands:

'Whither is fled the visionary gleam, Where is it now, the glory and the dream?'

Oh, for that historian who, with the open pen of truth, will bring to Africa's claim the strength of written proof. He will tell of a race whose onward tide was often swelled with tears, but in whose heart bondage has not quenched the fire of former years. He will write that in these later days when Earth's noble ones are named, she has a roll of honour too, of whom she is not ashamed. The giant is awakening! From the four corners of the earth Africa's sons, who have been proved through fire and sword, are marching to the future's golden door bearing the records of deeds of valour done.

Mr Calhoun, I believe, was the most philosophical of all the slave-holders. He said once that if he could find a black man who could understand the Greek syntax, he would then consider their race human, and his attitude toward enslaving them would therefore change. What might have been the sensation kindled by the Greek syntax in the mind of the famous Southerner, I have so far been unable to discover; but oh, I envy the moment that was lost! And woe to the tongues that refused to tell the truth! If any such were among the now living, I could show him among black men of pure African blood those who could repeat the Koran from memory, skilled in Latin, Greek and Hebrew – Arabic and Chaldaic – men great in wisdom and profound knowledge – one professor of philosophy in a celebrated German university; one corresponding member of the French Academy of Sciences, who regularly transmitted to that society meteorological observations, and hydrographical journals and papers on botany and geology: another whom many ages call 'The Wise', whose authority Mahomet himself frequently appealed to in the Koran in support of his own opinion – men of wealth and active benevolence, those whose distinguished talents and reputation have made them famous in the cabinet and in the field, officers of artillery in the great armies of Europe, generals and lieutenant-generals in the armies of Peter the Great in Russia and Napoleon in France, presidents of free republics, kings of independent nations which have burst their way to liberty by their own vigor. There are many other Africans who have shown marks of genius and high character sufficient to redeem their race from the charges which I am now considering.

Ladies and gentlemen, the day of great exploring expeditions in Africa is over! Man knows his home now in a sense never known before. Many great and holy men have evinced a passion for the day you are now witnessing – their prophetic vision shot through many unborn centuries to this very hour. 'Men shall run to and fro', said Daniel, 'and knowledge shall increase upon the earth.' Oh, how true! See the triumph of human genius today! Science has searched out the deep things of nature, surprised the secrets of the most distant stars, disentombed the memorials of everlasting hills, taught the lightning to speak, the vapors to toil and the winds to worship – spanned the sweeping rivers, tunnelled the longest mountain range – made the world a vast whispering gallery, and has brought foreign nations into one civilized family. This all-powerful contact says even to the most backward race, you cannot remain where you are, you cannot fall back, you must advance! A great century has come upon us. No race possessing the inherent capacity to survive can resist and remain unaffected by this influence of contact and intercourse, the backward with the advanced. This influence constitutes the very essence of efficient progress and of civilization.

From these heights of the twentieth century I again ask you to cast your eyes south of the Desert of Sahara. If you could go with me to the oppressed Congos and ask, What does it mean, that now, for liberty, they fight like men and die like martyrs; if you would go with me to Bechuanaland, face their council of headmen and ask what motives caused them recently to decree so emphatically that alcoholic drinks shall not enter their country – visit their king, Khama, ask for what cause he leaves the gold and ivory palace of his ancestors, its mountain strongholds and all its august ceremony, to wander daily from village to village through all his kingdom, without a guard or any decoration of his rank – a preacher of industry and education, and an apostle of the new order of things; if you would ask Menelik what means this that Abyssinia is now looking across the ocean – oh, if you could read the letters that come to us from Zululand – you too would be convinced that the elevation of the African race is evidently a part of the new order of things that belong to this new and powerful period.

The African already recognizes his anomalous position and desires a change. The brighter day is rising upon Africa. Already I seem to see her chains dissolved, her desert plains red with harvest, her Abyssinia and her Zululand the seats of science and religion, reflecting the glory of the rising sun from the spires of their churches and universities. Her Congo and her Gambia whitened with commerce, her crowded cities sending forth the hum of business and all her sons employed in advancing the victories of peace – greater and more abiding than the spoils of war.

Yes, the regeneration of Africa belongs to this new and powerful period! By this term regeneration I wish to be understood to mean the entrance into a new life, embracing the diverse phases of a higher, complex existence. The basic factor which assures their regeneration resides in the awakened race-consciousness. This gives them a clear perception of their elemental needs and of their undeveloped powers. It therefore must lead them to the attainment of that higher and advanced standard of life.

The African people, although not a strictly homogeneous race, possess a common fundamental sentiment which is everywhere manifest, crystallizing itself into one common controlling idea. Conflicts and strife are rapidly disappearing before the fusing force of this enlightened perception of the true intertribal relation, which relation should subsist among a people with a common destiny. Agencies of a social, economic and religious advance tell of a new spirit which, acting as a leavening ferment, shall raise the anxious and aspiring mass to the level of their ancient glory. The ancestral greatness, the unimpaired genius, and the recuperative power of the race, its irrepressibility, which assures its permanence, constitute the African's greatest source of inspiration. He has refused to camp forever on the borders of the industrial world; having learned that knowledge is power, he is educating his children. You find them in Edinburgh, in Cambridge, and in the great schools of Germany. These return to their country like arrows, to drive darkness from the land. I hold that his industrial and educational initiative, and his untiring devotion to these activities, must be regarded as positive evidences of this process of his regeneration.

The regeneration of Africa means that a new and unique civilization is soon to be added to the world. The African is not a proletarian in the world of science and art. He has precious creations of his own, of ivory, of copper and of gold, fine, plated willow-ware and weapons of superior workmanship. Civilization resembles an organic being in its development – it is born, it perishes, and it can propagate itself. More particularly, it resembles a plant, it takes root in the teeming earth, and when the seeds fall in other soils new varieties sprout up. The most essential departure of this new civilization is that it shall be thoroughly spiritual and humanistic – indeed a regeneration moral and eternal!

O Africa!
Like some great century plant that shall bloom
In ages hence, we watch thee; in our dream
See in thy swamps the Prospero of our stream;
Thy doors unlocked, where knowledge in her tomb
Hath lain innumerable years in gloom.
Then shalt thou, waking with that morning gleam,
Shine as thy sister lands with equal beam."

Distinguished Scholars: on behalf of myself and the Government and people of Ghana, it is my great pleasure to welcome you to Ghana and to this first Africanists' Conference to be held in Africa. I wish you every success.

18

Economic and regional groupings and organizations which have from time to time been formed in Africa, have achieved very little in terms of improving the standard of living of the African masses. It is not for nothing that such groupings are not opposed by international monopoly finance and the indigenous bourgeoisie, since these groupings and organizations are tailor-made to serve their interests. They represent just another form of balkanization, and as such retard the progress of the African Revolution.

In general, it has been the French-speaking independent African states which have consistently advocated a 'gradualist' approach to African liberation and unification, insisting that economic and regional co-operation must precede any form of political continental unification.

On 28th September, 1958, on the initiative of General de Gaulle, a referendum was held to determine the future status of French overseas territories. Each territory was given one of three choices:

(i) to achieve immediate independence by voting against the constitutional referendum;

(ii) to remain within the 'French Community' by

becoming integrated with France as an overseas department;
(iii) to become an autonomous state of the new Community. In this case it would have internal self-government but would entrust such federal powers as foreign affairs, defence, economic policy and currency to the Community as a whole.

Guinea was the only territory to vote 'NO', and to leave the French Community and become independent, on 2nd October, 1958. The other states chose the third option, and decided on membership of the Community, with associate membership of the European Economic Community (EEC).

These states held three conferences between October 1960 and March 1961. The first was in Abidjan (October 1960); the second in Brazzaville (December 1960); and the third in Yaounde (March 1961). Of these, the Brazzaville Conference was the most significant, since it was attended by all the ex-French countries which were then independent, with the exception of Guinea and Mali. These twelve countries, which came to be known as the 'Brazzaville Group' were: Cameroon, Central African Republic, Chad, Congo Brazzaville, Dahomey, Gabon, Ivory Coast, Malagasy, Mauritania, Niger, Senegal and Upper Volta. At the Brazzaville Conference these states took the first step towards the setting up of a joint Afro-Malagasy Economic Co-operation Organization (Organization Africaine et Malagache de Coopération Economique, OAMCE), and agreed to co-operate in economic, cultural and diplomatic spheres.

At the Yaounde Conference, the twelve states approved the proposal for the setting up of OAMCE, and the formation of a unified airline, Air Afrique. At a further conference held in Tananarive, Malagasy in September

1961, a new joint Afro-Malagasy Union (Union Africaine et Malagache, UAM) was set up which was to be open to all independent African states. The Charter of UAM provided for co-operation between member states to ensure their collective security, and to promote their economic development. A defence clause provided for the establishment of a Higher Defence Council consisting of one member state, with a permanent general secretariat and a general staff. Togo and Rwanda later joined the UAM, increasing the membership to fourteen.

At a meeting held in Dakar from 7–10 March 1964, UAM decided to dissolve. This decision was said to have been taken as a result of the formation of the OAU in 1963. In February 1965, UAMCE went out of existence when its member states formed a new body, the Organization Commune Africaine et Malagache (OCAM) with headquarters in Yaounde, Cameroon. The French-speaking states of OCAM, established as a group within the OAU, were mutually linked through their association with the EEC.

Six months after the Casablanca Conference (3–7 January 1961), delegates from nineteen independent African states had met in Monrovia from 8–13 May 1961. They were the twelve Brazzaville states, and Ethiopia, Liberia, Nigeria, Sierra Leone, Somalia, Togo and Tunisia. The Casablanca powers did not attend.

A further conference of the Monrovia Group was held in Lagos from 25–30 January 1962. A draft Charter for a permanent Inter-African and Malagasy Organization was accepted in principle, and confirmed with slight modifications four months later at a meeting of foreign ministers held in Lagos. The Charter defined the aims of the Organization which emphasized economic, cultural, health, educational and scientific co-operation between member states, and once again affirmed the principles of the sovereign equality of the African states, their territorial integrity, and the condemnation of any attempts by states to interfere in each other's domestic affairs. Membership was declared to be open to any sovereign, independent African state, and a Permanent Secretariat was set up to carry out the policies of the organization, and to create by stages an African – Malagasy Common Market. Political resolutions adopted by the conference dealt with the liberation movement throughout Africa, nuclear tests, and the formation of an African caucus at the United Nations.

But in spite of the many conferences held in Africa in the fifties and sixties, and the great number of high-sounding resolutions and declarations of intent agreed by the various regional, economic groupings, the economic and political condition of Africa has shown scant improvement. In fact, the plight of the African masses has deteriorated. Reactionary and puppet regimes continue, neocolonialism extends its grip; and political commentators refer openly to the 'reconquest of Africa'.

Furthermore, the people of Francophone Africa have not benefited to any significant degree from arrangements made with France and with the EEC. This is hardly surprising, since Associate status was defined by the EEC countries without reference to Africa, and to suit their own and quite separate interests.

The East African Community of Uganda, Kenya and Tanzania, formed by a treaty signed in Kampala on 1st December 1967, is facing problems and difficulties similar to those of the regional economic groupings of west and central Africa. The declared aim of the East African Community is:

> to strengthen and regulate the industrial, commercial and other relations of the Partner States to the end that there shall be accelerated, harmonious and balanced development and sustained expansion of

economic activities the benefits whereof shall be equitably shared.

But already, political and economic nationalism is causing friction and rivalry, which prevents genuine economic integration. At the same time, different levels of development in the member states cause problems which can only be solved within the framework of unified political machinery.

Full economic and social development in Africa can only be accomplished within the optimum zone of development, which is the entire African continent, and under the direction of an All-African Union Government pursuing policies of scientific socialism. Until then, the forces of reaction will continue to block progress which threatens the basic pillars of their positions of privilege.

It was my hope when I wrote *Africa Must Unite*, that it might contribute to the African Revolution by setting down the case for total liberation and unification. The book was first published in 1963, just before the opening of the Conference of African Heads of State and Government held in Addis Ababa in May 1963. The following Chapter 21 sums up the argument of the book.

AFRICA MUST UNITE

CHAPTER TWENTY-ONE

CONTINENTAL GOVERNMENT
FOR AFRICA

We have seen, in the example of the United States, how the dynamic elements within society understood the need for unity and fought their bitter civil war to maintain the political union that was threatened by the reactionary forces. We have also seen, in the example of the Soviet Union, how the forging of continental unity along with the retention of national sovereignty by the federal states, has achieved a dynamism that has lifted a most backward society into a most powerful unit within a remarkably short space of time. From the examples before us, in Europe and the United States of America, it is therefore patent that we in Africa have the resources, present and potential, for creating the kind of society that we are anxious to build. It is calculated that by the end of this century the population of Africa will probably exceed five hundred millions.

Our continent gives us the second largest land stretch in the world. The natural wealth of Africa is estimated to be greater than that of almost any other continent in the world. To draw the most from our existing and potential means for the achievement of abundance and a fine social order, we need to unify our efforts, our resources, our skills and intentions.

Europe, by way of contrast, must be a lesson to us all. Too busy hugging its exclusive nationalisms, it has descended, after centuries of wars interspersed with intervals of uneasy peace, into a state of confusion, simply because it failed to build a sound basis of political association and understanding. Only now, under the necessities of economic stringency and the threat of the new German industrial and military rehabilitation, is Europe trying – unsuccessfully – to find a *modus operandi* for containing the threat. It is deceptively hoped that the European Community will perform this miracle. It has taken two world wars and the break-up of empires to press home the lesson, still only partly digested, that strength lies in unity.

While we in Africa, for whom the goal of unity is paramount, are striving to concert our efforts in this direction the neo-colonialists are straining every nerve to upset them by encouraging the formation of communities based on the languages of their former colonizers. We cannot allow ourselves to be so disorganized and divided. The fact that I speak English does not make me an Englishman. Similarly, the fact that some of us speak French or Portuguese does not make us Frenchmen or Portuguese. We are Africans first and last, and as Africans our best interests can only be served by uniting within an African Community. Neither the Commonwealth nor a Franco-African Community can be a substitute.

To us, Africa with its islands is just one Africa. We reject the idea of any kind of partition. From Tangier or Cairo in the North to Capetown in the South, from Cape Guardafui in the East to Cape Verde Islands in the West, Africa is one and indivisible.

I know that when we speak of political union, our critics are quick to observe an attempt to impose leadership and to abrogate sovereignty. But we have seen from the many examples of union put forward, that equality of the states is jealously guarded in every single constitution and that sovereignty is maintained. There are differences in the powers allotted to the central government and those retained by the states, as well as in the functions of the executive, legislature and judiciary. All of them have a common trade and economic policy. All of them are secular, in order that religion might not be dragged across the many problems involved in maintaining unity and securing the greatest possible development.

We in Africa who are pressing now for unity are deeply conscious of the validity of our purpose. We need the strength of our combined numbers and resources to protect ourselves from the very positive dangers of returning colonialism in disguised forms. We need it to combat the entrenched forces dividing our continent and still holding back millions of our brothers. We need it to secure total African liberation. We need it to carry forward our construction of a socio-economic system that will support the great mass of our steadily rising population at levels of life which will compare with those in the most advanced countries.

But we cannot mobilize our present and potential resources without concerted effort. If we developed our potentialities in men and natural resources in separate isolated groups, our energies would soon be dissipated in the struggle to outbid one another. Economic friction among us would certainly lead to bitter political rivalry, such as for many years hampered the pace of growth and development in Europe.

At present most of the independent African States are moving in directions which expose us to the dangers of imperialism and neo-colonialism. We therefore need a common political basis for the integration of our policies in economic planning, defence, foreign and diplomatic relations. That basis for political action need not infringe the essential sovereignty of the separate African States. These States would continue to exercise independent authority, except in the fields defined and reserved for common action in the interests of the security and orderly development of the whole continent.

In my view, therefore, a united Africa – that is, the political and economic unification of the African Continent – should seek three objectives:

Firstly, we should have an over-all economic planning on a continental basis. This would increase the industrial and economic power of Africa. So long as we remain balkanized, regionally or territorially, we shall be at the mercy of colonialism and imperialism. The lesson of the South American Republics *vis-à-vis* the strength and solidarity of the United States of America is there for all to see.

The resources of Africa can be used to the best advantage and the maximum benefit to all only if they are set within an overall framework of a continentally planned development. An overall economic plan, covering an Africa united on a continental basis, would increase our total industrial and economic power. We should therefore be thinking seriously now of ways and means of building up a Common Market of a United Africa and not allow ourselves to be lured by the dubious advantages of association with the so-called European Common Market. We in Africa have looked outward too long for the development of our economy and transportation. Let us begin to look inwards into the African Continent for all aspects of its development. Our communications were devised under colonial rule to stretch outwards towards Europe and elsewhere, instead of developing internally between our cities and states. Political unity should give us the power and will to change all this. We in Africa have untold agricultural, mineral and water-power resources. These almost fabulous resources can be fully exploited and utilized in the interest of Africa and the African people, only if we develop them within a Union Government of African States. Such a Government will need to maintain a common currency, a monetary zone and a central bank of issue. The advantages of these financial and monetary arrangements would be inestimable, since monetary transactions between our several States would be facilitated and the pace of financial activity generally quickened. A central bank of issue is an inescapable necessity, in view of the need to re-orientate the economy of Africa and place it beyond the reach of foreign control.

Secondly, we should aim at the establishment of a unified military and defence strategy. I do not see much virtue or wisdom in our separate efforts to build up or maintain vast military forces for self-defence which, in any case, would be ineffective in any major attack upon our separate States. If we examine this problem realistically, we should be able to ask ourselves this pertinent question: which single State in Africa today can protect its sovereignty against an imperialist aggressor? In this connection, it should be mentioned that anti-*apartheid* leaders have alleged that South Africa is building a great military force with all the latest weapons of destruction, in order to crush nationalism in Africa. Nor is this all. There are grave indications that certain settler governments in Africa have already been caught in the dangerous arms race and are now arming themselves to the teeth. Their military activities constitute a serious threat not only to the security of Africa, but also to the peace of the world. If these reports are true, only the unity of Africa can prevent South Africa and these other governments from achieving their diabolical aims.

If we do not unite and combine our military resources for common defence, the individual States, out of a sense of insecurity, may be drawn into making defence pacts with foreign powers which may endanger the security of us all.

There is also the expenditure aspect of this problem. The maintenance of large military forces imposes a heavy financial burden on even the most wealthy States. For young African States, who are in great need of capital for internal development, it is ridiculous – indeed suicidal – for each State separately and individually to assume such a heavy burden of self-defence, when the weight of this burden could be easily lightened by sharing it among themselves. Some attempt has already been made by the Casablanca Powers and the Afro-Malagasy Union in the matter of common defence, but how much better and stronger it would be if, instead of two such ventures, there was one over-all (land, sea and air) Defence Command for Africa.

The third objective which we should have in Africa stems from the first two which I have just described. If we in Africa set up a unified economic planning organization and a unified military and defence strategy, it will be necessary for us to adopt a unified foreign policy and diplomacy to give political direction to our joint efforts for the protection and economic development of our continent. Moreover, there are some sixty odd States in Africa, about thirty-two of which are at present independent. The burden of separate diplomatic representation by each State on the Continent of Africa alone would be crushing, not to mention representation outside Africa. The desirability of a common foreign policy which will enable us to speak with one voice in the councils of the world, is so obvious, vital and imperative that comment is hardly necessary.

I am confident that it should be possible to devise a constitutional structure applicable to our special conditions in Africa and not necessarily framed in terms of the existing constitutions of Europe, America or elsewhere, which will enable us to secure the objectives

I have defined and yet preserve to some extent the sovereignty of each State within a Union of African States.

We might erect for the time being a constitutional form that could start with those states willing to create a nucleus, and leave the door open for the attachment of others as they desire to join or reach the freedom which would allow them to do so. The form could be made amenable to adjustment and amendment at any time the consensus of opinion is for it. It may be that concrete expression can be given to our present ideas within a continental parliament that would provide a lower and an upper house, the one to permit the discussion of the many problems facing Africa by a representation based on population; the other, ensuring the equality of the associated States, regardless of size and population, by a similar, limited representation from each of them, to formulate a common policy in all matters affecting the security, defence and development of Africa. It might, through a committee selected for the purpose, examine likely solutions to the problems of union and draft a more conclusive form of constitution that will be acceptable to all the independent States.

The survival of free Africa, the extending independence of this continent, and the development towards that bright future on which our hopes and endeavours are pinned, depend upon political unity.

Under a major political union of Africa there could emerge a United Africa, great and powerful, in which the territorial boundaries which are the relics of colonialism will become obsolete and superfluous, working for the complete and total mobilization of the economic planning organization under a unified political direction. The forces that unite us are far greater than the difficulties that divide us at present, and our goal must be the establishment of Africa's dignity, progress and prosperity.

Proof is therefore positive that the continental union of Africa is an inescapable desideratum if we are determined to move forward to a realization of our hopes and plans for creating a modern society which will give our peoples the opportunity to enjoy a full and satisfying life. The forces that unite us are intrinsic and greater than the superimposed influences that keep us apart. These are the forces that we must enlist and cement for the sake of the trusting millions who look to us, their leaders, to take them out of the poverty, ignorance and disorder left by colonialism into an ordered unity in which freedom and amity can flourish amidst plenty.

Here is a challenge which destiny has thrown out to the leaders of Africa. It is for us to grasp what is a golden opportunity to prove that the genius of the African people can surmount the separatist tendencies in sovereign nationhood by coming together speedily, for the sake of Africa's greater glory and infinite well-being, into a Union of African States.

19

In January 1963, six months before the Conference of Independent African States met in Addis Ababa, I sent proposals for the setting up of a unified political organization to heads of state and government of all independent African states. The purpose was to provide a basis of discussion from which a positive programme of African unification could be formulated. The text, dated 1st January, 1963, was as follows:

Your Excellency,

For some time now it has been the burning desire of the leaders and people of Africa to find a way of bringing about the unity of the African Continent. Various attempts have been made recently to give expression to this great impulse. Thus, a Conference of Independent African States was held at Accra in April 1958, and the All-African People's Conference in December of the same year. In 1958, Guinea and Ghana came together and formed a Union which was regarded as a nucleus for the achievement of African Unity. In an attempt to expand the basis of this nucleus, Guinea, Ghana and Liberia, met at Sanniquellie in 1959, where further advances were made in the concept of African Unity. Later, after the break-up of the Mali Federation, the Republic of Mali joined Guinea and Ghana to form a Union, which was reconstituted into the Union of African States. A further step towards the consolidation of African Unity was taken when Guinea, the United Arab Republic, Libya, Mali, Morocco, Algeria and Ghana met at Casablanca in January, 1961, to consider joint measures for dealing with the Congo problem and other dangers which threatened the freedom and independence of Africa. These efforts were calculated to stress the importance of political unity for dealing with the problems that confront the Independent African States.

Shortly afterwards, the Monrovia and Brazzaville Conferences also took place. All these conferences, as indicated in their respective Charters, were clear manifestations of the desire to achieve African Unity, which is the goal to which all of us greatly aspire. Indeed, there is a general feeling throughout Africa today that development into separate political or economic groupings is unfortunate, since it tends, among other things, to a dispersal of energy, resources and general inter-State or inter-territorial co-operative effort. We must therefore express concern not only about territorial balkanization but also regional balkanization of Africa. If we are to fulfil our purpose of achieving Continental Unity and avert foreign oppression, interference and intimidation, we must all work together and devise a common political framework within which the existing Independent African States and others soon to become independent can find free scope for development. For this reason, I am convinced that we the leaders and people of Africa have a duty, at this serious and critical moment in the history of our continent, to adopt concrete measures that can unite us all – States and Territories of our Continent – without necessarily involving changes in the territorial boundaries of the Independent African States or in their national sovereignty.

I hope that by this proposal we shall be able to steer clear of the superficial differences among us, which those who seek to dominate us in their interests have successfully emphasized and exaggerated in the past. I accordingly venture to put forward the following views for earnest and serious consideration.

I am convinced that under such a proposal frontier disputes, economic difficulties, political disagreements among African States and neo-colonialism, still hanging like the sword of Damocles over the Independent African States, can all be resolved within the framework of a Union Government of African States. In a united Africa there would be no frontier claims between Ethiopia and Somalia, Zanzibar and Kenya, Guinea and Liberia, Mauritania and Mali, or between Togo and Ghana, because we would regard ourselves as one great continental family within a Union of African States. There is no time to waste, for we must unite now or perish, since no single African State is large or powerful enough to stand on its own against the unbridled imperialist exploitation of her men and resources and the growing complexities of the modern world.

1. A COMMON FOREIGN POLICY AND DIPLOMACY

There are some sixty odd States in Africa, about thirty-two of which are at present independent. The burden of separate diplomatic representation by each State on the Continent of Africa alone would be crushing, not to mention representation outside Africa. The desirability of a Common Foreign Policy which will enable us to speak with one voice in the councils of the world is so obvious, vital and imperative that comment is hardly necessary.

2. COMMON CONTINENTAL PLANNING FOR ECONOMIC AND INDUSTRIAL DEVELOPMENT OF AFRICA

The resources of Africa can be used to the best advantage and the maximum benefit to all only if they are set within an overall framework of a continental planned development. An overall economic plan, covering an Africa united on a continental basis would increase our total industrial and economic power. We should therefore be thinking seriously now of ways and means of building up a Common Market of a United Africa and not allow ourselves to be lured by the dubious advantages of association with the so-called European Common Market. We in Africa have looked outward too long for development of our economy and transportation. Let us begin to look inwards into the African Continent for all aspects of its development. Our communications were devised under colonial rule to stretch outwards towards Europe and elsewhere, instead of developing internally between our cities and states. Political Unity should give us the power and will to change all this. We in Africa have untold agricultural, mineral and water-power resources. These almost fabulous resources can be fully exploited and utilized in the interest of Africa and the African people, only if we develop them within a Union Government of African States.

The advantages of this would be inestimable, since monetary transactions between our several States would be facilitated and the pace of financial activity generally quickened. A Central Bank of Issue is an inescapable necessity, in view of the need to orientate the economy of Africa and place it beyond the reach of foreign control.

4. A COMMON DEFENCE SYSTEM

Because we do not yet have a common system of defence, some African countries feel insecure and have therefore naturally entered into defence pacts with foreign Governments. This endangers the security of all Africa.

The present practice whereby each State tries to establish its own individual defence system is intolerably expensive at a time when money is most urgently needed for the compelling task of education and other social welfare activities. Some attempt has already been made by the Casablanca Powers and the Afro-Malagasy Union in the matter of common defence, but how much better and stronger it would be, if instead of two such ventures there were one over-all (land, sea and air) Defence Command for Africa?

To implement the above proposal, a Central Political Organization with its own constitution would have to be drawn up as a matter of urgency. It is suggested that this Union of African States should consist of an Upper House and a Lower House. Each State would have the right to send two representatives to the Upper House, irrespective of the size and population of the State; while admission to the Lower House would be secured on the basis of proportional representation in accordance with the population of each State. This proposal does not in any way interfere with the internal constitutional arrangements of any State. The overriding concern of the Union of African States would be to give political direction in regard to the implementations of the proposals mentioned above. From the standpoint of accessibility, the Central African Republic could provide the most central site for the *Union Government*, if the right approach is made.

This message has been addressed to all Heads of State and Governments of the Independent African States. I trust therefore that when the Foreign Ministers of the Independent African States meet, this could form the basis of discussion from which a positive programme of African Unity could be formulated. Such understanding among the Leaders of Africa will fling wide open the gates of continental unity, and Africa will be able to speak with one voice and some authority to the world. I am sure that we can achieve political unity without sacrificing our sovereignties.

Representatives of thirty-one Independent African States attended the Conference in Addis Ababa in May 1963, and signed the Charter of the Organization of African Unity (OAU) of the 25th of May. It seemed that at last the foundation had been laid for the freedom and political unification of Africa, and that the existing blocs and political groupings were at an end. It was with these high hopes that I addressed the Conference on the 24th of May 1963.

ADDRESS TO THE CONFERENCE OF AFRICAN HEADS OF STATE AND GOVERNMENT

24th May 1963

YOUR EXCELLENCIES, COLLEAGUES,
BROTHERS AND FRIENDS

I am happy to be here in Addis Ababa on this most historic occasion. I bring with me the hopes and fraternal greetings of the Government and people of Ghana to His Imperial Majesty Haile Selassie and to all Heads of African States gathered here in this ancient capital in this momentous period in our history. Our objective is African

233

Union now. There is no time to waste. We must unite now or perish. I am confident that by our concerted effort and determination we shall lay here the foundations for a continental Union of African States.

At the first gathering of African Heads of State, to which I had the honour of playing host, there were representatives of eight independent States, only. Today, five years later, here at Addis Ababa, we meet as the representatives of no less than thirty-two States, the guests of His Imperial Majesty, Haile Selassie, the First, and the Government and people of Ethiopia. To his Imperial Majesty, I wish to express, on behalf of the Government and people of Ghana my deep appreciation for a most cordial welcome and generous hospitality.

The increase in our number in this short space of time is open testimony to the indomitable and irresistible surge of our peoples for independence. It is also a token of the revolutionary speed of world events in the latter half of this century. In the task which is before us of unifying our continent we must fall in with that pace or be left behind. The task cannot be attacked in the tempo of any other age than our own. To fall behind the unprecedented momentum of actions and events in our time will be to court failure and our own undoing.

A whole continent has imposed a mandate upon us to lay the foundation of our Union at this Conference. It is our responsibility to execute this mandate by creating here and now the formula upon which the requisite superstructure may be erected.

On this continent it has not taken us long to discover that the struggle against colonialism does not end with the attainment of national independence. Independence is only the prelude to a new and more involved struggle for the right to conduct our own economic and social affairs; to construct our society according to our aspirations, unhampered by crushing and humiliating neo-colonialist controls and interference.

From the start we have been threatened with frustration where rapid change is imperative and with instability where sustained effort and ordered rule are indispensable.

No sporadic act nor pious resolution can resolve our present problems. Nothing will be of avail, except the united act of a united Africa. We have already reached the stage where we must unite or sink into that condition which has made Latin-America the unwilling and distressed prey of imperialism after one-and-a-half centuries of political independence.

As a continent we have emerged into independence in a different age, with imperialism grown stronger, more ruthless and experienced, and more dangerous in its international associations. Our economic advancement demands the end of colonialist and neo-colonialist domination in Africa.

But just as we understood that the shaping of our national destinies required of each of us our political independence and bent all our strength to this attainment, so we must recognize that our economic independence resides in our African union and requires the same concentration upon the political achievement.

The unity of our continent, no less than our separate independence, will be delayed if, indeed, we do not lose it, by hobnobbing with colonialism. African Unity is, above all, a political kingdom which can only be gained by political means. The social and economic development of Africa will come only within the political kingdom, not the other way round. The United States of America, the Union of Soviet Socialist Republics, were the political decisions of revolutionary peoples before they became mighty realities of social power and material wealth.

How, except by our united efforts, will the richest and still enslaved parts of our continent be freed from colonial occupation and become available to us for the total development of our continent? Every step in the decolonization of our continent has brought greater resistance in those areas where colonial garrisons are available to colonialism and you all here know that.

This is the great design of the imperialist interests that buttress colonialism and neo-colonialism, and we would be deceiving ourselves in the most cruel way were we to regard their individual actions as separate and unrelated. When Portugal violates Senegal's border, when Verwoerd allocates one-seventh of South Africa's budget to military and police, when France builds as part of her defence policy an interventionist force that can intervene, more especially in French-speaking Africa, when Welensky talks of Southern Rhodesia joining South Africa, when Britain sends arms to South Africa, it is all part of a carefully calculated pattern working towards a single end: the continued enslavement of our still dependent brothers and an onslaught upon the independence of our sovereign African states.

Do we have any other weapon against this design but our unity? Is not our unity essential to guard our own freedom as well as to win freedom for our oppressed brothers, the Freedom Fighters? Is it not unity alone that can weld us into an effective force, capable of

235

creating our own progress and making our valuable contribution to world peace? Which independent African State, which of you here will claim that its financial structure and banking institutions are fully harnessed to its national development? Which will claim that its material resources and human energies are available for its own national aspirations? Which will disclaim a substantial measure of disappointment and disillusionment in its agricultural and urban development?

In independent Africa we are already re-experiencing the instability and frustration which existed under colonial rule. We are fast learning that political independence is not enough to rid us of the consequences of colonial rule.

The movement of the masses of the people of Africa for freedom from that kind of rule was not only a revolt against the conditions which it imposed.

Our people supported us in our fight for independence because they believed that African Governments could cure the ills of the past in a way which could never be accomplished under colonial rule. If, therefore, now that we are independent we allow the same conditions to exist that existed in colonial days, all the resentment which overthrew colonialism will be mobilized against us.

The resources are there. It is for us to marshal them in the active service of our people. Unless we do this by our concerted efforts, within the framework of our combined planning, we shall not progress at the tempo demanded by today's events and the mood of our people. The symptoms of our troubles will grow, and the troubles themselves become chronic. It will then be too late even for Pan African Unity to secure for us stability and tranquillity in our labours for a continent of social justice and material well-being. Unless we establish African Unity now, we who are sitting here today shall tomorrow be the victims and martyrs of neo-colonialism.

There is evidence on every side that the imperialists have not withdrawn from our affairs. There are times, as in the Congo, when their interference is manifest. But generally it is covered up under the clothing of many agencies, which meddle in our domestic affairs, to foment dissension within our borders and to create an atmosphere of tension and political instability. As long as we do not do away with the root causes of discontent, we lend aid to these neo-colonialist forces, and shall become our own executioners. We cannot ignore the teachings of history.

Our continent is probably the richest in the world for minerals and industrial and agricultural primary materials. From the Congo alone, Western firms exported copper, rubber, cotton, and other goods to the value of 2,773 million dollars in the ten years between 1945 and 1955, and from South Africa, Western gold mining companies have drawn a profit, in the six years between 1947 to 1951, of 814 million dollars.

Our continent certainly exceeds all the others in potential hydro-electric power, which some experts assess as 42 per cent of the world's total. What need is there for us to remain hewers of wood and drawers of water for the industrialized areas of the world?

It is said, of course, that we have no capital, no industrial skill, no communications and no internal markets, and that we cannot even agree among ourselves how best to utilize our resources for our own social needs.

Yet all the stock exchanges in the world are pre-occupied with Africa's gold, diamonds, uranium, platinum, copper and iron ores. Our capital flows out in streams to irrigate the whole system of Western economy. Fifty-two per cent of the gold in Fort Knox at this moment, where the USA stores its bullion, is believed to have originated from our shores. Africa provides more than 60 per cent of the world's gold. A great deal of the uranium for nuclear power, of copper for electronics, of titanium for supersonic projectiles, of iron and steel for heavy industries, of other minerals and raw materials for lighter industries – the basic economic might of the foreign Powers – come from our continent.

Experts have estimated that the Congo Basin alone can produce enough food crops to satisfy the requirements of nearly half the population of the whole world and here we sit talking about regional-ism, talking about gradualism, talking about step by step. Are you afraid to tackle the bull by the horn?

For centuries Africa has been the milchcow of the Western world. Was it not our continent that helped the Western world to build up its accumulated wealth?

It is true that we are now throwing off the yoke of colonialism as fast as we can, but our success in this direction is equally matched by an intense effort on the part of imperialism to continue the exploitation of our resources by creating divisions among us.

When the colonies of the American Continent sought to free themselves from imperialism in the 18th century there was no threat of neo-colonialism in the sense in which we know it today in Africa. The American States were therefore free to form and fashion the unity which was best suited to their needs and to frame a constitution to hold their unity together without any form of interference from external sources. We, however, are having to grapple with outside interventions. How much more, then do we need to come together in the African unity that alone can save us from the clutches of neo-colonialism and imperialism.

We have the resources. It was colonialism in the first place that prevented us from accumulating the effective capital; but we ourselves have failed to make full use of our power in independence to mobilize our resources for the most effective take-off into thoroughgoing economic and social development. We have been too busy nursing our separate states to understand fully the basic need of our union, rooted in common purpose, common planning and common endeavour. A union that ignores these fundamental necessities will be but a sham. It is only by uniting our productive capacity and the resultant production that we can amass capital. And once we start, the momentum will increase. With capital controlled by our own banks, harnessed to our own true industrial and agricultural development, we shall make our advance. We shall accumulate machinery and establish steel works, iron foundries and factories; we shall link the various states of our continent with communications by land, sea and air. We shall cable from one place to another, phone from one place to the other and astound the world with our hydroelectric power; we shall drain marshes and swamps, clear infested areas, feed the under-nourished, and rid our people of parasites and disease. It is within the possibility of science and technology to make even the Sahara bloom into a vast field with verdant vegetation for agricultural and industrial developments. We shall harness the radio, television, giant printing presses to lift our people from the dark recesses of illiteracy.

A decade ago, these would have been visionary words, the fantasies of an idle dreamer. But this is the age in which science has transcended the limits of the material world, and technology has invaded the silences of nature. Time and space have been reduced to unimportant abstractions. Giant machines make roads, clear forests, dig dams, lay out aerodromes; monster trucks and planes distribute goods; huge laboratories manufacture drugs; complicated geological surveys are made; mighty power stations are built; colossal factories erected – all at an incredible speed. The world is no longer moving through bush paths or on camels and donkeys.

We cannot afford to pace our needs, our development, our security, to the gait of camels and donkeys. We cannot afford not to cut down the overgrown bush of outmoded attitudes that obstruct our path to the modern open road of the widest and earliest achievement of economic independence and the raising up of the lives of our people to the highest level.

Even for other continents lacking the resources of Africa, this is the age that sees the end of human want. For us it is a simple matter of grasping with certainty our heritage by using the political might of unity: All we need to do is to develop with our united strength the enormous resources of our continent. A United Africa will provide a stable field of foreign investment, which will be encouraged as long as it does not behave inimically to our African interests. For such investment would add by its enterprises to the development of the continental national economy, employment and training of our people, and will be welcome to Africa. In dealing with a united Africa, investors will no longer have to weigh with concern the risks of negotiating with governments in one period which may not exist in the very next period. Instead of dealing or negotiating with so many separate states at a time they will be dealing with one united government pursuing a harmonized continental policy.

What is the alternative to this? If we falter at this stage, and let time pass for neo-colonialism to consolidate its position on this continent, what will be the fate of our people who have put their trust in us? What will be the fate of our freedom fighters? What will be the fate of other African territories that are not yet free?

Unless we can establish great industrial complexes in Africa – which we can only do in a united Africa – we must leave our peasantry to the mercy of foreign cash crop markets, and face the same unrest which overthrew the colonialists. What use to the farmer is education and mechanization, what use is even capital for development; unless we can ensure for him a fair price and a ready market? What has the peasant, worker and farmer gained from political independence, unless we can ensure for him a fair return for his labour and a higher standard of living?

Unless we can establish great industrial complexes in Africa, what have the urban worker, and those peasants on overcrowded land gained from political independence? If they are to remain unemployed or in unskilled occupation, what will avail them the better facilities for education, technical training, energy and ambition which independence enables us to provide?

There is hardly any African State without a frontier problem with its adjacent neighbours. It would be futile for me to enumerate them because they are already so familiar to us all. But let me suggest to Your Excellencies that this fatal relic of colonialism will drive us to war against one another as our unplanned and unco-ordinated industrial development expands, just as happened in Europe. Unless we succeed in arresting the danger through mutual understanding on fundamental issues and through African Unity, which will render existing boundaries obsolete and superfluous, we shall have fought in vain for independence. Only African Unity can heal this festering sore of boundary disputes between our various states. Your Excellencies, the remedy for these ills is ready in our hands. It stares us in the face at every customs barrier, it shouts to us from every African heart. By creating a true political union of all the independent states of Africa, with executive powers for political direction we can tackle hopefully every emergency, every enemy, and every complexity. This is not because we are a race of supermen, but because we have emerged in the age of science and technology in which poverty, ignorance and disease are no longer the masters, but the retreating foes of mankind. We have emerged in the age of socialized planning, where production and distribution are not governed by chaos, greed and self-interest, but by social needs. Together with the rest of mankind, we have awakened from Utopian dreams to pursue practical blueprints for progress and social justice.

Above all, we have emerged at a time when a continental land mass like Africa with its population approaching three hundred million are necessary to the economic capitalization and profitability of modern productive methods and techniques. Not one of us working singly and individually can successfully attain the fullest development. Certainly, in the circumstances, it will not be possible to give adequate assistance to sister states trying, against the most difficult conditions, to improve their economic and social structures. Only a united Africa functioning under a Union Government can forcefully mobilize the material and moral resources of our separate countries and apply them efficiently and energetically to bring a rapid change in the conditions of our people.

If we do not approach the problems in Africa with a common front and a common purpose, we shall be haggling and wrangling among ourselves until we are colonized again and become the tools of a far greater colonialism than we suffered hitherto.

Unite we must. Without necessarily sacrificing our sovereignties, big or small, we can here and now forge a political union based on Defence, Foreign Affairs and Diplomacy, and a Common Citizenship, an African Currency, an African Monetary Zone and an African Central Bank. We must unite in order to achieve the full liberation of our continent. We need a Common Defence System with an

African High Command to ensure the stability and security of Africa.

We have been charged with this sacred task by our own people, and we cannot betray their trust by failing them. We will be mocking the hopes of our people if we show the slightest hesitation or delay in tackling realistically this question of African Unity.

The supply of arms or other military aid to the colonial oppressors in Africa must be regarded not only as aid in the vanquishment of the freedom fighters battling for their African independence, but as an act of aggression against the whole of Africa. How can we meet this aggression except by the full weight of our united strength?

Many of us have made non-alignment an article of faith on this continent. We have no wish, and no intention of being drawn into the Cold War. But with the present weakness and insecurity of our States in the context of world politics, the search for bases and spheres of influence brings the Cold War into Africa with its danger of nuclear warfare. Africa should be declared a nuclear-free zone and freed from cold war exigencies. But we cannot make this demand mandatory unless we support it from a position of strength to be found only in our unity.

Instead, many Independent African States are involved by military pacts with the former colonial powers. The stability and security which such devices seek to establish are illusory, for the metropolitan Powers seize the opportunity to support their neo-colonialist controls by direct military involvement. We have seen how the neo-colonialists use their bases to entrench themselves and even to attack neighbouring independent states. Such bases are centres of tension and potential danger spots of military conflict. They threaten the security not only of the country in which they are situated but of neighbouring countries as well. How can we hope to make Africa a nuclear-free zone and independent of cold war pressure with such military involvement on our continent? Only by counter-balancing a common defence force with a common desire for an Africa untrammelled by foreign dictation or military and nuclear presence. This will require an all-embracing African High Command, especially if the military pacts with the imperialists are to be renounced. It is the only way we can break these direct links between the colonialism of the past and the neo-colonialism which disrupts us today.

We do not want nor do we visualize an African High Command in the terms of the power politics that now rule a great part of the world, but as an essential and indispensable instrument for ensuring stability and security in Africa.

We need unified economic planning for Africa. Until the economic power of Africa is in our hands, the masses can have no real concern and no real interest for safeguarding our security, for ensuring the stability of our regimes, and for bending their strength to the fulfilment of our ends. With our united resources, energies and talents we have the means, as soon as we show the will, to transform the economic structures of our individual states from poverty to that of wealth, from inequality to the satisfaction of popular needs. Only on a continental basis shall we be able to plan the proper utilization of all our resources for the full development of our continent.

How else will we retain our own capital for our development? How else will we establish an internal market for our own industries? By belonging to different economic zones, how will we break down the currency and trading barriers between African States, and how will the economically stronger amongst us be able to assist the weaker and less developed States?

It is important to remember that independent financing and independent development cannot take place without an independent currency. A currency system that is backed by the resources of a foreign state is *ipso facto* subject to the trade and financial arrangements of that foreign country.

Because we have so many customs and currency barriers as a result of being subject to the different currency systems of foreign powers, this has served to widen the gap between us in Africa. How, for example, can related communities and families trade with, and support one another successfully, if they find themselves divided by national boundaries and currency restrictions? The only alternative open to them in these circumstances is to use smuggled currency and enrich national and international racketeers and crooks who prey upon our financial and economic difficulties.

No independent African State today by itself has a chance to follow an independent course of economic development, and many of us who have tried to do this have been almost ruined or have had to return to the fold of the former colonial rulers. This position will not change unless we have a unified policy working at the continental level. The first step towards our cohesive economy would be a unified monetary zone, with, initially, an agreed common parity for our currencies. To facilitate this arrangement, Ghana would change to a decimal system. When we find that the arrangement of a fixed common parity is working successfully, there would seem to be no reason for not instituting one common currency and a single bank of issue. With a common currency from one common bank of issue we should be able to stand erect on our own feet because such an arrangement would be fully backed by the combined national products of the states composing the union. After all, the purchasing power of money depends on productivity and the productive exploitation of the natural, human and physical resources of the nation.

While we are assuring our stability by a common defence system, and our economy is being orientated beyond foreign control by a Common Currency, Monetary Zone and Central Bank of Issue, we can investigate the resources of our continent. We can begin to ascertain whether in reality we are the richest, and not, as we have been taught to believe, the poorest among the continents. We can determine whether we possess the largest potential in hydroelectric power, and whether we can harness it and other sources of energy to our own industries. We can proceed to plan our industrialization on a continental scale, and to build up a common market for nearly three hundred million people.

Common Continental Planning for the Industrial and Agricultural Development of Africa is a vital necessity.

So many blessings flow from our unity; so many disasters must follow on our continued disunity, that our failure to unite today will not be attributed by posterity only to faulty reasoning and lack of courage, but to our capitulation before the forces of neo-colonialism and imperialism.

The hour of history which has brought us to this assembly is a revolutionary hour. It is the hour of decision. For the first time, the economic imperialism which menaces us is itself challenged by the irresistible will of our people.

The masses of the people of Africa are crying for unity. The people of Africa call for the breaking down of the boundaries that keep them apart. They demand an end to the border disputes between sister African states – disputes that arise out of the artificial barriers raised by colonialism. It was colonialism's purpose that divided us. It was colonialism's purpose that left us with our border irredentism, that rejected our ethnic and cultural fusion.

Our people call for unity so that they may not lose their patrimony in the perpetual service of neo-colonialism. In their fervent push for unity, they understand that only its realization will give full meaning to their freedom and our African independence.

It is this popular determination that must move us on to a Union of Independent African States. In delay lies danger to our well-being, to our very existence as free states. It has been suggested that our approach to unity should be gradual, that it should go piece-meal. This point of view conceives of Africa as a static entity with 'frozen' problems which can be eliminated one by one and when all have been cleared then we can come together and say: 'Now all is well. Let us now unite.' This view takes no account of the impact of external pressures. Nor does it take cognizance of the danger that delay can deepen our isolations and exclusiveness; that it can enlarge our differences and set us drifting further and further apart into the net of neo-colonialism, so that our union will become nothing but a fading hope, and the great design of Africa's full redemption will be lost, perhaps, forever.

The view is also expressed that our difficulties can be resolved simply by a greater collaboration through co-operative association in our inter-territorial relationships. This way of looking at our problems denies a proper conception of their inter-relationship and mutuality. It denies faith in a future for African advancement in African independence. It betrays a sense of solution only in continued reliance upon external sources through bilateral agreements for economic and other forms of aid.

The fact is that although we have been co-operating and associating with one another in various fields of common endeavour even before colonial times, this has not given us the continental identity and the political and economic force which would help us to deal effectively with the complicated problems confronting us in Africa today. As far as foreign aid is concerned, a United Africa would be in a more favourable position to attract assistance from foreign sources. There is the far more compelling advantage which this arrangement offers, in that aid will come from anywhere to a united Africa because our bargaining power would become infinitely greater. We shall no longer be dependent upon aid from restricted sources. We shall have the world to choose from.

What are we looking for in Africa? Are we looking for Charters, conceived in the light of the United Nations example? A type of United Nations Organization whose decisions are framed on the basis of resolutions that in our experience have sometimes been ignored by member States? Where groupings are formed and pressures develop in accordance with the interest of the groups concerned? Or is it intended that Africa should be turned into a loose organization of States on the model of the Organization of American States, in which the weaker States within it can be at the mercy of the stronger or more powerful ones politically or economically and all at the mercy of some powerful outside nation or group of nations? Is this the kind of association we want for ourselves in the United Africa we all speak of with such feeling and emotion?

Your Excellencies, permit me to ask: Is this the kind of framework we desire for our United Africa? An arrangement which in future could permit Ghana or Nigeria or the Sudan, or Liberia, or Egypt or Ethiopia for example, to use pressure, which either superior economic or political influence gives, to dictate the flow and direction of trade from, say, Burundi or Togo or Nyasaland to Mozambique or Madagascar?

We all want a united Africa, united not only in our concept of what unity connotes, but united in our common desire to move forward together in dealing with all the problems that can best be solved only on a continental basis.

When the first Congress of the United States met many years ago at Philadelphia one of the delegates sounded the first chord of unity by declaring that they had met in 'a state of nature'. In other words, they were not in Philadelphia as Virginians, or Pennsylvanians, but simply as Americans. This reference to themselves as Americans was in those days a new and strange experience. May I dare to assert equally on this occasion. Your Excellencies, that we meet here today not as Ghanaians, Guineans, Egyptians, Algerians, Moroccans, Malians, Liberians, Congolese or Nigerians but as Africans. Africans united in our resolve to remain here until we have agreed on the basic principles of a new compact of unity among ourselves which guarantees for us and our future a new arrangement of continental government.

If we succeed in establishing a New Set of Principles as the basis of a New Charter or Statute for the establishment of a continental unity of Africa and the creation of social and political progress for our people, then, in my view, this conference should mark the end of our various groupings and regional blocs. But if we fail and let this grand and historic opportunity slip by then we shall give way to greater dissension and division among us for which the people of Africa will never forgive us. And the popular and progressive forces and movements within Africa will condemn us. I am sure therefore that we shall not fail them.

I have spoken at some length, Your Excellencies, because it is necessary for us all to explain not only to one another present here but also to our people who have entrusted to us the fate and destiny of Africa. We must therefore not leave this place until we have set up effective machinery for achieving African Unity. To this end, I propose for your consideration the following:—

As a first step, Your Excellencies, a declaration of principles uniting and binding us together and to which we must all faithfully and loyally adhere, and laying the foundations of unity should be set down. And there should also be a formal declaration that all the Independent African States here and now agree to the establishment of a Union of African States.

As a second and urgent step for the realization of the unification of Africa, an All-Africa Committee of Foreign Ministers be set up now, and that before we rise from this Conference a date should be fixed for them to meet.

This Committee should establish on behalf of the Heads of our Governments, a permanent body of officials and experts to work out a machinery for the Union Government of Africa. This body of officials and experts should be made up of two of the best brains from each independent African State. The various Charters of the existing groupings and other relevant documents could also be submitted to the officials and experts. A Praesidium consisting of the heads of Governments of the Independent African States should be called upon to meet and adopt a Constitution and other recommendations which will launch the Union Government of Africa.

We must also decide on a location where this body of officials and experts will work as the new Headquarters or Capital of our Union Government. Some central place in Africa might be the fairest suggestion, either at Bangui in the Central African Republic or Leopoldville in Congo. My Colleagues may have other proposals. The Committee of Foreign Ministers, officials and experts should be empowered to establish:

(1) a Commission to frame a constitution for a Union Government of African States;

(2) a Commission to work out a continent-wide plan for a unified or common economic and industrial programme for Africa; this plan should include proposals for setting up:
    (a) A Common Market for Africa;
    (b) An African Currency;
    (c) An African Monetary Zone;
    (d) An African Central Bank, and
    (e) A continental Communication system.

(3) a Commission to draw up details for a Common Foreign Policy and Diplomacy.

(4) a Commission to produce plans for a Common System of Defence.

(5) a Commission to make proposals for a Common African Citizenship.

These Commissions will report to the Committee of Foreign Ministers who should in turn submit within six months of this Conference their recommendations to the Praesidium. The Praesidium meeting in Conference at the Union Headquarters will consider and approve the recommendations of the Committee of Foreign Ministers.

In order to provide funds immediately for the work of the permanent officials and experts of the Headquarters of the Union, I suggest that a special Committee be set up to work out a budget for this.

Your Excellencies, with these steps, I submit, we shall be irrevocably committed to the road which will bring us to a Union Government for Africa. Only a United Africa with central political direction can successfully give effective material and moral support to our freedom fighters, in Southern Rhodesia, Angola, Mozambique, South-West Africa, Bechuanaland, Swaziland, Basutoland, Portuguese Guinea, etc., and of course South Africa. All Africa must be liberated now. It is therefore imperative for us here and now to establish a liberation bureau for African freedom fighters. The main object of this bureau, to which all governments should subscribe, should be to accelerate the emancipation of the rest of Africa still under colonial and racialist domination and oppression. It should be our joint responsibility to finance and support this bureau. On their successful attainment of Independence these territories will automatically join our Union of African States, and thus strengthen the fabric of Mother Africa. We shall leave here, having laid the foundation for our unity.

Your Excellencies, nothing could be more fitting than that the unification of Africa should be born on the soil of the State which stood for centuries as the symbol of African independence.

Let us return to our people of Africa not with empty hands and with high-sounding resolutions, but with the firm hope and assurance that at long last African Unity has become a reality. We shall thus begin the triumphant march to the kingdom of the African Personality, and to a continent of prosperity, and progress, of equality and justice and of work and happiness. This shall be our victory – victory within a continental government of a Union of African States. This victory will give our voice greater force in world affairs and enable us to throw our weight more forcibly on the side of peace. The world needs peace in which the greatest advantage can be taken of the benefits of science and technology. Many of the world's present ills are to be found in the insecurity and fear engendered by the threat of nuclear war. Especially do the new nations need peace in order to make their way into a life of economic and social well-being amid an atmosphere of security and stability that will promote moral, cultural and spiritual fulfilment.

If we in Africa can achieve the example of a continent knit together in common policy and common purpose, we shall have made the finest possible contribution to that peace for which all men and women thirst today, and which will lift once and forever the deepening shadow of global destruction from mankind. Ethiopia shall STRETCH forth her hands unto God.

AFRICA MUST UNITE.

20

The Charter of the OAU, signed on the 25th of May, 1963 by the Heads of State and Governments of the Independent African States in Addis Ababa, provided rudimentary machinery for the implementation of the declared objectives of the Organization, which were clearly stated in Article 2 of the Charter. But most of those who signed the Charter on that historic day envisaged the development and strengthening of the institutions provided for in Article 7 as the processes of the African Revolution gained momentum. It was their intention to provide the framework through which could emerge effective All-African political direction which would make possible economic planning on a continental basis, and the full development of our resources.

It was a Charter of *intent*, rather than a Charter of *positive action*. But this was inevitable in view of the widely differing policies of those who took part in the Conference. All were agreed on the principles of African liberation and unification, and the need for close co-ordination and co-operation in economic, social and cultural spheres, but there were crucial differences of opinion when it came to questions of methods and procedures.

In addition, the nature of the embryonic institutions provided for in the Charter, and the lack of provision for an All-African High Command to give teeth to the Organization, meant that the OAU suffered from the start from inherent weaknesses. The signatories declared that they were 'DESIROUS that all African States should henceforth unite so that the welfare and well-being of their peoples can be assured'; and stated that their first purpose was 'to promote the unity and solidarity of the African States' (Article 2). Yet right from the start, differences within the OAU tended to develop along the lines of the old power blocs and alliances.

There were those who advocated a gradualist approach towards liberation and unification, and wished to concentrate on economic and cultural co-operation, and on regional groupings; and there were those who insisted that there could be no genuine improvement in the well-being of the African people without unified political machinery to plan economic development on a continental scale. Several signatories of the Charter appeared far more concerned with selfish national interests than with the condition of the African people as a whole, and particularly with those still suffering under colonial and settler minority regimes. There was much talk of the inviolability of 'sovereignty', and 'territorial integrity and independence', regardless of the fact that most of our national frontiers are relics of colonialism, and irrelevant within the context of the African nation.

As the years have passed, these fundamental differences of approach and emphasis, coupled with the stepping up of imperialist and neocolonialist pressures have led to compromise and delay in the OAU's handling of obstacles blocking the advance of the African Revolution. This has seriously weakened the authority of the OAU, and has caused growing lack of confidence in its ability to achieve the objectives for which it was created. In times of crisis it has failed to provide the dynamic leadership and decisive action expected of it. For example, the struggle in the Congo; the Nigerian civil war; UDI in Rhodesia; the question of South West Africa; the treatment of African political refugees; and problems arising from the rash of military coups which have taken place in recent years; all these, and other missed opportunities, have shown the inherent weakness of an organization which lacks cohesive political and military direction.

In the meantime, external reactionary forces in league with indigenous bourgeois elements, are mounting a new offensive to continue their oppression of the African masses. Imperialists and neocolonialists are unifying and concerting their political, economic and military strategy and tactics, while Africa continues in disunity and disarray.

In May 1963, when the OAU was formed, and rudimentary institutions and procedures for the total liberation and unification of the African continent were agreed upon, the stage was set for a great advance in the African Revolution. Yet the African people still await the implementation of the declared purposes of the OAU, and their living standards remain among the lowest in the world.

CHARTER OF THE ORGANIZATION OF AFRICAN UNITY

Signed in Addis Ababa on 25th May, 1963

WE, the Heads of African States and Governments assembled in the City of Addis Ababa, Ethiopia;

CONVINCED that it is the inalienable right of all people to control their own destiny;

CONSCIOUS of the fact that freedom, equality, justice and dignity are essential objectives for the achievement of the legitimate aspirations of the African peoples;

CONSCIOUS of our responsibility to harness the natural and human resources of our continent for the total advancement of our peoples in spheres of human endeavour;

INSPIRED by a common determination to promote understanding among our peoples and co-operation among our States in response to the aspirations of our peoples for brotherhood and solidarity, in a larger unity transcending ethnic and national differences;

CONVINCED that, in order to translate this determination into a dynamic force in the cause of human progress, conditions for peace and security must be established and maintained;

DETERMINED to safeguard and consolidate the hard-won independence as well as the sovereignty and territorial integrity of our States, and to fight against neo-colonialism in all its forms;

DEDICATED to the general progress of Africa;

PERSUADED that the Charter of the United Nations and the Universal Declaration of Human Rights, to the principles of which we reaffirm our adherence, provide a solid foundation for peaceful and positive co-operation among States;

DESIROUS that all African States should henceforth unite so that the welfare and well-being of the peoples can be assured;

RESOLVED to reinforce the links between our States by establishing and strengthening common institutions;

HAVE agreed to the present Charter.

Establishment
Article 1

1. The High Contracting Parties do by the present Charter establish an Organization to be known as the ORGANIZATION OF AFRICAN UNITY.

2. The Organization shall include the continental African States, Malagasy and other islands surrounding Africa.

Purposes
Article 2

1. The Organization shall have the following purposes:

(a) To promote the unity and solidarity of the African States:

(b) To co-ordinate and intensify their co-operation and efforts to achieve a better life for the peoples of Africa;

(c) To defend their sovereignty, their territorial integrity and independence;

(d) To eradicate all forms of colonialism from Africa; and

(e) To promote international co-operation, having due regard to the Charter of the United Nations and the Universal Declaration of Human Rights.

2. To these ends, the Member States shall co-ordinate and harmonize their general policies, especially in the following fields:
   (a) Political and diplomatic co-operation;
   (b) Economic co-operation, including transport and communications;
   (c) Educational and cultural co-operation;
   (d) Health, sanitation, and nutritional co-operation;
   (e) Scientific and technical co-operation; and
   (f) Co-operation for defence and security.

Principles
Article 3

The Member States, in pursuit of the purposes stated in Article 2, solemnly affirm and declare their adherence to the following principles:

1. The sovereign equality of all Member States;
2. Non-interference in the internal affairs of States;
3. Respect for the sovereignty and territorial integrity of each State and for its inalienable right to independent existence;
4. Peaceful settlement of disputes by negotiation, mediation, conciliation or arbitration;
5. Unreserved condemnation, in all its forms, of political assassination as well as of subversive activities on the part of neighbouring States or any other State;
6. Absolute dedication to the total emancipation of the African territories which are still dependent;
7. Affirmation of a policy of non-alignment with regard to all blocs.

Membership
Article 4

Each independent sovereign African State shall be entitled to become a Member of the Organization.

Rights and Duties of Member States
Article 5

All Member States shall enjoy equal rights and have equal duties.

Article 6

The Member States pledge themselves to observe scrupulously the principles enumerated in Article 3 of the present Charter.

Institutions
Article 7
The Organization shall accomplish its purposes through the following principal institutions:
1. The Assembly of Heads of State and Government;
2. The Council of Ministers;
3. The General Secretariat;
4. The Commission of Mediation, Conciliation and Arbitration.

The Assembly of Heads of State and Government
Article 8
The Assembly of Heads of State and Government shall be the supreme organ of the Organization. It shall, subject to the provisions of this Charter, discuss matters of common concern to Africa with a view to co-ordinating and harmonizing the general policy of the Organization. It may in addition review the structure, functions and acts of all the organs and any specialized agencies which may be created in accordance with the present Charter.
Article 9
The Assembly shall be composed of the Heads of State and Government or their duly accredited representatives and it shall meet at least once a year. At the request of any Member State and on approval by a two-thirds majority of the Member States, the Assembly shall meet in extraordinary session.
Article 10
1. Each Member State shall have one vote.
2. All resolutions shall be determined by a two-thirds majority of the members of the Organization.
3. Questions of procedure shall require a simple majority. Whether or not a question is one of procedure shall be determined by a simple majority of all Member States of the Organization.
4. Two-thirds of the total membership of the Organization shall form a quorum at any meeting of the Assembly.
Article 11
The Assembly shall have the power to determine its own rules of procedure.

The Council of Ministers
Article 12
1. The Council of Ministers shall consist of Foreign Ministers or such other Ministers as are designated by the Governments of Member States.

2. The Council of Ministers shall meet at least twice a year. When requested by any Member State and approved by two-thirds of all Member States, it shall meet in extraordinary session.

Article 13

1. The Council of Ministers shall be responsible to the Assembly of Heads of State and Government. It shall be entrusted with the responsibility of preparing conferences of the Assembly.

2. It shall take cognizance of any matter referred to it by the Assembly. It shall be entrusted with the implementation of the decision of the Assembly of Heads of State and Government. It shall co-ordinate inter-African co-operation in accordance with the instructions of the Assembly and in conformity with Article II (2) of the present Charter.

Article 14

1. Each Member State shall have one vote.

2. All resolutions shall be determined by a simple majority of the members of the Council of Ministers.

3. Two-thirds of the total membership of the Council of Ministers shall form a quorum for any meeting of the Council.

Article 15

The Council shall have the power to determine its own rules of procedure.

General Secretariat

Article 16

There shall be an Administrative Secretary-General of the Organization, who shall be appointed by the Assembly of Heads of State and Government. The Administrative Secretary-General shall direct the affairs of the Secretariat.

Article 17

There shall be one or more Assistant Secretaries-General of the Organization, who shall be appointed by the Assembly of Heads of State and Government.

Article 18

The functions and conditions of the services of the Secretary-General, of the Assistant Secretaries-General and other employees of the Secretariat shall be governed by the provisions of this Charter and the regulations approved by the Assembly of Heads of State and Government.

1. In the performance of their duties the Administrative Secretary-General and the staff shall not seek or receive instructions from any government or from any other authority external to the Organization.

They shall refrain from any action which might reflect on their position as international officials responsible only to the Organization.

2. Each member of the Organization undertakes to respect the exclusive character of the responsibilities of the Administrative Secretary-General and the staff and not to seek to influence them in the discharge of their responsibilities.

Commission of Mediation, Conciliation and Arbitration
Article 19

Member States pledge to settle all disputes among themselves by peaceful means and to this end decide to establish a Commission of Mediation, Conciliation and Arbitration, the composition of which and conditions of service shall be defined by a separate Protocol to be approved by the Assembly of Heads of State and Government. Said Protocol shall be regarded as forming an integral part of the present Charter.

Specialized Commissions
Article 20

The Assembly shall establish such Specialized Commissions as it may deem necessary, including the following:
1. Economic and Social Commission;
2. Educational and Cultural Commission;
3. Health, Sanitation and Nutrition Commission;
4. Defence Commission;
5. Scientific, Technical and Research Commission.

Article 21

Each Specialized Commission referred to in Article 20 shall be composed of the Ministers concerned or other Ministers or Plenipotentiaries designated by the Governments of the Member States.

Article 22

The functions of the Specialized Commissions shall be carried out in accordance with the provisions of the present Charter and of the regulations approved by the Council of Ministers.

The Budget
Article 23

The budget of the Organization prepared by the Administrative Secretary-General shall be approved by the Council of Ministers. The budget shall be provided by contributions from Member States in accordance with the scale of assessment of the United Nations; provided, however, that no Member State shall be assessed an amount exceeding twenty per cent of the yearly regular budget of the Organization. The Member States agree to pay their respective contributions regularly.

Signature and Ratification of Charter
Article 24

1. This Charter shall be open for signature to all independent sovereign African States and shall be ratified by the signatory States in accordance with their respective constitutional processes.

2. The original instrument, done, if possible in African languages, in English and French, all texts being equally authentic, shall be deposited with the Government of Ethiopia which shall transmit certified copies thereof to all independent sovereign African States.

3. Instruments of ratification shall be deposited with the Government of Ethiopia, which shall notify all signatories of each such deposit.

Entry into Force
Article 25

This Charter shall enter into force immediately upon receipt by the Government of Ethiopia of the instruments of ratification from two-thirds of the signatory States.

Registration of the Charter
Article 26

This Charter shall, after due ratification, be registered with the Secretariat of the United Nations through the Government of Ethiopia in conformity with Article 102 of the Charter of the United Nations.

Interpretation of the Charter
Article 27

Any question which may arise concerning the interpretation of this Charter shall be decided by a vote of two-thirds of the Assembly of Heads of State and Government of the Organization.

Adhesion and Accession
Article 28

1. Any independent sovereign African State may at any time notify the Administrative Secretary-General of its intention to adhere or accede to this Charter.

2. The Administrative Secretary-General shall on receipt of such notification communicate a copy of it to all the Member States

Admission shall be decided by a simple majority of the Member States. The decision of each Member State shall be transmitted to the Administrative Secretary-General, who shall, upon receipt of the required number of votes, communicate the decision to the State concerned.

Miscellaneous
Article 29
The working languages of the Organization and all its institutions shall be, if possible, African languages, English and French.
Article 30
The Administrative Secretary-General may accept on behalf of the Organization gifts, bequests and other donations made to the Organization, provided that this is approved by the Council of Ministers.
Article 31
The Council of Ministers shall decide on the privileges and immunities to be accorded to the personnel of the Secretariat in the respective territories of the Member States.

Cessation of Membership
Article 32
Any State which desires to renounce its membership shall forward a written notification to the Administrative Secretary-General. At the end of one year from the date of such notification, if not withdrawn, the Charter shall cease to apply with respect to the renouncing State, which shall thereby cease to belong to the Organization.

Amendment of the Charter
Article 33
This Charter may be amended or revised if any Member State makes a written request to the Administrative Secretary-General to that effect; provided, however, that the proposed amendment is not submitted to the Assembly for consideration until all the Member States have been duly notified of it and a period of one year has elapsed.
Such an amendment shall not be effective unless approved by at least two-thirds of all the Member States.
IN FAITH WHEREOF, We, the Heads of African States and Governments, have signed this Charter.
Done in the City of Addis Ababa, Ethiopia, this 25th day of May, 1963.

ALGERIA	MALI
BURUNDI	MAURITANIA
CAMEROUN	MOROCCO
CENTRAL AFRICAN	NIGER
REPUBLIC	NIGERIA
CONGO	RWANDA
(BRAZZAVILLE)	SENEGAL
CONGO	SIERRA LEONE
(LEOPOLDVILLE)	SOMALIA
DAHOMEY	SUDAN
ETHIOPIA	TANGANYIKA
GABON	TCHAD
GHANA	TOGO
GUINEA	TUNISIA
IVORY COAST	UGANDA
LIBERIA	UNITED ARAB
LIBYA	REPUBLIC
MALAGASY	UPPER VOLTA

ADDRESS TO THE NATIONAL ASSEMBLY ON THE OCCASION OF THE RATIFICATION OF THE CHARTER OF THE ORGANIZATION OF AFRICA UNITY

Friday, 21st June, 1963

Mr. Speaker, Members of the National Assembly,

I am here to invite you to ratify the Charter of African Unity adopted by the Addis Ababa Conference. This meeting of the Heads of State and Government of the existing Independent African States has rightly been acclaimed as the most momentous event in Africa's modern history. Addis Ababa will certainly be recorded as a crucial turning point in our struggle against the final bastions of colonialism in Africa and as the founding piece of Continental African Union.

The Charter adopted at Addis Ababa enjoins us all to go forward in unity. This Charter, the Charter of the Organization of African Unity, which I signed along with all the other Heads of State and Government of the Independent African States, and which has been placed before the House for ratification, contains the will and determination of our countries to achieve the unity of our Continent

The coming together on a basis of unity of all the Independent African States has created a new factor in the fight against imperialism and its twin instruments of colonialism and neo-colonialism. Our combined effort and our combined strength are to be placed at the service of our brothers waging an all-out struggle against oppressive colonialism in all those parts of our continent still under alien domination. We have covenanted together to co-ordinate and harmonize our general policies in the sphere of our political, diplomatic, economic, educational, cultural, health, scientific and technical activities, as well as in the sphere of defence and security.

These are wide enough areas of mutual co-operation that should lead us to a Centralized Continental Union and give effective protection to our sovereign Independence.

The Charter of African Unity must be regarded as the last but one step on the road to a Continental Union. Its provisions certainly challenge foreign political and economic domination of our Continent. The exploiters of Africa have grasped its implications. They realize that we are out to make ourselves masters in our own house and to drive out relentlessly from the length and breadth of our Continent those forces which batten upon us and keep us in political and economic subjection.

A Provisional Secretariat has been set up with a Provisional Headquarters at Addis Ababa. The Secretariat is composed of the representatives of Ghana, Nigeria, Egypt, Ethiopia, Niger and Uganda.

One of the major decisions of the Addis Ababa Conference is the setting up of a Co-ordinating Committee with Headquarters at Dar-es-Salaam in Tanganyika. This Committee will be responsible for regulating the assistance from African States and for managing the special fund which is being created by contributions from all the Independent African Governments.

This means that we must accept as our primary task the extension of independence to all territories of Africa. Apart from the sense of oneness and unity which impels us to go to the aid of our suffering compatriots in Angola, Mozambique, Southern Rhodesia, South Africa, and other parts of Africa still under colonial rule, we know that none of the Independent African States is safe so long as a single colonial ruler remains on African soil.

Freedom Fighters will take renewed hope and determination from the knowledge that their struggle is identified with the continued independence of the existing African States and is to be directed within a total strategy. No longer will these Freedom Fighters who have been in the vanguard of the African revolution and the colonial liberation movement feel isolated from the mainstream of African independence and unity. I am indeed happy that the goal which we set ourselves at our independence has been brought nearer. We shall strive for it now, not alone, but with our brothers from all the Independent African States.

Speaking of the liberation and unity of our Continent, I may mention that there are two main categories of Freedom Fighters:

(a) those fighting in colonial territories for the overthrow of exploitation and oppression by foreign governments; and
(b) those who consider that they have a duty to fight in order to strengthen the independence of their countries where colonial rule has been overthrown, but where it is still necessary to create conditions for the welfare of the people and for the elimination of neo-colonialist interference and influence.

As long as conditions in these countries are such as to assist the maintenance of neo-colonialism, discontent cannot be stifled or suppressed. The governments of such countries are a menace, not only to their own states but also to the safety and security of our entire continent.

The Government of Ghana fully appreciates the right of any State to grant political asylum to such Fighters under the accepted conventions of international law; it also appreciates that, unless conditions in their states change radically in the interest and welfare of the masses of the people, such Freedom Fighters cannot but resort to the use of constitutional, or even revolutionary, methods and activities aimed at securing a change of regime in their countries.

Most of these nationalists have sought refuge in African countries, other than their own, as a result of their struggle against neo-colonialism. We have quite a few of them in Ghana. There are others in other parts of Africa. We did not invite them here, but they naturally felt that they could enjoy sanctuary and be given the necessary protection in Ghana which has for the past six years since her attainment of independence and sovereignty played host to Freedom Fighters from all over the continent. The African Affairs Centre in Accra is a symbol of this determination.

These nationalists, some of whom were stalwart warriors in the struggle against colonialism, were received and accorded the traditional African and Ghanaian hospitality not as criminals fleeing from justice, but as victims of persecution by the neo-colonialists and their agents. But, Mr Speaker, at the Addis Ababa Conference, all the signatories to the Charter of African Unity solemnly pledged themselves to fight colonialism, neo-colonialism and imperialism in all its forms.

In order, therefore, to preserve the spirit of unity so happily engendered at Addis Ababa, I consider it essential that we should declare publicly the principles that must henceforth govern our granting of political asylum in Ghana to such refugees. These I set forth as follows:—

(a) Ghanaians and the nationals of the Independent African States are kinsmen and brothers and must be hospitable to one another. If, for any reason, such compatriots leave their territories the bond of fraternity that exists between us and their people makes it incumbent on Ghana to grant them hospitality.

(b) However, such hospitality cannot continue unless they observe the following conditions:

(i) the Government and the institutions which have been established by the will of the people in their respective territories, in accordance with the constitution freely chosen by them, must be respected;

(ii) they will be free to work in Ghana and earn their living here, but in no case can the Government of Ghana give them any material assistance, inasmuch as the Independent African States now maintain a central fund for the granting of such assistance to Freedom Fighters;

(iii) as long as the refugees remain in Ghana, they are forbidden to do anything whatsoever against the Government and the institutions of their country.

It is our earnest hope and belief that our own example in the creation of a Socialist pattern of Society, in which the free development of each is a condition for the free development of all is bound to have a striking impact on regimes in Africa in which the wealth and resources of the people are concentrated in the hands of neo-colonialists and their agents.

Now, Mr Speaker, Members of the National Assembly, in order to complete the liberation of our Continent, we must face the problem of South Africa and of Portuguese colonies on the Continent.

The arms which the Portuguese colonialists use in Angola and Mozambique, the bombs which they drop in Senegal, were not manufactured in Portugal, nor were they paid for by Portugal.

Portugal is the poorest State in Europe and the average Ghanaian, as our statistics show, is now wealthier than the average citizen of Portugal. Portugal by herself could not for a year continue to maintain the vast military apparatus which she employs for the suppression of the people and the exploitation of the resources of large areas of the African Continent.

Ghana has no quarrel in principle with the various treaty arrangements which States outside Africa make to secure their own defence, except where they impinge upon the sovereignty of Independent African States and the desire of the colonial territories in Africa to accede to independence. No one in Ghana could justifiably question, for instance, the avowed purpose of the North Atlantic Treaty Organization as set out in the words of its preamble, which I quote to you:

'The parties of this Treaty reaffirm their faith in the purposes and principles of the United Nations and their desire to live in peace with all peoples and all governments. They are determined to safeguard the freedom, common heritage, and civilization of their peoples, founded on the principles of democracy, individual liberty, and the rule of law. They seek to promote stability and well-being in the North Atlantic area. They are resolved to unite their efforts for collective defence for the preservation of peace and security. They therefore agree to this North Atlantic Treaty.'

But Angola and Mozambique are no part of North Atlantic defence. The Portuguese in Africa are not defending the freedom, common heritage, or civilization of the African people. They observe no principle of democracy, no individual liberty, nor the rule of law. In its conduct in Africa, Portugal acts continuously in defiance of the purposes and principles of the United Nations. Yet the truth is that NATO weapons and NATO support alone enable Portugal to survive as a colonial power in Africa even today.

I am certain that the moral case against NATO support for Portugal while she remains an oppressor of the African people, is so strong and overwhelming that the NATO powers must have no alternative but to withdraw their support. Appeals from individual African States may be passed over, unheeded. But the voice of a united Africa cannot go unheeded.

Portugal, unfortunately, is not the only colonial power which still retains control of African territory. With the exception of Madagascar and two small islands – one off the coast of Guinea and the other off the coast of Ethiopia – every single island belonging to the

African continent is still a colonial possession. On the African Continent itself, in addition to Portugal, Spain and France still maintain colonial possessions, and a large area of African territory is still under British colonial rule.

As I have said time and again, colonialism is an anachronism today and these various powers must give up their colonial possessions with grace and retire honourably. It is therefore with joy that we hail the beginning of the ending of the long struggle against colonialism in Kenya and applaud the successful conclusion of the recent elections there in favour of KANU. We equally rejoice at the clear prospect of independence for Nyasaland and Northern Rhodesia.

But Mr Speaker, it is the future of Southern Rhodesia which casts such a dark cloud on the horizon of Africa's freedom and independence.

Let us make our position perfectly clear on this vital issue. In the past, Britain, by force of arms, imposed upon the people of Southern Rhodesia or, to give it its natural, indigenous name, Zambia, an alien government designed to deprive the people of Zambia of their lands and their mineral wealth. Britain was a party to the establishment of a government composed exclusively of minority settlers who had, contrary to all conceptions of justice, possessed themselves of the lands and resources of the inhabitants. This settler government of Southern Rhodesia is now demanding that it should be granted independence. In other words, it is inviting the British Government to set up a second South Africa in the heart of our Continent without taking into account the wishes of the majority of the people in that territory.

No African States could in any way accept such a travesty of morality, justice and international law. Nor would we accept the undemocratic, racialist counter proposals which the British Government is reported to have made to the settler Southern Rhodesian Government. Any Government that is formed in Southern Rhodesia without the consent of the majority of its people will be unacceptable. Not only would we refuse to acknowledge any such government; we shall oppose its entry into the Commonwealth and into the United Nations. Our recognition will only go to a Government which in our view is fully representative of the people of Zambia. That is, a Government based upon universal adult suffrage, employing the principle of one man one vote.

You will recall, Mr Speaker, Members of the National Assembly, that on the very threshold of our independence, the British Govern-

264

ment compelled us to go to the polls more than once to prove to the world that the Convention People's Party enjoyed the fullest support of the majority of our people. The independence of Nigeria was similarly delayed in order that the British Government might satisfy itself that all sections of the population were properly represented in Parliament. Kenya had to endure a similar election for the same reason.

In all these cases, the United Kingdom Government sought to justify its position by maintaining that its actions were based on its avowed dedication to the principles of democracy and representative government. Let me ask now, Mr Speaker, what makes the case of Southern Rhodesia different from the pre-independence situation in Ghana, Nigeria and Kenya? There is no need to pause for a reply.

I cannot believe that any British Government could commit the supreme folly and blunder of setting up at this stage of our African struggle for independence and unity a second South Africa, whose examples of the appalling evils of apartheid and minority rule are so glaringly manifested against the African population every single day. I have left the British Government in no doubt about the stand we are prepared to take against the setting up of an unpopular minority independent Government of Southern Rhodesia.

This is a crucial and decisive moment in the history of Southern Africa. The attainment of political freedom by the people of Southern Rhodesia would not only mean the setting up of a free and indigenous Zambian state. It would bring a message of hope and encouragement to African peoples elsewhere in Southern Africa who are denied any right to control their own affairs. But Zambia will, in any event become free.

In truth, of course, the situation in Southern Rhodesia could have been solved as had been the Kenya situation, but for one factor – the proximity of Southern Rhodesia to South Africa. Indeed, the Southern Rhodesian settlers are nothing more than pawns in the game of chess now being played by the Foreign powers over South Africa. The independence of the people of Southern Rhodesia is not in reality being considered on its merits. It is considered only in relation to the South African situation.

South Africa is the biggest impediment to the liberation and unity of the African Continent, and it is a question which we must face squarely and realistically.

For some time now we have tried a line of policy, namely, that if only one was patient and negotiated and tried to understand the problems of South Africa, then the situation would gradually begin to improve, and little by little racial oppression would disappear.

However, Mr Speaker, our experience has proved this policy to be false. The sincerity of our approach can be judged from the fact that South Africa was invited to the first Conference of Independent African States here in Accra. It is of some significance that she refused to attend unless the other colonial powers were invited as well. We attempted to exchange High Commissioners; we met with South African whites at various African and international Conferences, and we tried in every way to follow a path of persuasion and conciliation. Our efforts were entirely without results, and I think it is now clear to everyone that the South African situation cannot be dealt with by attempts to maintain the normal channels of diplomatic and commercial association, or by appeals to morality and religion, justice and codes of ethics.

Unfortunately, the great powers, and some of the smaller ones, still continue to export arms to South Africa. Have those who have authorized the export of such arms made any enquiry as to the real purpose for which they are required by South Africa? Have they asked why so many small arms should be needed for the protection of South African whites? For what purpose do these States consider that Apartheid South Africa requires aircraft capable of and designed for carrying nuclear rockets and weapons? The Buccaneer aircraft with its limited range and about which there has recently been controversy in Britain is not such as could be employed against, say, the Soviet Union, or the United States of America or indeed against any State outside the African Continent. Against whom on the African Continent, then, are they intended to be employed?

These are questions all the Independent African States are asking and would like to have answered. But we would be helping the cause of world peace if the traffic in arms to South Africa were stopped. In the spirit and context of the Addis Ababa resolutions, I have instructed the Ghanaian representative on the Security Council to raise immediately as a matter of urgency with his African colleagues the question as to whether the United Nations should not call upon all nations to cease forthwith to supply arms to South Africa.

The decisions taken at Addis Ababa demand the breaking off of diplomatic and consular relations between all the African States and the Governments of Portugal and South Africa. They call for an effective boycott of foreign trade with the two countries. It is for all the Independent African States to see that their total economic and political boycott is made complete without delay. The allies of the colonial powers have also been given notice that they must choose between their friendship for the African peoples and their support of the powers that oppress African peoples. This reflects as well upon those countries which have accepted as a political principle the independence of colonial peoples, but which at times betray this principle out of expediency.

If the great powers, or even a large enough body of the smaller ones, were to support us by joining the boycott, the moral effect would have tremendous repercussions throughout the African Continent, besides serving notice on the Verwoerd and Salazar regimes that they can no longer continue a policy of racial segregation, oppression and genocide. Surely, it must be obvious to every reasonable person that no minority settlers of European origin, can keep us indefinitely in subjection in our own continent. Is it not a staggering thought to think that in South Africa the law as established by a sheer minority of 3 million white settlers enables and permits them to control the destiny of 12 million of our people? Where is justice? Where is morality? Where is democracy? Let us not forget that, like the rest of the world the African Continent cannot exist, and refuses to exist, half free and half colonized.

Mr Speaker and Members of the National Assembly, it is of great consequence that the States of the Organization of African Unity have, in Article Three of the Charter, solemnly affirmed and declared their adherence to the principle of a non-aligned policy.

Non-alignment is now a world factor and moral force in international relations. The contribution of Africa as a continent united in its observance of a truly non-aligned policy will give tremendous weight to that force. It will also give a great fillip to the search for permanent world peace.

Mr Speaker, Nothing has stood so firmly in the way of African freedom or hindered African unity as the existence of foreign bases on African soil and African involvement through military alliances and pacts with powers outside the African Continent. If we are to combine our forces and create a common strategy both in support of Africa's Freedom Fighters and in the defence and protection of our established independence, then it goes without saying that all such bases and all such pacts need to be annulled. Unless this is done, we stand exposed and our Charter will remain nothing but a mere scrap of paper.

In saying this, I am not unmindful of the grave difficulties which face some of us. Lack of capital, economic weakness and political instability are conditions that have been responsible for the acceptance of economic and military dependence upon former colonial powers. In some instances such assistance is obtained not only for development, but even for meeting normal recurrent budgetary expenses. It is an act of high courage on the part of Sister States thus boldly to have set their hand to a policy of non-alignment which can hardly be in keeping with the policy of those on whom, unhappily, they find themselves dependent.

Yet it is these States particularly that should find the greatest advantage in developing African Unity into a firmly welded concert of nations as a real political force with political direction under a central authority within which they can shed their economic and military dependence and regain their dignity. Proposals of aid need to be examined with care. Most of all we must beware of any kind of military help, for it can so easily place us in the hands of foreign powers and make them, in effect, the arbiters of our fate. Apart from drawing us into their orbit, they become intimately familiar with details of our defence structure and its strength. They can even become the designers of our defence structure and place us completely at their mercy. Aid of this kind, even where ostensibly free, can be most dangerous and costly in its consequences. For it creates pockets of cold-war presence on the African Continent and lets in the neo-colonialists with danger not only to the harbouring country but to its neighbours, to whom it poses an open threat. Above all, it creates frictions and disputes that disturb the unity upon which we have embarked and to which, I am convinced, all of us are sincerely dedicated. That is why it is so urgent for us to get together within a centralized framework that will give shape and purpose to the agreements which we made at Addis Ababa.

Co-ordination of our political and diplomatic policies, harmonization of our economic, educational and cultural activities, collaboration in health, sanitation and nutritional matters, co-ordination in scientific and technical fields, co-operation for defence and security will go their dilatory pace unless the Organization of African Unity is pivoted upon a centralized authority capable of giving effective political direction to these aims.

Political and diplomatic co-operation cannot function in a void. It needs some sort of a political constitution to direct it. Economic development in separate States is ineffective, but with our combined resources, governed by an overall plan, we can make Africa great, prosperous and progressive.

Above all, the full development of all our countries needs the most economic exploitation and husbanding of our natural and human resources. This is possible only on a continental scale, if we are to extract the greatest advantage from the latest industrial and administrative techniques as applied to our extensive land mass and population.

As a token of Ghana's dedication to the Charter of African Unity, I am setting on foot immediately plans for the exchange of students and for the provision at the University of Ghana of a course of studies in African Affairs and in History, Economics and Politics generally, which may be of value to other States who do not as yet possess universities in the training of their administrators. Educational and cultural co-operation in general demands effective co-ordination at inter-State level. A guide to the history of Africa should be produced to destroy once and for all the colonial myth that Africa has no past.

Mr Speaker, the structure of the social organizations in our New Africa must embrace all sections of our people. The goals of our endeavours have always been to secure the material basis for increasing the economic and social wealth of our farmers, peasants and workers. Our revolution, therefore, must be identified with the organizations of the workers and our peasant population. We cannot succeed very much in our aims if there should be conflict between the trade unions as the organization of the workers and our national Governments which are also serving the same interests. Our identical aims must make it possible for us to harmonize relations and work within a co-ordinated programme for solving the problems that face Africa.

The All-African Trade Union Federation must therefore be in a position to mobilize the exploited masses of Africa for the final onslaught in the battle against imperialism and neo-colonialism. In the Independent States of Africa AATUF has a vital role to play in evolving a Trade Union orientation which will enable the workers to play their full part in socialist construction.

An All-African Trade Union grouping independent of external conflicts can play a most useful part in fostering understanding within the International Labour Movement. International Labour Unity is essential for the preservation of peace and the security of mankind.

These, Mr Speaker, are some of the implications of the Charter which I and the other Heads of State and Government signed at Addis Ababa. With goodwill and honest striving on the part of us all the Charter can become a reality within a workable Centralized African Union. In the march forward to our continental growth and prosperity, it is our earnest hope that the principle of the free development of each as a condition for the free development of all will find general acceptance in Africa. For it is within the functioning of this principle that it will be possible to smooth out those inequalities in our societies that engender social friction and discontent imposed upon us by imperialism. We have arrived at national statehood in an epoch when the ordinary people will no longer tolerate the concentration of the national wealth and resources in the hands of a privileged few while the many go ragged, destitute and hungry. This is a factor of which we have to take full congnizance in designing our political, economic and social future, both at the national and continental levels. Otherwise we shall find ourselves in the sad position of stifling the hopes and aspirations of the vast masses of our people and being forced, in the face of their resentment and possible uprising, to resort to draconian measures which will sunder our societies and plunge us into civil strife, confusion and anarchy. Where such conditions arise, the neo-colonialists can enter unchecked to profit from them and menace the safety and security of our entire Continent.

This, then, is another most cogent argument for fashioning our African unity in a way that will bind us all closely in every field of endeavour and make the well-being and happiness of all our people its keynote. Only thus shall we achieve a calm and stable progress to that complete independence and unity which we desire to achieve in Africa.

With our continental liberation and unity, Africa will become a powerful force that will carry its total impact in the councils of the world. For that reason, no country in the world can afford to be indifferent to what we have set on foot at Addis Ababa.

Equally, in striving for African freedom and unity, we cannot be indifferent to events in other parts of the globe, which can vitally affect the progress which we make towards our goal. It is in this spirit that we have concerned ourselves about such grave international issues as the Sino-Indian border dispute and the Cuban situation. In doing so, we were not only serving the cause of world peace which is of vital importance to us. We were serving the cause of African liberation and unity as well.

I believe that the forces now pressing for freedom and unity in Africa will be strong enough to overcome any external obstacle. Yet we must not blind ourselves to the fact that one of the great causes of African disunity and of the maintenance of racialist and colonialist regimes on African soil is the disagreement and hostility which at present exists between the great powers.

Imperialism and the so-called white supremacy are the basic factors of instability in Africa and one of the contributory causes of world tension. Secondly, unless the situation in South Africa improves radically so as to afford opportunities for the majority of the citizens of that State to express their will in a Government of their own, this could be a theatre for a world conflict. Racial oppression and injustice in any form cannot be condoned or ignored. Racialism is a blot on the conscience of mankind, and the sooner it is removed the greater the prospects of world peace will be. It is in the same context that one has to consider the problem of racial discrimination in the United States. Although the efforts now being made by the Government of the United States to bring about a solution to this long-standing problem in America are appreciated, it must be stated that nothing except a bold and revolutionary assault on this moral obloquy and this grave crisis of racial confidence in the United States, can bring about a speedy solution.

The Afro-American has been taught to appreciate the dignity of the individual, living as he does in one of the most technically advanced countries of our time; and yet at the same time he is being denied what is his essential and inalienable right. The Afro-American did not choose to go to the New World. He was dragged into America to help establish the economy of that country. This he has done with great credit, distinguishing himself in all fields of human endeavour. In Music, Law, Diplomacy, Art, Science, Education, he has achieved great distinction for America. The United States has therefore a moral duty to accept the essential humanity of the Afro-American.

Now, Mr Speaker, let me turn to other problems that affect the position of the African and endanger world peace. The nuclear arms race in the Middle East is now an open secret. Instability in this area not only heightens world tension but jeopardizes the security of the African Continent. In the interests of world peace a way must therefore be found quickly to end the dangerous arms race between Israel and Egypt which could easily lead to disaster for Africa, the Middle East and the world. This arms race has already involved some of the major world powers who are aiding and abetting both sides in the struggle.

The world leaders must hasten to insulate the Middle East not only from the intensification of the Cold War crisis in that area but also from the threat of a nuclear arms clash between the Arabs and Israel. To this end, I have repeatedly called for a nuclear moratorium in the Middle East, for the creation of an Arab State for the refugees and for the permanent delimitation of the State of Israel. Time is running out, and I call again upon the United Nations to move as quickly as they can to save a very grave situation.

In the same way as the dispute between India and China over frontier delimitation heightens world tension and thus makes more difficult the tasks which we have set ourselves in Africa, so do the unhappy differences that have arisen between the United States and Cuba, which nearly sparked off a nuclear conflagration a few months ago. Whatever the causes of disagreement may be, the United States and Cuba must find a way to co-exist. Cuba has indicated her willingness to come to a settlement with the United States and to make appropriate restitution for United States assets nationalized by the Cuban Government. It would seem reasonable, therefore, for the United States which, in size, economic and military power, is far greater than Cuba, to express her greatness in an equal – if not greater – gesture of goodwill, magnanimity and statesmanship. Peaceful co-existence is essential and indispensable for the establishment of understanding between the nations at a time when nuclear weapons hang like the Sword of Damocles over the head of mankind.

Mr Speaker, Members of the National Assembly, we can safeguard our independence and economic interests in Africa only if we speak with one voice. Only a united Africa can obtain capital on a large scale and technical aid from the industrially advanced countries without undue pressures and restrictive conditions. The only alternative I can see to this is confusion in our ranks, economic retrogression and a pitiful sell-out of our patrimony to the colonialists and imperialists. Did we fight to secure sovereignty and independence only to exchange these precious attributes for a state of despair and despondency? We have proved at Addis Ababa that we are ready to build a united Africa, united in our conception of its importance and in our common desire to move forward together in a triumphant march to the great kingdom of the African Personality, where although we may be Ghanaians, or Nigerians or Ethiopians, Algerians, Egyptians or Sierra Leonians, we shall have a common purpose and a common objective in working for the destiny of our Continent as Africans. Until Africa achieves total independence and national unification the African revolution will not have completed its destined task. When we talk of African Unity, we are thinking of a political arrangement which will enable us *collectively* to provide solutions for our problems in Africa.

Mr Speaker, General de Gaulle is reported to have commented on the results achieved at the Addis Ababa Conference that the organization of Africa which the Independent African States envisage is 'a Federation of the various African regional groupings'. What made him arrive at that conclusion, I cannot tell.

It is, however, a matter of great interest to us to observe that this Great European, now engrossed with his grand design for Europe, should feel such unsolicited concern for the future of Africa. It should be quite clear to General de Gaulle that not only can he not be a greater African than the Africans themselves, but he cannot be both a Great European and a Great African.

Regional Groupings of any kind are a serious threat to the unity of Africa. Such groupings have decisive influences which can break the forces of cohesion and unity among us. General de Gaulle knows quite well that if regional federalism, this political commodity of dubious value, can be sold to Africa, the economic future of his Europe will be assured. Only by fomenting and nursing regional and sectional political groupings in Africa can the imperialists and ex-colonial powers be sure of retaining their rapidly waning influence in Africa. That is why, even after Addis Ababa, they wish to secure the political dismemberment of Africa. It is for the same reason that the British Government also is reported to have fervently supported the idea of a political federation in East Africa. This is surely timed to defeat the objectives of the Addis Ababa Conference. But all these manoeuvres will fail. Out of African Unity a new Africa will arise, life will be full and abundant; our culture and the arts, so long suppressed under colonial domination, will blossom again and flourish.

There can, therefore, be no co-existence between freedom and slavery on the African Continent, between African independence and colonial and neo-colonial domination, between Independent Africa and colonial imperialism. Such co-existence would mean denial of our African right to be free, a right as inalienable for us as for any other people of the world. It would be to condone the crime of apartheid, to accept the cruelties of Portuguese rule, to leave Africa at the mercy of even more ruthless suppression and exploitation. It would lay the independence of the sovereign African States wide open to the predatory attacks of the colonialists who still hold power in parts of our Continent. Africa would become a dark battleground of Western competitiveness that could only result in the miseries and horrors of open conflicts and civil wars.

Mr Speaker, One of our great hopes in pursuing the goal of total African liberation and unity is the vista of world peace that it opens up. For the culmination of that goal we envisage the end of colonialism

273

and neo-colonialism, the twin offspring of imperialism, the cause of much of the world's rivalry and divisions. Imperialism, which reached its zenith in the Western world in the period of capitalist democracy is finance capital and capitalist democracy run wild in other people's countries. Its first stage was during the period of direct political governance, known as colonialism. As colonialism is being forced to retreat under pressure of nationalist awakening the imperialists are making an all-out effort to consolidate and extend their domination by different means. These means are various and take on many forms; they can be direct or subtle. Mostly they are devious, often insinuating, frequently disguised. They may promise friendship or use political and economic blackmail. They add up to neo-colonialism, which is the last stage of imperialism in the epoch of rising independence among colonial peoples. With the widening of freedom's boundaries and the unification that now portends in Africa, the root of imperialism will undoubtedly weaken and it is difficult to forecast another stage to which it can go except to decline. But imperialism, colonialism and neo-colonialism will end only when conditions are such as to make their existence impossible. That is, when there are no nations and peoples exploiting others; when there are no vested interests exploiting the earth, its fruits and resources for the benefit of a few against the well-being of the many. And I am convinced that our march in Africa towards total independence and unity must hasten this end and thereby add to the peace of the world.

This at once raises the matter of speed and urgency. Time is everything in our march. We must in Africa crowd into a generation the experience and achievements attained through centuries of trial and error by the older nations of the world. We do not wish to see Africa set on a course in which her nations grow in different, separate and competing directions until they develop into a confused and disorderly economic tangle of 'Sixes and Sevens'. Because Europe has become the victim of such economic circumstances that is surely no reason why Africa should follow a similar course. Those who set the example of Europe as an illustration for the need to develop step by step in Africa do not seem to appreciate that Africa need not begin by imitating the mistakes of Europe. After all, what use is the experience of human progress if we who study its course fail to learn from its errors and muddles. As I said at Addis Ababa, this world is no longer moving on camels and donkeys. Speed has become a new potent factor in the progress of the world. The progress of the modern man, like the agile Kangaroo, leaps and jumps.

More than that, we have to remove the gap between those nations and ourselves if we are to emerge from the grip of the economic imperialism that will retard us the longer it remains master, or even a part, of our economy. We have to keep in mind, however, that the gap is not a static one, but that it grows as modern technology improves and its productive capacities and output potentials increase. Thus the gap can widen seriously and new dangers threaten us, unless we hasten forward at a much accelerated speed. Consciousness of the time element among the leaders of Independent Africa was clearly revealed in the course of our deliberations at Addis Ababa. This awareness enabled us to examine our problems with a striking sense of urgency. It was responsible for the speed with which we were able to adopt a Charter of Unity for Africa. Why, then, cannot we observe the same consciousness of time and the same sense of urgency, in pushing forward our unity into a form that will give it direction and authority, so that we can speed up our common development and advancement? In the horizon of Africa's future I see clearly the bright dawn of a Union Government, the birth of a great Nation which is no longer the dream of a new Utopia. Africa, the sleeping giant, is now awake and is coming into her very own.

21

The second Summit Conference of the OAU took place in Cairo from the 17th to the 21st of July, 1964. The OAU, just over a year old, was already in difficulties. There was deep dissatisfaction among freedom fighters at the ineffectiveness of the OAU Liberation Committee. They complained of lack of supplies and of training facilities. Serious disputes had broken out between Ethiopia and Somalia; between Morocco and Algeria; and between Somalia and Kenya. There had been army mutinies in Tanzania, Uganda and Kenya, which were suppressed not with the assistance of troops from a sister African state, but with the help of British troops. Foreign interference in the Congo's internal affairs was continuing to cause untold misery and suffering to the Congolese people. Mozambique, Angola, Guinea Bissau, Bechuanaland, Basutoland, Swaziland, and other territories in Africa were still suffering under colonialism. In Southern Rhodesia, a white settler minority regime was still refusing to allow even the most elementary of human rights to the vast majority of the population. And while African disunity and balkanization continued, virtually no improvement was being made in the living conditions of the African masses. Only foreign interests, and with them, the interests of the African bourgeoisie, flourished.

In the light of all that had taken place since the foundation of the OAU, I was more than ever convinced that the creation of a Union Government for Africa provided the only solution for Africa's continued political instability and underdevelopment. The OAU as established in Addis Ababa in 1963 had been shown to be unable to deal effectively with the problems facing it, and was by its very ineffectiveness blocking the advance of the African Revolution, and thereby aiding the forces of reaction. The whole purpose of my Address to the Conference on the 19th of July 1964 was, therefore, to stress the urgent need for the immediate setting up of a Union Government for Africa. The specific areas of unified action which I had in mind were: defence, foreign policy and economic development, the last implying a common currency for Africa.

To my great disappointment, it was clear from the speeches of some of the Conference members that there were some who were still not ready for such a radical step to be taken. There was general agreement on the need for a Union Government, but it was decided that the whole matter should be examined by specialized commissions of the OAU, and that the question should be discussed again at the next summit conference which it was agreed should be held in Accra in 1965.

SPEECH DELIVERED AT THE SUMMIT CONFERENCE OF THE ORGANIZATION OF AFRICAN UNITY

Cairo, 19th July 1964

PROPOSALS FOR A UNION GOVERNMENT OF AFRICA

Mr Chairman,
In the year that has passed since we met at Addis Ababa and

established the Organization of African Unity, I have had no reason to change my mind about the concrete proposals which I made to you then, or about the reasons I gave for my conviction that only a Union Government can guarantee our survival. On the contrary, every hour since then, both in the world at large and on our own Continent, has brought events to prove that our problems as individual states are insoluble except in the context of African Unity, that our security as individual states is indivisible from the security of the whole Continent, that the freedom of our compatriots still in foreign chains and under colonial rule awaits the redeeming might of an African Continental Government.

We took a monumental decision at the Summit Meeting in Addis Ababa last year. No amount of disappointment or impatience with the pace at which our Charter has been implemented, can detract from the epoch-making and irrevocable nature of our decision to affirm the unity of our Continent.

It was an act of faith, a recognition of reality. We forged the Organization of African Unity fully conscious of all the difficulties facing our various States in committing themselves to common obligations. We have passed through the first year victorious over trials on our loyalty, and over hostile forces seeking to disrupt our unity.

Wherever and whenever the subsidiary bodies set up by the Addis Ababa Charter have met, the spirit of unity, of co-operation and goodwill have prevailed. On that score, none of us can complain; none of us have cause to doubt the strength and permanence of the spirit of unity which found its expression in our Charter.

Yet, even more than last year, I must urge that the historical conditions in which African independence has emerged and the concrete manifestations of our weaknesses and difficulties, call for immense radical and urgent measures which the Addis Ababa Conference did not fulfil. Measures which would have been accounted adequate for dealing with our problems a few years ago, cannot now meet the exigencies of the African revolution.

It is not single States or single Continents which are undergoing de-colonialization, but the greater portion of the world. It is not one empire which is expiring, but the whole system of imperialism which is at bay. It is not individual communities, but the whole of humanity which is demanding a different and better way of life for the world's growing millions.

Great positive and social revolutions have created mighty nations and empires, and the waves of those revolutions lap our shores no less than they do those of other continents. Great technological and industrial revolutions have transformed the economies of large portions of the world, and the waves of those revolutions will not stop short on the Continent of Africa. A revolution in communications brings knowledge of every change in the world to the remotest corners of our continent. The world will not wait – nor will it move step by step, however much we may wish this.

It is against this background of great political, social, cultural, scientific and technological revolutions that the emergence of African independence and the development of Africa must be viewed. None of us imagines that we can keep our own pace, immune from interference, isolated from the world's upsurges and revolutions. What differences there are between us arise from a difference in appreciation of the sense of urgency, not in the understanding we have of our tasks and responsibilities.

Time, indeed, is the crucial factor, for time acts for those who use it with purpose, and not for those who let it slip by. Those who do not use time as their agent, give the advantage to those who do.

When we met last year we were at the beginning of an era of peaceful co-existence. The risk of a World War was abating, and the prospect of peacful co-operation between the Great Powers appeared to bring to an end the struggle of foreign influences in Africa. We embraced non-alignment in order to escape involving ourselves in the prevailing cold war politics. Instead, we have witnessed the menacing upsurge of imperialism and a revival of colonialism itself in Africa, and foreign interference and subversion in the internal affairs of our African States.

The one essential factor which united us at Addis Ababa – the over-riding factor which made all differences and difficulties seem trivial and irrelevant – was the need to free that part of our continent which is still in the grip of imperialism. In spite of our Charter, in spite of our common front at the United Nations and in other international gatherings, what have we witnessed?

Far from deterring the imperialists and neo-colonialists from giving support to the apartheid regime in South Africa and to the fascist regime in Portugal, the NATO Powers, on the contrary, have poured and are pouring vast sums of money and vast armaments into the apartheid regime of South Africa and Portugal. Not only is South Africa being assisted to grow stronger economically and militarily, but the cruelty, repression and exploitation of our African brothers have reached new heights.

At this point I must comment on the activities of the Liberation

Committee set up under the Organization of African Unity at Addis Ababa last year, on which both we and the Freedom Fighters pinned so much hope. It is with great regret that I raise the matter at all, but I would be failing in my duty to the Freedom Fighters and to the cause of African Liberation if I remain silent about the general dissatisfaction which exists regarding the functioning of this Committee.

The frequent and persistent reports from Freedom Fighters about the shortcomings of the aid and facilities for training offered to them, make it impossible for the Government of Ghana to turn over its contribution to this Committee until a reorganization has taken place for more effective and positive action.

This is not a situation in which individuals or individual governments can be held to blame. It is our first essay in a task of stupendous magnitude and with stupendous difficulties. But some of the failures of the Committee are inexcusable because they were so unnecessary.

It failed, for instance, to make the best use of our resources since some Military specialists have been excluded on ideological grounds.

If the Liberation Committee had made effective use of the military experience of Egypt and of Algeria, where neo-colonialist interference and espionage have been frustrated and held at bay, we would have given Freedom Fighters the necessary help in their liberation struggle.

The choice of the Congo (Leopoldville) as a training base for Freedom Fighters was a logical one, and there was every reason to accept the offer of the Congolese Government to provide offices and accommodation for the representatives of the Liberation Movements.

Africa's Freedom Fighters should not, however, have been exposed to the espionage, intrigues, frustrations and disappointments which they have experienced in the last eight months.

What could be the result of entrusting the training of Freedom Fighters against imperialism into the hands of an imperialist agent? Under the Liberation Committee set up at Addis Ababa, the Freedom Fighters had no real security, and were not provided with instruments for their struggle, nor were food, clothing and medicine given for the men in training. Thus, their training scheme collapsed within two months under the eyes of the Liberation Committee, and the Freedom Fighters became disappointed, disgruntled and frustrated.

I am giving you no more than the bare bones of the complaints of the Freedom Fighters. It will not avail us to have a lengthy post-mortem over past failures. But these failures must be understood and acknowledged. The disappointment and frustration of the Freedom Fighters must not be dismissed as unreal or unreasonable. Not only the Liberation Committee, but all of us are to blame, for the way in which we allowed the Liberation Committee to let down the Freedom Fighters.

We dare not say that they could have done their work better until we have all done better. The enormous task of liberating our continent cannot be undertaken in a spirit of compromise and surrender.

By raising a threat at Addis Ababa and not being able to take effective action against apartheid and colonialism, we have worsened the plight of our kinsmen in Angola, Mozambique, Southern Rhodesia and South Africa. We have frightened the imperialists sufficiently to strengthen their defences and repression in Southern Africa, but we have not frightened them enough to abandon apartheid supremacy to its ill-fated doom.

It must be said that by merely making resolutions on African Unity, and not achieving our goal of a Union Government of Africa, we have made our task of freeing the rest of the African Continent harder and not easier.

The North Atlantic Treaty Organization Powers have not been deterred one whit from sending all the arms needed by the Salazar regime to keep down our kinsmen in its colonies. The Portuguese fascist regime has not made a single move to negotiate with the United Nations or with the nationalist forces. It has become more insolent, more mendacious and more repressive since our Conference in Addis Ababa.

What has gone wrong?
The imperialists regard our Charter of Unity as token unity; they will not respect it until it assumes the form of a Union Government. It is incredible that they will defy a united Continent. But it is easy to understand that they do not believe that we will be able to accomplish the next stage – to organize and centralize our economic and military and political forces to wage a real struggle against apartheid, Portuguese fascism and those who support these evils with trade, investments and arms.

We have not yet made the imperialists to believe that we can set our continent in order as a mighty economic force, capable of standing together as a united and progressive people.

Serious border disputes have broken out and disturbed our Continent, since our last meeting. Fortunately, good sense and

African solidarity have prevailed in all those instances. But the disputes have been smothered, not settled. The artificial divisions of African States are too numerous and irrational for real permanent and harmonious settlements to be reached, except within the framework of a Continental Union.

How, for example, can we prevent the people of Western Somalia, whose whole livelihood is cattle-grazing, from continuing to look for fresh fields for grazing by travelling beyond traditional barriers without bringing them into clashes with their compatriots in Ethiopia?

And yet, in a united Africa, Ethiopian land and Somalian land, even though they may be separately sovereign within the framework of a Union Government of Africa, will belong to a common pool which would assist the general development of cattle-rearing in that part of our Continent, because there would be no artificial barriers to such development. The benefit of the development will be for the benefit of both Ethiopia and Somalia.

I said a little while ago, and I repeat, that the real border disputes will grow with the economic development and national strengthening of the African States as separate balkanized governmental units. That was the historical process of independent states in other continents. We cannot expect Africa, with its legacy of artificial borders, to follow any other course, unless we make a positive effort to arrest that danger now; and we can do so only under a Union Government. In other words, the careers and ambitions of political leaders, on the one hand, and balkanized nationalism on the other, if allowed to grow and become entrenched, could constitute a brake on the unification of African States. The Balkan States of Europe are a lesson for us.

History has shown that where the Great Powers cannot colonize, they balkanize. This is what they did to the Austro-Hungarian Empire and this is what they have done and are doing in Africa. If we allow ourselves to be balkanized, we shall be re-colonized and be picked off one after the other.

Now is the time for Africa's political and economic unification.

By far the greatest wrong which the departing colonialists inflicted on us, and which we now continue to inflict on ourselves in our present state of disunity, was to leave us divided into economically unviable States which bear no possibility of real development. As long as the chief consideration of the industrial Nations was our raw materials at their own prices, this policy made sense for them, if not for us.

Now that their technological impetus is such that they need Africa even more as a market for their manufactured goods than as a source of raw materials, our economic backwardness no longer makes sense for them any more than for us. The output of their great industrial complexes is no longer the primitive and simple implements like hoes and shovels. They now need vaster and more prosperous markets for heavy agricultural tractors and electronic machines. They wish to sell to us, not Ford motors propelled by magnetos or turbo-prop transport aircraft, but the latest in supersonic jets and atomic-powered merchant vessels. Which of us, trading separately in these highly developed market areas, can survive more than a year or two without remaining either economically backward, indebted, bankrupt or re-colonized?

There is much re-thinking on this score among the industrially-advanced countries, although their outlook is obscured because their economies are still geared to monopolistic devices for getting hold of our oil and gas deposits, uranium, gold, diamonds and other raw materials, cheap, and selling their manufactured goods back to us at exorbitant prices.

The poverty of the developing world has become a blot on the ethics and commonsense of the industrial nations. The recent United Nations Conference on Trade and Development was not organized by accident or solely by pressure from the developing nations. The growing economic gap between the two worlds spells misery for the developing countries, but it also threatens the industrialized nations with unemployment and with dangerous recessions and economic explosion.

We have reason to think that the imperialists themselves are in divided councils about the Unity of Africa. They must remain ambivalent, however, as long as they retain direct control over Southern Africa and neo-colonialist control of the Congo. The vast mineral wealth of those territories represents profits which they cannot willingly give up, even for greater markets in the rest of Africa.

But a Union Government of Africa would end the dilemma of the industrialized nations, because inevitably that wealth will be converted into capital for the development of Africa.

The fact that imperialism and neo-colonialism are in that dilemma should be for us the clearest indication of the course we must follow. We must unite for economic viability, first of all, and then to recover our mineral wealth in Southern Africa, so that our vast resources and capacity for development will bring prosperity for us and additional benefits for the rest of the world. That is why I have written elsewhere that the emancipation of Africa could be the emancipation of Man.

Is there any need to point out again that we are potentially the world's richest continent, not only in mineral wealth, but also in hydro-electric power? The wealth of the Sahara is yet untapped; the waters and rivers of Tanganyika and Ethiopia are yet unharnessed. All the capital we need for the development of these regions flows out of Africa today in gold, diamonds, copper, uranium and other minerals from Southern Africa, Northern Rhodesia, the Congo and other parts of the Continent. Every year in the Sahara and in other parts of Africa, new stores of mineral, chemical and petroleum wealth are discovered.

What is lacking for us in Africa, but the will and the courage to unite a divided but compact continent?

Today, in countless ways, our people learn that their poverty is not a curse from the gods or a burden imposed by the imperialists, but a political defect of our independence. The general realization grows that independence is not enough without the unity of Africa, for that is the only road towards the economic emancipation and development of our continent.

We in Africa are living in the most momentous era of our history. In a little less than one decade the majority of the territories in our continent have emerged from colonialism into sovereignty and independence. In a few years from now, we can envisage that all Africa will be free from colonial rule. Nothing can stem our onward march to independence and freedom.

While we have cause to rejoice in this achievement, our central problem as Independent States is the fragmentation of our territories into little independent States and of our policies and programmes into a patchwork of conflicting objectives and unco-ordinated development and plans.

While the post-war years have seen a phenomenal rise in the prices of manufactured goods which we need to sustain progress and development in our States, the prices of the raw materials which we export to these countries have shown an alarmingly steady decline. So the disparity between the 'haves' or the highly developed nations and the 'have-nots' or developing nations, becomes inevitably wider and wider as our needs grow greater and greater. How can we resolve this tragic paradox, except by uniting our forces and working together in Africa as a team?

Let us look further back on the year that has just passed since we first met at Addis Ababa last year. Think of the unfortunate clashes between Algeria and Morocco, between Somalia and Ethiopia and between Somalia and Kenya which nearly damaged and disrupted our new spirit of understanding and unity. If we had lived within a continental federal government in which the fortunes and fate of one were the fortunes and fate of all, could we have been drawn into such bloodshed with needless loss of precious African lives?

What shall I say of the military upheavals and mutinies in our sister States of Tanganyika, Uganda and Kenya? While no one among us here can tolerate indiscipline and mutiny in our armies, which of us was happy to learn that in their hour of need, our brothers were compelled to resort to the use of foreign troops – the troops of a former colonial power, at that – to bring these disturbances under control.

Before the damage was completely done, our brothers were able to send away these foreign troops and, in one case, called for the assistance of troops from a Sister African State.

Surely, these events have a clear lesson for us all! How can we maintain the safety and security of our respective States as our responsibilities increase and our problems become more complex, except through a united defence arrangement which will invest us with the effective and powerful means for joint action at short notice?

Last year at Addis Ababa I gave the warning that if we did not come together as speedily as possible under a Union Government, there would be border clashes and our people, in their desperation to get the good things of life, would revolt against authority. Subsequent events have fully endorsed that warning.

Look at events in the Congo. Why did they remain so confused, so frustrating and even so tragic for so long? If we had all been jointly responsible for bringing our brothers in the Congo the assistance they needed in their hour of travail, who would have dared to interfere from outside Africa in Congolese affairs? Instead of this, what did we see in the Congo?

On the one hand, internal disagreements and discord, endless manoeuvring for positions among the political leaders, and even the tragedy of fratricidal strife. On the other hand, foreign intervention and pressures, intrigues and coercion, subversion and cajolery.

In all this confusion, the power of imperialism has a fertile ground. It even dares to use openly certain African States to promote its selfish plans for the exploitation and degradation of the Congo.

We are unable to hold back foreign intrigues, because we are divided among ourselves. None of us is free and none of us can be safe, while there is frustration and instability in any part of this continent.

I do not need to go on citing specific instances of our common problems and difficulties to prove the urgency and the need for united action on a continental basis in Africa today. There is not one of us here now who does not suffer from the handicaps of our colonial past. Let us therefore move forward together in unity and in strength, confident in the knowledge that with such immense national and human resources as we possess in our continent, we cannot fail to make Africa one of the happiest, most prosperous and progressive areas of the world.

Two years ago we were exposed to the ridicule of the world because they saw us as a divided Africa. They called us names which helped to widen the apparent breach among us: the 'radical' Casablanca Powers, the 'moderate' Monrovia Group, and the 'pro-French' Brazzaville States. There was no justification for these labels, but to the imperialists they were a very convenient means of giving the dog a bad name and hanging him!

It is to our eternal credit that last year at Addis Ababa we put our enemies to shame by forging a common Charter from these groupings and emerging as the Organization of African Unity. Let it be said that at Cairo we put them to greater shame by agreeing to the establishment of a Union Government of Africa. Have you noticed, Brother Presidents and Prime Ministers, that so soon as we achieved this measure of agreement at Addis Ababa, the neo-colonialists and their agents proceeded to sow new seeds of disruption and dissension among us?

They became particularly active and vocal in preaching the new and dangerous doctrine of the 'step by step' course towards unity. If we take one step at a time, when they are in a position to take six steps for every single one of ours, our weakness will, of course, be emphasized and exaggerated for their benefit. One step now, two steps later, then all will be fine in Africa for imperialism and neo-colonialism. To say that a Union Government for Africa is premature is to sacrifice Africa on the altar of neo-colonialism. Let us move forward together to the wider fields of our heritage, strong in our unity, where our common aspirations and hopes find abundant expression in the power of our united endeavours.

All over Africa the essential economic pattern developed under colonialism remains. Not one of us, despite our political independence, has yet succeeded in breaking, in any substantial measure, our economic subservience to economic systems external to Africa. It is the purpose of neo-colonialism to maintain this economic relationship.

The developed countries need the raw materials of Africa to maintain their own industries and they are anxious to find markets in Africa for their manufactured goods. But there can be no market for these manufactured goods unless the people of Africa have the money with which to buy them. Therefore I say that the developed countries have a vested interest in Africa's prosperity.

In many cases our most valuable raw materials – such as minerals – are owned and exploited by foreign companies. Large parts of the wealth of Africa, which could be used for the economic development of Africa, are drained out of the continent in this way to bolster the economies of the developed nations.

It is true that the whole world is poised at a delicate economic balance and that economic collapse in any one part of the world would have grave repercussions on us. Our situation in Africa is so weak that we are bound to be the first and the worst sufferers if economic difficulties should set in in Europe or America, and the effect upon us would be absolute and catastrophic. We have nothing to fall back on. We have become so utterly dependent upon these outside economic systems that we have no means of resistance to external economic fluctuations. We have no economic resilience whatsoever within our own continent.

We are so cut off from one another that in many cases the road systems in each of our countries peter out into bush as they approach the frontier of our neighbour. How can we trade amongst ourselves when we do not even have proper means of physical communication? It is now possible to travel by air from Accra to London in six hours. I can fly from Accra to Nairobi or from Accra to Cairo in half a day. It is easy for us to get together to talk. But on the ground over which we fly with such ease and nonchalance, it is frequently impossible to engage in the most elementary trade simply because there are no proper roads, and because we are artificially divided and balkanized.

Our few and negligible roads and railways always lead, ultimately, to some port. In a sense they have become symbols of our economic subservience and our dependence on trade outside the African Continent.

We have inherited from colonialism an economic pattern from which it is difficult to escape. Great forces are arrayed to block our escape. When individually we try to find some economic independence, pressures are brought against us that are often irresistible owing to our disunity.

I am not arguing that we should cut off all economic relationships with countries outside Africa. I am not saying that we should spurn foreign trade and reject foreign investment. What I am saying is that we should get together, think together, plan together and organize our African economy as a unit, and negotiate our overseas economic relations as part of our general continental economic planning. Only in this way can we negotiate economic arrangements on terms fair to ourselves.

The Organization of African Unity was a declaration of intention to unite. It was an optimistic beginning. But we need more than this. We must unite NOW under a Union Government if this intention is to have any meaning and relevance.

Talk is worthless if it does not lead to action. And so far as Africa is concerned, action will be impossible if it is any further delayed. Those forces which endanger our continent do not stand still. They are not moving step by step. They are marching in double step against us.

Every day we delay the establishment of a Union Government of Africa, we subject ourselves to outside economic domination. And our political independence as separate States becomes more and more meaningless.

Brother Presidents and Prime Ministers: as I said a few minutes ago, this decade is Africa's finest hour. Great things are in store for us if we would but take our courage in our hands and reach out towards them. How would South Africa dare to sentence Nelson Mandela and his seven brave colleagues against protests of a United Africa? How could Portugal dare think of continuing the violation of the sovereignty of Angola and Mozambique or so-called 'Portuguese Guinea', if these formed part of a United Government of Africa? How could a white settler minority Government in Southern Rhodesia dare to lock up Nkomo and Sithole?

We have gone to Geneva to seek a major victory in our quest for fair play and justice in international trade. There were no less than seventy-five of us in one group set against the few of the great industrialized communities of Europe and the United States. And yet how weak was our bargaining power because of our political and economic disunity and divisions.

How much more effective would our efforts have been if we had spoken with the one voice of Africa's millions. With all our minerals and waterpower and fertile lands, is it not a cause for shame that we remain poor and content to plead for aid from the very people who have robbed us of our riches in the past? How can Egypt, strategically situated as it is, combat the imperialism and neo-colonialism and solve the pressing and urgent problems of the Middle East unless it has the backing of a Union Government of Africa? Only a Union Government can assist effectively in the solution of the problems of the Middle East, including the Palestinian question.

Mr Chairman,

Let us remember, Brother Presidents and Prime Ministers, the Sahara no longer divides us. We do not see ourselves merely as Arab Africa, Black Africa, English Africa or French Africa. We are one people, one Continent with one destiny.

I see no way out of our present predicament except through the force and power of a Union Government of Africa. By this I do not mean the abrogation of any sovereignty. I seek no regional unions as a basis for unity. Indeed, the more Independent States there are within our Union Government, the stronger will be our unity, and the freer will be each sovereign State within the Union to attend to its specific and exclusive problems.

The specific fields of common action I have in mind are: Defence, Foreign Policy and Economic Development (including a common currency for Africa).

In this way, instead of a Charter which operates on the basis of peripatetic or widely-separated commissions under the control of an administrative secretariat without political direction, we shall have a government for joint action in three fields of our governmental activity.

It has been suggested from this rostrum, and it is on our agenda also, that we should decide at this Conference as to the location of the Permanent Headquarters of the Organization of African Unity and appoint a permanent Secretary-General. If, as I hope, we agree in principle, at this Conference to move on to the establishment of a Union Government of Africa, we shall require quite a different set of criteria for selecting the Headquarters of the Organization and its permanent officials. We should also be careful to avoid being drawn into discussions at this stage which could lead to a clash of interests as to which country should have the Headquarters or provide a Secretary-General. This could harm the very unity which we are trying now to establish. I feel very strongly that the status quo should remain.

I see no objection, however, to the proposal that we should

appoint a Secretary-General, provided it is agreed that the appointment is made on a provisional basis only. I feel that Addis Ababa should continue as the Provisional Headquarters of our Organization.

Mr Chairman,

I would like to express on behalf of Ghana our sincere thanks to His Imperial Majesty Haile Selassie I and to the Ethiopian Government for maintaining the Provisional Secretariat up to now. I feel, however, that before we rise we should make appropriate contributions from our various States for the upkeep of this our Organization. The burden should not be Ethiopia's alone.

I would like to state in this connection that Ghana is not interested in either the Headquarters or the Secretary-Generalship of the Organization.

Mr Chairman,

Two-hundred-and-eighty million people in strength with a common destiny and a common goal could give progress and development in Africa a new momentum and an impetus which go beyond our wildest dreams. Do not let us speak and act as if we are not aware of the revolutionary forces surging through Africa today. Even the industrialized nations outside Africa recognize this now.

Today, there may be frustration, doubt and distrust in every part of our Continent, but tomorrow will see a new hope and a new march to glory, under a United Government capable of speaking with one voice for all Africa.

Mr Chairman,

For a few moments, please permit me to refer to the pattern of economic structure which we inherited from the colonialists in Africa. All of us, under colonial rule, were encouraged to produce a limited number of primary commodities, mainly agricultural and mineral, for export overseas. Capital for development was owned by foreigners and profits were vigorously transferred abroad.

A trade pattern of this sort stagnated the rest of our national economy, and our resources remained undeveloped. In consequence, indigenous capital formation was negligible, leaving all our countries in a state of abject poverty.

Since independence, we have been making energetic efforts to reverse and overhaul these unsatisfactory features in our economy. In some of the Independent African States great efforts have been made to relax traditional economic links with the ex-colonial Powers, but none of us can say that we have succeeded in breaking those dangerous links completely.

Another handicap which we suffered from colonialism was the restriction of our economies which has hampered economic development in many ways. The very fact that all the Independent African States produce and maintain development plans is an indication of our deep concern for realizing nationalist aspirations and improving the conditions of living of our people.

But however deep our concern, however strong our determination, these development plans will avail us nothing if the necessary capital is not available. This capital, as we all know, is everywhere desperately short. The men with the know-how are few and scattered. It is by our coming together and pooling our resources that we can find a solution to this problem. In other words, only by unified economic planning on a continental basis with a central political direction within a Union Government can we hope to meet the economic challenge of our time.

It takes millions of pounds to build the basic industries, irrigation and power plants which will enable us to escape from our present economic stagnation. Our various individual, separate, balkanized States cannot mobilize the enormous amounts of money required for these major projects and industrial complexes. We cannot bargain effectively for the essential funds from foreign sources on the best possible terms. What we are doing now is to compete between ourselves for the little capital available from foreign sources. In our scramble to get this capital we grant foreign firms extensive and lucrative concessions for the exploitation of our natural resources. These Concessions to secure this capital exacerbate the colonial pattern of our economy. We invest more in raw materials output than in industrial development, and the continued drain abroad of profits which should have been re-invested in economic development retards the progress of our industrialization plans.

In a continental federal union, we can easily mobilize the amount of capital available to the African States by the establishment of a Central Monetary Development Finance Bank. Already our various States have agreed to form an African Development Bank. This, however, cannot succeed without a continental economic plan and without the necessary political direction which only a Union Government of Africa can provide.

An African Monetary Development Bank of the kind I envisage will enable us to formulate continental agreements concerning the terms of loans and investments by foreign interests. Together, we can bargain far more effectively with foreign firms and governments for investments and loans for the kinds of industries we desire and not those they desire. We can bargain on the terms of these loans and we can ensure that the increased savings which will arise from continental development of Africa's huge resources will enable us to develop even more rapidly. The unnecessary competition amongst us for capital would cease and moreover we can work up continental tariff policies designed to protect newly developing African industries. The great risks involved in investing in our individual countries will be reduced, for in an African economic union our development projects would be backed by all the African States together. But even this healthy sign of development is in grave danger of driving us against one another. As the general conditions of our economy are similar in all the Independent African States, and as our national development plans are not being co-ordinated, this can only lead to a concomitant expansion of our separate productive capacities in excess of the quantity which can be profitably marketed either internally or abroad. The result of this is obviously the certainty of establishing cut-throat competition among us with heavy financial losses to our respective economies.

The problem of African Unity must therefore be examined against the background of the economic position of the Independent African States, our aspirations for rapid development and the difficulties with which we are confronted in our separate existence. If we examine these problems carefully, we cannot evade the conclusion that the movement towards African political unity will substantially and immediately contribute to the solution of the economic problems of the Independent African States.

Indeed, I will make bold to state that African Unity based on a Continental Union Government is the only, I repeat only, possible framework within which the economic difficulties of Africa can be successfully and satisfactorily settled. The appeal for a Union Government of Africa is therefore not being made merely to satisfy a political end. It is absolutely indispensable for our economic survival in this modern world of ours.

We must remember that just as we had to obtain political independence from colonial rule as a necessary pre-requisite for establishing new and progressive communities for our respective States, so we cannot achieve economic stability in Africa as a whole without the pre-requisite of a continental Union Government.

Indeed, we cannot hope to sustain the economic development of Africa without first accepting the necessity for a continental division of labour to ensure that particular States specialized in their respective fields for which geographical, economic and social factors make them the most suitable, can develop to their fullest capacity with the best interest of the Continent as a whole in mind.

Take, for example, the steel industry. This could be developed to the highest possible limit in Nigeria, Egypt or Mauretania, or Liberia or Ghana, to mention only a few instances. If we do not unite under a federal government, it is clear that each of the States mentioned will wish in their own national interests to pursue the possibility of establishing and expanding its own steel mill.

Indeed, this is being done already by some of us to the benefit, profit and gain of foreign concerns.

If, however, our resources were combined to set up steel mills on a continental basis, at strategically chosen points in Africa, we would be in a position to make the greatest possible contribution to the industrial progress of the whole continent. Without a conscious effort based on a common governmental programme, we cannot hope to achieve this end. We might even find ourselves using the resources of one area of Africa to retard the progress and development of one or more other areas by cut-throat competition.

How then, at this moment of history, shall we meet this great challenge?

Certainly, we cannot blink at the harsh facts of life which are all too tragically familiar to us. This is especially true when we consider the economic development of Africa, on which all our other aspirations depend.

The most casual glance at our continent should convince anyone that the price of our disunity is continued exploitation from abroad and foreign interference in our internal matters. No matter where we look in the continent, we will find that, to a greater or lesser degree, the same pattern of exploitation persists.

For example: the economy of the Congo (Leopoldville) is still dominated by three foreign groups which represent Belgian, French, British and American interests. Herein lies the woe and tragedy of our beloved Congo. Two foreign firms – the Rhodesian Anglo-American Corporation and the Rhodesian Selection Trust – control the mining output of Zambia. Copper makes up eighty to ninety per cent of Zambia's exports, yet profits and interest shipped abroad annually often mount to as high as *half* of Zambia's total export earnings!

Thus you can see that despite political independence, nearly all of us here today are unable to exploit our agricultural and mineral resources in our own interests. Under a strong union government we would have the material resources for rapid industrialization, whereby all of us – big or small – would be benefited. But so long as we are divided, we will, to this extent, remain colonies in an economic sense. We shall remain puppets and agents of neo-colonialism.

The truth of this is even more evident when we examine monetary zones and customs unions. Most African States are still in monetary zones linked to the former colonial power. One-fourth of these States are in the sterling zone and one-half are in the franc zone. Owing to this currency arrangement, trade between the Independent African States is restricted and hampered. Indeed, trade is practically impossible within this financial environment.

An example of our present economic limitations as separate independent Governments, may be cited from our experience in our economic relations with our brothers from Upper Volta and Togo. Two years ago, in furtherance of our natural desire for closer collaboration in all fields of development with our Sister States, we performed a historic ceremony by breaking down the physical barriers established between Ghana and Upper Volta. The two Governments signed a long-term Trade and Payments Agreement under which each Government agreed to grant a non-interest bearing 'swing' credit of about two-hundred-and-fifty-thousand pounds sterling. The Bank of Ghana on behalf of the Government of Ghana was appointed as the technical Agent to operate the Payments Agreement. In the case of the Upper Volta Government, the Banque de l'Afrique Occidental was nominated by the Upper Volta Government as its Agent. To this day, the Banque de l'Afrique Occidental in Ouagadougou have refused to execute the banking arrangements drawn up by the bank of Ghana to implement the Agreement. Payment instructions issued by the Bank of Ghana to the Banque de l'Afrique Occidental have so far not been honoured.

On the other hand, the Bank of Ghana has been requested by the Banque de l'Afrique Occidental to transfer sterling in their favour before the Payments instructions will be carried out, in spite of the fact that it is expressly laid down in the Agreement that all payments to or from either country should be effected through the Clearing Account to be maintained by the two banks.

If the Agreement instituted between Ghana and Upper Volta had worked successfully, the operation of the French currency arrange-ments, which are the medium of commercial undertakings in Upper Volta, would have been seriously undermined. Is it therefore any wonder that the Banque de l'Afrique Occidental made the operation of an Agreement signed between two Sister African States with the best of intentions unworkable and inoperative? Our difficulties with the Republic of Togo arise from the same limitations.

It will be clear from these examples that until we in Africa are able to establish our own independent currency and financial institutions, we shall continue to be at the mercy of the financial arrangements imposed by foreign Governments in their own, and not in our, interest.

As long as the States of Africa remain divided, as long as we are forced to compete for foreign capital and to accept economic ties to foreign powers because in our separate entities we are too small, weak and unviable to 'go it alone', we will be unable to break the economic pattern of exploitation established in the days of outright colonialism.

Only if we can unite and carry out co-ordinated economic planning within the framework of African political unity, will it be possible for us to break the bonds of neo-colonialism and reconstruct our economies for the purpose of achieving real economic independence and higher living standards for all our African States, big or small.

Mr Chairman,

After all these arguments that have been advanced, can it still be maintained that a Union Government for Africa is premature? Have we not got the men? Have we not got the resources? Have we not got the will? What else are we waiting for? I know, and some of you know, that we can, right now, if we have the will and determination to do so. Mere resolutions cannot help us. Not even another Charter. The Ghana-Guinea Union, Casablanca Charter, Monrovia Charter and others, have long completed this Resolution and Charter-writing exercise.

Mr Chairman,

It is therefore with great honour and privilege that I now propose to you, Your Majesties, Brother Presidents and Prime Ministers, the framework for a Union Government of Africa.

This Union Government shall consist of an Assembly of Heads of State and Government headed by a President elected from among the Heads of State and Government of the Independent African States. The Executive of the Union Government will be a Cabinet or Council of Ministers with a Chancellor or Prime Minister as its head, and a Federal House consisting of two Chambers – The

Senate and a House of Representatives. If you agree, we can appoint our Foreign Ministers, assisted by experts, to work out a constitution for a Union Government of Africa.

Brother Presidents and Prime Ministers: with our common suffering and aspirations, we should be one and a united people. Our Continent, surrounded on all sides by oceans, is one of the most compact land masses in the world. Nature has endowed us with the richest and the best of natural resources. Circumstances and our common experience in history have made all of us a people with one destiny. Let us not betray the great promise of our future or disappoint the great hopes of the masses of our people by taking the wrong turning in this critical and momentous hour of decision.

We cannot save ourselves except through the unity of our continent based on common action through a Continental Union Government. Only a united Africa under a Union Government can cure us of our economic ills and lift us out of our despair and frustration.

I make this sincere and serious appeal in the interest of our common progress, our security and our future well-being. I hope that all of us will accept this appeal with equal sincerity. But I know that, for various reasons, some of us may not be ready or prepared to take this historic and momentous decision now.

Nevertheless, I charge those of us who are ready to do so now – even if we are only a few (and how I wish it could be all of us) – firstly, to come away from Cairo having agreed to the establishment of a Union Government of Africa.

Secondly, those of us who subscribe to this solemn agreement must designate our Foreign Ministers to constitute a Working Committee to draft the Constitution for the Federal Union Government of Africa.

Thirdly, those who subscribe to this agreement should, within six months, meet at a place to be agreed upon, to adopt and proclaim to the world the Federal Union Government of Africa.

Mr Chairman, Brother Presidents and Prime Ministers: It has been said that 'great things from little causes spring'. How true this saying is, can be judged from the beginnings of some of the world's Great Powers of today. The United States started within thirteen weak economically non-viable colonies exposed to serious political and economic hardships. Yet today, the United States of America is a world power with not less than fifty constituent states.

The Soviet Union, whose scientists have astounded the world with their interplanetary exploits, began their Union amid untold hardships and difficulties with but three States. Today, the Soviet Union is composed of sixteen federated States!

We cannot wait, we dare not wait, until we are encompassed by our doom for failing to seize this grand opportunity rising to the call of Africa's finest hour.

This is the challenge which history has thrust upon us. This is the mandate we have received from our people, that we set about to create a Union Government for Africa now; and this is also the challenge which Providence and destiny has thrust upon us. We cannot, we must not, we dare not fail or falter.

22

As soon as the decision was taken to hold the 1965 OAU Summit Conference in Accra, enemies of the African Revolution set to work to try to prevent the conference taking place in Ghana. Imperialist and neocolonialist agents did all they could to split the OAU, and whipped up vicious press campaigns. A deputation was sent to visit OAU States in an attempt to persuade them to boycott the conference if it was held in Accra. The excuse was made that Ghana was sheltering political refugees, and was assisting in the subversion of other African states.

The governments of Ivory Coast, Upper Volta, Dahomey, Niger (the 'Entente' States), and Togo, used this excuse to declare that they would not attend the conference if it was held in Accra. In order to remove the supposed grievance, the Ghana government expelled a number of political refugees whose presence had been resented, and their expulsions were confirmed by independent OAU observers. But the objecting states did not reciprocate by banishing Ghanaian political dissidents operating from their territories, nor did they agree to attend the Conference. It was clear that their real objection to the OAU Conference being held in Accra went far deeper than the question of political refugees, and concerned the proposals for Union Government which it was anticipated I would place before the member States. By boycotting the conference, the object was either to prevent it being held in Accra, or if it did take place, to sabotage it by making it very difficult for any real progress to be made towards a Union Government of Africa.

Although the opposition to the Accra Summit came from French-speaking African states not all the former French colonies were involved. Guinea and Mali, for example, were among the radical states supporting political unification.

It is an old imperialist tactic to try to use superficial differences to divide peoples they wish to continue to oppress and exploit. But they are up against a fundamental unifying factor which they cannot destroy, and that is the common experience of oppressed and exploited *peoples*, which binds them together and ignores differences of language, culture and traditions.

The underlying conflict, reflected in the feverish diplomatic manoeuverings before the Accra Summit in 1965, was not between the peoples of Africa, but between Africa as a whole and imperialism and neocolonialism working through puppet, reactionary regimes representing a small minority of indigenous bourgeois elements.

As it was, the opening of the conference had to be postponed for a month. The new conference buildings specially constructed for the occasion, had been completed within ten months, but the dates of the OAU conference coincided with the postponed Afro-Asian Conference in Algiers. In addition, it was hoped that a later start for the OAU conference might give time for a change of attitude on the part of the Entente States. But when in fact the conference opened in Accra on the 21st of October, 1965, the five Entente States and Togo were absent. Instead of going to Accra they met in Ouagadougou in Upper Volta, and announced that they would not attend the Accra Summit because the government of Ghana had not expelled all the families of the so-called subversive elements.

The absence of Ivory Coast, Upper Volta, Dahomey, Niger and Togo from the conference was a stab in the back for the OAU, but it did not prevent more than three quarters of the member states from voting in favour of my proposal for an OAU Executive Council to act as the executive arm of the Assembly of the Heads of State and Government. Of the 28 independent states which attended the conference, 22 voted for the immediate adoption of the proposals. But a two thirds vote, i.e. 24 of the total membership was needed to pass the resolution, and so it was agreed that the proposal should be referred back to the governments of the member states for further consideration, and a report be submitted to the next session of the Assembly. It was a disappointment not to get the proposals adopted there and then, but at least it had been clearly shown that the majority of states supported them, and I gave notice that I would place the question of the setting up of an Executive Council as an amendment to the Charter of the OAU.

I considered the setting up of an Executive Council was key to the future of the OAU, for without effective political machinery it could not hope to fulfil the purposes for which it was created. Already, by 1965, it had been powerless to deal with some of Africa's most pressing problems, and was being derided by some critics as a mere 'talking shop'. Freedom fighters engaged in a life and death struggle with imperialism are not impressed with the passing of resolutions unless they result in positive action in the form of supplies, training facilities, and so on. The OAU like the UN, was proving to be no better than the governments which controlled it, and the peoples whose interests it was formed to serve were in danger of being betrayed.

The first question to be discussed when the Accra conference opened was the crisis in Rhodesia. Somalia and other member states called for the immediate adoption of a resolution prepared at the meeting of foreign ministers which preceded the conference. At the request of Dr Banda of Malawi the conference at once went into secret session, and from then on the sessions remained private except for formal announcements and the concluding session. After much discussion there was agreement on a resolution on Rhodesia which called on the British government to suspend the 1961 constitution and to take over the administration of the country. The resolution went on to urge Britain to release all political prisoners, including Joshua Nkomo and the Reverend Sithole, and to call a constitutional conference of representatives of the entire population. Independence should be based only on one man one vote, and free elections. It called on the UN to regard a unilateral declaration of independence (UDI) as a threat to international peace, and to take steps to deal with any such contingency. It further urged all governments and international bodies not to recognize a white minority government in Rhodesia, and to apply sanctions against it. If Britain granted or tolerated UDI, all OAU members should reconsider their economic, diplomatic and financial relations with the British government, and use all possible means, including the use of force, to oppose UDI.

The conference went on to call on the UN Security Council and General Assembly to regard the situation in South Africa, and the increasing collaboration between S. Africa, Portugal and the minority government in Rhodesia as a serious threat to international peace and security. A strong call was made to all states to give maximum help to the liberation movements.

On the question of political refugees, member states agreed that they must be given shelter provided that they did not engage in subversive activities against any OAU state. Representatives of liberation movements throughout Africa met in Accra at the time of the OAU Summit, and discussed common problems. It was hoped that they might create a united liberation movement and a common strategy for all oppressed areas. But although there were very useful discussions, no unified organization was established to combine strategy and tactics, and to organize the struggle as a whole. Similarly, the OAU failed to set up a single African High Command, though a resolution was passed agreeing to the principle of co-ordination in the military field.

Developments in Africa since the 1965 OAU Summit Conference in Accra have shown with tragic clarity the hopelessness of trying to solve Africa's problems without unified political machinery to carry through the complete liberation of the continent and the full development of Africa's economic potential, through the optimum zone of development, for the benefit of her own people.

A NEW AFRICA—SPEECH AT THE OPENING OF THE SUMMIT CONFERENCE OF THE O.A.U., ACCRA, 21 OCTOBER 1965

YOUR IMPERIAL MAJESTY, BROTHERS AND COLLEAGUES,

No honour is greater for me personally and for the Government and people of Ghana than that we should have the privilege of extending to you, distinguished and eminent sons of Africa, our humble hospitality and sincere welcome.

I am particularly happy that I should have lived long enough to witness with you here the historic and momentous spectacle of this great assembly of the leaders and representatives of the Independent States of Africa.

We are glad to recall today memories of our struggles for independence; our prophetic imaginings of a new Africa emancipated from colonial chains, standing united and ready to play its historic role in world affairs. The dreams of generations are being steadily realized and fulfilled in many ways. Today, we raise our voices above the earth and to the world, not as the oppressed and downtrodden of mankind, but with the reborn dignity and strength of a people confident in themselves and certain of their future. It is in this spirit and with humility but with a sense of pride in our destiny that I stand before you to offer you, distinguished compatriots, a truly African welcome to Ghana.

Let me take this opportunity to welcome into our midst Brother Dawda Jawara, Prime Minister of the Gambia, who takes his seat among us for the first time. Gambia's accession to independence is of great significance to us because her independence closes the chapter of British and French colonialism in this part of our Continent.

Among us here also in the capacity of observers are the representatives of our courageous Freedom Fighters in the remaining territories of Africa still under the yoke of colonial rule.

On this historic occasion our minds must be filled with the suffering and heroism of our brothers in South Africa, Angola, Mozambique, Basutoland, Swaziland, Bechuanaland, South West Africa and the so-called Portuguese and Spanish possessions in Africa, whose mounting struggle for freedom and independence is also our struggle. Every minute, every moment, that passes sees the intensification of this struggle. Our Freedom Fighters refuse to bend their knees to colonial oppression. We salute them. Allow me to assure them in your name, that we stand by them; their struggle is our struggle, and we are determined that they shall soon come to share with us the benefits of freedom and independence, and the responsibilities of managing their own affairs in a united Africa.

The liberation of the whole of our continent, and the restoration of freedom and dignity to those of our brothers who are still under the colonial yoke remain our most important and immediate tasks, but we cannot forget that we are an integral part of humanity involved in all conflicts, perils, strivings and hopes of the human race all over the globe.

We cannot ignore the fact that the same imperialist forces which exploit and subvert our independent States, and which exploit and oppress our peoples in the remaining colonial enclaves of Africa, are the very same forces which breed armed conflicts, civil strife and economic impoverishment on other continents.

It would be folly for us to dream of Africa as a peaceful and thriving continent in the midst of a world convulsed by armed conflicts, tormented by hunger and disease and continually menaced by imperialist intrigue and aggression.

The armed conflict in Vietnam presents a grave peril to world peace. We must find a way to end that conflict permanently, if the world is to live in peace. In the same way, we must find the means to end the conflict over Kashmir permanently.

We in Africa believe that the unhappy conflict between India and Pakistan can be of benefit to nobody except the imperialists, the colonialists and the neo-colonialists.

We must also find a way of putting an end to the current wave of aggression and armed conflicts which are today threatening the peace of the world and causing so much suffering.

We in Africa therefore demand the establishment of an Atom Free Zone; we demand the ultimate destruction of nuclear stock-piles wherever they may be and the banning of their manufacture. On these and other issues we expect the world to respect our point of view, our stand, our heritage and our freedom and independence.

Brothers and Colleagues, we are enjoined by the Charter of the OAU to harness the material and human resources of our great and ancient continent for the well-being of all our people. From the experience of the last two years, are we sure that the Charter as it stands at present contains adequate provisions to enable us to achieve this?

The people of Africa are waiting in anxious expectation for a concrete and constructive programme which will assist them to realize their hopes and aspirations. They know their suffering; they know how heavy is their burden and we who are here today know too that if we fail them – woe betide us!

It is true that all of us here are dedicated to the progress of Africa, and that we are determined to forge stronger bonds of unity in the interests of the welfare and happiness of the African people as a whole.

It is also true that a number of resolutions and declarations have been made and adopted, not only by our Summit Conference, but also by the Council of Ministers and by the various Commissions of the OAU. It is proper that we should have made and adopted these resolutions in the interests of African Unity, but unless an effective political machinery is devised, to implement these resolutions, they remain no more than words on paper.

In spite of these resolutions and declarations, in spite of all good intentions, in spite of our plans, the naked fact, alas, is that Africa is still an impoverished continent, immobilized by the lack of political cohesion, harrassed by imperialism and ransacked by neocolonialism. That is so because our unity is still incomplete and ineffective in the face of grave threats to our existence. What use is it to us then that our continent is so rich in material and human resources? Brothers and Colleagues, the fault is in ourselves, not in our stars.

As I speak to you now the situation in Southern Rhodesia constitutes a grave threat to the peace of Africa. The racialist minority which has been allowed to assume power in this British Colony now believes that its colonial constitution is not designed to enable it to introduce a complete version of apartheid in that colony. The racialist regime now threatens to take the law into its own hands and to make a unilateral declaration of independence. We recognize that Britain, as the metropolitan power bears the ultimate responsibility for the conduct of the colonial regime and for the maintenance of law and order in the colony. But we in Africa cannot remain indifferent to the fate of four million Africans in that territory, and cannot allow an extension of the vile, inhuman system of apartheid to other parts of Africa. We call on the British Government to do its duty and to fulfil its obligations towards all the citizens in its colony of Southern Rhodesia. If armed force is required to bring the rebellious elements in the Colony to order, we expect the United Kingdom Government to use force to quell the rebellion. In the event of the United Kingdom Government failing in its duty, I am sure that the member states of the OAU will take whatever steps are necessary in support of the four million Africans who form the majority in Southern Rhodesia.

Whatever the outcome of the present crisis, the struggle for the liberation of our brothers in Southern Rhodesia will not be abandoned by the Organization of African Unity any more than it can be abandoned by the oppressed majority. We call on the British Government to realize that the peace of Africa is immediately involved in the present crisis in Rhodesia and that the only safety and prosperity which the white settler minority can find is in a just and democratic constitution which allows the majority to rule for the benefit of all the people in the territory.

Another issue which requires our urgent attention at this Conference is the problem of political refugees. Political refugees are a recent phenomenon in this continent, and they have arisen as an outcome of the struggle for independence. Indeed so extensive is this question that there is perhaps not one independent African State today which has no political refugee problem. While in the fight against colonialism, we can expect a large measure of political cohesion and unity of purpose, what happens thereafter is a different matter. The responsibility for safeguarding political freedom, once it has been won, and the responsibility for fostering national development are not seen in the same light by those who only yesterday were colleagues and comrades-in-arms.

Thus we find that Ivory Coast opposition elements come into hiding in Ghana; that Ghanaian dissidents go to live in Nigeria Togo and the Ivory Coast. We find similar problems and difficulties virtually everywhere in Africa.

We are all aware of the international convention which recognizes that any sovereign state can permit political refugees from another country to dwell in its territory. In a speech to the National Assembly on the Geneva Agreement which Ghana, and some other African States have ratified, I added an over-riding condition that they do not carry out on our soil political activities aimed against their own country. It would indeed be a sad reflection on our organization, if even one African, whose well-being and progress is the duty of everyone of us here, is permitted to wander around this continent, a reproach and a by-word among all men, an outcast, deprived of food and shelter, a stateless individual, hounded from State to State, from country to country, without friends, and every man's hands against him.

As long as political boundaries persist in Africa, boundaries which we have inherited at independence and were drawn arbitrarily, with no heed to the ethnic, economic, and social realities of Africa, so long shall we be plagued by the political refugee problem.

The political refugee problem is a social and political problem, and its only solution lies in an all-African Union Government within which our present boundaries will become links instead of barriers.

In the national Constitution of Ghana, we have provision for the full or partial surrender of our sovereignty to an all-African Union. No member State should or can be expected to surrender its sovereignty for any lesser cause.

History is made only by bold ventures and not by retreating in the face of difficulties.

Those who argue that the time is not ripe or that the difficulties are too great for the establishment of a Continental Union Government are not recognizing the imperative needs of the African Continent or the overwhelming wishes and desires of the masses of the people of Africa.

We can delay no longer in taking the economic destiny of Africa into our own hands. Since the founding of the Organization of Africa Unity at Addis Ababa, world trade has moved further and faster into the channels prepared by neo-colonialism. The increased productivity of our wealthy continent has benefited not us, but the industrial nations. By depressing the prices of our raw materials and metals, they have stunted our economic progress. By raising the prices of their manufactured goods they have drained away any surpluses we might have acquired. The deliberate policy of neo-colonialism emerges, not only to rob us of our wealth, but to prevent us from acquiring capital for our own development.

Those of us who are in the European Common Market and those of us outside it are equally rocked by economic storms and in danger of economic shipwreck. Everywhere in Africa, our economies are crumbling, our treasuries are getting empty, we are becoming client States, none of us can stand alone. We will remain in that condition until we take the economic and political destiny of Africa into our own hands.

An African Common Market of three hundred million producers and consumers should have a productivity, a purchasing and bargaining power equal to any of those trading and currency blocs which now rule the commerce of the world.

Who is there to oppose or frustrate us, if we only have the courage to form an all-African Union Government. Can the industrialized nations do without our copper, our uranium, our iron ore, our bauxite, our coffee, cocoa, cotton, groundnuts, palm oil – or will they come running to us, as we have been running to them for trade on equitable terms? It is courage that we lack, not wealth.

It is true that we have made half-hearted attempts at economic co-operation, but without the drive and authority which can only come from political action. In this connection, let me quote the words of Brother Nyerere of Tanzania:

'For Africa, the lesson of our East African experience is that although economic co-operation can go a long way without political integration, there comes a point when movement must be either forward or backward – forward into political decision or backward into reduced economic co-operation.'

The OAU must face such a choice now – we can either move forward to progress through an effective African Union or step backward into stagnation, instability and confusion – an easy prey for foreign intervention, interferences and subversion.

We have a market which can absorb the produce of modern giant enterprises. We have already through the efforts of the United Nations established an African Development Bank. There are recommendations adopted by the Addis Ababa Summit Conference as well as by the ECA concerning the establishment of a common monetary zone. What is left now is to create a Union Central Bank to back our individual currencies. The decision to create a Central Bank for Africa is a political one. Why is it that we are finding it difficult to take this decision in spite of so many resolutions, declarations and attempts ? If Africa had one political front, a central machinery, such a decision would not be difficult to take and achieve.

Nothing that has happened since our Addis Ababa or Cairo meetings has caused me to alter my mind about the necessity of a Union Government for Africa. On the contrary the growing perils in Africa and on the international scene, the growing strictures on world trade, the growing impoverishment of our primary producers, the persistent border disputes in Africa, the increasing instability caused by interference and subversive activities, the continued defiance and insolence of the racist minority regimes in South Africa and Southern Rhodesia – all these urge me to continue our pursuit for the political unification of Africa.

Our poverty, in the midst of our unbounded wealth; our weakness in spite of our unbounded might; the greatness of our need and the justice of our cause; the cry of our hungry and oppressed countrymen, as well as the courage and readiness to make further sacrifices by our liberation forces – all these urge me to restate my conviction that we must give political form or reality to our unity.

I am more than ever convinced that Africa should unite into one state with a Union Government. This is the view which I stated at Addis Ababa in 1963 and in Cairo last year, and I still hold to this position.

It is clear from the shortcomings and difficulties experienced in the running of the OAU that it is necessary to strengthen the Charter of the OAU by providing an effective machinery which will enable us to work effectively and successfully for the realization of our noble aims and objectives. Furthermore, the Heads of State and Government and the Council of Ministers cannot in practice meet as often as the imperative issues of a great continent demand.

I have never wavered in my conviction that the most effective form for the unity of Africa is a single African State, wielding its power through a Continental Union Government. In fact, everything that has happened since our first meeting in Addis Ababa has strengthened me in this conviction.

At the same time, in order to meet the views expressed by some of my Brothers and Colleagues, and to achieve as much unity as is possible now, I put forward the following proposals.

We should set up now a full-time body or Executive Council of the OAU to act as the Executive arm of the Assembly of the Heads of State and Government. The Assembly of Heads of State and Government shall appoint from among themselves a Chairman for the Executive Council which will be responsible for implementing the decisions of the Assembly of Heads of State and Government.

I also propose that this body shall be responsible for initiating policies and making recommendations to the Assembly of Heads of State and Government on matters pertaining to the aims and objectives of the OAU as set out in Article Two of the Charter.

Under my proposals, the Assembly of Heads of State and Government shall continue to be the supreme Governing Body of the OAU in Article Eight of our Charter. I further propose that the Assembly shall elect a Union President and a number of Union Vice-Presidents to meet periodically during the ensuing year in order to review the work of the Executive Council when the Assembly is not in session.

The General Secretariat of the OAU shall be the Secretariat of the Executive Council.

I am confident, Brothers and Colleagues, that from our deliberations we shall leave yet another significant mark on the history of our times. A United Africa is destined to be a great force in world affairs. So the battle is joined, and we cannot disengage, until the wishes and aspirations of our people have been met. Just as in the 1950's we stood abreast and solid in the vanguard of Africa's liberation movement, so in the 1960's we shall see an even greater struggle for the fruits of the African revolution – a new and unified society without which the peoples of Africa cannot independently survive or prosper: Africa shall be a bright star among the constellation of Nations.

23

My purpose in writing *Neo-Colonialism: The Last Stage of Imperialism* was to expose the workings of international monopoly capitalism in Africa in order to show the meaninglessness of political freedom without economic independence, and to demonstrate the urgent need for the unification of Africa and a socialist transformation of society.

The US State Department reacted sharply to the publication of the book, and in an Aide Memoire protested particularly against Chapter 18 where I drew attention to the activities in Africa of the Peace Corps, the US Information Services, the US Agency for International Development, and to the World Bank. The State Department considered the book 'anti-American in tone', though it was neocolonialist practices and not governments which were attacked in the book.

The State Department followed up its protest with the rejection of a request from my government for 35 million dollars' worth of surplus food shipments. A headline in the New York Herald Tribune of Wednesday, 24th November, 1965 declared: 'Ghana Bites US hand so Feeding is Halted'. The State Department protest was conveyed orally by Mennen Williams, the Assistant Secretary of State for African Affairs, in a meeting with

Miguel Augustus Ribeiro, the Ghanaian ambassador to the USA. The rejection of the food-for-peace aid request followed two days later. The text of the US Aide Memoire delivered by Mennen Williams to Ribeiro on 18 November 1965 was contained in a telegram from Ribeiro to the Ministry of Foreign Affairs in Accra. It read as follows:

I refer to my cyphered message WA/484 of 2nd November on American reaction to Osagyefo's latest book 'Neo-Colonialism'.

At 12.30 this afternoon Governor Mennen Williams, on behalf of the United States Government, handed me a formal Aide-Memoire protesting against alleged attacks by Osagyefo on the (United States) in (public). I quote below the text of the protest:

'The United States has noted with profound alarm the attacks against the United States in President Nkrumah's book, *Neo-Colonialism: The Last Stage of Imperialism*. This represents an unprecedented attack by the Head of State of a friendly country against the United States, a country which has by word and deed shown repeatedly over the years its desire to maintain friendly relations with the people and government of Ghana.

The book appears to have been designed for the specific purpose of creating in the minds of its readers suspicion and distrust of the motives, intentions and actions of the United States. The hostility of the book exhibits, particularly in Chapter 18, and its general provocation and anti-American tone, are deeply disturbing and offensive to the Government's goodwill.

The Government of the United States actually therefore holds the Government of Ghana fully responsible for whatever consequences the book's publication may have.'

Before handing in the protest Mr Mennen Williams expressed his personal disappointment and that of his government at the attacks on the United States which are considered by them to be very hostile.

I explained that nothing had been stated in the book which had not been said before even by American writers as evidenced by the profuse quotations from the book entitled 'Invisible Government' and that (far from) sharp sentences intending to attack the United States, it could be inferred from arguments and conclusions in the book that Osagyefo's real intention was to point out to his fellow African leaders the dangers that disunity exposes them to, and the need for the formation of a Union Government of Africa. I assured him also of Osagyefo's high regard for the person of President Johnson and pointed out that neither from books created from Osagyefo's past record could anyone justifiably accuse Osagyefo of indulging in personal attacks on heads of Governments even though some other heads of Governments had from time to time attacked Osagyefo personally. I emphasized that what Osagyefo has attacked is a system and not the American President and Government. Needless to say the Governor Williams was not convinced.

I was given the impression that the protest may not be the last word of the issue. I advise that the protest be taken seriously and an appropriate reply be sent at an early date through me or the United States Charge d'Affaires and copied to me.

According to an article which appeared in the *Baltimore Sun* on 23 November 1965, State department officials denied that the rejection of Ghana's request for food-for-peace aid was directly connected with the publication of *Neo-Colonialism*. But they did not deny that relations between the USA and Ghana had reached 'a new low as a result of Nkrumah's charges that the United States is foremost among the neocolonialist powers seeking to exploit and subjugate the African continent'. What appeared to annoy the State Department was the timing of the publication, and the fact that copies of the book were circulated among the African heads of state and their delegations attending the OAU Summit meeting in Accra in October 1965.

Neocolonialism is a stage in the development of imperialism. In the sub-title of my book I refer to it as the 'last stage' since I considered it the last thrust of imperialism before the ultimate and inevitable victory of the masses over all forms of oppression and exploitation. The 'last stage' may be said to have developed with full force after the Second World War, in 1945. Before then, neocolonialism had reared its head in Latin America and elsewhere, though it was not until after the Second World War that neocolonialism became the predominant expression of imperialism.

Neocolonialism is more insidious, complex and dangerous than the old colonialism. It not only prevents its victims from developing their economic potential for their own use, but it controls the political life of the country, and supports the indigenous bourgeoisie in perpetuating the oppression and exploitation of the masses. Under neocolonialism, the economic systems and political policies of independent territories are managed and manipulated from outside, by international monopoly finance capital in league with the indigenous bourgeoisie.

The policy of balkanization pursued by the imperialist powers when forced to concede political independence in Asia, Africa and Latin America, reflects the strategy of neocolonialism – the intention being to ensure their continued exploitation and oppression.

In Africa, most of the independent states are economically unviable, and still have the artificial frontiers of colonialism. They are easy prey for the voracious appetites of neocolonialist empire builders. Where political balkanization has not been successful for the imperialists, economic balkanization has been pursued. A single productive process is divided between states. Communications, banking, insurance, and other key services are controlled by neocolonialists. Then regional economic groupings in Africa have been encouraged, controlled by neocolonialists, which therefore further strengthen international finance capital. Backing up these processes, the power of international monopoly finance is used to force down the price of raw materials, and to keep up the price of foreign manufactured goods.

In recent times, a further tactic of neocolonialism is to appear to support liberation movements, and even to give donations to them, where such movements are thought to be the expression of bourgeois nationalism, and not the outcome of genuine socialist revolutionary effort. For the ending of direct colonial rule and the emergence of a puppet government facilitates neocolonialism by opening the door to exploitation from a wider range of neocolonialists than those represented by a single former colonial power. By concentrating on political struggles to end direct colonial rule, or to force minority regimes to grant reforms, attention is diverted from economic and domestic issues, and the insidious processes of neocolonialism can proceed. Meanwhile, many of the puppet rulers of Africa masquerade as 'revolutionaries' and 'liberators', and serve the interest of their neocolonialist masters by trying to mask the reactionary nature of their regimes.

It is very significant, that of all my books, *Neo-colonialism* is the only one which has caused a government to register a formal protest.

EXTRACTS FROM *NEO-COLONIALISM: THE LAST STAGE OF IMPERIALISM*

INTRODUCTION

The neo-colonialism of today represents imperialism in its final and perhaps its most dangerous stage. In the past it was possible to convert a country upon which a neo-colonial regime had been imposed – Egypt in the nineteenth century is an example – into a colonial territory. Today this process is no longer feasible. Old-fashioned colonialism is by no means entirely abolished. It still constitutes an African problem, but it is everywhere on the retreat. Once a territory has become nominally independent it is no longer possible, as it was in the last century, to reverse the process. Existing colonies may linger on, but no new colonies will be created. In place of colonialism as the main instrument of imperialism we have today neo-colonialism.

The essence of neo-colonialism is that the State which is subject to it is, in theory, independent and has all the outward trappings of international sovereignty. In reality its economic system and thus its political policy is directed from outside.

The methods and form of this direction can take various shapes. For example, in an extreme case the troops of the imperial power may garrison the territory of the neo-colonial State and control the government of it. More often, however, neo-colonialist control is exercised through economic or monetary means. The neo-colonial State may be obliged to take the manufactured products of the imperialist power to the exclusion of competing products from elsewhere. Control over government policy in the neo-colonial State may be secured by payments towards the cost of running the State, by the provision of civil servants in positions where they can dictate policy and by monetary control over foreign exchange through the imposition of a banking system controlled by the imperial power.

Where neo-colonialism exists the power exercising control is often the State which formerly ruled the territory in question, but this is not necessarily so. For example, in the case of South Vietnam the former imperial power was France, but neo-colonial control of the State has now gone to the United States. It is possible that neo-colonial control may be exercised by a consortium of financial interests which are not specifically identifiable with any particular State. The control of the Congo by great international financial concerns is a case in point.

The result of neo-colonialism is that foreign capital is used for the exploitation rather than for the development of the less developed parts of the world. Investment under neo-colonialism increases rather than decreases the gap between the rich and the poor countries of the world.

The struggle against neo-colonialism is not aimed at excluding the capital of the developed world from operating in less developed countries. It is aimed at preventing the financial power of the developed countries being used in such a way as to impoverish the less developed.

Non-alignment, as practised by Ghana and many other countries, is based on co-operation with all States whether they be capitalist, socialist or have a mixed economy. Such a policy, therefore, involves foreign investment from capitalist countries, but it must be invested in accordance with a national plan drawn up by the government of the non-aligned State with its own interests in mind. The issue is not what return the foreign investor receives on his investments. He may, in fact, do better for himself if he invests in a non-aligned country than if he invests in a neo-colonial one. The question is one of power. A State in the grip of neo-colonialism is not master of its own destiny. It is this factor which makes neo-colonialism such a serious threat to world peace. The growth of nuclear weapons has made out of date the old-fashioned balance of power which rested upon the ultimate sanction of a major war. Certainty of mutual mass destruction effectively prevents either of the great power blocs from threatening the other with the possibility of a world-wide war, and military conflict has thus become confined to 'limited wars'. For these neo-colonialism is the breeding ground.

Such wars can, of course take place in countries which are not neo-colonialist controlled. Indeed their object may be to establish in a small but independent country a neo-colonialist regime. The evil of neo-colonialism is that it prevents the formation of those large units which would make impossible 'limited war'. To give one example: if Africa was united, no major power bloc would attempt to subdue it by limited war because from the very nature of limited war, what can be achieved by it is itself limited. It is only where small States exist that it is possible, by landing a few thousand marines or by financing a mercenary force, to secure a decisive result.

The restriction of military action of 'limited wars' is, however, no guarantee of world peace and is likely to be the factor which will ultimately involve the great power blocs in a world war, however much both are determined to avoid it.

Limited war, once embarked upon, achieves a momentum of its own. Of this, the war in South Vietnam is only one example. It escalates despite the desire of the great power blocs to keep it limited. While this particular war may be prevented from leading to a world conflict, the multiplication of similar limited wars can only have one end – world war and the terrible consequences of nuclear conflict.

Neo-colonialism is also the worst form of imperialism. For those who practise it, it means power without responsibility and for those who suffer from it, it means exploitation without redress. In the days of old-fashioned colonialism, the imperial power had at least to explain and justify at home the actions it was taking abroad. In the colony those who served the ruling imperial power could at least look to its protection against any violent move by their opponents. With neo-colonialism neither is the case.

Above all, neo-colonialism, like colonialism before it, postpones the facing of the social issues which will have to be faced by the fully developed sector of the world before the danger of world war can be eliminated or the problem of world poverty resolved.

Neo-colonialism, like colonialism, is an attempt to export the social conflicts of the capitalist countries. The temporary success of this policy can be seen in the ever widening gap between the richer

316

and the poorer nations of the world. But the internal contradictions and conflicts of neo-colonialism make it certain that it cannot endure as a permanent world policy. How it should be brought to an end is a problem that should be studied, above all, by the developed nations of the world, because it is they who will feel the full impact of the ultimate failure. The longer it continues the more certain it is that its inevitable collapse will destroy the social system of which they had made it a foundation.

The reason for its development in the post-war period can be briefly summarized. The problem which faced the wealthy nations of the world at the end of the second world war was the impossibility of returning to the pre-war situation in which there was a great gulf between the few rich and the many poor. Irrespective of what particular political party was in power, the internal pressures in the rich countries of the world were such that no post-war capitalist country could survive unless it became a 'Welfare State'. There might be differences in degree in the extent of the social benefits given to the industrial and agricultural workers, but what was everywhere impossible was a return to the mass unemployment and to the low level of living of the pre-war years.

From the end of the nineteenth century onwards, colonies had been regarded as a source of wealth which could be used to mitigate the class conflicts in the capitalist States and, as will be explained later, this policy had some success. But it failed in its ultimate object because the pre-war capitalist States were so organized internally that the bulk of the profit made from colonial possessions found its way into the pockets of the capitalist class and not into those of the workers. Far from achieving the object intended, the working-class parties at times tended to identify their interests with those of the colonial peoples and the imperialist powers found themselves engaged upon a conflict on two fronts, at home with their own workers and abroad against the growing forces of colonial liberation.

The post-war period inaugurated a very different colonial policy. A deliberate attempt was made to divert colonial earnings from the wealthy class and use them instead generally to finance the 'Welfare State'. As will be seen from the examples given later, this was a method consciously adopted even by those working-class leaders who had before the war regarded the colonial peoples as their natural allies against their capitalist enemies at home.

At first it was presumed that this object could be achieved by maintaining the pre-war colonial system. Experience soon proved that attempts to do so would be disastrous and would only provoke colonial wars, thus dissipating the anticipated gains from the continuance of the colonial regime. Britain, in particular, realized this at an early stage and the correctness of the British judgement at the time has subsequently been demonstrated by the defeat of French colonialism in the Far East and Algeria and the failure of the Dutch to retain any of their former colonial empire.

The system of neo-colonialism was therefore instituted and in the short run it has served the developed powers admirably. It is in the long run that its consequences are likely to be catastrophic for them.

Neo-colonialism is based upon the principle of breaking up former large united colonial territories into a number of small non-viable States which are incapable of independent development and must rely upon the former imperial power for defence and even internal security. Their economic and financial systems are linked, as in colonial days, with those of the former colonial ruler.

At first sight the scheme would appear to have many advantages for the developed countries of the world. All the profits of neo-colonialism can be secured if, in any given area, a reasonable proportion of the States have a neo-colonialist system. It is not necessary that they *all* should have one. Unless small States can combine they must be compelled to sell their primary products at prices dictated by the developed nations and buy their manufactured goods at the prices fixed by them. So long as neo-colonialism can prevent political and economic conditions for optimum development, the developing countries, whether they are under neo-colonialist control or not, will be unable to create a large enough market to support industrialization. In the same way they will lack the financial strength to force the developed countries to accept their primary products at a fair price.

In the neo-colonialist territories, since the former colonial power has in theory relinquished political control, if the social conditions occasioned by neo-colonialism cause a revolt the loyal neo-colonialist government can be sacrificed and another equally subservient one substituted in its place. On the other hand, in any continent where neo-colonialism exists on a wide scale the same social pressures which can produce revolts in neo-colonial territories will also affect those States which have refused to accept the system and therefore neo-colonialist nations have a ready-made weapon with which they can threaten their opponents if they appear successfully to be challenging the system.

These advantages, which seem at first sight so obvious, are, however, on examination, illusory because they fail to take into consideration the facts of the world today.

The introduction of neo-colonialism increases the rivalry between the great powers which was provoked by the old-style colonialism. However little real power the government of a neo-colonialist State may possess, it must have, from the very fact of its nominal independence, a certain area of manoeuvre. It may not be able to exist without a neo-colonialist master but it may still have the ability to change masters.

The ideal neo-colonialist State would be one which was wholly subservient to neo-colonialist interests but the existence of the socialist nations makes it impossible to enforce the full rigour of the neo-colonialist system. The existence of an alternative system is itself a challenge to the neo-colonialist regime. Warnings about 'the dangers of Communist subversion' are likely to be two-edged since they bring to the notice of those living under a neo-colonialist system the possibility of a change of regime. In fact neo-colonialism is the victim of its own contradictions. In order to make it attractive to those upon whom it is practised it must be shown as capable of raising their living standards, but the economic object of neo-colonialism is to keep those standards depressed in the interest of the developed countries. It is only when this contradiction is understood that the failure of innumerable 'aid' programmes, many of them well intentioned, can be explained.

In the first place, the rulers of neo-colonial States derive their authority to govern, not from the will of the people, but from the support which they obtain from their neo-colonialist masters. They have therefore little interest in developing education, strengthening the bargaining power of their workers employed by expatriate firms, or indeed of taking any step which would challenge the colonial pattern of commerce and industry, which it is the object of neo-colonialism to preserve. 'Aid', therefore, to a neo-colonial State is merely a revolving credit, paid by the neo-colonial master, passing through the neo-colonial State and returning to the neo-colonial master in the form of increased profits.

Secondly, it is in the field of 'aid' that the rivalry of individual developed States first manifests itself. So long as neo-colonialism persists so long will spheres of interest persist, and this makes multilateral aid – which is in fact the only effective form of aid – impossible.

Once multilateral aid begins the neo-colonialist masters are faced by the hostility of the vested interests in their own country. Their manufacturers naturally object to any attempt to raise the price of the raw materials which they obtain from the neo-colonialist territory in question, or to the establishment there of manufacturing industries which might compete directly or indirectly with their own exports to the territory. Even education is suspect as likely to produce a student movement and it is, of course, true that in many less developed countries the students have been in the vanguard of the fight against neo-colonialism.

In the end the situation arises that the only type of aid which the neo-colonialist masters consider as safe is 'military aid'.

Once a neo-colonialist territory is brought to such a state of economic chaos and misery that revolt actually breaks out then, and only then, is there no limit to the generosity of the neo-colonial overlord, provided, of course, that the funds supplied are utilized exclusively for military purposes.

Military aid in fact marks the last stage of neo-colonialism and its effect is self-destructive. Sooner or later the weapons supplied pass into the hands of the opponents of the neo-colonialist regime and the war itself increases the social misery which originally provoked it.

Neo-colonialism is a mill-stone around the necks of the developed countries which practise it. Unless they can rid themselves of it, it will drown them. Previously the developed powers could escape from the contradictions of neo-colonialism by substituting for it direct colonialism. Such a solution is no longer possible and the reasons for it have been well explained by Mr Owen Lattimore, the United States Far Eastern expert and adviser to Chiang Kai-shek in the immediate post-war period. He wrote:

'Asia, which was so easily and swiftly subjugated by conquerors in the eighteenth and nineteenth centuries, displayed an amazing ability stubbornly to resist modern armies equipped with aeroplanes, tanks, motor vehicles and mobile artillery.

Formerly big territories were conquered in Asia with small forces. Income, first of all from plunder, then from direct taxes and lastly from trade, capital investments and long-term exploitation, covered with incredible speed the expenditure for military operations. This arithmetic represented a great temptation to strong countries. Now they have run up against another arithmetic, and it discourages them.'

The same arithmetic is likely to apply throughout the less developed world.

This book is therefore an attempt to examine neo-colonialism not only in its African context and its relation to African unity, but in world perspective. Neo-colonialism is by no means exclusively an African question. Long before it was practised on any large scale in Africa it was an established system in other parts of the world. Nowhere has it proved successful, either in raising living standards or in ultimately benefiting the countries which have indulged in it.

Marx predicted that the growing gap between the wealth of the possessing classes and the workers it employs would ultimately produce a conflict fatal to capitalism in each individual capitalist State.

This conflict between the rich and the poor has now been transferred on to the international scene, but for proof of what is acknowledged to be happening it is no longer necessary to consult the classical Marxist writers. The situation is set out with the utmost clarity in the leading organs of capitalist opinion. Take for example the following extracts from *The Wall Street Journal*, the newspaper which perhaps best reflects United States capitalist thinking.

In its issue of 12th May, 1965, under the headline of 'Poor Nations' Plight', the paper first analyses 'which countries are considered industrial and which backward'. There is, it explains, 'no rigid method of classification'. Nevertheless, it points out:

'A generally used breakdown, however, has recently been maintained by the International Monetary Fund because, in the words of an IMF official, "the economic demarcation in the world is getting increasingly apparent". The breakdown, the official says, "is based on simple common sense".

In the IMF's view, the industrial countries are the United States, the United Kingdom, most West European nations, Canada and Japan. A special category called "other developed areas" includes such other European lands as Finland, Greece and Ireland, plus Australia, New Zealand and South Africa. The IMF's "less developed" category embraces all of Latin America and nearly all of the Middle East, non-Communist Asia and Africa.'

In other words the 'backward' countries are those situated in the neo-colonial areas.

After quoting figures to support its argument, *The Wall Street Journal* comments on this situation:

'The industrial nations have added nearly $2 billion to their reserves, which now approximate $52 billion. At the same time, the reserves of the less-developed group not only have stopped rising, but have declined some $200 million. To analysts such as Britain's Miss Ward, the significance of such statistics is clear: the economic gap is rapidly widening "between a white, complacent, highly bourgeois, very wealthy, very small North Atlantic elite and everybody else, and this is not a very comfortable heritage to leave to one's children".

"Everybody else" includes approximately two-thirds of the population of the earth, spread through about 100 nations.'

This is no new problem. In the opening paragraph of his book, *The War on World Poverty*, written in 1953, the present British Labour leader, Mr Harold Wilson, summarized the major problem of the world as he then saw it:

'For the vast majority of mankind the most urgent problem is not war, or Communism, or the cost of living, or taxation. It is hunger. Over 1,500,000,000 people, something like two-thirds of the world's population, are living in conditions of acute hunger, defined in terms of identifiable nutritional disease. This hunger is at the same time the effect and the cause of the poverty, squalor and misery in which they live.'

Its consequences are likewise understood. The correspondent of *The Wall Street Journal*, previously quoted, underlines them:

'... many diplomats and economists view the implications as overwhelmingly – and dangerously – political. Unless the present decline can be reversed, these analysts fear, the United States and other wealthy industrial powers of the West face the distinct possibility, in the words of British economist Barbara Ward, "of a sort of international class war".'

What is lacking are any positive proposals for dealing with the situation. All that *The Wall Street Journal*'s correspondent can do is to point out that the traditional methods recommended for curing the evils are only likely to make the situation worse.

It has been argued that the developed nations should effectively assist the poorer parts of the world, and that the whole world should be turned into a Welfare State. However, there seems little prospect that anything of this sort could be achieved. The so-called 'aid' programmes to help backward economies represent, according to a rough UN estimate, only one half of one per cent of the total income of industrial countries. But when it comes to the prospect of increasing such aid the mood is one of pessimism:

'A large school of thought holds that expanded share-the-wealth schemes are idealistic and impractical. This school contends climate, undeveloped human skills, lack of natural resources and other factors – not just lack of money – retard economic progress in many of these lands, and that the countries lack personnel with the training or will to use vastly expanded aid effectively. Share-the-wealth schemes, according to this view, would be like pouring money down a bottomless well, weakening the donor nations without effectively curing the ills of the recipients.'

The absurdity of this argument is demonstrated by the fact that every one of the reasons quoted to prove why the less developed parts of the world cannot be developed applied equally strongly to to the present developed countries in the period prior to their development. The argument is only true in this sense. The less developed world will not become developed through the goodwill or generosity of the developed powers. It can only become developed through a struggle against the external forces which have a vested interest in keeping it undeveloped.

Of these forces, neo-colonialism is, at this stage of history, the principal.

I propose to analyse neo-colonialism, first, by examining the state of the African continent and showing how neo-colonialism at the moment keeps it artificially poor. Next, I propose to show how in practice African Unity, which in itself can only be established by the defeat of neo-colonialism, could immensely raise African living standards. From this beginning, I propose to examine neo-colonialism generally, first historically and then by a consideration of the great international monopolies whose continued stranglehold on the neo-colonial sectors of the world ensures the continuation of the system.

THE MECHANISMS OF NEO-COLONIALISM

In order to halt foreign interference in the affairs of developing countries it is necessary to study, understand, expose and actively combat neo-colonialism in whatever guise it may appear. For the methods of neo-colonialists are subtle and varied. They operate not only in the economic field, but also in the political, religious, ideological and cultural spheres.

Faced with the militant peoples of the ex-colonial territories in Asia, Africa, the Caribbean and Latin America, imperialism simply switches tactics. Without a qualm it dispenses with its flags, and even with certain of its more hated expatriate officials. This means, so it claims, that it is 'giving' independence to its former subjects, to be followed by 'aid' for their development. Under cover of such phrases, however, it devises innumerable ways to accomplish objectives formerly achieved by naked colonialism. It is this sum total of these modern attempts to perpetuate colonialism while at the same time talking about 'freedom', which has come to be known as *neo-colonialism*.

Foremost among the neo-colonialists is the United States, which has long exercised its power in Latin America. Fumblingly at first she turned towards Europe, and then with more certainty after world war two when most countries of that continent were indebted to her. Since then, with methodical thoroughness and touching attention to detail, the Pentagon set about consolidating its ascendancy, evidence of which can be seen all around the world.

Who really rules in such places as Great Britain, West Germany, Japan, Spain, Portugal or Italy? If General de Gaulle is 'defecting' from US monopoly control, what interpretation can be placed on his 'experiments' in the Sahara desert, his paratroopers in Gabon, or his trips to Cambodia and Latin America?

Lurking behind such questions are the extended tentacles of the Wall Street octopus. And its suction cups and muscular strength are provided by a phenomenon dubbed 'The Invisible Government', arising from Wall Street's connection with the Pentagon and various intelligence services. I quote:

'The Invisible Government . . . is a loose amorphous grouping of individuals and agencies drawn from many parts of the visible government. It is not limited to the Central Intelligence Agency, although the CIA is at its heart. Nor is it confined to the nine other agencies which comprise what is known as the intelligence community: the National Security Council, the Defense Intelligence Agency, the National Security Agency, Army Intelligence, Navy Intelligence and Research, the Atomic Energy Commission and the Federal Bureau of Investigation.

The Invisible Government includes also many other units and agencies, as well as individuals, that appear outwardly to be a normal part of the conventional government. It even encompasses business firms and institutions that are seemingly private.

To an extent that is only beginning to be perceived, this shadow government is shaping the lives of 190,000,000 Americans. An informed citizen might come to suspect that the foreign policy of the United States often works publicly in one direction and secretly through the Invisible Government in just the opposite direction.

This Invisible Government is a relatively new institution. It came into being as a result of two related factors: the rise of the United States after World War II to a position of pre-eminent world power, and the challenge to that power by Soviet Communism. . . .

By 1964 the intelligence network had grown into a massive hidden apparatus, secretly employing about 200,000 persons and spending billions of dollars a year.'*

Here, from the very citadel of neo-colonialism, is a description of the apparatus which now directs all other Western intelligence set-ups either by persuasion or by force. Results were achieved in Algeria during the April 1961 plot of anti-de Gaulle generals; as also in Guatemala, Iraq, Iran, Suez and the famous U-2 spy intrusion of Soviet air space which wrecked the approaching Summit, then in West Germany and again in East Germany in the riots of 1953, in Hungary's abortive crisis of 1959, Poland's of September 1956, and in Korea, Burma, Formosa, Laos, Cambodia and South Vietnam; they are evident in the trouble in Congo (Leopoldville) which began with Lumumba's murder, and continues till now; in events in Cuba, Turkey, Cyprus, Greece, and in other places too numerous to catalogue completely.

And with what aim have these innumerable incidents occurred? The general objective has been mentioned: to achieve colonialism in fact while preaching independence.

On the economic front, a strong factor favouring Western

* *The Invisible Government*, David Wise and Thomas B. Ross, Random House, New York, 1964.

monopolies and acting against the developing world is international capital's control of the world market, as well as of the prices of commodities bought and sold there. From 1951 to 1961, without taking oil into consideration, the general level of prices for primary products fell by 33·1 per cent, while prices of manufactured goods rose 3·5 per cent (within which, machinery and equipment prices rose 31·3 per cent). In that same decade this caused a loss to the Asian, African and Latin American countries, using 1951 prices as a basis, of some $41,400 million. In the same period, while the volume of exports from these countries rose, their earnings in foreign exchange from such exports decreased.

Another technique of neo-colonialism is the use of high rates of interest. Figures from the World Bank for 1962 showed that seventy-one Asian, African and Latin American countries owed foreign debts of some $27,000 million, on which they paid in interest and service charges some $5,000 million. Since then, such foreign debts have been estimated as more than £30,000 million in these areas. In 1961, the interest rates on almost three-quarters of the loans offered by the major imperialist powers amounted to more than five per cent, in some cases up to seven or eight per cent, while the call-in periods of such loans have been burdensomely short.

While capital worth $30,000 million was exported to some fifty-six developing countries between 1956 and 1962, it is estimated this interest and profit alone extracted on this sum from the debtor countries amounted to more than £15,000 million. This method of penetration by economic aid recently soared into prominence when a number of countries began rejecting it. Ceylon, Indonesia and Cambodia are among those who turned it down. Such 'aid' is estimated on the annual average to have amounted to $2,600 million between 1951 and 1955; $4,007 million between 1956 and 1959, and $6,000 million between 1960 and 1962. But the average sums taken out of the aided countries by such donors in a sample year, 1961, are estimated to amount to $5,000 million, in profits, $1,000 million in interest, and $5,800 million from non-equivalent exchange, or a total of $11,800 million extracted against $6,000 million put in. Thus, 'aid' turns out to be another means of exploitation, a modern method of capital export under a more cosmetic name.

Still another neo-colonialist trap on the economic front has come to be known as 'multilateral aid' through international organizations: the International Monetary Fund, the International Bank for Reconstruction and Development (known as the World Bank), the International Finance Corporation and the International Development Association are examples, all, significantly, having US capital as their major backing. These agencies have the habit of forcing would-be borrowers to submit to various offensive conditions, such as supplying information about their economies, submitting their policy and plans to review by the World Bank and accepting agency supervision of their use of loans. As for the alleged development, between 1960 and mid-1963 the International Development Association promised a total of $500 million to applicants, out of which only $70 million were actually received.

In more recent years, as pointed out by Monitor in *The Times*, 1st July, 1965, there has been a substantial increase in communist technical and economic aid activities in developing countries. During 1964 the total amount of assistance offered was approximately £600 million. This was almost a third of the total communist aid given during the previous decade. The Middle East received about 40 per cent of the total, Asia 36 per cent, Africa 22 per cent and Latin America the rest.

Increased Chinese activity was responsible to some extent for the larger amount of aid offered in 1964, though China contributed only a quarter of the total aid committed; the Soviet Union provided a half, and the East European countries a quarter.

Although aid from socialist countries still falls far short of that offered from the west, it is often more impressive, since it is swift and flexible, and interest rates on communist loans are only about two per cent compared with five to six per cent charged on loans from western countries.

Nor is the whole story of 'aid' contained in figures, for there are conditions which hedge it around: the conclusion of commerce and navigation treaties; agreements for economic co-operation; the right to meddle in internal finances, including currency and foreign exchange, to lower trade barriers in favour of the donor country's goods and capital; to protect the interests of private investments; determination of how the funds are to be used; forcing the recipient to set up counterpart funds; to supply raw materials to the donor; and use of such funds – a majority of it, in fact – to buy goods from the donor nation. These conditions apply to industry, commerce, agriculture, shipping and insurance, apart from others which are political and military.

So-called 'invisible trade' furnished the Western monopolies with yet another means of economic penetration. Over 90 per cent of world ocean shipping is controlled by the imperialist countries. They control shipping rates and, between 1951 and 1961, they increased them some five times in a total rise of about 60 per cent, the upward trend continuing. Thus, net annual freight expenses incurred by Asia, Africa and Latin America amount to no less than an estimated $1,600 million. This is over and above all other profits and interest payments. As for insurance payments, in 1961 alone these amounted to an unfavourable balance in Asia, Africa and Latin America of some additional $370 million.

Having waded through all this, however, we have begun to understand only the *basic* methods of neo-colonialism. The full extent of its inventiveness is far from exhausted.

In the labour field, for example, imperialism operates through labour arms like the Social Democratic parties of Europe led by the British Labour Party, and through such instruments as the International Confederation of Free Trade Unions (ICFTU), now apparently being superseded by the New York Africa-American Labor Centre (AALC) under AFL-CIO chief George Meany and the well-known CIA man in labour's top echelons, Irving Brown.

In 1945, out of the euphoria of anti-fascist victory, the World Federation of Trade Unions (WFTU) had been formed, including all world labour except the US American Federation of Labor, (AFL). By 1949, however, led by the British Trade Union Congress (TUC), a number of pro-imperialist labour bodies in the West broke away from the WFTU over the issue of anti-colonialist liberation, and set up the ICFTU.

For ten years it continued under British TUC leadership. Its record in Africa, Asia and Latin America could gratify only the big international monopolies which were extracting super-profits from those areas.

In 1959, at Brussels, the United States AFL-CIO union centre fought for and won control of the ICFTU Executive Board. From then on a flood of typewriters, mimeograph machines, cars, supplies, buildings, salaries and, so it is still averred, outright bribes for labour leaders in various parts of the developing world rapidly linked ICFTU in the minds of the rank and file with the CIA. To such an extent did its prestige suffer under these American bosses that, in 1964, the AFL-CIO brains felt it necessary to establish a fresh outfit. They set up the AALC in New York right across the river from the United Nations.

'As a steadfast champion of national independence, democracy and social justice', unblushingly stated the April 1965 Bulletin put out by this Centre, 'the AFL-CIO will strengthen its efforts to assist the advancement of the economic conditions of the African peoples. Toward this end, steps have been taken to expand assistance to the African free trade unions by organizing the African-American Labour Centre. Such assistance will help African labour play a vital role in the economic and democratic upbuilding of their countries.'

The March issue of this Bulletin, however, gave the game away: 'In mobilizing capital resources for investment in Workers Education, Vocational Training, Co-operatives, Health Clinics and Housing, the Centre will work with both private and public institutions. It will also *encourage labour-management co-operation to expand American capital investment in the African nations.*' The italics are mine. Could anything be plainer?

Following a pattern previously set by the ICFTU, it has already started classes: one for drivers and mechanics in Nigeria, one in tailoring in Kenya. Labour scholarships are being offered to Africans who want to study trade unionism in – of all places – Austria, ostensibly by the Austrian unions. Elsewhere, labour, organized into political parties of which the British Labour Party is a leading and typical example, has shown a similar aptitude for encouraging 'Labour-management co-operation to expand . . . capital investment in African nations.'

But as the struggle sharpens, even these measures of neo-colonialism are proving too mild. So Africa, Asia and Latin America have begun to experience a round of coups d'état or would-be coups, together with a series of political assassinations which have destroyed in their political primes some of the newly emerging nations' best leaders. To ensure success in these endeavours, the imperialists have made widespread and wily use of ideological and cultural weapons in the form of intrigues, manoeuvres and slander campaigns.

Some of these methods used by neo-colonialists to slip past our guard must now be examined. The first is retention by the departing colonialists of various kinds of privileges which infringe on our sovereignty: that of setting up military bases or stationing troops in former colonies and the supplying of 'advisers' of one sort or another. Sometimes a number of 'rights' are demanded: land concessions, prospecting rights for minerals and/or oil; the 'right' to collect customs, to carry out administration, to issue paper money; to be exempt from customs duties and/or taxes for expatriate enterprises; and, above all, the 'right' to provide 'aid'. Also demanded and granted are privileges in the cultural field; that Western information services be exclusive; and that those from socialist countries be excluded.

Even the cinema stories of fabulous Hollywood are loaded. One has only to listen to the cheers of an African audience as Hollywood's heroes slaughter red Indians or Asiatics to understand the effectiveness of this weapon. For, in the developing continents, where the colonialist heritage has left a vast majority still illiterate, even the smallest child gets the message contained in the blood and thunder stories emanating from California. And along with murder and the Wild West goes an incessant barrage of anti-socialist propaganda, in which the trade union man, the revolutionary, or the man of dark skin is generally cast as the villain, while the policeman, the gum-shoe, the Federal agent – in a word, the CIA-type spy – is ever the hero. Here, truly, is the ideological under-belly of those political murders which so often use local people as their instruments.

While Hollywood takes care of fiction, the enormous monopoly press, together with the outflow of slick, clever, expensive magazines, attends to what it chooses to call 'news'. Within separate countries, one or two news agencies control the news handouts, so that a deadly uniformity is achieved, regardless of the number of separate newspapers or magazines; while internationally, the financial preponderance of the United States is felt more and more through its foreign correspondents and offices abroad, as well as through its-influence over international capitalist journalism. Under this guise, a flood of anti-liberation propaganda emanates from the capital cities of the West, directed against China, Vietnam, Indonesia, Algeria, Ghana and all countries which hack out their own independent path to freedom. Prejudice is rife. For example, wherever there is armed struggle against the forces of reaction, the nationalists are-referred to as rebels, terrorists, or frequently 'communist terrorists'!

Perhaps one of the most insidious methods of the neo-colonialists is evangelism. Following the liberation movement there has been a veritable riptide of religious sects, the overwhelming majority of them American. Typical of these are Jehovah's Witnesses who recently created trouble in certain developing countries by busily teaching their citizens not to salute the new national flags. 'Religion' was too thin to smother the outcry that arose against this activity, and a temporary lull followed. But the number of evangelists continues to grow.

Yet even evangelism and the cinema are only two twigs on a much bigger tree. Dating from the end of 1961, the US has actively developed a huge ideological plan for invading the so-called Third World, utilizing all its facilities from press and radio to Peace Corps.

During 1962 and 1963 a number of international conferences to this end were held in several places, such as Nicosia in Cyprus, San José in Costa Rica, and Lagos in Nigeria. Participants, included the CIA, the US Information Agency (USIA), the Pentagon, the International Development Agency, the Peace Corps and others. Programmes were drawn up which included the systematic use of US citizens abroad in virtual intelligence activities and propaganda work. Methods of recruiting political agents and of forcing 'alliances' with the USA were worked out. At the centre of its programmes lay the demand for an absolute US monopoly in the field of propaganda, as well as for counteracting any independent efforts by developing states in the realm of information.

The United States sought, and still seeks, with considerable success, to co-ordinate on the basis of its own strategy the propaganda activities of all Western countries. In October 1961, a conference of NATO countries was held in Rome to discuss problems of psychological warfare. It appealed for the organization of combined ideological operations in Afro-Asian countries by all participants.

In May and June 1962 a seminar was convened by the US in Vienna on ideological warfare. It adopted a secret decision to engage in a propaganda offensive against the developing countries along lines laid down by the USA. It was agreed that NATO propaganda agencies would, in practice if not in the public eye, keep in close contact with US Embassies in their respective countries.

Among instruments of such Western psychological warfare are numbered the intelligence agencies of Western countries headed by those of the United States 'Invisible Government'. But most significant among them all are Moral Re-Armament (MRA), the Peace Corps and the United States Information Agency (USIA).

Moral Re-Armament is an organization founded in 1938 by the American, Frank Buchman. In the last days before the second world war, it advocated the appeasement of Hitler, often extolling Himmler, the Gestapo chief. In Africa, MRA incursions began at the end of World War II. Against the big anti-colonial upsurge that followed victory in 1945, MRA spent millions advocating collaboration between the forces oppressing the African peoples and those same peoples. It is not without significance that Moise Tshombe and Joseph Kasavubu of Congo (Leopoldville) are both MRA supporters. George Seldes, in his book *One Thousand Americans*, characterized MRA as a fascist organization 'subsidized by . . . Fascists, and with a long record of collaboration with Fascists the world over. . . .' This description is supported by the active participation in MRA of people like General Carpentier, former commander of NATO land forces, and General Ho Ying-chin, one of Chiang Kai-shek's top generals. To cap this, several newspapers, some of them in the Western world, have claimed that MRA is actually subsidized by the CIA.

When MRA's influence began to fail, some new instrument to cover the ideological arena was desired. It came in the establishment of the American Peace Corps in 1961 by President John Kennedy, with Sargent Shriver, Jr., his brother-in-law, in charge. Shriver, a millionaire who made his pile in land speculation in Chicago, was also known as the friend, confidant and co-worker of the former head of the Central Intelligence Agency, Allen Dulles. These two had worked together in both the Office of Strategic Services, US wartime intelligence agency, and in the CIA.

Shriver's record makes a mockery of President Kennedy's alleged instruction to Shriver to 'keep the CIA out of the Peace Corps'. So does the fact that, although the Peace Corps is advertised as a voluntary organization, all its members are carefully screened by the US Federal Bureau of Investigation (FBI).

Since its creation in 1961, members of the Peace Corps have been exposed and expelled from many African, Middle Eastern and Asian countries for acts of subversion or prejudice. Indonesia, Tanzania, the Philippines, and even pro-West countries like Turkey and Iran, have complained of its activities.

However, perhaps the chief executor of US psychological warfare is the United States Information Agency (USIA). Even for the wealthiest nation on earth, the US lavishes an unusual amount of men, materials and money on this vehicle for its neo-colonial aims.

The USIA is staffed by some 12,000 persons to the tune of more than $130 million a year. It has more than seventy editorial staffs working on publications abroad. Of its network comprising 110 radio stations, 60 are outside the US. Programmes are broadcast for Africa by American stations in Morocco, Eritrea, Liberia, Crete, and Barcelona, Spain, as well as from off-shore stations on American ships. In Africa alone, the USIA transmits about thirty territorial and national radio programmes whose content glorifies the US while attempting to discredit countries with an independent foreign policy.

The USIA boasts more than 120 branches in about 100 countries, 50 of which are in Africa alone. It has 250 centres in foreign countries, each of which is usually associated with a library. It employs about 200 cinemas and 8,000 projectors which draw upon its nearly 300 film libraries.

This agency is directed by a central body which operates in the name of the US President, planning and co-ordinating its activities in close touch with the Pentagon, CIA and other Cold War agencies, including even armed forces intelligence centres.

In developing countries, the USIA actively tries to prevent expansion of national media of information so as itself to capture the market-place of ideas. It spends huge sums for publication and distribution of about sixty newspapers and magazines in Africa, Asia and Latin America.

The American government backs the USIA through direct pressures on developing nations. To ensure its agency a complete monopoly in propaganda, for instance, many agreements for economic co-operation offered by the US include a demand that Americans be granted preferential rights to disseminate information. At the same time, in trying to close the new nations to other sources of information, it employs other pressures. For instance, after agreeing to set up USIA information centres in their countries, both Togo and Congo (Leopoldville) originally hoped to follow a non-aligned path and permit Russian information centres as a balance. But Washington threatened to stop all aid, thereby forcing these two countries to renounce their plan.

Unbiased studies of the USIA by such authorities as Dr R. Holt of Princeton University, Retired Colonel R. Van de Velde, former intelligence agents Murril Dayer, Wilson Dizard and others, have all called attention to the close ties between this agency and US Intelligence. For example, Deputy Director Donald M. Wilson was a political intelligence agent in the US Army. Assistant Director for Europe, Joseph Philips, was a successful espionage agent in several Eastern European countries.

Some USIA duties further expose its nature as a top intelligence arm of the US imperialists. In the first place, it is expected to analyse the situation in each country, making recommendations to its Embassy, thereby to its Government, about changes that can tip the local balance in US favour. Secondly, it organizes networks of monitors for radio broadcasts and telephone conversations, while recruiting informers from government offices. It also hires people to distribute US propaganda. Thirdly, it collects secret information with special reference to defence and economy, as a means of eliminating its international military and economic competitors. Fourthly, it buys its way into local publications to influence their policies, of which Latin America furnishes numerous examples. It has been active in bribing public figures, for example in Kenya and Tunisia.

Finally, it finances, directs and often supplies with arms all anti-neutralist forces in the developing countries witness Tshombe in Congo (Leopoldville) and Pak Hung Ji in South Korea. In a word, with virtually unlimited finances, there seems no bounds to its inventiveness in subversion.

One of the most recent developments in neo-colonialist strategy is the suggested establishment of a Businessmen Corps which will, like the Peace Corps, act in developing countries. In an article on 'US Intelligence and the Monopolies' in *Internatinal Affairs* (Moscow, January 1965), V. Chernyavsky writes: 'There can hardly be any doubt that this Corps is a new US intelligence organization created on the initiative of the American monopolies to use Big Business for espionage.'

It is by no means unusual for US Intelligence to set up its own business firms which are merely thinly disguised espionage centres. For example, according to Chernyavsky, the CIA has set up a firm in Taiwan known as Western Enterprises Inc. Under this cover it sends spies and saboteurs to South China. The New Asia Trading Company, a CIA firm in India, has also helped to camouflage US intelligence agents operating in South-east Asia.

Such is the catalogue of neo-colonialism's activities and methods in our time. Upon reading it, the faint-hearted might come to feel that they must give up in despair before such an array of apparent power and seemingly inexhaustible resources.

Fortunately, however, history furnishes innumerable proofs of one of its own major laws: that the budding future is *always* stronger than the withering past. This has been amply demonstrated during every major revolution throughout history.

The American Revolution of 1776 struggled through to victory over a tangle of inefficiency, mismanagement, corruption, outright subversion and counter-revolution the like of which has been repeated to some degree in every subsequent revolution to date.

The Russian Revolution during the period of Intervention, 1917 to 1922, appeared to be dying on its feet. The Chinese Revolution at one time was forced to pull out of its existing bases, lock stock and barrel, and make the unprecedented Long March; yet it triumphed. Imperialist white mercenaries who dropped so confidently out of the skies on Stanleyville after a plane trip from Ascension Island thought that their job would be 'duck soup'. Yet, till now, the nationalist forces of Congo (Leopoldville) continue to fight their way forward. They do not talk of *if* they will win, but only of *when*.

334

Asia provides a further example of the strength of a people's will to determine their own future. In South Vietnam 'special warfare' is being fought to hold back the tide of revolutionary change. 'Special warfare' is a concept of General Maxwell Taylor and a military extension of the creed of John Foster Dulles: let Asians fight Asians. Briefly, the technique is for the foreign power to supply the money, aircraft, military equipment of all kinds, and the strategic and tactical command from a General Staff down to officer 'advisers', while the troops of the puppet government bear the brunt of the fighting. Yet in spite of bombing raids and the immense build-up of foreign strength in the area, the people of both North and South Vietnam are proving to be unconquerable.

In other parts of Asia, in Cambodia, Laos, Indonesia, and now the Philippines, Thailand and Burma, the peoples of ex-colonial countries have stood firm and are winning battles against the allegedly superior imperialist enemy. In Latin America, despite 'final' punitive expeditions, the growing armed insurrections in Colombia, Venezuela and other countries continue to consolidate gains.

In Africa, we in Ghana have withstood all efforts by imperialism and its agents; Tanzania has nipped subersive plots in the bud, as have Brazzaville, Uganda and Kenya. The struggle rages back and forth. The surging popular forces may still be hampered by colonialist legacies, but nonetheless they advance inexorably.

All these examples prove beyond doubt that neo-colonialism is *not* a sign of imperialism's strength but rather of its last hideous gasp. It testifies to its inability to rule any longer by old methods. Independence is a luxury it can no longer afford to permit its subject peoples, so that even what it claims to have 'given' it now seeks to take away.

This means that neo-colonialism *can* and *will* be defeated. How can this be done?

Thus far, all the methods of neo-colonialists have pointed in one direction, the ancient, accepted one of all minority ruling classes throughout history – *divide and rule*.

Quite obviously, therefore, *unity* is the first requisite for destroying neo-colonialism. Primary and basic is the need for an all-union government on the much divided continent of Africa. Along with that, a strengthening of the Afro-Asian Solidarity Organization and the spirit of Bandung is already under way. To it, we must seek the adherence on an increasingly formal basis of our Latin American brothers.

Furthermore, all these liberatory forces have, on all major issues and at every possible instance, the support of the growing socialist sector of the world.

Finally, we must encourage and utilize to the full those still all too few yet growing instances of support for liberation and anti-colonialism inside the imperialist world itself.

To carry out such a political programme, we must all back it with national plans designed to strengthen ourselves as independent nations. An external condition for such independent development is neutrality or *political non-alignment*. This has been expressed in two conferences of Non-Aligned Nations during the recent past, the last of which, in Cairo in 1964, clearly and inevitably showed itself at one with the rising forces of liberation and human dignity.

And the preconditions for all this, to which lip service is often paid but activity seldom directed, is to develop ideological clarity among the anti-imperialist, anti-colonialist, pro-liberation masses of our continents. They, and they alone, make, maintain or break revolutions.

With the utmost speed, neo-colonialism must be analysed in clear and simple terms for the full mass understanding by the surging organizations of the African peoples. The All-African Trade Union Federation (AATUF) has already made a start in this direction, while the Pan-African Youth Movement, the women, journalists, farmers and others are not far behind. Bolstered with ideological clarity, these organizations, closely linked with the ruling parties where liberatory forces are in power, will prove that neo-colonialism is the symptom of imperialism's weakness and that it is defeatable. For, when all is said and done, it is the so-called little man, the bent-backed, exploited, malnourished, blood-covered fighter for independence who decides. And he invariably decides for freedom.

CONCLUSION

In the Introduction I attempted to set out the dilemma now facing the world. The conflict between rich and poor in the second half of the nineteenth century and the first half of the twentieth, which was fought out between the rich and the poor in the developed nations of the world ended in a compromise. Capitalism as a system disappeared from large areas of the world, but where socialism was established it was in its less developed rather than its more developed parts and, in fact, the revolt against capitalism had its greatest successes in those areas where early neo-colonialism had been most actively practised. In the industrially more developed countries, capitalism, far from disappearing, became infinitely stronger. This strength was only achieved by the sacrifice of two principles which had inspired early capitalism, namely the subjugation of the working classes within each individual country and the exclusion of the State from any say in the control of capitalist enterprise.

By abandoning these two principles and substituting for them 'welfare states' based on high working-class living standards and on a State-regulated capitalism at home, the developed countries succeeded in exporting their internal problem and transferring the conflict between rich and poor from the national to the international stage.

Marx had argued that the development of capitalism would produce a crisis within each individual capitalist State because within each State the gap between the 'haves' and the 'have nots' would widen to a point where a conflict was inevitable and that it would be the capitalists who would be defeated. The basis of his argument is not invalidated by the fact that the conflict, which he had predicted as a national one, did not everywhere take place on a national scale but has been transferred instead to the world stage. World capitalism has postponed its crisis but only at the cost of transforming it into an international crisis. The danger is now not civil war within individual States provoked by intolerable conditions within those States, but international war provoked ultimately by the misery of the majority of mankind who daily grow poorer and poorer.

When Africa becomes economically free and politically united, the monopolists will come face to face with their own working class in their own countries, and a new struggle will arise within which the liquidation and collapse of imperialism will be complete.

As this book has attempted to show, in the same way as the internal crisis of capitalism within the developed world arose through the uncontrolled action of national capital, so a greater crisis is being provoked today by similar uncontrolled action of international capitalism in the developing parts of the world. Before the problem can be solved it must at least be understood. It cannot be resolved merely by pretending that neo-colonialism does not exist. It must be realized that the methods at present employed to solve the problem of world poverty are not likely to yield any result other than to extend the crisis.

Speaking in 1951, the then President of the United States, Mr Truman, said, 'The only kind of war we seek is the good old fight against man's ancient enemies ... poverty, disease, hunger and illiteracy.' Sentiments of a similar nature have been re-echoed by all political leaders in the developed world but the stark fact remains: whatever wars may have been won since 1951, none of them is the war against poverty, disease, hunger and illiteracy. However little other types of war have been deliberately sought, they are the only ones which have been waged. Nothing is gained by assuming that those who express such views are insincere. The position of the leaders of the developed capitalist countries of the world are, in relation to the great neo-colonialist international financial combines, very similar to that which Lord Macaulay described as existing between the directors of the East India Company and their agent, Warren Hastings, who, in the eighteenth century, engaged in the wholesale plunder of India. Macaulay wrote:

'The Directors, it is true, never enjoined or applauded any crime. Far from it. Whoever examines their letters written at the time will find there are many just and humane sentiments, many excellent precepts, in short, an admirable code of political ethics. But each exultation is modified or nullified by a demand for money. ... We by no means accuse or suspect those who framed these dispatches of hypocrisy. It is probable that, written 15,000 miles from the place where their orders were to be carried into effect, they never perceived the gross inconsistency of which they were guilty. But the inconsistency was at once manifest to their lieutenant in Calcutta. ... Hastings saw that it was absolutely necessary for him to disregard either the moral discourses or the pecuniary requisitions of his employers. Being forced to disobey them in something, he had to consider what kind of disobedience they would most readily pardon; and he correctly judged that the safest course would be to neglect the sermons and to find the rupees.'

Today the need both to maintain a welfare state, i.e. a parasite State at home, and to support a huge and ever-growing burden of armament costs makes it absolutely essential for developed capitalist countries to secure the maximum return in profit from such parts of the international financial complex as they control. However much private capitalism is exhorted to bring about rapid development and a rising standard of living in the less developed areas of the world, those who manipulate the system realize the inconsistency between

338

doing this and producing at the same time the funds necessary to maintain the sinews of war and the welfare state at home. They know when it comes to the issue they will be excused if they fail to provide for a world-wide rise in the standard of living. They know they will never be forgiven if they betray the system and produce a crisis at home which either destroys the affluent State or interferes with its military preparedness.

Appeals to capitalism to work out a cure for the division of the world into rich and poor are likely to have no better result than the appeals of the Directors of the East India Company to Warren Hastings to ensure social justice in India. Faced with a choice, capitalism, like Hastings, will come down on the side of exploitation.

Is there then no method of avoiding the inevitable world conflict occasioned by an international class war? To accept that world conflict is inevitable is to reject any belief in co-existence or in the policy of non-alignment as practised at present by many of the countries attempting to escape from neo-colonialism. A way out is possible.

To start with, for the first time in human history the potential material resources of the world are so great that there is no need for there to be rich and poor. It is only the organization to deploy these potential resources that is lacking. Effective world pressure can force such a redeployment, but world pressure is not exercised by appeals, however eloquent, or by arguments, however convincing. It is only achieved by deeds. It is necessary to secure a world realignment so that those who are at the moment the helpless victims of a system will be able in the future to exert a counter pressure. Such counter pressures do not lead to war. On the contrary, it is often their absence which constitutes the threat to peace.

A parallel can be drawn with the methods by which direct colonialism was ended. No imperial power has ever granted independence to a colony unless the forces were such that no other course was possible, and there are many instances where independence was only achieved by a war of liberation, but there are many other instances when no such war occurred. The very organization of the forces of independence within the colony was sufficient to convince the imperial power that resistance to independence would be impossible or that the political and economic consequences of a colonial war outweighed any advantage to be gained by retaining the colony.

In the earlier chapters of this book I have set out the argument for African unity and have explained how this unity would destroy neo-colonialism in Africa. In later chapters I have explained how strong is the world position of those who profit from neo-colonialism. Nevertheless, African unity is something which is within the grasp of the African people. The foreign firms who exploit our resources long ago saw the strength to be gained from acting on a Pan-African scale. By means of interlocking directorships, cross-shareholdings and other devices, groups of apparently different companies have formed, in fact, one enormous capitalist monopoly. The only effective way to challenge this economic empire and to recover possession of our heritage, is for us also to act on a Pan-African basis, through a Union Government.

No one would suggest that if all the peoples of Africa combined to establish their unity their decision could be revoked by the forces of neo-colonialism. On the contrary, faced with a new situation, those who practise neo-colonialism would adjust themselves to this new balance of world forces in exactly the same way as the capitalist world has in the past adjusted itself to any other change in the balance of power.

The danger to world peace springs not from the action of those who seek to end neo-colonialism but from the inaction of those who allow it to continue. To argue that a third world war is not inevitable is one thing, to suppose that it can be avoided by shutting our eyes to the development of a situation likely to produce it is quite another matter.

If world war is not to occur it must be prevented by positive action. This positive action is within the power of the peoples of those areas of the world which now suffer under neocolonialism but it is only within their power if they act at once, with resolution and in unity.

24

The unilateral declaration of independence (UDI),
by the minority government of Rhodesia on 11 November
1965, was not only the expression of racist, settler politics,
but an exposure of the workings of imperialism and neo-
colonialism in Africa. For the settler government, representing capitalism, made it clear in UDI that the intention
was to continue indefinitely, the exploitation and repression of the African people of Zimbabwe. It was the culmination of a settler policy evolved with the direct and
indirect support of the British government, and of the
imperialist and capitalist interests of the West.

As I said in my speech at the United Nations on 23
September 1960:

> The problem of Africa, looked at as a whole, is a wide and diversi-
> fied one. But its true solution lies in the application of one principle,
> namely, the right of a people to rule themselves. No compromise
> can affect this cardinal and fundamental principle, and the idea
> that when a handful of settlers acquire a living space on our
> continent the indigenes must lose this right, is not only a serious
> travesty of justice, but also a woeful contradiction of the very
> dictates of history.
>
> Out of a total African population of over two hundred and
> thirty million people some three per cent are of non-African
> origin. To suppose that such a small minority could in any other
> continent produce acute political difficulties would be unthinkable.

Yet such is the sub-conscious feeling of certain European settlers in Africa that to them the paramount issue in Africa is not the welfare of the ninety-seven per cent but rather the entrenchment of the rights of the three per cent of this European settler minority in Africa.

To these minority settlers a solution seems impossible unless what they describe as 'justice' is done to the foreign three per cent. Justice, they say, must be done to this group irrespective of whether it means that injustice continues to be done to the remaining inhabitants.

I believe that a reasonable solution can be found to the African problem which would not prejudice the minorities on the continent. No effective solution, however, can be found, if political thinking in regard to a solution begins with the rights of the three per cent and only considers the rights of the ninety-seven per cent within the framework which is acceptable to the rest.

The world must begin at last to look at African problems in the light of the needs of the African people and not only of the needs of the minority settlers.

When the OAU Summit meeting took place in Accra in October 1965, the question of Rhodesia was high on the Agenda, since UDI appeared to be imminent, and Britain was apparently unprepared to deal firmly with the rebellion. The situation was made worse for us because the OAU still lacked force to implement any decisions reached. We still had no African High Command, and no unified political machinery. It was my great hope that the Accra Summit would at last set in motion the formation of an All-African High Command, and also an Executive Council as the initial step in the establishment of an All-African Union Government. But although the Rhodesian situation cried out for bold, revolutionary steps, the opportunity was missed, and instead, a series of resolutions were passed. The Assembly called on the United Nations to declare that a unilateral declaration of independence was a threat to international peace, and called for the putting into effect of all the measures necessitated by such a situation in accordance with the UN

Charter to help in bringing into office a government of Rhodesia representing the majority of the people. A further resolution called on Britain to abrogate the Rhodesia constitution of 1961, and to take all necessary measures, even in the use of armed force, for the restoration of the administration of the territory, and to release political prisoners. The Assembly also called on Britain to hold a constitutional conference to be attended by representatives of all the people of Rhodesia with a view to agreeing to a new constitution ensuring the right of general elections, the right to vote and the holding of free elections. All governments and international organizations were asked to refuse recognition of the minority government in the event of UDI, and to apply sanctions against it. Further, OAU states were recommended to reconsider their political, economic, diplomatic and financial relations with Britain if Britain accepted the independence of Rhodesia on the basis of minority rule. The resolution stated that member states would use all possible means, including force, against UDI, and they would support the African people of Zimbabwe in their fight to establish majority rule in the country. They also agreed in principle on the following measures to be taken in the event of a negotiated independence:

(i) Refusal to recognize the new Rhodesian government.

(ii) Continued efforts to reconcile the two African nationalist parties – the Zimbabwe African Peoples Union and the Zimbabwe African National Union – with a view to forming a government in exile, and giving it financial, political, diplomatic and military help.

(iii) An emergency meeting of the OAU Council of Ministers to consider further action, including the most effective means of involving the United Nations.

(iv) A call to African members of the Commonwealth, and other African countries, to reconsider their relations

343

with Britain, and bring the utmost pressure to bear on the British government; and

(v) Generally to treat Rhodesia like South Africa and the Portuguese African territories in applying such measures as an economic boycott. A committee was formed, including Egypt, Tanzania, Kenya, Zambia and Nigeria, to follow up the resolutions of the Conference.

The futility of paper resolutions and declarations of intent without effective political and military machinery to implement them, has been amply demonstrated in the case of Rhodesia by subsequent events. The settler government declared UDI on 11 November 1965 confident that the OAU was powerless to act, and that there would be no really meaningful pressures brought to bear by Britain or the United Nations. They were prepared for economic sanctions, and did not fear them, knowing that they would be ineffective, and that South Africa would become Rhodesia's economic support. As events proved, after some initial dislocation, the total value of Rhodesia's imports increased beyond the level attained before UDI; and as a whole, the Rhodesian economy probably suffered less than it did in the recession which accompanied the dissolution of the Federation.

A few days after UDI, on 19 November 1965, I sent the following Note to the Heads of State of Guinea, Zambia, Tanzania, Uganda, Sudan, Congo (Brazzaville), and Congo (Leopoldville) now Zaire.

Mr President and Dear Brother,
The illegal and unilateral declaration of independence by the minority settler Government of Southern Rhodesia has flouted and shocked African and world opinion. Apart from declarations condemning the action of the Rhodesian settler regime, and the application of sanctions, it is clear that neither the United Kingdom Government, nor the other world powers intend to take the necessary effective measures, including the use of force, to crush the Rhodesian rebellion.

344

The Rhodesian situation is a serious and direct threat to the peace of Africa, and unless the Organization of African Unity can act quickly to meet the situation, the consequences to our continent will be incalculable.

As you know I have been advocating for a long time the establishment of an African High Command which could resist such acts which threaten the territorial integrity and sovereignty of the African States. It was for this same reason that I proposed the creation of an Executive Council for the Organization of African Unity.

The present situation therefore provides an urgent opportunity for us to mount an African Force capable of being deployed against the illegal minority Government of Southern Rhodesia.

The machinery of the Organization of African Unity works very slowly, and I am convinced that we must do something now to demonstrate that we are planning realistically to deal with the situation created by the racialist rebellion in Southern Rhodesia.

I suggest, in order to make our efforts more effective and realistic, that a Treaty of Mutual Defence and Security be signed between as many African States as possible, but beginning with:

The Revolutionary Government of the Congo (Brazzaville)
The Democratic Republic of the Congo (Leopoldville)
Sudan
Uganda
Tanzania
Zambia
Guinea
Ghana

The object of this Treaty would be to deal with the possibility of hostilities breaking out between any of the States, subscribing to the Treaty and Southern Rhodesia, Portugal and South Africa. Each member State of the Treaty shall pledge itself to go to the assistance of any country or countries subscribing to the Treaty. In other words, an attack on any of these countries would be an attack on all of them. There would be no objection to other African countries adhering to this Treaty at any time they find it fit to do so.

If you are in favour of such a Treaty it is, I am sure, desirable that we formalize it as soon as possible. I suggest therefore that we should have a meeting in Accra attended by the Defence Ministers of those States which adhere to the Treaty to draw up the precise terms of the Treaty, and plan action. It will be valuable also if the meeting could be attended by the Military Advisers and Chiefs of Staff so that all technical points could be covered.

Please accept, Mr President, and dear Brother my fraternal sentiments.

(Kwame Nkrumah)
President of the Republic of Ghana

The reactionary coup in Ghana in February 1966, greeted so jubilantly in Salisbury by the settler government, prevented follow up action. Zambia under the leadership of my good friend Kenneth Kaunda was left to bear the brunt of the continuing aggression of Smith's rebel regime. In 1971 the OAU still lacks unified political and military machinery, and the racist, minority government in Salisbury continues to defy the people of Africa who are the rightful owners of the land of Zimbabwe.

CALL FOR ACTION ON RHODESIA—ADDRESS TO THE NATIONAL ASSEMBLY

25 November 1965

Mr Speaker, Members of the National Assembly,

Exactly two weeks ago today, some European settlers in the British Colony of Southern Rhodesia revolted against the Government of the United Kingdom and seized control of the colonial machinery of government. It is now time that we took stock of the situation thus created and decided on what practical steps we should take.

Since then there have been directed against these settlers millions of words of denunciation. If words could kill, the entire rebel regime would be now in their graves. But rebellions are put down by action not by words. It is true there have been many calls for action but these have been calls for action by others. We must avoid the habit of looking outside the African Continent to some former colonial power to set right those problems which are our duty to settle. The time has now come for us to take action ourselves. This means that we must examine the Southern Rhodesian rebellion with utmost realism and in the realities of the African revolution.

At first sight the rebellion in Southern Rhodesia appears to be aimed at enabling the settlers to continue unimpeded their policy of oppression and degradation of the African population. If we examine the circumstances of the revolt, however, it will be seen that this is not the explanation. The British Government had already conceded to the settlers everything for which they asked short of formal independence. They could have continued as long as they liked to practise apartheid under the shadow of the Union Jack and with the assurance that whatever crime against humanity they committed they would be defended by the United Kingdom Government at the United Nations.

Despite the fact that the present British Government when in opposition had denounced the Southern Rhodesian Constitution, despite the fact that the British Prime Minister had described Southern Rhodesia as a police state, the United Kingdom Government were perfectly prepared to allow the settlers to continue to rule so long as they wished – provided only that they acknowledged the sovereignty of Britain. Why were they unwilling to do this? In such circumstances there can only be one reason for the rebellion, namely, that the settlers wished to demonstrate to the world that they were powerful enough to defy the might of Britain. Naturally they would not have embarked on this course unless previously they had obtained promises of support from South Africa and from Portugal. What we are facing is an alliance of the three apartheid countries aimed at taking over the whole of Southern Africa. The talk of Bechuanaland becoming independent in the near future becomes meaningless when viewed against this terrible background.

Let me first state the position of Ghana, which remains unchanged. We consider that the United Kingdom has under the Charter of the United Nations certain positive obligations towards the African people of Southern Rhodesia which are set out in Article 73. If Britain is unwilling or unable to fulfil these obligations the United Nations must step in. Ghana considers that the proper organ through which the United Nations should intervene is the Organization for African Unity. This view has now been supported by the Security Council of the United Nations.

In a Resolution passed five days ago the Security Council called on the United Kingdom – and I quote – 'to quell this rebellion of the racist minority and to take all other appropriate measures which would prove effective in eliminating the authority of the usurpers and in bringing the minority regime to an immediate end'. Further, the Resolution – and again I quote – 'called upon the Organization of African Unity to do all in its power to assist in the implementation of this Resolution in accordance with chapter 8 of the Charter'. Chapter 8 provides that Regional Organizations such as the Organization of African Unity may be empowered by the Security Council to take all suitable action, including military action.

In response to this decision of the Security Council, for which the United Kingdom Government voted in favour, and in accordance with the Resolution on Southern Rhodesia, unanimously passed at the Assembly of Heads of State and Government of the Organization of African Unity held in Accra last month, a Bill will be placed before you tomorrow which will enable Ghana to play its full part in any action that may be decided upon.

I would remind you that in their Resolution on Southern Rhodesia the Heads of State and Government decided that in the event of the failure of the United Kingdom Government to take decisive action on the Southern Rhodesian issue, the African States would – and once again I quote – 'use all possible means, including the use of force, with a view to opposing a unilateral declaration of independence'. In addition, the Heads of State and Government decided – and I quote once more – 'to give immediate and every necessary assistance to the people of Zimbabwe with a view to establishing a majority government in the Country'. The Bill which you will be asked to consider tomorrow will make it quite clear that Ghana is prepared to play its full part in implementing this Resolution.

Ghana's position is that the United Kingdom Government, having affirmed that it has full authority and responsibility for dealing with the Southern Rhodesian situation, should act to quell the rebellion. In my view, for the various reasons which I will explain later, it will prove impossible to quell the rebellion by purely economic means. From the very beginning of all this, I have made it clear to the British Prime Minister that I consider it would be necessary for Britain to use armed force against the rebels. I am still of this opinion. Even Christ had to use the whip to drive the wicked money changers from the temple. That is why the Government of Ghana believes that it is only by the use of force that this rebellion can be checked. I am extremely doubtful as to whether sanctions could be operated effectively; and I can foresee that in the end it will be necessary either for the United Nations or the Organization of African Unity to use military force to put down the rebellion, if the United Kingdom is unwilling to act.

I believe that it is possible, if a complete trade boycott were feasible, for the rebel regime to be overthrown in this way. Even so, nothing would be achieved by this except the creation of a state of anarchy, and unless there was an alternative government prepared and ready to take over from the rebels.

The British Colony of Southern Rhodesia is a land-locked territory some one hundred and fifty thousand square miles in extent; in other words, it is about $1\frac{1}{2}$ times the size of Ghana. Southern Rhodesia is bounded on the north by Zambia and on the west by the British Protectorate of Bechuanaland. It has a southern frontier with South Africa, and on the east a common frontier with Mozambique. Its rail communications are through Bechuanaland and through Portuguese territory. There is road but no rail communication direct with South Africa. An economic blockade of Southern Rhodesia would thus require the co-operation of four countries; the United Kingdom – which still controls the external relations of Bechuanaland, South Africa, Portugal and Zambia. Britain and Zambia are agreed on blockading Southern Rhodesia provided this is ordered by the United Nations. South Africa and Portugal have given no indication that they would accept a decision of the Security Council to impose economic sanctions. There is no economic reason why the United Kingdom should not enforce a blockade since Rhodesian trade with Britain represents less than one per cent of the United Kingdom total trade turnover. In contrast to this the sacrifice demanded of Zambia is colossal. One-third of Zambia's trade is with Southern Rhodesia. Further, all the essential imports required to keep the Zambian economy running are supplied through a railway system which passes through Southern Rhodesia.

If, therefore, as the United Kingdom Government suggests, the only method of bringing down the Smith regime is to be an economic blockade, this will impose on both Zambia and Malawi an intolerable economic burden, while the sacrifice made by Britain will be minimal. In any event if any economic blockade of Southern Rhodesia is to be effective, either the United Nations must compel Portugal and South Africa to join in economic sanctions or else all the other nations in the world must agree to extend sanctions so that they apply equally to the Portuguese colony of Mozambique and to South Africa. I hope that the United Nations would be prepared to take this action but I have doubts whether the Security Council, as at present composed, would vote in favour of this. If they are not prepared to do so, all talk of economic sanctions is nonsense.

It is possible, of course, in the coming elections to the Security

Council for the African States to insist that only such states as are prepared to support a blockade of not only Southern Rhodesia but South Africa and Mozambique in addition, are elected to the Council. Even so, there is no guarantee that the United Nations Security Council has the authority to see that such a blockade was effectively enforced. For these reasons I believe that it will be extremely difficult, if not impossible, to defeat the Southern Rhodesian rebels by purely economic means.

If the United Kingdom Government and the other major powers are sincere in their professed desire to carry out an effective blockade of Southern Rhodesia, the first step is clearly to inform Portugal and South Africa that United Nations inspectors will be sent to their territory to ensure that no goods are sent to Southern Rhodesia or are exported from it. If South Africa and Portugal refuse to accept this proposal then the Security Council must order that the same sanctions are applied against Mozambique and South Africa as are applied against Southern Rhodesia.

The enforcing of such sanctions would result in, at least, a naval and air blockade of the whole of Southern Africa and would thus involve the use of far more military force than would be required if direct military action were taken against the Southern Rhodesian rebels.

It is for this reason that I think the economic sanctions are unrealistic and that the only sensible course is for direct military action against the rebels.

No one African State by itself can undertake this military action and if it were left to African States alone, they might well have to seek assistance from outside the African continent in order to deal with the situation which might arise if Portugal or South Africa came militarily to the assistance of the rebels.

What then are we to do? Our first step must be to mobilize the conscience of the world so that in the last resort if African States are compelled to act on their own, they will have the sympathy of all peoples outside the African Continent.

At the moment far too little is known of the sordid history of Southern Rhodesia and the oppression suffered by its African inhabitants. We all have a duty to make the facts known.

A year ago when I was writing *Neo-Colonialism: The Last Stage of Imperialism*, I described the Southern Rhodesian situation, as it was then, in these words:

'Rhodesia, while theoretically a colony, is really a fossilized form of the earliest type of neo-colonialism which was practised in Southern Africa until the formation of the Union of South Africa. The essence of the Rhodesia system is not to employ individuals drawn from the people of the territory itself to run the country, as in the newer type of neo-colonial State, but to utilize instead an alien minority. The majority of the European ruling class of Rhodesia only came to the Colony after the Second World War, but it is they and not the African inhabitants, who out-number them 16 to 1, that Britain regards as "the Government". This racialist State is protected from outside pressure because under international law it is a British colony, while Britain herself excuses her failure to exercise her legal rights to prevent the oppression and exploitation of the African inhabitants (of which, of course, she officially disapproves) because of a supposed British parliamentary convention. In other words, by maintaining Rho-desia nominally as a colony, Britain in fact gives her official protection as a second South Africa and the European racialists are left free to treat the African inhabitants as they will.

The Rhodesian system thus has all the hallmarks of the neo-colonial model. The patron power, Britain, awards to a local government over which it claims to have no control unlimited rights and exploitation within the territory. Yet Britain still retains powers to exclude other countries from intervening either to liberate its African population or to bring its economy into some other zone of influence. The manoeuvring over Rhodesia's "independence" is an excellent example of the workings of neo-colonialism and of the practical difficulties to which the system gives rise. A European minority of less than a quarter of a million could not maintain, in the conditions of Africa today, rule over four million Africans without external support from somewhere. When the settlers talk of "independence" they are not thinking of standing on their own feet but merely of seeking a new neo-colonialist master who would, in their view, be more reliable than Britain.'

That is what I wrote a year ago.

Southern Rhodesia came into existence by trickery and force of arms. At the close of the 19th century, Cecil Rhodes, the South African Diamond buccaneer who had become Prime Minister of what was then the British dependency of Cape Colony, invaded Southern Rhodesia and Zambia. Rhodes, dreaming of the Cape to Cairo British empire, pushed from Matabeleland into Mashonaland across the Zambesi, into the country now called Zambia. Thus he drove a wedge between the Portuguese colonies of Mozambique and Angola. This expedition was undertaken by a pioneer column of mercenary free-booters who were recruited from among the English and Boer populations of South Africa. Each man who took part in the expedition was promised not less than fifteen gold claims and a farm of three thousand acres. These individuals were the first white settlers in Rhodesia and the National Day of Southern Rhodesia is described as 'Pioneer Day'.

It commemorates the arrival on the 12th of September, 1890, of this pioneer column at the spot where the present capital of Salisbury is now situated. Thus the first white settlers only arrived in Rhodesia and Zambia seventy-five years ago and they were a tiny minority among the African population. For the fifty years prior to the arrival of Rhodes' Pioneer Column, what is now Southern Rhodesia had been dominated by the Africans of Matabele. Their famous chief, Lo Bengula, was tricked into signing an agreement with Rhodes' agents under which he gave away to Rhodes' British South Africa Company all the mineral rights in his domain.

When Lo Bengula woke up to the bitter realization of the trickery that had divested him and his people of the rights in their own land, he petitioned Queen Victoria. Despite the fact that Lo Bengula's letter showed clearly the nature of the fraud which had been per-petrated on him the British Government of the day did nothing. Rhodes was allowed to bring in additional troops. He picked a quarrel with the Matabele, declared war on them and crushed them. The British Government granted a Charter to Rhodes' British South Africa Company which continued to rule Southern Rhodesia and Zambia up to 1923. In that year the British Government organized a referendum among the white settlers of Southern Rhodesia so that they could decide whether they wished in future to join South Africa, or to be a 'self-governing British Colony'. The then popula-tion of some three million Africans were not allowed to vote and the only people participating in the plebiscite were some fourteen thousand European settlers. By a narrow majority they decided against joining South Africa.

In the same year the British Government made a famous statement of policy known as 'The Devonshire Declaration' which is now reproduced in substance in Article 73 of the Charter of the United Nations. The Devonshire Declaration declared, and I quote: 'His Majesty's Government think it necessary definitely to record their considered opinion that the interests of the African natives must be paramount and if and when those interests and the interests of the immigrant races should conflict, the former should prevail'. In the spirit of this declaration the British Parliament insisted on maintaining some control at least over how the settlers treated the African majority of the colony. Since that date the whole history of Southern Rhodesia has consisted of the efforts made by the settlers to throw off this restraint and to obtain complete freedom to oppress and degrade the African population as they wished.

Their first attempt consisted of a plan to extend Southern Rhodesian settler control over what is now Zambia and Malawi.

At first they had some success. In 1953, despite the opposition of the great majority of the African population of the territories concerned, the British Government set up a Federation composed of the Colony of Southern Rhodesia and the then two British Protectorates of Northern Rhodesia and Nyasaland. The constitution of this Federation, enacted by Britain, gave the political control of its Government to the European settlers.

This Federation lasted for only ten years. The heroic resistance of the peoples of Zambia and Malawi made it impossible for the European settlers to continue ruling and at the end of 1963 the Federation was dissolved and Malawi and Zambia became independent. During the period of the Federation's existence the present Rhodesian Front Party was born. It was called then 'the Dominion Party' because it had as its policy the creation of independent racial dominion which would include the rich copper belt areas of Zambia and Katanga as well as Southern Rhodesia. In 1962 this Dominion Party, re-christened the 'Rhodesian Front Party', won the settler general elections in Southern Rhodesia. They have ruled the colony ever since.

In a sense, the rebellion of Southern Rhodesia has been inevitable since September, 1963, when the British Government frustrated a move by the Security Council of United Nations to prevent the arming of the Rhodesian settlers. What happened was this.

During the time of the Federation of Rhodesia and Nyasaland the British Government built up a strong army and air force in the territory. In practice these forces were under the control of Britain though in name they belonged to the Federation. When the Federation broke up and its assets were being shared up neither Malawi nor Zambia was independent. And in any event these two States did not have the revenue or the facilities to keep hold of any but a very small part of the Federation's air force and army. The British Government proposed that the bulk of these armed forces should be handed over to the racist settlers of Southern Rhodesia.

353

As soon as it became known that Britain was intending to hand over the armed forces to the racist settlers, Ghana took the initiative of raising the question in the Security Council of the United Nations.

This move was backed by all the African States. In the Security Council itself not only the African members, Ghana and Morocco, but also all the other non-permanent members representing other regions of the world supported the Ghana Resolution. Except for Britain, no single member of the Security Council was opposed to it. The Resolution, moved by Ghana, would have prevented the handing over of any armed forces or military aircraft to the racist regime of Ian Smith. This regime was then already in power and had already boasted of its intention to seize independence by force. The Resolution would have been carried and the subsequent revolt prevented except for the fact that the United Kingdom Government used its veto to prevent it being passed.

Why did the United Kingdom Government hand over these armed forces?

The United Kingdom Government may have genuinely believed that by handing over these armies to Rhodesia, the Settler government would be persuaded to accept the conditions demanded as a basis for the independence of Rhodesia and that an independent Rhodesia would act as a bulwark of Britain's east of Suez policy.

This explains what is otherwise not clear about Britain's policy towards the rebellion in Rhodesia. The British quarrel with the settlers is that the Ian Smith regime has broken the implied bargain with Britain, and is now insisting on using Rhodesian armed forces for his own purpose. This purpose can only be one of aggression against other African States, in league with South Africa and Portugal.

Under previous settler Governments the condition of the African population was bad enough. Under the Rhodesian Front Party it became intolerable. Indeed the persecution of the African population of Southern Rhodesia has reached such a pitch that the continuation of settler rule in any form is impossible.

Just before the rebellion began, three recently recruited Southern Rhodesian policemen from Britain deserted, horrified at the conditions in Rhodesia. Now back in Britain they have been telling British newspapers of their experiences. They say they were told by the settler officers to shoot Africans to kill and thus save hospital fees. They were advised not to hit Africans on the head, 'as it's four times thicker than a European's, but to 'remember that the African has a weak stomach' – and aim for that. They claim that the police deliberately incite African riots. Nor are they the only witnesses to the callous brutality with which the four million African population is treated. The Roman Catholic Archbishop and Bishops of Southern Rhodesia have declared and I quote from their pastoral letter:

'Wages are inadequate, housing conditions in many instances are unworthy of human beings, and terms of employment are such that husbands are separated for long periods from their wives. Such a state of affairs cries to heaven for vengeance and even in the natural order can only breed crime and chaos.'

Under the Land Apportionment Act passed by the settler government all the best land is given to the Europeans. Four million Africans are compelled to live on the worse land while the 217,000 Europeans occupy one-half of the total farming area. The treatment of African domestic servants, of whom there are some 80,000 is little short of slavery. There are no schools for their children. Husbands and wives are not allowed to live together or have their children with them. A servant cannot see a film, go to a dance, attend an athletic event, hear a lecture or go for a walk at night. If he stays at home and drinks an alcoholic beverage he is guilty of a criminal offence for which he can be punished by a term of imprisonment.

Similar conditions apply to most of the industrial workers. They are compelled to live in African 'locations' where, as often as not, they are separated from their families. Eighty per cent of the accommodation provided for the African workers of Salisbury is for single men. Usually four men are compelled to live and cook in one small room. The African town worker may only have a visitor to stay with him if he obtains the permission of a Superintendent of a location; he may only leave his lodging for two weeks unless he obtains special permission; and in many cases may not be out of doors after 9 p.m. He automatically loses his home if he is dismissed by his employer or if he is convicted of any political offence or even if he transgresses some of the provisions of the 'Pass' Laws.

Against these conditions the African population of Southern Rhodesia has sought to establish political parties which could organize opposition to oppression. The Zimbabwe African Peoples Union – ZAPU – was established after the African People's Conference in Accra in 1958 and campaigned against the efforts of the settlers to negotiate with the British Government a constitution which would give the settlers a freer hand than they had already possessed for ill-treating and oppressing the bulk of the population. In spite of the opposition of ZAPU, Britain insisted on granting to the settlers the notorious 1961 Constitution. This Constitution was at the time denounced in the British Parliament by the British Labour Party, then in opposition. It was condemned by overwhelming majority of the General Assembly in the United Nations which asked Britain not to bring it into force. Nevertheless the Constitution was established and it has subsequently provided the means by which Ian Smith has established his illegal regime.

Ghana believes, as I think do all other African States, that it is a tragic misfortune that ZAPU has now been split and that there are in Southern Rhodesia two nationalist African parties, each claiming to speak for the African people. Nevertheless such disunity is bound to occur in conditions where all political activity is forbidden, the leaders of both parties are imprisoned, and there is no opportunity to test by free elections which party the people support. At all costs we must avoid a situation in which we refuse to support the masses of the African people of Southern Rhodesia merely on the ground that two parties are claiming their allegiance. A simple election on a universal franchise could easily decide this.

It is clear that the African people of Southern Rhodesia are today putting up a strong resistance to the illegal Smith regime and they deserve our full support.

There is nothing now to be gained by recrimination over past events. The United Kingdom Government has stated it is determined to end the rebellion and to establish a new regime in Southern Rhodesia. As a member of the United Nations of the Organization of African Unity and of the Commonwealth, Ghana has a duty to make positive and constructive proposals to Britain as to how this may be done. The problem can be looked at under two heads. First, how is the rebellion to be ended? And, secondly, when the rebellion is over what type of Government is to be substituted for the present regime? These two questions are closely inter-related. If the United Kingdom rules out military intervention by its own forces and is opposed to military intervention by the United Nations or by the Organization of African Unity, then the only way the Smith regime can be overthrown is by an internal revolt against the present illegal Government. But such an internal revolt can only be brought about if those seeking to restore law and order within Southern Rhodesia are given positive assurances as to what will happen to them after they have overthrown Smith. No single person in Southern Rhodesia is prepared to move a finger to restore the discredited 1961 Constitution. Therefore, it seems clear that if the United Kingdom Government really wants to create an effective opposition to Smith within Southern Rhodesia, it must not only revoke the 1961 Constitution forthwith but also hold out hopes for something better in the future.

Up till now, according to the United Kingdom Government, that one obstacle to holding a Southern Rhodesia Constitutional Conference at which all political parties would be represented, was that Smith's settler government was opposed to the holding of such a Conference and the British Government could not over-ride his wishes. Well, the Smith Government is no more. From Britain's point of view, Smith and his Cabinet are private citizens and what they say or do has no constitutional validity. In any event, even if Smith had continued as the legal Prime Minister of Southern Rhodesia, the British Government were pledged to considering the holding of a Constitutional Conference despite his opposition. I will quote to you the exact words of this pledge as set out in the Final Communique of the last Commonwealth Prime Minister's Conference:

'In this process of seeking to reach agreement on Rhodesia's advance to independence a constitutional conference would, at the appropriate time, be a natural step. If the discussions did not develop satisfactorily in this direction in a reasonably speedy time, the British Government having regard to the principle enunciated by the Commonwealth Secretary of unimpeded progress towards majority rule would be ready to consider promoting such a conference in order to ensure Rhodesia's progress to independence on a basis acceptable to the people of Rhodesia as a whole.'

What should be the theme of this Constitutional Conference? Again, I quote from the same Communiqué, which states that the other Commonwealth Heads of Government 'welcomed the statement of the British Government that the principle of "one man one vote" was regarded as the very basis of democracy and this should be applied to Rhodesia'.

In my view the United Kingdom Government should summon immediately a Constitutional Conference to devise a Constitution for Southern Rhodesia which would provide for the establishment of majority rule in the shortest practical time. The United Kingdom Government should state that once majority rule had been established on a firm basis, Zimbabwe should become independent, but that there should be no question of Southern Rhodesia becoming independent on any other basis than 'one man one vote'.

But we must be realistic. The downfall of the Smith regime will create a vacuum. This vacuum must immediately be filled by the United Kingdom. Britain must establish immediately a system of direct rule through agencies immediately responsible to the British Government so that conditions can be created for the emergence of a constitutional Government based on universal adult suffrage.

If the people of Southern Rhodesia are to rise against Smith without any external military aid, they have a hard and desperate task before them. They cannot be expected to undertake that task unless they have a clear goal before them. A Constitutional Conference now is the first requirement of the situation.

There is only one basic problem in Southern Rhodesia. It is the presence of the white settlers. It is therefore Britain's duty to consider means by which those of them who will not cooperate with a majority Government can be induced to leave. It is quite wrong to suppose that the majority of these settlers are people who have lived in Southern Rhodesia for generations. The majority of them came there after the last world war to escape the austerity and high taxation which had to be faced in Britain as a result of Britain's part in the struggle against Hitler. Clifford Dupont, the so-called officer administering the rebel government, is still enrolled as a Solicitor in London. He only left England in 1948 and it would be no hardship to him if he was compelled to resume his British law practice. The majority of Rhodesian Front supporters are similarly situated.

At the time of Indonesian independence, the Netherlands, which is a small country and heavily populated, nevertheless repatriated to Holland over two hundred thousand colonial residents of the former East Indian colonies.

I propose that discussions should take place immediately among Commonwealth Governments to see how many settlers could be resettled in other Commonwealth countries. At the moment, Australia, for example, is calling out for European immigrants. Grants and assisted passages are provided by Australia for tens of thousands of settlers from Austria, Germany and other European countries. The older Commonwealth countries could, I believe, make a positive contribution by agreeing to take a fixed quota of such Southern Rhodesian settlers as wished to leave.

Short of these major measures, there are certain other positive steps which Britain could take here and now. The United Kingdom Government has now taken power to legislate for Southern Rhodesia and it has used this power to declare illegal the Press censorship imposed by Smith. Britain should, I consider, immediately use these same powers to revoke all the detention orders in force against African nationalists who have been imprisoned for opposing the Smith Regime. How can Britain possibly hope that Smith will be overthrown and British authority reasserted if the United Kingdom Government do nothing to aid those who have been imprisoned for opposing the rebels? It seems to me extraordinary that even in the case of Mr Garfield Todd, who was a missionary from New Zealand and was for five years Prime Minister of Southern Rhodesia, nothing has been done by the British Government to free him from detention.

Finally, there is the question of the armed forces and the police. Almost all the European officers in the police are British, as are about one-third of the officers in the Army and Air Force. Southern Rhodesian citizens only comprise a small fraction of the Rhodesian armed forces and police and, next to Britain, South Africa provides the largest contingent. Without their British officers, Southern Rhodesian Air Force, Army and Police would be crippled. It seems to me imperative that Britain should recall at once all British Air Force and Police Officers and should state that the United Kingdom Government would regard as treason the action of any British subject who continued to serve in the Smith forces after a certain date.

Many of these officers are in receipt of pensions from Britain for past services in the United Kingdom Police or defence forces. It should be made clear that the pensions of any officers who continue to serve under Smith will be forfeited.

If the United Kingdom Government were to take the various steps which I have outlined, it is possible that these would bring the rebels down but there is no certainty of this. It is therefore much more appropriate that the Southern Rhodesian question is dealt with by the United Nations.

Hitherto the United Kingdom Government has always claimed that Southern Rhodesia is a purely internal matter. Such a claim is nonsense today. British authority does not extend beyond a deserted villa in the suburbs of Salisbury where the British Governor wanders through the empty corridors.

The Resolution of the Security Council taken five days ago states – and I quote its actual words:

'That the situation resulting from the proclamation of independence by the illegal authorities in Southern Rhodesia is

359

extremely serious, that the United Kingdom Government should put an end to it and that its continuance in time constitutes a threat to international peace and security.'

It is important to note that this wording places the Southern Rhodesia issue under Chapter 7 of the Charter of the United Nations which is the Chapter that deals with threats to world peace and which enables the Security Council to give mandatory instructions to all member states.

Under this Chapter the United Nations can halt all road, rail and air communication with Southern Rhodesia. It can also order military sanctions. I consider that the Security Council must, if the United Nations is to survive as an effective force, order such military sanctions if the present economic sanctions are proved ineffective against the Rhodesian rebellion.

It is necessary to point out that the Security Council can order military intervention without necessarily setting up a United Nation's force. In my view it would be much better if the Security Council in the United Nations were to authorize African States, either collectively or individually, to intervene militarily to suppress the rebellion in Southern Rhodesia in the event of the United Kingdom Government being unable or unwilling to do so. It would be desirable if all permanent members of the Security Council guaranteed against attack by Portugal or South Africa the African States undertaking these police measures on behalf of the United Nations. But it would not be necessary in practice for all the permanent members to give such a guarantee. If it could be obtained from one of them it would be sufficient.

Finally, it is necessary to consider the possible role of the Organization of African Unity.

It could, of course, act in concert with the United Kingdom Government if the members were convinced that Britain genuinely intended to put down the revolt. The Zambian Government has already offered the United Kingdom military bases in Zambia if Britain desires to place forces in Africa either to suppress the rebellion or at least to protect those African States which are threatened by the rebels. The United Kingdom has not accepted Zambia's generous offer. Nevertheless, in order to make Ghana's position clear, I wish to state that if the British Government desires to use Ghanaian territory for any purpose connected with the suppression of the Southern Rhodesian Government we shall accord every facility possible.

The second possible role which the Organization of African Unity might undertake is to act as a peace force of the United Nations. For this purpose it is essential that we establish as soon as possible a unified military command and engage in detailed planning so that we deploy our military forces to the best advantage.

Finally, the Organization of African Unity must consider what action it will take if both Britain and the United Nations fail within a given time effectively to deal with the Southern Rhodesian situation.

If a cry for help comes to us from the victims of oppression in Southern Rhodesia, we, the African States, must answer it. It is for this reason that the National Assembly is being asked tomorrow to enact legislation to give the Government power to prepare for any military eventuality. The Bill which will be introduced under a certificate of urgency seeks to give the Government general powers to make all laws necessary for mobilization. Already the first steps in this direction have been taken. Members of the Armed Forces who have completed their time of service are being retained in the forces. As a precaution all military leave has been stopped.

Under existing law we are going to establish a militia. This militia will be a voluntary force. Its members will not be paid. Their training will be on a part-time basis and their enrolment is to start on Monday next.

Under the Bill which you will be asked to pass the Government is given power to requisition Ghanaian aircraft and ships. You may remember that at the time of the Congo crisis the Western powers failed to provide us with air transport which they had promised. The Government cancelled all internal and external services of Ghana Airways and used the aircraft to transport our troops. We shall not hesitate to do the same thing again. The Bill also enables airports, seaports and roads to be closed in whole or in part in order to facilitate troop movements. I must warn you that a mobilization on the scale which we have in mind must entail considerable disorganization of civilian life but in a crisis of this nature we must put military necessity first.

In everything we must be realistic; it would not be possible for Ghana alone to defeat the forces of the Southern Rhodesian settlers. Nevertheless Ghana forces, if properly mobilized and deployed could provide very powerful support for any African State which was threatened by the Smith Regime. Ghana, in conjunction with a number of other African States who may have taken the same steps of military preparedness as we have done, would certainly be able to defeat the rebels.

Any war against the rebels would not be like a normal war. For every racialist in Southern Rhodesia there are sixteen Africans. Once arms have been put in their hands the war is as good as over. As I see it, if African armed forces are compelled to put down the Smith regime by force then this will not be done by means of conventional warfare but by organizing a rising in mass by the people.

I consider that when the African States meet at Addis Ababa on the 3rd December, there is one other step which should be considered most seriously. Outside the African continent there are thousands – indeed hundreds of thousands – of individuals with military training who are prepared to fight against racialism. In fact I have already received numerous telegrams and letters from individuals and organizations outside Africa who are prepared to fight for the liberation of Zimbabwe. We must consider realistically how we can mobilize and equip them. In some countries voluntary contributions could be organized by which these volunteers would be provided with the necessary equipment. This is a proposal we must consider in all its implications.

In any event it is my firm view that at the forthcoming Addis Ababa meeting the African Defence Organization, which was approved by the Heads of State at the recent Accra Summit Conference, should be set up immediately.

It is unfortunate that the proposal which I made two years ago for the setting up of an African High Command was not taken up, otherwise Africa would not find itself in this predicament.

I am reminded of a story. A little boy had read many stories in his Children's books about many a life and death struggle between a man and a lion. In all the stories no matter how fearlessly and ferociously the lion fought the man each time emerged the victor. This puzzled the boy so he asked his father: 'Why is it, father, that in all those stories the man always beats the lion when everybody knows quite well that the lion is the toughest and strongest animal in all the jungle?' The father answered: 'Son, those stories will always end like that until the lion learns how to write.'

These are serious days for the world. I wish that I could believe that the United Kingdom Government was sincere in its desire to put down the rebellion but from their past actions I see no sign of it. I hope that time may prove me wrong. If it does not, then a heavy responsibility will fall upon all African States and we in Ghana must today begin to prepare to take our share in that responsibility.

GHANA BREAKS DIPLOMATIC RELATIONS WITH BRITAIN—ADDRESS TO THE NATIONAL ASSEMBLY ON THE SOUTHERN RHODESIAN SITUATION

16th December 1965

Mr Speaker, Members of the National Assembly,

The House will recall that at the Summit Conference of the Organization of African Unity held at Accra last October, it was unanimously decided that in the event of the failure on the part of the United Kingdom to use all possible means, including the use of force, to oppose a unilateral declaration of independence by the Southern Rhodesian Settlers, all members of the Organization of African Unity would reconsider, among other matters, their diplomatic relations with the United Kingdom. In accordance with this resolution, when it became clear that the United Kingdom Government was not using effective means to quell the rebellion, the Council of Ministers meeting recently at Addis Ababa unanimously decided that all Member States of the Organization of African Unity should break off diplomatic relations with Britain. The decision was that if by the 15th of December, that is yesterday, Britain had not put down the rebellion, we of the Independent African States should sever diplomatic relations with Britain.

The breaking of diplomatic relations is a serious step, and the Ghana Government had therefore hoped that the United Kingdom Government would take some action which might justify African States refraining from making a move which, however valuable as a protest, must have grave consequences.

Since 1963, I have continuously emphasized to the British Government the seriousness of the situation in Southern Rhodesia and the dangers it could pose for our relationship, unless it were handled firmly and effectively. In particular, I pointed out the serious consequences inherent in the transfer of the attributes of sovereignty to Rhodesia without majority rule. I have also stressed time and again that the handing over of the armed forces which the British had built up for the former Central African Federation to a minority Settler regime whose avowed policy has always been to maintain a racialist state was bound to lead to a situation such as confronts us today. It is against this background that Ghana raised this question at the Security Council in September, 1963, and urged the Council to call upon the United Kingdom Government not to hand over these armed forces and other attributes of sovereignty to the Southern Rhodesian minority settler regime. As you know, Mr Speaker, all my warnings went unheeded, and my forebodings have come true. Indeed, by vetoing Ghana's resolution the United Kingdom Government actually made the present situation inevitable. History thus holds Britain responsible.

It is therefore clear that my Government has taken all possible steps to let the British Government know of Africa's concern in an effort to avoid the present crisis. We have consistently urged on the United Kingdom Government policies which could have averted the present unhappy situation. Only last Tuesday, I sent a special delegation to deliver a personal message from me to the Prime Minister of the United Kingdom, Mr Harold Wilson. In that message I made it clear to the British Prime Minister that as there was no evidence that Britain was taking positive and effective action to quell the rebellion in Southern Rhodesia, the Government of Ghana was in honour bound to carry out the decision taken by the Organization of African Unity at Addis Ababa on the 3rd December this year.

I have considered very carefully a reply which Mr Wilson sent to me yesterday. There is nothing in Mr Wilson's letter which could justify a change in our position. Ghana's position is that sanctions alone are inadequate, unless backed by military intervention. I am still of the view that the measures which Britain proposes to take are inadequate to deal with the situation. The United Kingdom Government shows no intention of taking military action to quell this rebellion.

The Government of Ghana has, therefore, severed diplomatic relations with Britain as from yesterday, and the United Kingdom Government has been informed accordingly.

Mr Speaker, I would like to make it clear that the rupture of relations with Britain does not affect British business interests or individuals in Ghana, nor does it affect the services of British technical and professional personnel (including those in the Armed Forces) recruited directly by the Ghana Government or on loan to us through Technical Assistance from the United Kingdom.

If and when the United Kingdom Government succeeds in crushing the Ian Smith rebellion and solves the Rhodesian crisis in the interests of the majority of the Rhodesian people, the Government of Ghana will normalize relations.

It would appear that British policy in regard to Southern Rhodesia is to treat what is essentially an African problem as though it were exclusively a British concern. Up to the very last moment I was hoping that the United Kingdom Government would show some response to the initiative of the Organization of African Unity. In all this, the British Prime Minister has gone to the utmost lengths to make every concession to the Ian Smith regime. Throughout, Mr Wilson has disregarded the feelings of the African people in this matter. In this connection, it is futile to talk of further Commonwealth Prime Ministers' meetings at this time, when the undertakings given by the British Government at the last Prime Ministers' Conference in London have been totally ignored.

Mr Speaker, the Southern Rhodesian issue has brought to a head a more fundamental question affecting the interests and destiny of Africa. Upon this issue all African States must take a definite stand. I would like to clarify this point further. By the accident of history almost all the Independent African States were once colonies of European powers and because of this the relationships and associations formed during the colonial period have continued in one form or another even after independence. Typical of such associations is the French Community or the British Commonwealth, to which Ghana chose to belong of her own free will after independence.

On the other hand, our policy in Africa has been based on the fundamental necessity to establish an all-African approach to the problems of the African continent. This is why I have been advocating the establishment of a Continental Union Government of Africa all these years.

The movement for African Unity has now made considerable progress and will continue to grow until it reaches its goal: a Union Government for all Africa. It is clear, however, that the Commonwealth connection is misunderstood by the non-Commonwealth countries in Africa and is used by them as an argument for setting up other groupings which seek to foster active links with former Colonial powers.

Mr Speaker, as you know, Ghana has participated actively as a member of the Commonwealth and had even proposed the establishment of a Commonwealth Secretariat in order to make the Commonwealth more in tune with the common aspirations of its members. However, Ghana's membership within the Commonwealth has made it difficult for her to pursue boldly and effectively her African objectives, namely, the struggle against colonialism and neo-colonialism and the establishment of an All-African Union Government. This difficulty has been high-lighted by the present crisis in Southern

Rhodesia and by the inadequate manner in which the United Kingdom Government has so far handled the rebellion.

The conception of the Commonwealth was built up upon the idea that it provided a bridge between peoples of all races and of all stages of development. The manner in which events in Southern Rhodesia have been handled by the United Kingdom Government has undermined and betrayed this conception.

Mr Speaker, in these circumstances, and in order to preserve African Unity so as to facilitate the earliest formation of a Union Government for Africa, the Government of Ghana must consider withdrawing from the Commonwealth. To this end, we propose to hold the necessary consultations within the Organization of African Unity as to the severance from ex-colonial powers of ties which militate against African Unity.

As I said before, African Unity and our endeavours to establish a Union Government for Africa are imperilled by African States forming links with their ex-colonial masters. Our unity can only be preserved and a Union Government achieved and stabilized if we sever links with former colonial powers whose continuing interest in our Continent only breeds disunity amongst us.

For this reason, the Government of Ghana will place before the next Organization of African Unity Summit conference a resolution calling upon all member states of the Organization of African Unity to sever such links as stand in the way of African Unity or impede its progress, whether such links be with the French, British, Spanish, Portuguese, Belgian or what have you. Such united action by all member states of the Organization of African Unity is the best means and the surest way of guaranteeing the unity and security of the independent States of Africa.

Mr Speaker, I have taken this opportunity to make Ghana's position clear to the world and in particular to our brothers and colleagues of our Sister States of Africa. It is my view that, in the interest of African Unity, there should be no political or economic re-grouping or blocs in Africa in alliance with an ex-colonial power or any foreign power for that matter. And any economic grouping in Africa must be only under the aegis and umbrella of the Organization of African Unity.

In pursuit of this objective the time has now come for the Organization of African Unity to create and develop the essential machinery for African Unity, namely,

(a) a Common Monetary Authority which will enable us to

pool our resources in order to survive the pressures which can be applied to us;

(*b*) an All-African Common Market to serve our expanding economies;

(*c*) an African High Command which can defend our Continent and ensure the security of the member states, and

(*d*) an Executive to co-ordinate and harmonize our efforts on an all-African basis.

Mr Speaker, the Southern Rhodesian crisis has once again exposed the weakness of the Organization of African Unity. If, as I had proposed at the Accra Summit Conference, an Executive of the Organization of African Unity had been established, we would now have been fully prepared to carry out the decisions of the Accra Summit Conference and the Addis Ababa meeting of the Council of Ministers in regard to the Rhodesian crisis. If we had had an African High Command we would now be in a better position to give military assistance to our brothers in Zambia and Zimbabwe. As I have said before, military operations are a complex and difficult matter. They cannot be suddenly improvised. If we blame Britain for not having taken steps in advance to deal with the Southern Rhodesian rebels, the African states must equally blame themselves for not having made adequate preparations to deal with such situations.

Mr Speaker, today Africa is facing a great challenge – in fact the greatest challenge in its chequered history. And we must act in such a way as to uphold her honour and dignity. Let no one underrate or miscalculate the strength of a United Africa.

25

The failure of the OAU, and of Britain and the United Nations, to act decisively to put down the rebellion in Rhodesia in November 1965, was a major factor in triggering off the rapid succession of coup d'etats which have taken place in Africa since then. Our continued disunity, shown clearly in the failure of the Accra OAU Summit of October 1965 to set up an African High Command and an Executive Council, stimulated imperialist and neocolonialist forces operating throughout our continent. While the independent African states hang so tenaciously to their separate identities and interests, the enemies of the African people, the imperialists and neocolonialists and their local agents, strengthen the bonds which unite them, and set us an example in planning on a continental scale. The Pan-African barometer had been tested over the Rhodesian issue, and had been seen to be virtually static.

The months following UDI were ones of chaos and confusion. Ghana broke diplomatic relations with Britain, and gave notice of a probable withdrawal from the Commonwealth. But the strongly worded OAU resolutions of October 1965 were in the main disregarded by most of the member states. A hastily summoned OAU conference was held in Lagos. It was poorly attended, and failed to achieve any positive results. There followed a military coup in Nigeria on 15 January 1966, when the government of Balewa was toppled. At that time, the opinion was widely expressed in political circles throughout the world that Africa was 'going the way of South America', and was rapidly becoming a continent of great political instability, and fertile ground for an indefinite period of neocolonialist exploitation. We could expect a succession of military coups, and increasingly oppressive and reactionary regimes as revolutionary movements of workers and peasants, and liberation movements, gained momentum and challenged the new breed of military rulers.

In Ghana, at the beginning of 1966, we were at a critical point in our struggle to win economic independence, and to push forward our socialist policies. On 23 January 1966, I inaugurated the completed Volta River Project at Akosombo. This great project was designed to provide the electricity needed for our industrialization programme. In addition, sufficient power was to be generated to cater also for the need of sister African states. We were all set, with the implementation of the Seven Year Development Plan, for an economic and socialist transformation of our society. Ghana was developing the resources to become a power house of the African Revolution.

A week later, on 1 February 1966, I addressed the National Assembly. Some three weeks afterwards, on the 24th February 1966, while I was on my way to Hanoi at the invitation of President Ho Chi Minh, with proposals for ending the war in Vietnam, a clique of army and police traitors, supported by neocolonialists and certain reactionary elements within Ghana, seized power. In the name of 'national liberation' they halted, and then turned back the processes of socialist revolution in Ghana, and

369

so betrayed the African people in their struggle for total
liberation and unification.

SESSIONAL SPEECH TO THE
NATIONAL ASSEMBLY

1st February, 1966

Mr Speaker, Members of the National Assembly,
The opening of this session of Parliament, the first of the new
year, and also our budget session, comes at a critical period in the
history of the African Revolution. All over our continent, we are
beset by forces created by neo-colonialism, forces which must be
faced, fought and vanquished.

The liberation movement is, however, awake to this threat. It will
continue to resist and fight this menace until its final collapse, and
we shall erect in the place of neo-colonialism the edifice of a continental union government. Until this is achieved, we shall continue
to witness the crises and shocks which we are now experiencing in
many parts of our continent.

Two years ago, at Addis Ababa, I warned my brother African
Heads of State and Government that the fruits of our disunity
would spell chaos and confusion, *coup d'etats* and boundary disputes
and be a breeding ground for corruption and neo-colonialist con-
spiracies and intrigues in our individual States.

As we all know, within the last few months there have been unfortunate military intrusions into the political life of several independent African States. And if we do not establish an all-African political
union such intrusions will continue to occur in some of the remaining
states of Africa.

Normally, the duty of the armed forces is to defend and support
the Civil Government, and not to overthrow it. It is not the duty of
the army to rule or govern, because it has no political mandate and
its duty is not to seek a political mandate. The army only operates
under the mandate of the civil government. If the national interest
compels the armed forces to intervene then immediately after the
intervention the army must hand over to a new civil government

elected by the people and enjoying the people's mandate under a constitution accepted by them. If the Army does not do this then the position of the army becomes dubious and anomalous and involves a betrayal of the people and the national interest. The substitute of a military regime or dictatorship is no solution to the neo-colonialist problem.

What therefore has led to the military intrusions and interference and violence which we are now witnessing? Why is it that the armies of certain African States have been forced to take the steps which they have taken? We must examine critically and carefully the underlying forces and circumstances which have given rise to these upheavals. Their root cause can be found not in the life and traditions of the African people, but in the manouevres of neo-colonialism.

In a neo-colonialist State, the leaders of the Government allow themselves to be used and manipulated by foreign states and financial interests. The whole regime of a neo-colonialist state is therefore subject to remote control. In other words, the rulers and governors of the neo-colonialist regime are tele-guided from afar. These foreign powers and interests seek to maintain the exploitation and oppression of the people even after independence. Corruption, bribery, nepotism, shameless, and riotous and ostentatious living become rife among the leaders of the neo-colonialist regime. This brings untold suffering on the workers and people as a whole. The masses become lethargic and see no reason to make any sacrifices for their country. They see plainly and clearly before their eyes a conspiracy of their leaders and the neo-colonialists to defraud them and to drain the fruits of their labours into the pockets of the neo-colonialists and their agents in the regime.

In these circumstances, the real fruits of independence are denied to the people, and they become incensed and frustrated. Even though disillusioned and frustrated, the masses are once again mobilized even more militantly to remove the neo-colonialist and client regime, knowing full well that the regime, supported by the neo-colonialists, will not hesitate to use the army to crush them.

If the masses persist in their protest, they are sure to come in conflict with the army, and civil war results. The masses of the people have then nowhere to turn for redress. They therefore have no choice but to organize to isolate the army from the corrupt regime, if the army itself is free from the taint of corruption. But if the army itself is corrupt or if it proves impossible to detach it from the corrupt regime, then the people have no choice but to take up arms against the neo-colonialist regime. The people's struggle for freedom and justice would have reached the phase of civil conflict which invariably takes the form of guerrilla war, that is, people's war – a nationalist revolutionary war. Let us remember always that in the final analysis the masses are the final arbiter. They will always choose freedom and justice, as against oppression and corruption. They will always find a way to give expression to their will as against neo-colonialism and against the betrayal of the people by the armed forces.

As part of the neo-colonialist strategy, the independent African States are made to believe that their constitutions must be based on an imitation of Western Parliamentary systems. Before they quit, the colonial power imposes a Constitution which is alien to the traditions and true aspirations of the people. It is this state of affairs which fosters the development of neo-colonialism and breeds discontent and frustration among the people. But the chaos, confusion, corruption, nepotism and misery engendered by such unreflecting imitation have exposed the futility and ineffectiveness of the Western Parliamentary system in Africa.

It is for this reason that the Western Parliamentary system is being forsaken in Africa, and there is a growing tendency towards the establishment of one-Party States, and rightly so. Because of our egalitarian society, this development becomes natural and understandable. The multi-party system which exists in western countries is in fact a reflection of a social cleavage and the kind of class system which does not exist in African countries. A multi-party system introduced into Africa results in the perpetuation of feudalism, tribalism and regionalism and an inordinate power struggle and rivalry.

We have established in Ghana a people's parliamentary socialist democracy, that is, a one-party State within a people's parliamentary socialist democracy where the will of the people, expressed through their majority, is supreme. In fact, here in Ghana, political power resides in the people. It is they, and they alone, who make, enshrine and uphold our Constitution – the fundamental law of our land.

But let me emphasize that a one-party system of Government is an effective and safe instrument only when it operates in a socialist society. In other words, it must be a political expression of the will of the masses working for the ultimate good and welfare of the people as a whole. On the other hand, a one-party system of government in a neo-colonialist client state, subject to external pressures and control, can quickly develop into the most dangerous form of tyranny, despotism and oppression. It can become, in the hands of a few privileged rascally-minded and selfish individuals in a neo-colonialist state, a weapon and tool for suppressing the legitimate aspirations of the people in the interests of foreign powers and their agents. I repeat, a one-party state can only function for the good of the people within the framework of a socialist state or in a developing state with a socialist programme. The government governs through the people, and not through class cleavages and interests. In other words, the basis of government is the will of the people.

It is in the face of these considerations, that I have made a constant appeal to my brother African Heads of State and Government for continental unity based on a Union Government and warned them of the dangers of our present disunity. I shall continue to appeal and warn until the political unification of Africa is achieved.

Alone, few of the Independent African States have the markets, the raw materials or the capital to build even a single large scale modern industrial complex. United in a continental Union Government, we could plan the use of our rich natural resources, our markets, and our capital to build giant complexes, iron and steel industries, hydro-electric projects in key areas throughout the continent. Such projects, planned on a continental scale, could assist in our endeavours for continental economic reconstruction.

United, we could bargain more effectively with foreign investment and governments. Our united economies could provide large markets [and would make large-scale efficient industries profitable for all concerned. Together, we could borrow funds to finance our hydro-electric schemes, construction of essential transport, factories and infrastructure facilities to ensure the necessary specialization and division of labour for continental economic growth. Together, in a mighty continent-wide political union, we could ensure the stability and resources necessary to guarantee that loans and investments were paid off at reasonable rates. Thus the potential of a new life can be provided for all Africa, if we establish a continent-wide Union Government.

A Union Government of Africa would be in a position to provide ready assistance on a continental scale to the independent African States, whose resources are inadequate to meet their expanding needs. It will also prevent them from seeking such help outside the African continent. The African States will thus be assisted in their efforts to safeguard their national independence and sovereignty against the pressures and plunder of foreign powers and foreign interests. Thus all the Independent African States, big or small, have everything and little to lose by a continental Union Government of Africa.

This month we shall welcome the independence of Bechuanaland. The fact that Bechuanaland can become independent shows how false is the suggestion that the African majority of Southern Rhodesia are not ready for self-rule. By virtue of the same argument why can't the other neighbouring colonized territories in Southern Africa be free and independent? Nevertheless, Bechuanaland, which is surrounded by South Africa and Southern Rhodesia, will obviously be in need of outside assistance. Such assistance should come from Africa. If the assistance comes from outside Africa on terms which militate against the interest of the people, Bechuanaland will cease to be independent, and neo-colonialism will set in.

This problem will also have to be faced by a few other African territories expected to accede to Independence shortly. If the interests of the Africans who inhabit these territories are to be upheld then this problem must be solved within the context of an all-African political union.

As you know, the Rhodesian question remains unresolved. In spite of our repeated warnings and advice, the British Government has consistently refused to resort to the use of the one effective weapon, namely military and police action, to crush the rebellion. As we foresaw, the Lagos Conference served no useful purpose and sanctions have so far not succeeded in bringing down the Ian Smith illegal regime. Action by the Independent African States is therefore more urgent than ever. My Government will put forward concrete proposals for joint action when the OAU Council of Ministers meets in Addis Ababa on the 17th of this month.

Here at home, our general economic situation is, to a large extent, dictated by the overall balance of economic power in the world. So far as cocoa, our principal export is concerned, if Africa were united under a union government, Africa would be able to set a price for world cocoa in exactly the same way as developed countries set a price for their exports of machinery and manufactured goods. As it is at the moment, however, the price of cocoa, like the price of many primary commodities produced by other developing countries is at the mercy of a capitalist-controlled world market, which is oriented to the disadvantage of the developing countries. What we obtain for our exports in hard cash depends not primarily on how much of these exports we can produce but on the price which powerful world forces, over which we have no control, are prepared to pay for them.

The manipulation of our cocoa price is only one illustration of this general world economic system. The gap between the developed countries and the developing countries, instead of narrowing year by year is widening. So long as Africa remains divided they will lack the strength to obtain a fair and equitable treatment from the developed nations of the world.

It will be seen, therefore, that the securing of a just cocoa price is essentially a political question. It cannot be solved by Ghana alone. It could be solved by the cocoa producing states of Africa if they were united in a Union Government which had effective overall economic planning powers. Our experience with the price of cocoa is the same as other primary commodities, like groundnuts, coffee, sisal and many others which are grown and exported by our sister African States. A Union Government for Africa is therefore a necessity, and a prerequisite for Africa's economic progress and survival.

In economic terms our policy of non-alignment means that we must not depend upon any one country or group of countries for capital investment and trade. Our aim must be to trade with and to secure investment from all countries in the world, irrespective of their economic systems and political ideologies. As I have repeatedly emphasized, we are not against foreign investment as such. We welcome foreign investment provided that there are no strings attached to it, and also provided that it fits in with our plans for national development and our socialist policy. And we insist that foreign investment should not interfere or meddle with the political life of our country.

It is important to make this point quite clear. The experience of developing countries is that foreign capital tends to entrench itself and to influence the political and economic life of the receiving country. Where the foreign capital is guaranteed by its government, that government sometimes attempts to involve itself in the life and development of the country under the guise of protecting its capital. It is vital both for the developed and developing countries that foreign governments and investors should desist from any attempt, overt or covert, at political domination in the developing countries in which they invest. When foreign investment interferes in or meddles with the political life of the country in which it invests, it then becomes part of the neo-colonialist system.

But as I have pointed out elsewhere, in the last analysis a solution to this problem may be the establishment of an international insurance agency which would provide a guarantee for foreign governments and investors on the same basis for example, as Lloyd's provides insurance cover for shipping interests and investments throughout the world.

We cannot look to foreign investment to provide an automatic solution to our problems. Foreign, private or public investment will not provide the bulk of the capital needed for our industrialization. The bulk of it must come from our own savings. We therefore intend to mount a vigorous savings campaign throughout the country. We must strengthen our economy. We must make sure that the progress which we have made already is not jeopardized by over straining our resources. We have now reached the point in our national development where we need to pause for a while, take stock of what we have achieved so far, which by any standard is remarkable. We shall then be ready to move ahead with increased momentum. We must therefore look upon this year, 1966 as a year of stocktaking, but not of stagnation.

An impartial look at our development effort since independence should leave no one in doubt as to the success of our national endeavours in the field of economic and social reconstruction. Within the short span of eight years since independence, we have built some of the finest roads in the world; we have provided adequate medical and health services for the large majority of our people; we have built universities, secondary schools, training colleges and provided opportunities for free education for the great mass of the population. We have completed the gigantic Volta River Project one year ahead of schedule.

This industrial growth and development has created a number of problems with which we must tackle. As a result of this vast and unprecedented development programme, there is more money available in the pockets of the people than there are goods to buy. Secondly, as I have explained, we have failed to obtain the foreign exchange to which our exports including our greatly increased cocoa export entitle us. This has resulted in foreign exchange earnings not rising as we had every right to expect they would, in view of our greatly increased production.

For this reason, I have directed that the size of the 1966 Budget should be reduced to a level which can be supported by available revenue. We may, therefore have to rephase some of our development projects so as to reduce their impact on our total expenditure budget. The purpose of these arrangements will be to produce an expenditure plan, which while ensuring sustained economic growth, will at the same time reduce our dependence on outside sources for help to complete projects under our Seven-Year Development Plan. In this connection a number of other steps have already been taken by the Bank of Ghana. These include credit control arrangements,

376

designed to restrain expenditure in the economy of our country. They also involve arrangements to ensure the careful and wise utilization of our foreign exchange earnings.

In spite of the comparatively heavy cuts in our total planned expenditure this financial year, the Budget which will be presented to you will make large sums of money available for expenditure on the Public Services, the State Enterprises and Public Boards. It is the intention of the Government that every pesewa voted should be properly accounted for. To this end, I have given directions that the Auditor-General's Department should conduct a detailed scrutiny of all revenue and expenditure, and expose all irregularities that may be committed in any sector of the economy.

As a further measure of ensuring that State Corporations and Industries manage their affairs efficiently and profitably a State Enterprises Audit Corporation has been established to examine the accounts of all State and Joint State Enterprises.

We will continue to follow the policy of producing, as much as possible, a very high proportion of essential goods and services that are consumed here from day to day. This will enable us to reduce our dependence on the importation of foreign imports. It will also create opportunities for employment, and for exploiting our other natural resources endowments. During this year, we shall devote more of our resources to productive investments, namely, agriculture and industry and mining, so that we may be able by the end of our Seven-Year plan to reach our planned growth rate of 5·5% per annum. For this purpose, I have already directed that over one-half of the 1966 budget shall be devoted to productive investments.

When I addressed this House a year ago, there were thirty-five State Enterprises in operation. Today, there are fifty-two, including twenty-five manufacturing and industrial enterprises. Among the new enterprises which have recently been commissioned are the Glass Manufacturing Corporation at Aboso, the Cement Works, Tema, the Government Electronics Industry at Tema and the Cocoa Processing Factories at Takarodi and Tema; the Publishing Corporation which now prints our school textbooks and the Textile Corporation now producing here in Ghana cloths and wax prints for the people. The Ghana People's Trading Corporation has also been recently established along-side the Ghana National Trading Corporation to assist the Consumer Co-operative Societies to distribute and sell both local and imported goods cheaply in the rural areas.

Very soon, further industrial projects will start production. These will include the corned beef factory at Bolgatanga, the Sugar Factory at Akuse and a Television Assembly Plant at Tema.

We hope to establish over next five years a thousand rural industrial projects throughout the country. Already two Coir Fibre Factories, each with a total capacity of 990,000 lb. of Coir fibre and over 1,000 lb. of door and floor mats are in operation. Bamboo factories are presently being established at Manso-Amenfi, Assin Foso and Axim to manufacture bamboo cups and trays which can artistically adorn the dinner table of a Ghanaian family in a Ghanaian way.

The Rattan Factory established at Asamankese is already in production and five other factories at Nkawkaw, Enyiresi, Oppon Valley, Asanwinso and Bobikuma will go into production this year. A factory at Axim will be developed into a training centre for Rattan, Bamboo, Coir and wood projects. It will have laboratory facilities to enable experiments to be conducted into improved methods of production, using local materials.

In the re-organization and development of the Co-operative Movement in the country, we must place emphasis on the establishment of a strong net-work of Consumer Co-operatives in the rural areas. These will assist in the fair and equitable distribution of available Consumer goods throughout the country.

Our progress in industry must be closely linked to a vigorous agricultural programme. We must ensure that we apply the right techniques that can maximize the benefits of modern science and technology in agriculture. To this end an Agricultural Council has been established to serve as a forum for the exchange of ideas between the Government Agencies, Universities, the Ghana Academy of Sciences and other institutions concerned with agriculture.

In addition to cocoa and other farm crops, our national economy can be firmly buttressed by a progressive programme of afforestation, conservation and the exploitation of timber from our forests. Ghana timber is renowned and popular on the world market, and every effort will be made to increase its production.

The recently created Ministry of Animal Husbandry has been directed to establish a livestock industry to cater for the meat requirements of the country, including milk and other livestock products from local resources.

Alongside these developments including improved poultry, pig and cattle production, sheep and goat multiplication ranches have been sited at Ejura and Wenchi to provide breeding stocks to farmers and improve the meat supply on the market.

A Dairy Production Unit has been established within the Ministry of Animal Husbandry to undertake a positive programme of increasing dairy products from local sources, so as to reduce our present dependence on supplies from foreign sources. The Government is seriously examining plans for the setting up of a chemical fertilizer plant.

In view of the importance of agriculture to Ghana, plans have been made to establish a University College of Agriculture. In the meantime, an Inter-Faculty Committee, composed of staff from the University of Ghana and the Kwame Nkrumah University of Science and Technology has been set up. They are preparing a single plan of higher education in agriculture to be brought immediately into operation when the University College is physically established.

Next in importance to the provision of food comes the housing needs of our people. Let us remember that our population is increasing faster than our expectation. I have therefore directed that during the financial year, 1966, the Housing Corporation should embark on the construction of additional estates throughout the country.

The new giant pre-fabricated housing factory now under construction will start full-scale production this year. As a result, our housing programme throughout the country will be accelerated.

During 1966, more and larger water conservation and irrigation schemes will be completed to supply farms in Northern and Southern Ghana with water throughout the year and at all times.

We attach great importance to the communications system in the country and we also intend to construct those major roads and bridges included in the Seven-Year Development Plan, and I will continue to pursue a comprehensive programme of road maintenance.

The Tano Bridge linking Navrongo to Tumu in the Upper Region as well as the bridge over River Ankase on the Western Border will be completed in the year. Preliminary work will start on the construction of a bridge over the River Ankobra on the Axim-Half Assini Road and a bridge over the River Oti on the new Dodi-Papase-Bimbila Road. Work on the Lower Volta Bridge continues to make very satisfactory progress, and will be completed by the end of the year.

In Accra, new roads will be constructed and work will continue on the widening of more and more major roads to avoid traffic congestion in the City. Already, the new concrete double carriage motorway linking Tema with Accra has been opened and this motorway will be extended to link up with the Nsawam and Winneba roads.

The construction of two new Berths at the Tema Harbour has been completed, and work on the Tema Shipyard and Drydock and the Fishing Harbour will continue as planned. By December this year the new Drydock will be brought into use, as an important centre for the building and repair of ships. Already Tema is beginning to feel the strain of our expanding trade and soon the construction of new berths may become necessary.

In order to support expansion of our industrial programme it is vital that we should establish and maintain a first class and modern telephone system. To this end the modernization of our telephone and telecommunication services is being given top priority. In Accra alone there are over 35,000 subscribers, more than double the position at independence in 1957. A new telephone exchange is now under construction near the Kwame Nkrumah Circle which when completed next year will provide over 8,000 additional lines. Even this will prove inadequate in view of our rapidly expanding industrial and commercial development.

In keeping with our policy of forging close links with the Independent African States, direct telegraph and telephone communications between Accra and the capitals of African States will be completed this year.

Our educational programme continues to expand at a very fast rate. No less than 400 new Middle and Primary Schools were opened at the beginning of the current academic year, resulting in an increase in the enrolment by 200,000. At present, therefore, there are 1,480,000 children in 10,388 Primary and Middle Schools.

Eleven new Secondary schools have been added to the list of assisted schools. There are, therefore, 101 secondary schools in the public system with an enrolment of over 35,000 which is almost half the target of 72,000 set for 1970.

During the current academic year, thirty-four new Teacher Training Colleges have been opened. This has resulted in an additional intake of 2,720 student teachers. The number of teachers in training is therefore 12,720 and the number of training colleges is now 80 as against 46 last year. Thus, in one year we have almost doubled the number of Teacher Training Colleges in Ghana.

It is only by planned expansion of this sort that effective universal education can be secure and maintained.

We are laying very strong emphasis on the teaching of science and science teaching is being given priority in the curricula of both elementary and secondary schools. Modern Science Laboratories for use by elementary schools have been built at Accra, Kumasi, Cape Coast, Sekondi and Ho. Others are to be constructed at Tamale and Bolgatanga. This is part of a pilot project in elementary schools. In addition to this, more and more teachers are being trained to teach science in schools in rural areas.

Technical education is also progressing steadily. Already a Technical Teacher Training College has been built at Kumasi to train teachers; and it is expected that within five years this College will have trained an adequate number of technical teachers for our Polytechnics, Technical Institutes and Training Centres. A third Government Secondary Technical School was opened in Obuasi in November last year and a fourth one, under construction at Koforidua is nearing completion.

Since my last sessional address, the Ministry of Science and Higher Education has been set up, replacing the former National Council for Higher Education.

While higher education advances on a broad front, I have directed that emphasis be laid on education in science and technology with a view to Ghana producing in the shortest possible time not only the Administrators and Managers required to implement our development programme, but also the Scientists, Technologists and Technicians needed in industry and agriculture.

In barely four years, student enrolment in Legon has risen by more than 300 per cent. To bring such large numbers of students up to the high levels of qualification and skill demanded in Ghana, the University has found ways of using its resources and facilities with the greatest economy and efficiency. The Institute of Statistics has made good progress towards providing Ghana with fully-trained statisticians, without whom much of our planning will be based on mere guesswork. Special attempts have been made to increase the intake of science students, and in this way also to introduce a correct balance between the Faculties. Already post-graduate students are being produced from our Universities to satisfy some of our manpower demands.

At the Kwame Nkrumah University of Science and Technology, the former Faculty of Science has been reconstituted into two Faculties, namely, the Faculty of Applied Science and the Faculty of Technology. In the new Faculty of Applied Science courses in Meteorology, Nuclear Physics and Applied Bio-Chemistry have been introduced, while courses in Chemical and Textile Technology and Glassware are planned for the Faculty of Technology.

The student intake at the University College of Science Education in Cape Coast is expected to reach 1,400 in October this year and this College will attain full University status. When this happens, Cape Coast will be declared a University City.

The Ghana Medical School recently established will enter upon its first course of clinical studies in April this year.

The Ghana Academy of Sciences which celebrated its 6th Anniversary last November has been rapidly expanding its scope of scientific research activities to provide the necessary scientific and technological basis for our economic and social development. Last year, the Academy established no less than five new research institutes in the field of food science and technology, aquatic biology, geology and geophysics, industrial standards and marine fisheries. Many more research institutes are in an advanced stage of physical development or of planning. These include the Institute of Glass and Ceramics, the Institute of Metallurgy, the Institute of Wild Life Research, the Institute for Research Development and a Centre for the Production of Scientific instruments.

The Academy, as a full-time national research organization is conducting development research required in the utilization of natural resources of the country. This work should proceed up to the pilot plant stage so that the Academy can advise Government on the feasibility of agricultural and industrial projects being established by Ministries and Corporations, and also render Scientific service to all Ministries and Corporations. The Academy is thus the spearhead to the scientific and technological development of the country. The Academy will also assist the Universities in the training of postgraduate students by providing facilities in its research institutes.

In order to ensure that the rich mineral resources of Ghana are exploited to the full, an intensive oil exploration programme has been launched in the Tano Basin, the Keta Basin and other areas of the country. Actual drilling for oil will be started at Anloga, near Keta in March this year.

The Government attaches the greatest importance to the health needs of the people. To this end we are concentrating on preventive medicine and measures to improve public health services throughout the country.

Health centres will continue as in the past to play a vital role in the promotion of health, and new Health centres will get set up at strategic points in the country.

As part of our programme for the expansion of our health services, three new Institutes of Maternal and Child Health, Tropical Medicine and Aviation Medicine will be established.

With the creation of a Ministry of Tourism, Parks and Gardens, we will intensify our efforts in the development of parks and gardens and tourist attractions throughout the country. We already have evidence of this new and dynamic approach to the beautification of our towns and cities. Ghana's natural attraction for Tourism is second to none in the world. The Government therefore has plans in hand for making a first-class tourist industry in Ghana.

The welfare of women continues to engage our special attention. Quite apart from the several Mass Education Women's Groups operating in our towns and villages, we have established many Girls Vocational Training Centres throughout the country with the aim of catering for the training and welfare of the future mothers of Ghana. Further, a crash programme designed specially for the women of the Northern and Upper Regions has been launched and we have already achieved commendable results with our women in these two Regions.

It is our policy to abolish illiteracy entirely from Ghana. Much has already been done in this field that we are in sight of the complete abolition of illiteracy in Ghana. To this end, a mass assault on the remaining pockets of illiteracy in the country will soon be launched.

The popularity of our television service is increasing daily. It is serving a useful role not only in entertainment but also in education and the fight against illiteracy. Next month I shall open a factory at Tema, jointly established by the Government of Ghana and a Japanese firm (Sanyo) which will mass-produce television sets and thus bring the service within the reach of all our people.

The structural changes in our Local Government set-up which were recommended by the pre-election Delimitation Commission have been brought into effect and the number of Councils increased as a consequence of this from 155 to 183. The working of local Authorities will continue to be reviewed in order to secure greater efficiency and reliability. Irregularities, waste and duplication of efforts, corruption and nepotism in our local government administration must be eliminated. Our pattern of local government must conform with the socialist ideology of the nation.

I am happy to announce that the progress of the Social Security (Pensions) Scheme has fully justified our determination to establish this scheme. The fund is growing steadily. Within the next few years, it is our intention to extend the scheme to cover everybody in Ghana.

Six years ago, I inaugurated the preparatory Committee of the All-African Trade Union Federation. On that occasion, I expressed the hope that the world would understand the aspirations of the African workers to build a non-aligned All-African Trade Union

Federation which, while playing a vital part in the anti-imperialist and anti-neo-colonialist struggle, would remain forever loyal to Africa.

Today, the All-African Trade Union Federation which is fighting in the forefront of the African revolution, has become a living reality. The workers of Africa cannot co-exist with the forces of colonialism and exploitation. They cannot co-exist with Imperialism and Neo-colonialism. Seeing poverty and exploitation around them and seeking a new way of life for themselves, they will continue to strive for a better life for all the people in Africa.

It is the inescapable role of the All-African Trade Union Federation to mobilize, educate and guide the activities of the African workers into new and creative channels which must open up Africa for the all-round development that will benefit the mass of the people. For it is when the workers and farmers have understood the fundamental aims of the African Revolution that we can move forward together in unity and progress.

At home the Ghana Trade Union Congress has the greatest responsibility for ensuring that the workers are given the correct leadership and orientation. Our workers must be mobilized to achieve the production targets of the Seven-Year Development Plan through higher productivity. This calls for labour and enthusiasm, industrial harmony and a clear understanding of our goals.

With the completion of the Volta River Project, Ghana is now poised for a positive break-through in our agricultural and industrial revolution. We have travelled a long way from our colonial past in which our initiative and energies were bottled up by the restrictive conditions of colonial rule. We can now look forward with renewed confidence and inspiration to the greater opportunities made available to us by our Party and Government. In all this, you, Members of Parliament have a great part to play. Ghana looks to you for an example of service, hard work and dedication to duty.

You who are Members of Parliament and all others in the country – teachers, farmers, peasants, market women, workers, civil and public servants – must be awake to your responsibilities in this regard. Let us remember that State property is public property, that is to say, it is property belonging to the people and for which we are all responsible. It is therefore the duty of every person who is put in charge of any State property to realize that he must guard it and protect it jealously in the interest of the Nation. We have made such progress towards a better life for all that anyone who neglects or misuses or misappropriates State property is undermining the Nation, and wilfully holding back our progress.

A basic problem now facing us is to improve the efficiency of our economic administration. If we can solve this problem, all will be well with us. The policies of the Government are clear, sound and well conceived and formulated. And our people have pledged their support for these policies. It is but for us to achieve and maintain a high level of efficiency in giving practical effect to these policies. In particular, our Ministries, Civil Servants, our public officers, Managing Directors of our Boards and Corporations and factories and all functionaries of the Party and the Government need to show a fuller grasp of the detailed administrative steps which must be taken to give effect to our policies. In other words, we need a closer degree of co-ordination and harmony among our economic Ministries and Agencies. A closer co-ordination is required among Ministries, the State Planning Commission, the Banks and other Economic Institutions and Commercial Agencies connected with our national economy. We should not spend so much time rectifying the things that have gone wrong; we must concentrate rather on preventing the things going wrong, and finding remedies for them. Let me give you an example. If there are no drugs for the hospitals, we should not waste so much time establishing which Ministry or agency is to blame. Instead, we should devise positive steps and crash procedures for eliminating such shortages. I am sure you can think of other examples.

It is only by such careful and painstaking economic co-ordination and husbanding of our resources that we can provide the means for better housing, education, health services, and all the other amenities which we must have, in order to create a fuller life for all our people.

I am confident that through your loyalty to the Party and Government, your sacrifice and devotion we can make still further gains in our national reconstruction and development. Only thus can we justify the confidence placed in us by our people. Only thus can we promote the upliftment of Ghana, the redemption of Africa, and make our contribution to world peace and to the welfare and happiness of mankind.

PART THREE

CLASS STRUGGLE, AND THE ARMED PHASE OF THE AFRICAN REVOLUTION

INTRODUCTION TO SECTIONS 26 TO 33

On Wednesday, the 2nd of March 1966, I arrived in Conakry, Guinea, at the invitation of President Sékou Touré and the Guinean people, and here began what I consider to be one of the most fruitful periods of my life. For, in a secluded villa by the sea, my enforced freedom from the day to day work of government leaves me time to study, to contemplate deeply on the problems of Africa, to write, and to prepare actively for the next vital phase of the African Revolution when all methods of struggle, including the use of armed force both conventional and unconventional, may be employed.

Apart from Section 26, the documents which follow are articles and selections from books written in Conakry between 1966 and 1970. They reflect my views on current problems and on the long term aspects of the African Revolution and the world socialist revolutionary struggle. Section 26 is the text of the first broadcast I made to the people of Ghana on Radio Guinea's 'Voice of the African Revolution'. It was made on the 6th of March 1966, on the ninth anniversary of Ghana's independence. I broadcast to the people of Ghana several times after that, and the full text of the broadcasts have been published as a book under the title *Voice from Conakry*.

In 1969, I revised Chapter 3 of *Consciencism*, in order

to emphasize my conviction of the class nature of the struggle being waged in Africa and throughout the world between the forces of reaction and the forces of progress. This revision necessitated the publication in 1970 of a new edition of *Consciencism**. Sections 32 and 33, which contain extracts from the *Handbook of Revolutionary Warfare*, and *Class Struggle in Africa*, reflect my conclusions on the various processes of the African Revolution, the nature of the struggle which lies ahead, and the practical implementation of our socialist revolutionary objectives.

---

* Panaf Books 1970 (paperback).

26

VOICE FROM CONAKRY

The first broadcast to the people of Ghana on Radio Guinea's 'Voice of the African Revolution', 6th March 1966

1. I expect you all at this hour of trial to remain firm in determination and resistance despite intimidation.

FELLOW countrymen, Chiefs and people, I am speaking to you from Radio Guinea, Conakry. On the eve of the 6th of March, Ghana's Independence Day, I send to you all, greetings and warm regards.

It was on this day that the combined forces of the Ghana people secured Independence from British imperialism. This achievement was not an easy task. It involved sacrifice, suffering and deprivation on the part of all of us.

It was only when I arrived at Peking in China that I was informed that some members of my Armed Forces, supported by some members of my Police had attempted to overthrow my Government. I know that you are always loyal to me, the Party and the Government and I expect you all at this hour of trial to remain firm in determination and resistance despite intimidation.

The people of Ghana built up the Convention People's Party which became the vanguard of the national liberation movement in Ghana. By indomitable will the Convention People's Party overcame all difficulties, triumphed over adversities and won independence and planned for the economic, political and social construction of our dear Ghana. The Party and Government fought not only for political independence but evolved a work and happiness programme of reconstruction. We also joined in the great movement for the liberation and political unification of Africa.

The achievement of the Convention People's Party under my leadership is an open book. It can be seen by all, and today, anyone who visits Ghana can be a witness of this great achievement. Internationally, independent Ghana has been playing her role in world affairs. She has supported peace and will always continue to support any movement that can lead to the peace and security of the world.

In all this struggle, the Convention People's Party, and its Government have not shed a single drop of a Ghanaian's blood. I shuddered when I learned of the shooting and killing of defenceless men and women, and the arrest, intimidation and imprisonment of many of the leading patriots of the country. The blood of these gallant men and women cry to heaven for redress. Their blood shall not be shed in vain. Those who have died, may they rest in peace.

By the arrest, detention and assassination of Ministers, the Party's civil servants, trade unionists and by the blind massacre of defenceless men and women, the authors of these insane acts of robbery, violence, intimidation and assassination have added brutality to their treason.

Never before in the cherished history of our new Ghana have citizens, men and women, been assassinated in cold blood and never have their children become orphans for political reasons. Never before have Ghanaians been shot down because of their political convictions. This is a tragedy of monstrous proportions.

But I know your courage and determination: I see the extent of your indignation against this wanton rebellion. I know that at the appropriate time you will take the initiative to crush it. The Party's dynamism will rise up again to save your dignity and personality. As far as I am concerned I will do my very best to crush this criminal rebellion.

The integral wings of the Convention People's Party, the Farmers Co-operative Council, the Trades Union Congress, the National Council of Ghana Women, the Young Pioneers, the Workers' Brigade have been established by the Party and the spirit that motivates these organizations cannot be destroyed. They now suffer in silence but they will rise up again and speak. The present rebellion has not only committed treason against the sovereign state of Ghana but has attacked the very foundation upon which our culture was based – the position of Chieftaincy which has been irrevocably enshrined in our Constitution.

In the Party's struggle for independence we have had opponents and enemies. Imperialism and neo-colonialism and their agents and stooges have not been our friends. They have tried in many ways to undo what the Convention People's Party has done. In all attempts they failed; and even several attempts on my personal life have failed. And so, if today we celebrate our 9th Anniversary of Independence, we have a lot to be thankful for.

Experience has given us added wisdom to continue the struggle. No one can destroy the socialist gains we have achieved. For no reason other than morbid ambition, inordinate and selfish desire for power, certain officers of my Armed Forces took advantage of my absence from Accra to subvert and rebel against constitutional authority. This reactionary rebellion sought to perpetrate subversive activities against the lawfully constituted Government of Ghana.

What has taken place in Ghana is not a coup d'état but a rebellion and it shall be crushed by its own actions. At the moment you are being suppressed at the point of guns and bayonets and you are made speechless by these same instruments. You are forbidden to hold your rallies and meetings. But, I know that even in silence you are determined and resisting. Be assured that I am standing firm behind you. There is a Russian proverb which says that one cannot screen the sun by the palm of a hand; nor can I be destroyed by telling lies about me. Very soon I shall be with you again.

The perpetrators of this rebellion have committed an act of high treason. Those soldiers of my army who have taken power in my absence have issued orders that our 9th Anniversary of Independence, a great national day, should not be celebrated. This shows that they are suppressing you at the points of guns and bayonets. They cannot destroy what we have taken years to build. For, what we have achieved is built on rock foundations and is indestructible. Forward Ever, Backward Never. There is Victory for Us.

I am safe and well. I will be with you in due course. Have courage and bear your humiliation and sufferings with fortitude. What has happened is only a phase of our struggle and it shall pass.

Long live the people of Ghana
Long live the Convention People's Party
Long live the liberation movement of Africa
Long live the African continental government that must be.

27

THE BIG LIE

It has been said that the fabrication of the 'big lie' is essential in the planning of any usurpation of political power. In the case of Ghana, the big lie told to the world was that Ghana needed to be rescued from 'economic chaos'. Various other lies were hinged on this central lie. The country was said to be hopelessly in debt and the people on the verge of starvation. Among the lies aimed against me personally was the one that I had accumulated a large private fortune; this was to form the basis for an all-out character assassination attempt. But these lies were subsidiary to the one big lie of 'economic mismanagement', which was to provide an umbrella excuse for the seizure of power by neo-colonialist inspired traitors.

If Ghana was in such a serious economic condition, why was there no lack of investment in her growing industries? Investors do not put their money into mismanaged enterprises and unstable economies. Why did the imperialist powers try to exert an economic squeeze on Ghana? No one in his right mind bothers to attack an already-dying concern. Who made up the figures of Ghana's supposed 'debt'? Why was only one side of the ledger shown – why no mention of assets? How can the obvious evidence of the modernization and industrialization of Ghana, such as the new roads, factories, schools and hospitals, the harbour and town of Tema, the Volta and Teffle bridges and the Volta dam be reconciled with the charge of wasted expenditure? If the Ghanaian people were starving, why no evidence of this, and why no popular participation in the 'coup'? How was it that Ghana had the highest living standard in Africa per capita, the highest literacy rate, and was the nearest to achieving genuine econ-

394

mic independence? All these questions, and many related to them, are now being asked. An examination of our development plans and of their implementation reveals the truth – that it was their success, and not their failure which spurred our enemies into action. Ghana, on the threshold of economic independence, and in the vanguard of the African revolutionary struggle to achieve continental liberation and unity, was too dangerous an example to the rest of Africa to be allowed to continue under a socialist-directed government.

In the first ten years of its administration, the Ghana government drew up the First and Second Five Year Development Plans (1951–1956 and 1959–1964), and the Consolidation Plan, which covered the two-year gap between these Plans (1957–1959). Under these Plans the foundations were to be laid for the modernization and industrialization of Ghana. A skilled labour force was to be trained and an adequate complement of public services built up such as transport, electricity, water and tele-communications.

We had to work fast. Under colonial rule, foreign monopoly interests had tied up our whole economy to suit themselves. We had not a single industry. Our economy was dependent on one cash crop cocoa. Although our output of cocoa is the largest in the world, there was not a single cocoa processing factory.

Before we took office in 1951 there was no direct railway between Accra and Takoradi, in those days our main port. Passengers and freight had to travel by way of Kumasi. This was because Kumasi was the centre of the timber and mining industries, both of which served foreign interests and were therefore well supplied with the necessary communications. There were few roads, and only a very rudimentary public transport system. For the most part, people walked from place to place. There were very few hospitals, schools or clinics. Most of the villages lacked a piped water supply. In fact the nakedness of the land when my government began in 1951 has to have been experienced to be believed.

Failure to promote the interests of our people was due to the insatiable demands of colonial exploitation. It was not until we had grasped political power that we were in a position to challenge this, and to develop our resources for the benefit of the Ghanaian people. Those who would judge us merely by the heights we have achieved would do well to remember the depths from which we started.

The condition of Ghana in 1964 showed that our first two Development Plans had been carried out with a high degree of success. We had one of the most modern network of roads in Africa. Takoradi harbour had been extended, and the great artificial harbour at Tema the largest in Africa, built from scratch. Large extensions to the supply of water, and to the telecommunication network had been constructed, and further extensions were under construction. Our agriculture was being diversified and mechanized. Above all, the Volta River Project, which was designed to provide the electrical power for our great social, agricultural and industrialization programme, was almost completed.

In education, progress was equally impressive. In ten years we had achieved more than in the whole period of colonial rule. The figures below show the great increase in the numbers of children in primary and middle schools, and of students in secondary and technical schools and in colleges of higher education.

	1951	1961	% Increase
Primary Schools	154,360	481,500	211·9
Middle Schools	66,175	160,000	141·7
Secondary and Technical Schools	3,559	19,143	437·8
Teacher Training Colleges	1,916	4,552	137·5
University Students	208	1,204	478·8

The building of schools and colleges was given top priority in our development plans. We took the unprecedented step in Africa of making all education free, from primary to university level. In addition, textbooks were supplied free to all pupils in primary, middle and secondary schools.

In the 1964–65 school year there were 9,988 primary and middle schools with an enrolment of 1,286,486. There were 89 secondary schools with 32,971 pupils; 47 teacher training colleges with and enrolment of 10,168; 11 technical schools and 3 universities. All this, in a population of 7,500,000 put Ghana in the lead among independent African states. At the same time, a mass literacy campaign has made Ghana the most literate country in the whole of Africa.

A look at some of the other social achievements during the Party's first ten years of office reveals a similar rate of progress.

BASIC SERVICE	1951	1961	% Increase
Health			
Number of hospital beds	2,368	6,155	159·9
Rural and urban clinics	1	30	—
Doctors and dentists	156	500	220·5

	1951	1961	% Increase
Transport and Communications			
Roads (in miles) –			
Class I (Bitumen)	1,398	2,050	46·7
Class II (Gravel)	2,093	3,346	59·8
(Since 1961 the mileage of motor roads has risen to 19,236. Feeder roads connect most villages to the trunk road network.)			
Post Offices	444	779	75·4
Telephones	7,383	25,488	345·2
Electricity			
Installed electrical capacity (kW)	84,708	120,860	42·7
Electrical power generated (kW '000)	281,983	390,174	38·4

In 1962 the government adopted what was known as the Party's Programme of Work and Happiness. It proclaimed our fundamental objective as the building of a socialist state devoted to the welfare of the masses.

The concrete programme of action for this was worked out in the Seven Year Development Plan launched on 11th March, 1964. In presenting the Plan to the National Assembly I said that its main tasks were first, to speed up the rate of growth of our national economy; secondly, to enable us to embark upon the socialist transformation of our economy through the rapid development of the state and co-operative sectors; thirdly, to eradicate completely the colonial structure of our economy.

The Plan embodied measures aimed to achieve a self-sustaining economy founded on socialist production and distribution – an economy the people and supporting secondary industries based on the products of our agriculture. Ghana was to be as soon as possible a socialist state. The people, through the state, would have an effective share in the economy of the country and an effective control over it. Thus the principles of scientific socialism would be applied to suit our own particular situation.

The Party has always proclaimed socialism as its objective. But socialism cannot be achieved without socialists, much hard work and sacrifice, and detailed economic planning to provide a vast improvement in the level of material wealth of the country, and distribution of this wealth among the population. It was decided in the Seven Year Plan that Ghana's economy would for the time being remain a mixed one, with a vigorous public and co-operative sector operating alongside the private sector. Our socialist objectives demanded, however, that the public and co-operative sectors should expand faster than the private sector, especially those strategic areas of production upon which the economy of the country essentially depended.

Various state corporations and enterprises were to be established as a means of securing our economic independence and assisting in the national control of the economy. They were, like all business undertakings, expected to maintain themselves efficiently, and to show profits which could be used for further investment and to help finance public services. A State Management Committee was set up to ensure their efficient and profitable management.

Many state enterprises were quick to show results. The Ghana National Trading Corporation (GNTC) made a net profit of £4,885,900 in 1965, and had become the largest trading concern in the country. Other state enterprises, by their very nature, took a longer time to develop, and by February 1966 were only just beginning to make a profit. A few, notably in the agricultural sector, were in their infancy and were not expected to yield significant results for some time to come. A certain period of adaptation is necessary for all young industries, particularly in developing countries where the patterns of production are still mainly agricultural and elementary. But it is noteworthy that the traitors of February 1966 found no less than 63 state enterprises which they could put on the market.

In our Seven Year Plan we recognized the value of foreign investment in the private sector, particularly in the production of consumer goods, the local processing of Ghanaian raw materials and the utilization of Ghana's natural resources in the areas of economic activity where a large volume of investment was required. But we welcomed foreign investors in a spirit of partnership. We did not intend to allow them to operate in such a way as to exploit our people. They were to assist in the expansion of our economy in line with our general objectives, an agreed portion of their profits being allocated to promote the welfare and happiness of the Ghanaian people.

The State retained control of the strategic branches of the economy, including public utilities, raw materials, and heavy industry. The state also participated in light and consumer goods industries in which the rates of return on capital were highest. We intended that those industries which provided the basic living needs of the people should be state-owned in order to prevent any exploitation.

It was estimated that during the seven years there would be a total expenditure of £1,016 million. Total government investment in the Plan was to be £476 million. Foreign investors, individual Ghanaians, local authorities and the co-operative sector were expected to invest about £440 million. Ghanaians, it was hoped, would contribute nearly £100 million of direct labour in the construction of buildings, in community development and in the extension of their farms.

Special attention was given to the modernizing of agriculture, so that a greater yield and a diversity of crops could be produced. We needed to produce more food locally so that we could reduce our imports of foodstuffs and at the same time improve the health of the people by increasing the protein content in the average diet. Most developing countries face nutritional problems of one kind or another. In our case, the great need was for more fish and meat to provide a properly balanced diet. We planned to increase the output of fish from an estimated 70,000 tons in 1963 to 250,000 tons in 1969. Livestock production, including poultry and eggs, was to increase from 20,080 tons to 37,800 tons.

Immediate steps were taken to expand the fishing fleet and to develop fish processing and marketing facilities. We bought 29 fishing trawlers from Russia. The immense man-made lake formed as part of the Volta River Project was being stocked with fish, and this too was about to bring a big improvement in the diet of the Ghanaian people.

As for meat and poultry, the government subsidized the development of many poultry farms, and the rearing of large herds of cattle. In colonial days, fresh meat, milk and eggs were available to Europeans only. Before the setback of February 1966, however, they were becoming part of the regular diet of the Ghanaian masses.

The task of correcting the imbalance in our food economy was regarded as the greatest challenge to the agricultural sector of the Plan. Far-reaching schemes were initiated for major improvements in irrigation and water conservation in the Northern and Upper Regions of Ghana. Peasant farmers throughout the country were informed that they would be able to make use of the agricultural machinery of state and co-operative farms. It was not the government's intention to squeeze out the peasant farmer. Far from it, we needed the maximum effort of every individual farmer if we were to achieve our agricultural targets.

During the period of the Plan, Ghana's production of raw materials was to be considerably increased, Cocoa, our main export, earned the country 1,680 million cedis between 1951 and 1961. Of this, the farmers received 1,008 million cedis and the remainder was used by the government and the Cocoa Marketing Board for maintaining public services and for the general development of the country. We increased our cocoa production from 264,000 tons in 1956–57, to 590,000 tons in 1963–64, and huge silos had been built, able to store half the cocoa crop, to enable us to restrict exports and so ensure a fair price for our cocoa in the world market.

Plans were also far advanced to increase exports of timber, and to develop new species of wood for buildings, furniture and other wood products, and for use in paper factories. Efforts were being made to revive our once-flourishing export crop of palm oil. Rubber production was being increased. In the Western Region, a vast new plantation, 18 miles long, had been sown. Within two to three years Ghana was to be one of the greatest rubber producers in Africa. The production of palm oil, cotton, sugar cane and tobacco was being stepped up. By 1970, there were to be four factories in operation producing 100,000 tons of sugar a year, more than sufficient to eliminate the item from our list of imports.

Greatest of all our development projects was the Volta dam. When the Seven Year Plan was launched, the Volta Project was expected to begin to generate electrical power by September 1965. Completion of the Project would enable us to develop the full industrial potential of Ghana. It would increase by nearly 600 per cent the installed electrical capacity of the country. Nearly one-half of this new capacity would be taken up by the aluminium smelter in Tema; it is estimated that Ghana has sufficient bauxite to last for 200 years. But apart from this the Volta Project would have an ample reserve of power for other users, and Ghana would have liberated herself decisively from the possibility of a power shortage becoming a brake on the rate of economic progress.

Construction targets for the various parts of the Volta River Project were achieved, some of them ahead of schedule, and the official inauguration ceremony took place on 23rd January, 1966. At that time, building was about to start on a large subsidiary dam at Bui. Plans were also well advanced for the construction of an alumina plant which would have given Ghanaians control of the whole process of aluminium production, As it was, we were exporting bauxite to the United Kingdom for processing while we were importing alumina manufactured in the United States from bauxite mined in Jamaica for our aluminium smelter.

In keeping with my government's policy of linking Ghana's

progress with Africa's total development, provision was made in the Plan for economic co-operation with other African states. As I said in my address to the National Assembly on 11th March, 1964:

'While we wait for the setting up of a Union Government for Africa, we must begin immediately to harmonize our plans for Africa's total development. For example, I see no reason why the independent African states should not, with advantage to each other, join together in an economic union and draw up together a joint Development Plan which will give us greater scope and flexibility to our mutual advantage. By the same token, I see no reason why the independent African states should not have common shipping and air lines in the interests of improved services and economy. With such rationalization of our economic policies, we could have common objectives and thus eliminate unnecessary competition and frontier barriers and disputes.'

When in fact I inaugurated the completed Volta River Project on 23rd January, 1966, I said:

'We are ready and prepared to supply power to our neighbours in Togo, Dahomey, Ivory Coast and Upper Volta. As far as I am concerned this project is not for Ghana alone. Indeed, I have already offered to share our power resources with our sister African states.'

On that day at Akosombo, some 60 miles north-east of Accra, when I switched on illuminating lights signifying the official opening of hydro-electric power from the Volta, one of my greatest dreams had come true. I had witnessed the wide-scale electrification of Ghana and the breakthrough into a new era of economic and social advance. The Volta Dam permitted not only a large aluminium plant at Tema processing the country's rich bauxite deposits, but a broad range of other industrial projects. The initial power output is 512,000 kW (588,000 kW at full load) and the ultimate power output will be 768,000 kW (882,000 kW at full load). There are 500 miles of transmission lines. The main grid carries 161,000 volts.

The water building up behind the dam is forming the largest man-made lake in the world. It will cover an area of 3,275 square miles with a capacity of 120 million acre feet of water, and will be 250 miles long, with a shore-line of 4,500 miles. Approximately 80,000 people had to be moved from the area submerged by the lake. This necessitated the construction of 50 new villages and towns to accommodate them, the provision of modern housing, schools, piped water, electricity, medical facilities and new forms of employment. Thousands of acres of land had to be cleared, and people settled on farms and smallholdings with up-to-date methods of cultivation and animal husbandry. All this was achieved.

The creation of the Volta Lake has already provided facilities for an important fresh-water fishing industry. The Volta River contained numerous excellent indigenous fish; and research has shown which fish to breed to increase the supply, and how to control weed growth. A number of ports and fishing villages being formed round the lake-side provide bases for a cheap means of transport from the north to the south of Ghana. Furthermore, the lake forms a vast reservoir, making possible the improvement of water supplies to towns and villages and the irrigation of land for agriculture. The natural seasonal fluctuation in the level of the lake will immediately affect 650 square miles of land, permitting the cultivation of rice and other crops. Lake Volta was also to be developed as a holiday and tourist attraction.

Ghanaians are justifiably proud that their own government provided £35,000,000, that is half of the cost of the Volta River Project as well as meeting the cost of the new port and township of Tema, which was an essential part of the scheme. The balance of the £70,000,000 required was to be raised by international loans as follows:

International Bank for Reconstruction and Development	£16,790,000
Agency for International Development of the United States Government	£9,640,000
Export-Import Bank of the United Kingdom Government	£3,570,000
United Kingdom Board of Trade acting for the Export Credits Guarantee Department	£5,000,000

Incidentally, at a time when our detractors talk much of bribery and corruption in the developing countries, it is noteworthy that not a single penny went astray or was misappropriated in the entire Volta undertaking, which involved countless contracts over many years.

Apart from completing the Volta River Project, the Seven Year Development Plan provided for certain further improvements in the physical services. These were mostly intended to improve upon the existing system of transport, communications, water supply and electricity services in order to make them fully capable of supporting the proposed level of industrial and agricultural development.

A considerable proportion of the increase in material wealth that was expected to accrue to the country during the seven years of the Plan's operation was to be used to promote public welfare services. Education, the health services and housing were all to benefit. As far as health services were concerned, the Plan proposed to change the main orientation which had hitherto been more curative than preventive. Rural health services were developed in such a way that the rate of infant mortality was lowered, and maternity and post-natal care improved. The main cause of poor health in Ghana is the prevalence of endemic diseases such as malaria. The Plan put emphasis on the fight against these endemic diseases.

New regional hospitals, equipped with all specialist facilities were under construction in Tamale, Koforidua, Ho and Sunyani, and existing hospitals were being improved. Arrangements had been made to build six new district hospitals and four more urban poly-clinics to assist in the decentralization of out-patient work. In addition, five new mental hospitals with accommodation for 1,200 patients were designed to be ready by 1970. They were to be backed up by psychiatric units providing treatment for as many mental patients as possible.

The urgent need for more doctors was being met by sending Ghanaian medical students to study abroad, and by the setting up of our own medical school. In 1962, 51 pre-medical students were enrolled at the University of Ghana. When our own medical school is functioning fully it will be empowered to provide a screening system for all doctors trained abroad who wish to practise in Ghana. The medical programme under the Seven Year Development Plan was intended to achieve the following ratios:

- 1 doctor to 10,000 people
- 1 nurse to 5,000 patients (including patients in public health centres)
- 1 technician (laboratory, X-ray, etc.) to 5,000 patients
- 1 health inspector to 15,000 people
- 1 health auxiliary (vaccinators, dressing room attendants, etc.) to 1,000 people.

A large network of health centres was being built all over Ghana to serve the rural population, and regional health officers were being provided with training and facilities to enable them to carry out their important work.

The only nursing school which existed in 1945 produced only 8 nurses a year by 1950. In 1961–62 six schools of nursing turned out 265 new nurses and midwives.

Perhaps the most outstanding contribution to public health has come from the Medical Field Unit. This unit was formed to seek out and control trypanosomiasis, and it has been successful in containing the disease. It has also carried out a massive vaccination programme, and played a leading role in the control of epidemics of cerebrospinal meningitis. It is currently actively engaged in combating malaria, leprosy and tuberculosis.

In launching the Seven Year Development Plan, with all its detailed programmes for our country's economic and social progress, I warned about the existence of Ghanaian private enterprise in our midst. It was necessary, I told members of the National Assembly, to distinguish between the two types of business which had grown up within recent years. The first was the type which it was the government's intention to encourage that of the small businessman who employed his capital in an industry or trade with which he was familiar, and which fulfilled a public need. The second consisted of that class of Ghanaian businesses which were modelled on the old colonial pattern of exploitation. In this category were those who used their capital, not in productive endeavour, but to purchase and resell, at high prices, commodities such as salt, fish and other items of food and consumer goods which were in demand by the people. This type of business served no social purpose, and steps would be taken to see that the nation's banking resources were not used to provide credit for them.

Even more harmful to the economy was another type of enterprise in which some Ghanaians had been participating. This was the setting up of bogus agencies for foreign companies which were in fact nothing more than organizations for distributing bribes and for exerting improper pressures on behalf of foreign companies. The government intended to carry out a thorough investigation into the activities of these agencies and to suppress them.

The initiative of Ghanaian businessmen would not be cramped, but we intended to take steps to see that it was channelled towards desirable social ends and was not expended in the exploitation of the community. We would discourage anything which threatened our socialist objectives. For this reason, no Ghanaian would be allowed to take up shares in any enterprise under foreign investment. Instead, our people would be encouraged to save by investing in the state sector and in co-operative undertakings.

This, in essence, was our Seven Year Development Plan, a Plan scientifically worked out with the participation of some of the world's leading experts on economic and social planning. It was to integrate educational, industrial and agricultural programmes to bring full employment and to make possible the achievement of economic independence and a big rise in our living standards. And this was the Plan the rebel military regime scrapped as soon as it usurped power.

No possible justification can be given for its abandonment and the sell-out of Ghana's increasing assets. The first phase of the Plan was going well, and according to schedule. During the first year, £48,900,000 was spent on development projects, and of this amount, £16 million went into the key sectors, agriculture and industry. In agriculture, the emphasis was on diversification. State farms cultivated 24,000 acres of rubber, oil palm, banana, urena, lobata, coconut and citrus. Together with the agricultural wing of the Workers Brigade, which alone had 12,500 acres, the two institutions cultivated large areas for cereals and vegetables. During this period also, improvements were made in the modernization and productivity of private and co-operative farms.

In the industrial sphere, during this period, nearly all the initiative was in the public sector. The construction of many new industrial plants were undertaken. These included a steelworks (30,000 tons), two cocoa processing plants, one at Takoradi (28,000 tons) and the other at Tema (68,600 tons), two sugar refineries, a textile printing plant, a glass factory, a chocolate factory, a meat processing plant, a radio assembly plant and a large printing works at Tema. All these factories were brought into production during the first phase of the plan.

In addition, work was well advanced on a textile mill and a complex of food industries at Tema, a gold refinery at Tarkwa, and asbestos, cement, shoe and rubber-tyre factories at Kumasi. The buildings for an atomic reactor at Kwabinya were almost finished. So also was a plant for the manufacture of pre-fabricated houses. In fact, the basic policy underlying the Seven Year Development Plan, to change the structure of our mainly agricultural economy into a balanced modern economy, was going ahead with great speed and efficiency. We were successfully managing to use our local raw materials for establishing industries, and were beginning to satisfy local demand for certain consumer goods. For example, we produced matches, shoes, nails, sweets, chocolate, soft drinks, whisky, beer, gin, etc., cigarettes, biscuits, paints, canned fruit, insecticides and other chemicals. An indication of the build-up of our industrial strength may be seen in the fact that at the beginning of January 1966 imports of raw materials amounted to about 9 per cent of Ghana's total imports.

Before the February action, the government was investing £25 million annually in manufacturing projects, and the country's main exports:

Cocoa	180	million cedis annually		
Timber	31·2	,,	,,	,,
Minerals	48	,,	,,	,,

were providing a sound basis for profitable industrial enterprise.

On an average, Ghana annually imports about 264 million cedis of semi-finished and finished products consisting mainly of food and drinks, textiles and clothing, construction materials and capital equipment. Annual exports average some 254·4 million cedis of primary produce, mainly cocoa, timber, gold, diamonds and manganese. Our growing industries were to make possible a cut in imports, particularly of consumer goods, and an increase in our exports, not only of primary produce but of our own locally-manufactured products.

A look at the orientation of Ghana's investment policy during recent years throws further light on the direction in which Ghana was moving. In 1951–1959, 90 per cent (i.e. £127·8 million) of government expenditure was allocated to provide social services and to create the infrastructure of economic growth, while 10 per cent (£13·4 million) went to the productive sector. During the 1951–1962 period, an average amount of £15·5 million was allocated yearly to the public sector during the First Development Plan, and during the Consolidated Plan an average of £21·4 million yearly. Under the Second Development Plan an average amount of £50 million yearly went to the public sector. Under the Seven Year Development Plan an average of £68 million was going to the public sector yearly, representing a total investment of £442 million for development projects belonging to the public sector. To the above-mentioned £68 million, £34 million were added for the Volta complex – in all £476 million for the public sector.

Investments during the Seven Year Development Plan period (1964–1970) were therefore distributed between social services and infrastructure (62%) and the directly productive sector (38%). This represented for Ghanaians an investment of £10 per head, per year (to be compared with the maximum investment of 8 shillings per head, per year, in countries asssociated with the Common Market during the 1958–1962 period). It may also be noted that Ghana has a 240 cedis per capita income, that is to say, practically the highest in independent Africa – and in real terms, the highest in Africa, since it cannot be considered that the distribution of gross national product is equitable in countries like South Africa, Rhodesia and most of the neo-colonialist states.

The qualitative aspect of Ghana's imports reveals that while consumer goods dropped from one-half of total imports in 1961 to two-fifths in 1963, industrial equipment and goods increased from 50·6 per cent of total imports in 1961 to 60·6 per cent in 1963.

On the question of ownership, it is worth noting that in 1965 the State controlled between 60 per cent and 65 per cent of the national production (this percentage was to rise in 1970), and that since 1963, the total gold and foreign exchange assets of Ghana, and total capital exports, were under state financial control.

Apart from a 41 per cent control over consumer goods imports, the State was controlling in 1965 over 60 per cent of the exports in the most important sectors such as gold, diamonds, cocoa. In the case of timber, the Timber Marketing Board had increased its foreign exchange earnings from £5·7 million in 1962 to £8 million in 1964, and was able during the same period, to grant revolving loans of £2 million to Ghanaian producers organized into co-operatives.

When the Party came to power in 1951, all imported goods were in the hands of a few big foreign firms, especially the monopolist United Africa Company, part of the Unilever complex. Foreign firms dominated Ghana's trade and virtually controlled the economy. By 1965, however, the grip was being broken. The nationalized Ghana National Trading Corporation was distributing 32 per cent of all imports.

My government was also breaking through the stranglehold of the big international banking houses. In 1958, foreign banks held one-third of Ghana's foreign currency reserves; in 1965 they held none.

Our success in breaking the web of economic control which Western capitalism has imposed across the whole of the African continent, and our clear socialist policies, provoked the hostility of the imperialist powers. They knew that as long as I was alive and at the head of the Party in Ghana the process could not be halted and neo-colonialist exploitation could not be re-imposed. Ours was a system they could neither penetrate nor manipulate.

Significantly, one of the first acts of the 'NLC' was to announce the abandonment of the Seven Year Development Plan, which would have given the Ghanaian people the only worthwhile independence – real economic independence. The 'NLC' replaced it with a two-year 'review period' during which the socialized industries would be dismantled and the door opened once more to unrestricted 'private enterprise' – in fact, they were establishing a neo-colonialist economic subjugation of Ghana.

The only Ghanaians to benefit from such a sell-out were the African middle-class hangers-on to neo-colonialist privilege and the neo-colonialist trading firms. For the mass of workers, peasants and farmers, the victims of the capitalist free-for-all, it meant a return to the position of 'drawers of water and hewers of wood' to Western capitalism.

Of course, the Ghanaian economy was not without its problems, but is this not true of all national economies, and particularly those of developing countries in the context of the growing gap between rich and poor nations? In any event, these difficulties were not determinant. It was no mean achievement that in January 1965, after five years as a Republic, Ghana had 63 state enterprises and a budget of £200 million, including a supplementary budget, for its population of nearly eight million; while Nigeria, richer in national resources and with a population of 55 million, had a budget of £78 million.

Imperialist circles have talked much about Ghana's external debt, given as £250 million. Apart from the dubious accounting which arrived at this conveniently round sum, a figure such as this means nothing unless it is set in the context of the overall Ghanaian economic situation. To implement our various Development Plans it was necessary to borrow considerable sums of money, but it was borrowed on the basis of building capital assets such as the Volta dam, and over 100 industries established in Ghana since independence. The government made sure that the international agreements signed were based on economic feasibility, and that the money borrowed could create something lasting and beneficial not only for us in our lifetime but for the generations to follow. Seen in the light of Ghana's growing industries and increasing exports, her 'indebtedness' is put in proper perspective – as an index of the investors' confidence in the enterprise and the management they helped to finance. In addition, it should be noted that only some £20 million was due to be paid in 1967, and this did not prevent the government from refusing the political conditions attached to a loan from the International Monetary Fund (IMF).

Long faces are pulled at the drop in our foreign reserves since independence. In 1957, Ghana, had a sterling balance of £200 million.

This has not been 'squandered' as the imperialist press would have its readers believe. It has been used to pay off successive balance of payments deficits due to the rise in prices of imported consumer goods, and the drastic fall in the price of our main export crop – cocoa. It should be remembered that the sterling balance was in fact a forced loan at negligible interest which Britain acquired from Ghana during and after the Second World War. Its accumulation was made possible by the Cocoa Marketing Board which prevented Ghanaian cocoa growers from receiving the bulk of the proceeds from the sale of their cocoa. The capital the growers might have amassed from cocoa profits and later might have invested in industry was locked up in London 'to maintain the confidence of the foreign investor'.

Our imperialist critics would be better employed examining the economic situation in their own countries, many of which are in grave financial difficulties. In Britain, for example, the £1 is de-valued, there is a continuous 'balance of payments crisis' and unemployment is a serious problem.

In Ghana, before 24th February, 1966, unemployment was vir-tually unknown. All salaries were regularly paid and new jobs were constantly being created as the Seven Year Development Plan was being implemented. It was estimated that more than one million new workers would be needed to fill the new jobs which would be created, and also to replace those who left the labour force during the Plan period. More than 500,000 of them would be employed in industry and agriculture, and another 400,000 would be needed in government services, commerce and construction. The remainder were to be employed in transport, mining and the public utility services. In fact, plans were being made to import labour.

When neo-colonialist inspired traitors seized power in February 1966, we were expanding our educational system to provide the necessary number of qualified people to meet these new demands. Changes were made to shorten and to improve educational courses. For example, there was a reduction made in the number of school years so that University graduates would be ready for employment at the age of 21 or 22 instead of 24 or 25 as used to be the case. Under the new plan, the time spent in middle school was reduced by two years and the secondary school period by one year. Primary educa-tion took six years and was followed by two years of vocationally oriented training for those who did not intend to proceed to secondary schools. The reduction by two years of the ten-year middle school programme was designed to permit 300,000 additional young people to join the labour force during the seven-year period, and to equip them with basic training in technical and agricultural skills.

The figures below illustrate the planned growth in school enrolment 1963-1970:

	Total enrolment	
	1963	1970
Primary – Middle	1,200,000	2,200,000
Secondary	23,000	78,000
Teacher Training	6,000	21,000
Technical Schools	4,000	6,000
Clerical Training	100	5,000
Universities	2,000	5,000

The intake would be such that from 1968 nearly 250,000 children would complete primary-middle school and 20,000 others would leave secondary school each year. For the entire Plan period, the output from all educational institutions was to have been approximately as follows:

Middle and continuing schools	750,000
Secondary schools	46,000
Universities	9,000
Technical schools	14,000
Secretarial schools	11,000
Teacher training	31,000

The tremendous rate of our educational growth created certain difficulties. We needed many more trained teachers, and more school and college buildings. We were successfully overcoming these problems. The government allocated 153·6 million cedis (£64 million) for the construction of post-primary school buildings to feed the new secondary and higher educational institutions. The University of Ghana, the Kwame Nkrumah University of Science and Technology, and Cape Coast University College were supplying a large number of teachers; and expatriate teachers had been recruited to fill other vacancies until our own output of teachers was sufficient to cope with the demand. The Cape Coast University College was to have become a fully-fledged University in September 1966, but the 'NLC' has abandoned the plan.

Local authorities and individual communities were primarily responsible for the provision of elementary school facilities, though the government provided teachers, textbooks and other services for primary schools. Special subsidies were given to less favoured parts of the country to help in the development of primary education.

To assist in solving the manpower problem, the Trades Union Congress, the Ministry of Labour and employers' associations launched and rapidly expanded in-service training schemes to augment the knowledge and technical skill of all new employees. Adult education facilities were also being improved to provide part-time and evening classes for craftsmen, foremen, technicians and managers. The Institute of Public Education, the Workers' College, the Universities and other specialized institutions were redoubling their efforts to make this type of education available throughout the country.

Ghana was going ahead. The nation's economy was almost completely controlled by Ghanaians, and our educational planning was producing educated and skilled personnel to meet the demand. Likewise, thorough-going machinery had been established for the political education of the masses so that our socialist objectives, and Ghana's role in the wider African revolution, might be clearly understood. This was the purpose of the Young Pioneers, the TUC educational programme, and the Ideological Institute of Winneba where cadres were being trained. It was to make possible the unfolding of the next phase of the Ghanaian revolution: the establishment of a socialist republic, the principle of which was enshrined in the 1961 Constitution of the Republic of Ghana.

This process was well on its way when in 1965, the imperialists and neo-colonialists stepped up their pressure on Ghana in the form of an economic squeeze. In that year, the price of cocoa on the world market was artificially forced down from £476 in 1954 to £87 10s. a ton (1965). This meant that although Ghana exported 500,000 tons of cocoa, she earned only £77 million, or less than her receipts in the mid-1950's for 250,000 tons.

When the Seven Year Development Plan was drawn up, it was assumed that the price of cocoa on the world market would be at least £200 a ton. This was not an unreasonable assumption. Between 1953 and 1963, prices fell only once below £190 a ton. In 1954 the price was £476, and in 1957–58 it was £352. But the very year the Seven Year Development Plan was launched, cocoa prices began to fall steeply. At the same time, the prices of capital and manufactured goods needed for industrial and agricultural projects under the Plan were rapidly rising. Between 1950 and 1961 they had risen by over 25 per cent.

In 1964, the imperialist powers, the principal consumers of cocoa, promised at the Geneva meeting of the United Nations Conference on Trade and Development (UNCTAD) that they would 'lift barriers in the form of tariffs and duties on primary products, either raw, processed or semi-processed'. This would have meant that cocoa-grindings, cocoa butter and chocolate products whose price was firm, could have been sold in the metropolitan markets to cushion the effects of the low cocoa prices. But Britain and the USA did not keep their promise to lower trade barriers against processed and semi-processed primary products. Ghana, regarded by them as a pace-setter in Africa, could not be allowed to succeed in building socialism.

When I spoke to the Ghana cocoa farmers on 22nd September, 1965, I drew attention to the breach of faith of the cocoa consumers and said that if tariff walls prevented us from selling our chocolate abroad we could still sell it in Ghana and in other African countries at a price well within the means of all. I announced that cocoa powder was being distributed to school children, and that the production of cocoa butter, in demand for the manufacture of cosmetics and pharmaceuticals, was being expanded.

We constructed silos which, when completed, would enable us to withhold more than half of our cocoa crop from the world market. This amount would be more than the combined world cocoa surplus of production over consumption. We were, in fact, breaking through the cocoa price squeeze. The USA, however, was stockpiling a record quantity of cocoa to be used to keep prices down. In its 1966 Commodity Review, the United Nations Food and Agricultural Organization (FAO), reported that the total stocks of cocoa beans in consuming countries at the end of 1964 amounted to 500,000 tons, and that by December 1965 this total was further increased.

The USA and Britain could, if they had wanted, have fixed a reasonable price for cocoa and so have eased the economic situation in Ghana. They had no wish to do so. On the contrary, the forcing down of the price of cocoa was part of their policy of preparing the economic ground for political action in the form of a 'coup' and a change of government.

Throughout 1965, and before then, the US government exerted various other forms of economic pressure on Ghana. It withheld investment and credit guarantees from potential investors, put pressure on existing providers of credit to the Ghanaian economy, and negated applications for loans made by Ghana to American-dominated financial institutions such as the IMF.

This pressure ended smartly after 24th February 1966 when the US State Department's political objective had been achieved. The price of cocoa suddenly rose on the world market, and the IMF rushed to the aid of the 'NLC'.

If further proof were needed of America's political motives it may be seen in the US government's hysterical reaction to the publication of my book *Neo-Colonialism – The Last Stage of Imperialism* in October 1965. In this book I exposed the economic stranglehold exercised by foreign monopolistic complexes such as the Anglo-American Corporation, and illustrated the ways in which this financial grip perpetuated the paradox of Africa: poverty in the midst of plenty. The American Government sent me a note of protest, and promptly refused Ghana $35 million of 'aid'.

The fact that our enemies decided finally on subversion and violence as the only effective way in which to achieve their objective of halting the Ghanaian revolution and bringing Ghana into the neo-colonialist fold, is a measure of the success of our economic policies. We had proved that we were strong enough to develop independently, not only without foreign tutelage, but also in the context of active imperialist and neo-colonialist resistance.

28

GHANA: THE WAY OUT

People of Ghana, the NLC must be forcibly overthrown now, by Positive Action in the form of a counter-coup if our beloved country is to be saved from complete political, social and economic disintegration. The time for non-violent action has passed. A quick, knock-out blow must now be delivered to clear the way for a radical, new, national reconstruction.

In this immense task of reconstruction we shall need the active participation of every single Ghanaian who has the will to work, and the love of country to wish to make Ghana great and prosperous. No one need fear revenge and time-wasting recrimination. The slate has been wiped clean. We must start afresh in the light of the tragic experience of the past two years. New thinking and action is needed.

As each day passes, Ghana is being dragged further and further down into the mud. The independent economy we strove so hard to build has broken down completely.

There is large-scale unemployment. All indigenous development has stopped, and the puppet NLC has handed over our national assets one by one to foreign interests. Almost a hundred state corporations have been sold.

You have seen with your own eyes the shameful disposal of Ghana's assets. Our state hotels are now foreign owned. The 20-mile rubber plantation developed by the State Farms Corporation has been handed over to the Firestone Rubber Company of America. The whole economic situation is the negation of an independent economic policy; and a downright sellout to American and other foreign, capitalist financial interests.

The balance of payments problem is being tackled in the classic capitalist way of creating unemployment and devaluation of the cedi. Unemployment suits capitalism.

It is an excellent thing for so-called private enterprise. It weakens the bargaining power of the workers (who have only their labour to sell), and it makes sure of a steady pool of cheap labour.

The basic principle of capitalism and so-called private enterprise (which in Africa generally means foreign private enterprise) is that an industrial or commercial project shall depend for its initiation or continuance according to how much profit it makes for the individual or group of individuals, such as shareholders. Capitalists or private entrepreneurs always seek projects which provide them with the greatest profit for the least investment in the shortest time. This is the principle on which they operate.

It means that in Ghana they are only going to support or introduce such projects as will show them the maximum possible profits for the smallest effort in the shortest time, and in the most convenient place to fulfil these conditions.

They are not going to do something in Ghana if they can do it more cheaply and with greater profit somewhere else. Nor are they going to do it in Ghana if it is in competition with some similar project they already have somewhere else.

This is why the treacherous NLC has failed completely in persuading its foreign capitalist sponsors to undertake a single new project in Ghana. All they have succeeded in doing is to allow foreign capitalists to take over certain existing projects which are already extremely profitable, or which were already at such a stage of development that they are certain to show a good profit in the near future.

This is why the incompetent NLC has had to close down or seriously curtail a whole series of our national projects which are of no interest to foreign profiteers. And why it has had to cut down social services, including education and health, to a point where they are in danger of total collapse. It has even become necessary now to pay a visiting fee when calling to see relatives and friends in hospital.

What foreign capitalists like about the ignorant NLC is that they have provided them with free access to Ghana's raw materials, and a plentiful supply of cheap labour to pick and choose as they wish. These are the classical conditions of colonialism. They are also the conditions of neo-colonialism, which is only the old colonialism with a façade of African stooges.

415

National development is impossible under this system. How can we develop Ghana as a whole if the test of every project is its attractiveness to foreign investors and its rapid profitability? Which foreign investor is going to develop the Northern Region of Ghana, for example, when the quickest source of profit is in the Southern Region?

The terrible neglect which is now taking place in large areas in Ghana is a direct result of neo-colonialist policies, and the abandonment of the principles of socialist planning. Even around Accra, which is economically convenient to capitalists, nothing of real value is taking place because foreign capitalists do not find it profitable enough. All they have done so far is to take over the industries and state enterprises which we worked so hard to build.

Ghana is no longer being run by an African government; it is being administered by a small clique of corrupt army and police officers, and behind the Ghanaian façade, the decisions are being made by foreign interests. There are some 250 American 'experts' in Ghana who are actively aiding and advising the NLC. The US Ambassador in Accra attends all official functions, and occupies a position similar to that held by the French official advisers in the Francophone states.

During last year, it is estimated that the US government and the IMF provided 70 million dollars credit to bolster up the regime. A team of economists from Harvard has had the effrontery to advise a 'development' plan for Ghana. What a miserable substitute for our own Seven Year Development Plan, drawn up by economists dedicated solely to the interests and welfare of the Ghanaian people.

Our economic problems are not being treated as Ghanaian problems, but as the problems of the United States of America, Britain, West Germany and other countries which have substantial economic interests in Ghana.

The solutions being dictated by advisers from these countries are not intended to strengthen the economy in the interests of the people of Ghana, but in the interests of the foreign companies and governments which today dominate and exploit the treachery and ignorance of the NLC. Ghana has become a neo-colony.

Mass unemployment has led to a crime wave of a type previously unknown in the history of our country. With growing unemployment and rising prices, living conditions have become intolerable. Many Ghanaians are finding it impossible to earn a living or to get enough food to eat. Groups of desperate men, some of them armed, are roaming the countryside at will, and in many places our peaceful citizens cannot travel in safety, or even sleep secu rely in their bed at night. Thus, formerly peaceful citizens have become criminals in order to survive.

The democratic pretences of the NLC are exposed by the deceptive draft constitution which they have produced after two years of misrule. This is a further attempt to deceive the Ghanaian people and to pull the wool over their eyes. It solves nothing. Under the infamous Disenfranchisement Decree thousands of Ghanaians are to be denied the vote and banned from the political life of the country simply because they are members of the Convention People's Party and believe in socialism. Hiding behind the cloak of a so-called civilian government there will remain the same clique of traitors and their neo-colonialist manipulators.

Yet the implementation of even these phoney constitutional proposals have been put off into the indefinite future, the NLC admitting that a return to civilian rule could 'hardly bear realistic examination'. The truth is that the traitorous clique dare not permit any form of popular political activity, even though the CPP and all its wing organizations have been banned.

The NLC and their foreign masters know how tenuous is the authority they wield, and fear that any genuinely free political expression would immediately bring about their total collapse.

Under my government, all our policies were devised and implemented with one object only, to promote the well-being and happiness of the Ghanaian people as a whole, and to strive to bring about the complete liberation of Africa and the establishment of an All-African Union Government.

The result of that method of thinking and planning is apparent to you all. You have only to look around you to see what we achieved. We built more roads, bridges and other forms of national communication than any other independent African state. We built more schools, clinics and hospitals. We provided more clean, piped water. We trained more teachers, doctors and nurses. We established more industries.

In the first nine years of independence our country was transformed. From a colony subsisting mainly on agriculture, notably cocoa-growing, it had become a dynamic independent state with a diversified and rapidly expanding economy.

Hundreds of thousands of acres of more land were brought into cultivation. With state and co-operative farming, with modern technology and irrigation schemes, agriculture was boosted and food production increased.

We launched the Workers Brigade, a national service organization whereby young men and women and workers without employment could play a decisive part in Ghana's national construction. With the plans for industrialization, there was need to train artisans and builders in public construction work to supplement Ghana's manpower. Feeder roads and dams were built, and farms were under cultivation by the Workers Brigade.

Education was free at all levels and students in teacher training colleges and universities received additional monthly allowances to meet their private expenses. Three universities were established, and the student population rose to 5,000. Plans were nearing completion for the building of a University of Agriculture at Somanya.

According to a UNESCO Report in 1963, Ghana spent more on education in proportion to her size and population than any country in the world.

Medical facilities were, to a large extent, free; and the many hospitals, clinics, child welfare centres and nurseries are there for all to see.

As you know, one of my main preoccupations was the electrification of Ghana – for without abundant electric power large-scale industrialization such as we envisaged was impossible. Always in the forefront of my mind, therefore, was the vital importance of the Volta River Project. Completion of this mighty multi-purpose project was the key to all our dreams of an economically independent Ghana.

It was no mere coincidence that it was only a few weeks after the completion of the Volta River Project in its initial stage of providing hydro-electric power, that traitors and neo-colonialists struck to destroy everything for which we had worked so long.

Plans were far advanced for the construction of the Bui dam, and for other smaller dams in various parts of the country. Ghana was at the point of breakthrough into national economic self-reliance.

Our national assets had never stood so high. We had laid the infrastructure for the development of Ghana into a modern, industrial state. Our real wealth – our roads, communications, Tema harbour the Volta River Project, our educational and public health systems, our factories, state corporations, hotels and public buildings – was reflected in actual achievement and in productive potential.

Economic experts the world over, unless the tools of vested commercial interests, acknowledged that the progress we had made in Ghana was amazing and beyond what even the most optimistic had believed possible.

But for the treachery of the NLC, the whole of Ghana would by now have been electrified. Industrialization would have taken place not only in the South, but in every region including the far North. Every town and village would have had ample electricity and piped water. There would have been further expansion of both the health and education services.

There would have been a tremendous increase in food production. We had developed plans for the vast grasslands of the North. Only days before the 'coup', I had signed a contract for the irrigation and agricultural development of the Accra plains. Our scheme to create an inland fishing industry and inland water transport on the Volta Lake was near to operation. We were waiting only for the water to rise.

All these schemes, and they were nation-wide, would have required the active participation of tens of thousands more of our people. Every young man and woman was needed as soon as he or she had completed the necessary education. How criminal that our resources of people and materials should now be wasted in mass unemployment, and that our immense productive potential should be put at the disposal of neo-colonialists serving their own selfish interests.

The Ghanaian, who was before a proud African, courageous and with head held high, today appears head-bowed as a collaborator with neo-colonialists. He is suffering as a result of the shame that has been brought on Ghana by the imperialist-inspired coup of February 24th, 1966.

Ghana, under my government, was a haven for the oppressed from all parts of Africa. Freedom fighters trained there. Ghana was revered all over the African continent, as a country which all who fought oppression and exploitation could depend upon. Our political and economic achievements were closely studied and admired.

Today, Ghana might not exist for all the impact the country makes in Africa and in world affairs. It is as if the heart has been torn out of the body, and only a lifeless robot remains, the mechanism controlled by a clique of traitors who in their turn are slavishly following the instructions of their neo-colonialist masters.

Yet there is no need to despair or to abandon hope. We have the mind, the will and the means to rebuild our country for the prosperity and happiness of all our people. All that stands in the way is the NLC and their abject subservience to foreign exploiters.

People of Ghana, stir yourselves. Rise up as free men and women. Be proud of your heritage and of your national independence. What the criminal NLC has destroyed can be rebuilt. Our development plans can once again be put into operation.

I have been following events in Ghana very closely. The economic situation is very serious, but it is not beyond recovery if action is taken quickly. Recently, Sierra Leone has shown the world how a corrupt military-police dictatorship can be removed, and constitutional government restored. Those who carried out the removal of the military junta in Sierra Leone were not even high-ranking officers. They were from the lower ranks of the army.

But they possessed the necessary ingredient for complete victory: true patriotism and the confidence of knowing that they were fulfilling the wishes of the vast majority of the people.

I have not been wasting my time in Conakry. I have been working, studying and drawing up plans for the reconstruction of our country. I am able to tell you, as a result of my very deep study of the economic situation, that it would be possible to put Ghana on the road again towards meaningful economic progress in a matter not of years, but a few months.

You will not expect me to tell you in any sort of detail of the plan I have worked out. To do so would open the door for foreign vested interests to prepare new sabotage. Your own common sense will tell you that things have gone basically wrong in Ghana, and that a completely new approach is needed.

I would like everybody to organize in secret groups. Organize in the villages and in the localities in the towns. Organize at your work places. Organize in your trade unions. The power of the people is irresistible once it is organized. Nothing can withstand it. The majority of the army and police are behind me and long for my early return to Ghana. Tribalism should not be allowed to confuse the issue.

The NLC must be overthrown now. There is no other way, than by force, to liberate our country from neo-colonialism and its stooges. Only then can the great work of national reconstruction again begin, and Ghana once more assume its true role in Africa and in world affairs.

Long live Ghana, and long live Africa's total emancipation and unity!

29

THE SPECTRE OF BLACK POWER

To
ERNESTO CHÉ GUEVARA
BEN BARKA
MALCOLM X

We could mourn them
but they don't want our tears.
We scorn death knowing
that we cannot be defeated.

INTRODUCTION

Pan-Africanism has its beginnings in the liberation struggle of
African-Americans, expressing the aspirations of Africans and
peoples of African descent. From the first Pan-African Conference,
held in London in 1900, until the fifth and last Pan-American
Conference held in Manchester in 1945, African-Americans provided the main driving power of the movement. Pan-Africanism
then moved to Africa, its true home, with the holding of the First
Conference of Independent African States in Accra in April 1958,
and the All-African People's Conference in December of the same
year.

The work of the early pioneers of Pan-Africanism such as

Sylvester Williams, Dr W. E. B. Du Bois, Marcus Garvey, and H. George Padmore, none of whom were born in Africa, has become a treasured part of Africa's history. It is significant that two of them, Dr Du Bois and George Padmore, came to live in Ghana at my invitation. Dr Du Bois died, as he wished, on African soil, while working in Accra on the Encyclopedia Africana. George Padmore became my Adviser on African Affairs, and spent the last years of his life in Ghana, helping in the revolutionary struggle for African unity and socialism.

The close links forged between Africans and peoples of African descent over half a century of common struggle continue to inspire and strengthen us. For, although the outward forms of our struggle may change, it remains in essence the same, a fight to the death against oppression, racism and exploitation.

Most of Africa has now achieved political independence. But imperialism has not been vanquished. International finance capital appearing now in its new guise of neo-colonialism seeks to maintain and extend its stranglehold over the economic life of our continent. Imperialists and neo-colonialists are resorting to every kind of stratagem to achieve their purposes. They have allied with reactionary elements in our midst to organize military coups and other forms of direct action in an attempt to halt the progress of the African Revolution. They are at the same time working in more insidious ways to undermine our morale and to divert our attention from the main purpose of our struggle – the total liberation of the African continent, an All-African Union Government and socialism.

The Organization of African Unity has been rendered virtually useless as a result of the machinations of neo-colonizalists and their puppets. Yet it is being preserved as an innocuous organization in the hope that it may delay the formation of a really effective Pan-African organization which will lead to genuine political unification. Encouragement is being given to the formation of African regional economic organizations in the knowledge that without political cohesion they will be ineffective and serve to strengthen, not weaken, neo-colonialist exploitation and domination.

All manner of red herrings are being used to distract and deflect us from our purpose. There is talk of 'African socialism', Arab socialism, democratic socialism, Muslim socialism, and latterly, the 'pragmatic pattern of development', their advocates claiming they have found the solution to our problems.

Just as there is only one true socialism, scientific socialism, the principles of which are universal and abiding, there is only one way to achieve the African revolutionary goals of liberation, political unification and socialism. That way lies through armed struggle. The time for speechifying, for conferences, for makeshift solutions and for compromise is past.

Similarly, with the emergence of Black Power in the United States of America, the liberation movement of African-Americans has become militant and armed. But as in Africa, the movement is having to be on its guard against the internal as well as the external enemy. There must be a closing of ranks and tenacious, united effort to carry the struggle through to a successful conclusion.

THE SPECTRE OF BLACK POWER

With a decisiveness and force which can no longer be concealed the spectre of Black Power has descended on the world like a thundercloud flashing its lightning. Emerging from the ghettoes, swamps and cotton-fields of America, it now haunts the streets, legislative assemblies and high councils and has so shocked and horrified Americans that it is only now that they are beginning to grasp its full significance, and the fact that Black Power, in other manifestations, is in confrontation with imperialism, colonialism, neo-colonialism, exploitation and aggression in many parts of the world.

In America, the 'Negro problem' has been a more or less polite conversation piece since the first African slaves were landed in James Town in 1619. For three hundred and fifty years, however, the subject of 'slave revolts' has been tabooed and eliminated from text-books. For the past thirty years stringent efforts have been made to whitewash and obscure the real issue of the United States Civil War: whether African slavery should be continued or not. Indeed, it is no longer considered proper in the United States to mention the 'Civil War'. Polite references are sometimes made to the 'unfortunate war between the states'.

After the Civil War, the 13th, 14th and 15th Amendments to the United States Constitution did abolish African slavery and granted citizenship rights to the freed men. Immediately, the majority of states passed laws nullifying these rights, and in general, public opinion all over the country supported their action. There were some legislators who pointed out the injustice and even dangers of this course, and in 1875 Congress passed a mild Civil Rights Bill for the freed men. But in 1884 this Bill was repealed by the United States Supreme Court. And so, down through the years, people of

African descent in the United States of America have been petition-ing, pleading, going to court and demonstrating for 'rights' freely granted to every naturalized immigrant.

As the United States grew richer, more powerful and imperialistic, as it expanded and extended its influence and control throughout Latin America and the islands of the Caribbean, its racialism, oppres-sion and contempt for the peoples of African descent became accepted as an American way of life.

Russia's October Revolution did not penetrate the masses of African-Americans. A few intellectuals, however, did hail it as a triumph of the oppressed and the exploited, a proletarian socialist victory. Some travelled to the newly established Soviet Union. Several remained there, and contributed their strength and skills in building the world's first socialist state. But those who returned found no means of applying what they had seen to the situation in the United States. Meanwhile, white workers were agitating for better working conditions. But until the organization of the Committee for Industrial Organization (CIO) and the Second World War, African-Americans were regularly excluded from labour organizations. The need for increased manpower during this period encouraged immigration from the South of thousands of black workers who crowded into northern cities finding jobs, but no place to live except in slums amid conditions far worse than the rural shacks they had left in the South.

In spite of the long and untiring work in education and organiza-tion of the pioneers of 'Civil Rights'; in spite of the painstaking efforts made by African-American citizens of the United States to educate their children, and by hard work to achieve 'acceptance' in American society, African-Americans have remained only barely tolerated aliens in the land of their birth, the vast mass of them outside consideration of basic human justice.

This is a fact which is now being called to the attention of all those who through the years have had in their power the means to order and fashion the world according to their interests. White interests controlled the economic wealth; white interests have been able to establish the 'moral' standards by which America must live; white domestic imperialism made all the laws, rules and regulations. This was the modern world up to, and throughout, the first half of the twentieth century.

The independence of Ghana, achieved on March 6th, 1957, ushered in the decisive struggle for freedom and independence throughout Africa – freedom from colonial rule and settler domina-tion. On that day I proclaimed to the world 'the independence of

Ghana is meaningless unless it is linked with the total liberation of the African continent'. Immediately, the beating drums sent this message across rivers, mountains, forests and plains. The people heard and acted. Liberation movements gained strength, and freedom fighters began to train. One after another, new African states came into being, and above the world's horizon loomed the African Personality. African statesmen went to the United Nations; Africans proudly wore the ancient regalia of their ancestral land; Africans stood up and spoke on the rostrum of the world forum, and they spoke for Africans and the people of African descent wherever they might be.

I experienced the immediate impact on Africa's dispossessed in the United States – Black dignity could be achieved. Black beauty was a reality. I know how determined and inspired African-American students went out from their colleges in the South and 'sat down' in those places which laws and customs had reserved for 'whites' only. They were heard to say when they were being dragged to jail by infuriated police: 'All Africa will be liberated before we here can get a lousy cup of coffee!'

American text-books shy away from discussion of slave revolts, though riots and insurrection form a large part of African-American history. We know how black men and women fought through the swamps of Louisiana, how Virginian planters cowed before the name of the rebel, Nat Turner, how Harriet Tubman led armed bands of runaway slaves out of the South, and of her fame as a sharp-shooter. The largest slave revolt was planned and led by a white man whose name has been immortalized in song. It was on Harpers Ferry bridge that John Brown began the Civil War which led inevitably to the freeing of the slaves.

The young African-American 'sit-downers' of recent years committed no violence, nor did the many white students who, following their example, poured out of the great northern universities to demonstrate against racialism, segregation and discrimination. But their petitions and pleas for justice were met with violence, with savage beatings, with jail sentences. Some of them died in the struggle.

Then, on August 18th, 1965, in the Negro ghetto of Watts, in the city of Los Angeles, African-Americans took up arms to meet their aggressors. Since then, practically every major city in the United States has seen guns, rifles and fire bombs in the hands of black men, who, with every shot fired, are claiming their birthright. Since 1966, the cry of the rebellion has been 'Black Power'.

425

What is Black Power? I see it in the United States as part of the vanguard of world revolution against capitalism, imperialism and neo-colonialism which have enslaved, exploited and oppressed peoples everywhere, and against which the masses of the world are now revolting. Black Power is part of the world rebellion of the oppressed against the oppressor, of the exploited against the exploiter. It operates throughout the African continent, in North and South America, the Caribbean, wherever Africans and people of African descent live. It is linked with the Pan-African struggle for unity on the African continent, and with all those who strive to establish a socialist society.

Analysis of the United States social structure indicates that black Americans comprise the proletariat base of the country. On their backs, their toil, sweat, enslavement and exploitation have been built the wealth, prosperity and high standard of living enjoyed by America today. Until recently, African-Americans sought to alleviate their oppression through integration into the majority white population. They demonstrated for an end of social discrimination and for 'equal rights', wanting to gain access to schools and colleges, restaurants, hotels and other places from which they had been excluded. Such were the demands of the Civil Rights Movement. Yet large numbers of African-Americans had no jobs, no decent housing, and no money to enjoy the restaurants, hotels and swimming pools reserved for 'whites only'. The Civil Rights Movement did not speak for the needs of the African-American masses.

It was, however, thought that the plea for civil rights would be met, because the United States Constitution, with its various amendments, supports these demands. Instead, thousands of African-Americans have been jailed, intimidated, beaten, and some murdered for agitating for those rights guaranteed by the American constitution.

The masses grasp instinctively the meaning and goal of Black Power: the oppressed and exploited are *without power*. Those who have power have everything, those without power have nothing: if you don't believe in guns, you are already dead.

Black Power gives the African-American an entirely new dimension. It is a vanguard movement of black people, but it opens the way for all oppressed masses. Unfortunately, the Trade Unions in the United States are as capitalist in make-up and goals as any million dollar corporation. And the majority of white skilled workers with their well-furnished houses, two cars, televisions and long vacations are complacent. They have much more to 'lose than their chains'. But there are potentially revolutionary white masses in the United

States. Consider the lot of the 'poor whites' in the hills of Georgia, Tennessee and the Carolinas, the white share-croppers in the low-lands of Alabama and Mississippi. Too often these are written off as 'poor white trash'. But they, too, are dispossessed; often they are without hope. Yet 'poor whites' and blacks' have not been pushed as far down as their backs will lie. When they see a way ahead for them, the oppressed and exploited do revolt. Black Power is leading the way; Black Power is already a spearhead.

At this momentous period of history, as the era of people's armed revolution gets under way in Africa, I see coming the triumph of the human spirit, the collapse of the forces of inhumanity and the emergence of the glorious effort finally to free mankind from sense-less and inhuman exploitation, degradation and wars. The old Africa is crumbling down; the new Africa is being constructed.

In Africa, we thought we could achieve freedom and independence, and our ultimate goals of unity and socialism by peaceful means. This has landed us in the grip of neo-colonialism. We could not succeed using non-violent methods. The same power structure which is blocking the efforts of African-Americans in the United States is also now throwing road-blocks in Africa's way. Imperialism, neo-colonialism, settler domination and racialism seek to bring us down and re-subjugate us.

In Africa, Latin America, the Caribbean, the Middle East and South East Asia, imperialists and neo-colonialists, with the help of local stooges, attempt to master with guns. They are united in their determination to extend and prolong their domination and exploita-tion. So we must fight wherever imperialism, neo-colonialism and racialism exist. We too must combine our strength and co-ordinate our strategy in a unified armed struggle. Non-violent methods are now anachronistic in revolution. And so I say to the progressive, revolutionary forces of the world, in the words of Ernesto Ché Guevara: 'Let us develop a true proletarian internationalism, with international proletarian armies; the flag under which we fight shall be the sacred cause of redeeming humanity.'

It must be understood that liberation movements in Africa, the struggle of Black Power in America or in any other part of the world, can only find consummation in the political unification of Africa, the home of the black man and people of African descent throughout the world. African-Americans have been separated from their cultural and national roots. Black children overseas are not taught of the glory of African civilization in the history of mankind, of pillaged cities and destroyed tribes. They do not know the millions

427

of black martyrs who died resisting imperialist aggression. The imperialists and neo-colonialists inside or outside the United States designate everything 'good' as 'white', and everything 'bad' as 'black'. Black Power says: 'We will define ourselves'. For centuries, African-Americans have been the victims of racialism. They have now taken up arms to abolish it for ever, and to destroy its fertile breeding ground, the capitalist system. For it is only with the building of a socialist society that peace and racial harmony can be ultimately achieved. It is only world socialism which can provide the solution to the problems of the world today.

For us in Africa, for the people of African descent everywhere, there can be no turning back, no compromise, no fear of failure or death. Africa must and shall fulfil her destiny. Even though revolution in other parts of the world may wither or go astray, the African revolution must reach its goal of unity and socialism. We have taken the correct road, even though hazardous. We face death as we face life with head up, eyes lifted, proud and unafraid. The seed dies that life may come forth. So, we may meet death knowing that we cannot be defeated. For the oppressed peoples of the world will one day triumph. Hundreds and thousands of us have died in many an imperialist war. If we die in the struggle of black emancipation it will be as men bringing into this world the wholesome, rich benefits of Black Power.

And so for us Black Power heralds the long-awaited day of liberation from the shadows of obscurity. We take our place among the peoples of the world without hate or apologies, with confidence and with goodwill towards all men. The spectre of Black Power has taken shape and form and its material presence fights to end the exploitation of man by man.

CONCLUSION

Racial discrimination is the product of an environment, an environment of a divided class society, and its solution is to change that environment. This presupposes the fact that it is only under socialism in the United States of America that the African-American can really be free in the land of his birth.

30

THE STRUGGLE CONTINUES

MESSAGE TO THE BLACK PEOPLE OF BRITAIN

Members of the Black Panther Movement and all my Black Brothers and Sisters, comrades and friends from the Caribbean, Africa, Asia, Latin America and all corners of the socialist world.

Greetings:

History rarely moves in a straight line; its course is uneven. Today as a result of the contradictions in capitalism, neo-colonialism and racism, Black Power is emerging on the stage of history. The oppressed of the earth are seeking a new way out to resolve these contradictions and achieve total emancipation.

What is Black Power? By Black Power we mean the power of the four-fifths of the world population which has been systematically damned into a state of undevelopment by colonialism and neo-colonialism. In other words, Black Power is the sum total of the economic, cultural and political power which the black man must have in order to achieve his survival in a highly developed technical society, and in a world ravaged by imperialism, colonialism, neo-colonialism and fascism.

Black Power epitomizes a new stage of revolutionary consciousness of the yearning and aspiration of the black man. Since the black man is the most oppressed of the races of mankind, Black Power, therefore, is the struggle for the possession of the economic, cultural, social and political power which he, in common with the oppressed and the exploited of the earth, must have in order to stampede and overthrow the oppressor. Unless we are prepared to do this then we are prepared to be enslaved.

Your organization is therefore part of this revolutionary upsurge in the world today.

You are in Britain not by chance or by choice; you are in Britain for historical reasons; you are in Britain because Britain colonized you and reduced the various countries to which you belong to the level of colonial status. You are in Britain because British neo-colonialism is strangling you in your home countries. Where else can you go to seek survival, except in the 'mother country' which has enslaved you?

But don't forget that your homes, at the moment, are under the yoke of colonialism or neo-colonialism. You all know that even though your organizations are anti-racist, they face racism in Britain. You have been so long confused that you have become victims of white racism. There is no solution to the race question until all forms of racial discrimination and segregation anywhere are made criminal offences. Under real socialism racism vanishes.

You who are in Britain have a significant role to play in the international black revolutionary movement. You live in the centre of the very citadel of British imperialism and neo-colonialism.

The finger of history is now pointing to the right direction. In my days in London we organized the Coloured Men's Association, and today in the emergence of Black Power you have in Britain organizations like the RASS headed by Michael X and the Black Panther Movement headed by Obi Egbuna. These two organizations are advocates of Black Power, and must mobilize, educate, and re-awaken the black people of Britain to the full realization of their revolutionary potential.

We know the difficulties you are going through in Britain: discrimination, prejudice and racial hostility. You know that what goes on in Britain, goes on in many parts of the world where white establishment holds power; be it in the United States of America, apartheid South Africa, Latin America, Australia, Rhodesia, Angola, Mozambique, or 'Portuguese' Guinea.

Your homes are under puppet regimes teleguided by neo-colonialism. Real black freedom will only come when Africa is politically united. It is only then that the black man will be free to breathe the air of freedom, which is his to breathe, in any part of the world.

To those of you who want to make Britain your home I say, remember that what is important is not where you are but what you do. And to those who want to come back home and fight for Africa's total emancipation, unity and independence I say, come home. We need you.

I want you all to understand that I am not in exile in Conakry. Every country and town in Africa is my home, and so I am at home in Conakry, Guinea, as I would be at home in any part of the black world. I am fit, alive and alert. The struggle for the political unification of Africa has never been clearer and better charted.

You have asked me to be your patron. My answer is, YES, I will stand behind you in all your Black Power revolutionary endeavours, and I hope you will answer my call when the clarion sounds.

I wish you good luck and success.

AFRICA DAY SPECIAL MESSAGE

As the armed phase of the African Revolution for total liberation and unity gains momentum in central and southern Africa, racist settlers, imperialists and neo-colonialists are intensifying and diversifying their efforts to consolidate and extend their domination.

They are faced with a protracted guerrilla struggle which in the long run they know they cannot win. But they are seeking by joint military action to contain it, and by devious and insinuating economic and political penetration to undermine its strength.

They see their opportunity in the continuing disunity of independent Africa, the lack of continental planning and direction of the liberation struggle, and in the willingness of certain African leaders to allow their countries to become client states.

Collective imperialism confronts a disunited, weakened, independent Africa.

The situation demands immediate and drastic remedy. We must throw the full weight of a united, revolutionary Africa into the struggle. Each day that we delay, we fail our gallant freedom fighters and betray our people.

It is an open secret that South Africa, Portugal and Rhodesia are co-operating in the military sphere to crush guerrilla campaigns in their territories. They exchange information about freedom fighter activities, allow overflights and landings of military aircraft in each other's countries, and in the case of South Africa, supply armed forces and helicopters to assist in the counter-offensive.

A military intelligence board, known as the Council of Three, is said to meet regularly in Pretoria, Salisbury, Lourenço Marques or Luanda, to prepare joint action.

The world first heard of the participation of South African forces in military action outside their own borders in August 1967, when a strong force of freedom fighters went into action around the Wankie game reserve in Rhodesia. A large contingent of South African police in armoured cars was rushed to the scene.

Since then, there have been innumerable reports of South African intervention. In Rhodesia, South West Africa, Angola and Mozambique, South African helicopters are being used to hunt freedom fighters. Armed South African police are operating against nationals in South West Africa. South African troops are reported in both Angola and Mozambique.

Nor is enemy co-operation confined to defensive operations. There are clear indications that the members of the Council of Three are planning offensive action against independent states.

Zambia has been openly threatened. Furthermore, some ten miles from her border, on the Caprivi strip, the South Africans have built an enormous airfield, said to have a two mile runway. There are many reports of armed incursions of Rhodesians, South Africans and Portuguese over the borders between Zambia, Rhodesia and Mozambique.

The example of the recent Israeli aggression against Arab states has not passed unnoticed in Pretoria, and has been publicly proclaimed in South Africa as an effective way of dealing with a so-called 'threat' from neighbouring states.

Faced with the combined military strength of the South Africans, Portuguese and Rhodesian settlers, African freedom fighters must close their ranks and put an end to internecine rivalries. They must also be supported by united and determined action on the part of the whole of independent Africa.

No part of Africa is free while any of our national territory remains unliberated. There can be no co-existence between African independence and imperialist and neo-colonialist domination; between independent Africa and racist, minority, settler governments.

The military obstacles we have to overcome if we are to achieve our goal of total liberation and an All-African Union Government are obvious and surmountable. Less easy to recognize and to combat are the insidious, often disguised workings of neo-colonialism – the economic and political pressures which seek to undermine our independence and to perpetuate and extend the grip of foreign monopoly finance capital over the economic life of our continent.

Many of our so-called independent states are in fact neo-colonies. They have all the outward appearance of sovereignty, but their economy and therefore their political policy is directed from outside.

Some have been in the grip of neo-colonialism since independence. Others have been subjected to neo-colonialism by means of military coups engineered by neo-colonialists acting in conjunction with indigenous reactionaries.

In recent months, with the intensification of the guerrilla struggle in central and southern Africa, pressure has been strongly directed towards those states which have common frontiers with South Africa, Rhodesia, Angola and Mozambique. The object is to dominate them politically and economically, and thus hold up the advance of the African Revolution and at the same time to improve their own neo-colonialist position.

The tragedy is that some African heads of state are themselves actually aiding and abetting imperialists and neo-colonialists. In February 1967 Malawi became the first independent African state to conclude a trade agreement, and later to establish diplomatic relations with South Africa.

Since then, other African states have also been lured into the South African neo-colonialist web by a mixture of 'aid' and carefully-veiled threats.

The withdrawal of Britain from the High Commission territories, the break between Britain and Rhodesia as a result of UDI, and the outbreak of guerrilla warfare in the Portuguese colonies, has given South Africa a golden opportunity to jump in.

South Africa is in the classic, imperialist position of a manufacturing country seeking new outlets for its capital and goods. Its policy is to exploit the labour and resources of its hinterland, thereby strengthening South Africa's economy and at the same time delaying the advance of the African Revolution.

South Africa's 'new policy' of improved relations with African states has been described as the building of 'bridges' rather than 'forts'. The crux of the matter was revealed clearly in the editorial of the South African 'Financial Gazette' of May 10th, 1968:

'We must build more bridges and less forts. The might of our armed forces are not enough to shield off hostilities still being built up against South Africa in some African states. We must build more bridges into Africa. In Malawi we have virtually spanned a bridge into the heart of Africa.'

A delighted broadcaster in Salisbury on October 8th, 1967 praised

Dr Banda for what he called his 'realistic policy', and added: 'the nations which are nearest to South Africa have been the quickest to realize the side on which their bread is buttered'. He referred here to Lesotho and Botswana.

South Africa is daily increasing her economic and political penetration into African territories. The Lesotho government in 1967 appointed three South Africans to 'advise' on political and economic affairs. In Rhodesia, South African capital investment already exceeds that of Britain; and it is mainly the support of South Africa which has enabled Ian Smith's rebel regime to survive.

The South African government has recently granted eight million rand to Malawi for the building of the new capital city of Lilongwe. Of the five million rand set aside for 'economic co-operation' two million has already been ear-marked for Malawi as a 'first instalment' this year.

Since 1964, when Malawi became independent, imports from South Africa have doubled; while the main force behind capital investment in Malawi is increasingly the South African government itself.

The South African liberation movement together with the peoples of independent Africa and freedom fighters, wherever they are operating must be alert to this new challenge. Neo-colonialism, like colonialism and imperialism can only be banished from our midst by armed struggle.

In east, central and west Africa, neo-colonialism is hard at work fostering regional economic groupings, in the knowledge that without political cohesion they will remain weak and subject to neo-colonialist pressures and domination. The US government in its latest statement on 'aid' has said that it will favour those states which are grouped together in this way.

As each new attempt is made to divide us and to divert us from our purpose, it must be exposed and attacked. Already, the ordinary men and women of Africa are talking the language of the African Revolution. They speak of freedom, unity and socialism, and know that these objectives are synonymous, and can only be attained through armed struggle.

In some cases, the people of Africa are ahead of their governments. But the pressures they are exerting will inevitably compel the pace forward.

We must recognize and fight the external and the internal enemy, and combine all our resources in the great struggle which lies ahead. With cohesive planning and with a full awareness of our united strength, nothing can halt the progress towards final victory.

434

31

TWO MYTHS

THE MYTH OF THE 'THIRD WORLD'

First published in 'Labour Monthly', October 1968.

There is much loose talk and woolly writing about the so-called Third World. To some it means all the developing nations; to some it suggests the coloured peoples of the world; others think of it as referring to a vague, amorphous mass of uncommitted peoples, the oppressed and exploited of the earth who are neither 'east' nor 'west' but who are a kind of third, neutral force in the world.

To Franz Fanon, the 'Third World' clearly meant the colonies and ex-colonies, and in his book 'The Wretched of the Earth' he makes a specific case study of the problems of decolonization. For him, the 'wretched' are those who have suffered the oppression and exploitation of colonialism. 'The Third World is not cut off from the rest. Quite the contrary, it is at the middle of the whirlpool', and is characterized by 'neutralism'. Its peoples are committed to a non-capitalist road, since capitalist exploitation is their enemy. But the 'Third World' should refuse to become a factor in the fierce competition which exists between the capitalist and socialist systems, and ought 'to find their own particular values and methods and a style which shall be peculiar to them'.

Fanon did not mean non-commitment or non-alignment in the commonly-accepted sense, though both have come to be associated with the term. The very mention of the 'Third World' suggests to some a kind of passivity, a non-participation, an opting out of the conflict between the two worlds of capitalism and socialism.

It is this concept which seems to have led to most of the misuse of the term 'Third World', and renders its use so misleading. There is no middle road between capitalism and socialism.

Two questions must be asked. First, does a 'Third World' really exist? Secondly, is it possible, either in terms of ideology or practical politics, in the ever-sharpening conflict between revolutionary and counter-revolutionary forces in the world to adopt a position of neutrality or non-alignment?

Clearly, the 'Third World' is not definable on a racial or colour basis, though in fact most of the oppressed peoples are non-white. Is it then the apparently uncommitted or non-aligned who form the 'Third World'?

The expression first came to be widely used when two Conferences of Non-Aligned States had been held. The first was in Belgrade in 1961. There were 25 participating states and three observer countries. The cold war and nuclear arms race was at its height and there seemed a very real possibility that the world might be plunged into a war which would mean the end of civilization as we know it. The main purpose of the Conference, therefore, was to employ all the efforts of the participating countries to bring about the destruction of nuclear stockpiles and to divert the vast scientific and technological resources at the disposal of the great powers to positive and progressive channels.

The Second Conference of Non-Aligned States was held in Cairo in October 1964. There were then 46 participating states and ten observer countries. Non-alignment seemed to be practical politics. In my address at that Conference I said:

'We are all here as Non-Aligned nations but the term "Non-Aligned" as applied to us has not yet covered every form of policy which it connotes. We came into existence as a protest and a revolt against the state of affairs in international relations caused by the division of the world into opposing blocs of east and west. We came into existence as a revolt against imperialism and neo-colonialism which are also the basic cause of world tension and insecurity.'

I went on to say that these states which claimed to be non-aligned had the right to choose the political and economic philosophy which was considered the most suitable for their rapid development and advancement. The fact that Ghana accepted socialism did not

436

necessarily imply opposition to any other country or people. 'Social-ism', I said, 'does not belong to the Soviet Union or China, or for that matter to any other country; it is an international idea.'

Many of us thought at that time that it was the duty of the Non-Aligned States to assert their full weight against the senseless build-up of nuclear weapons which threatened the whole world. With 'east' and 'west', two power blocs of roughly equal strength, poised it seemed on the brink of nuclear warfare, there appeared to be reprieve for the world only in the holding of a balance of power by some third force which would prevent either of the two sides from starting a major war.

After the First Conference, Pandit Nehru and I went to Moscow on behalf of the Non-Aligned States, and President Modibo Keita of Mali and President Sukarno of Indonesia went to Washington.

Although there was no sudden and dramatic lessening of world tension as a result of these missions, the threat of nuclear warfare has to some extent lessened.

However, in the present world situation, with the armed phase of the revolutionary struggle well-launched in Africa, Asia and Latin America, and in the USA itself by the Black Power Movement, it is no longer possible to adopt a third position outside the main con-flict. The world struggle, and the cause of world tension, has to be seen not in the old political context of the cold war, that is, of nation states and power blocs, but in terms of revolutionary and counter-revolutionary peoples. It cuts right across territorial boundaries and has nothing to do with colour or race. It is a war to the finish between the oppressed and the oppressors, between those who pursue a capitalist path, and those committed to socialist policies.

Yet old beliefs die hard. Although non-alignment is an anachron-ism, there are still a few politicians and heads of state who cling to the idea of neutralism and who advocate the holding of more Conferences of Non-Aligned States. Their thinking is a form of political escapism – a reluctance to face the stark realities of the present situation.

The oppressed and exploited peoples are the struggling revolution-ary masses committed to the socialist world. Some of them are not yet politically aware. Others are very much aware, and are already en-gaged in the armed liberation struggle. At whatever stage they have reached in their resistance to exploitation and oppression, they belong to the permanent socialist revolution. They do not constitute a 'Third World'. They are part of the revolutionary upsurge which is everywhere challenging the capitalist, imperialist and neo-colonialist power structure of reaction and counter-revolution. There are thus two worlds only, the revolutionary and the counter-revolutionary world – the socialist world trending towards communism, and the capitalist world with its extensions of imperialism, colonialism and neo-colonialism.

Today then, the 'Third World' is neither a practical political concept nor a reality. It is merely a misused expression which has come to mean everything and nothing. It has been used with equal looseness both by those committed to the revolutionary struggle and by those who are its deadly enemies. The western press has gladly made use of it to serve its own ends by associating it with racism, and by equating it with concepts such as non-alignment, neutralism and co-existence. It has thus helped to prevent the full weight of the so-called 'Third World' being identified openly and decisively as part of the socialist world.

If we are to achieve revolutionary socialism then we must avoid any suggestion that will imply that there is any separation between the socialist world and a 'Third World'.

Misused and misleading political terms must be either abandoned or defined clearly. Where the revolutionary struggle is in the armed phase as in Africa, Asia and Latin America, it is particularly important that there should be the utmost clarity of political expression.

The purpose of an article I wrote in 1966 under the title 'African Socialism Revisited' published in African Forum, Vol. 1, No. 3, was to show that there is no such thing as 'African Socialism'. The term had come to be employed as proof of the existence of brands of socialism peculiar to Africa, such as Arab socialism, pragmatic socialism, and this or that socialism, when in fact there is only one true socialism: scientific socialism.

I do not deny the existence of the struggling 'wretched of the earth', but maintain that they do not exist in isolation, as the 'Third World'. They are an integral part of the revolutionary world, and are committed to the hilt in the struggle against capitalism to end the exploitation of man by man.

'AFRICAN SOCIALISM' REVISITED

Reprint of an article in African Forum, *Vol. 1, No. 3, 1966*

The term 'socialism' has become a necessity in the platform diction and political writings of African leaders. It is a term which unites in the recognition that the restoration of Africa's humanist and egalitarian principles of society calls for socialism. All of us, therefore even though pursuing widely contrasting policies in the task of reconstructing our various nation-states, still use 'socialism' to describe our respective efforts. The question must therefore be faced: What real meaning does the term retain in the context of contemporary African politics? I warned about this in my book 'Consciencism':

'And yet, socialism in Africa today tends to lose its objective content in favour of a distracting terminology and in favour of a general confusion. Discussion centres more on the various conceivable types of socialism than upon the need for socialist development.'

Some African political leaders and thinkers certainly use the term 'socialism' as it should in my opinion be used: to describe a complex of social purposes and the consequential social and economic policies organizational patterns, state structure, and ideologies which can lead to the attainment of those purposes. For such leaders, the aim is to remould African society in the socialist direction; to reconsider African society in such a manner that the humanism of traditional African life reasserts itself in a modern technical community. Consequently, socialism in Africa introduces a new social synthesis in which modern technology is reconciled with human values, in which the advanced technical society is realized without the staggering social malefactions and deep schisms of capitalist industrial society. For true economic and social development cannot be promoted without the real socialization of productive and distributive processes. Those African leaders who believe these principles are the socialists in Africa.

There are, however, other African political leaders and thinkers who use the term 'socialism' because they believe that socialism would, in the words of Chandler Morse, 'smooth the road to economic development'. It becomes necessary for them to employ the term in a 'charismatic effort to rally support' for the policies that do not really promote economic and social development. Those African leaders who believe these principles are supposed to be the 'African socialists'.

It is interesting to recall that before the split in the Second International, Marxism was almost indistinguishable from social democracy. Indeed, the German Social Democratic Party was more or less the guardian of the doctrine of Marxism, and both Marx and Engels supported that Party. Lenin, too, became a member of the Social Democratic Party. After the break-up of the Second International, however, the meaning of the term 'social democracy' altered, and it became possible to draw a real distinction between socialism and social democracy. A similar situation has arisen in Africa. Some years ago, African political leaders and writers used the term 'African socialism' in order to label the concrete forms that socialism might assume in Africa. But the realities of the diverse and irreconcilable social, political and economic policies being pursued by African states today have made the term 'African socialism' meaningless and irrelevant. It appears to be much more closely associated with anthropology than with political economy. 'African socialism' has now come to acquire some of its greatest publicists in Europe and North America precisely because of its predominant anthropological charm. Its foreign publicists include not only the surviving social democrats of Europe and North America, but other intellectuals and liberals who themselves are dyed in the wool of social democracy. It was no accident, let me add, that the 1962 Dakar Colloquium made such capital of 'African socialism'; but the uncertainties concerning the meaning and specific policies of 'African socialism' have led some of us to abandon the term because it fails to express its original meaning and because it tends to obscure our fundamental socialist commitment.

Today, the phrase 'African socialism' seems to espouse the view that the traditional African society was a classless society imbued with the spirit of humanism and to express a nostalgia for that spirit. Such a conception of socialism makes a fetish of the communal African society. But an idyllic, African classless society (in which there were no rich and no poor) enjoying a drugged serenity is certainly a facile simplification; there is no historical or even anthropological evidence for any such a society. I am afraid the realities of African society were somewhat more sordid.

All available evidence from the history of Africa, up to the eve of the European colonization, shows that African society was neither classless nor devoid of a social hierarchy. Feudalism existed in some parts of Africa before colonization; and feudalism involves a deep and exploitative social stratification, founded on the ownership of land. It must also be noted that slavery existed in Africa before European colonization, although the earlier European contact gave slavery in Africa some of its most vicious characteristics. The truth remains, however, that before colonization, which became widespread in Africa only in the nineteenth century, Africans were prepared to sell, often for no more than thirty pieces of silver, fellow tribesmen and even members of the same 'extended' family and clan. Colonialism deserves to be blamed for many evils in Africa, but surely it was not preceded by an African Golden Age or paradise. A return to the pre-colonial African society is evidently not worthy of the ingenuity and efforts of our people.

All this notwithstanding, one would still argue that the basic organization of many African societies in different periods of history manifested a certain communalism and that the philosophy and humanist purposes behind that organization are worthy of recapture. A community in which each saw his well-being in the welfare of the group certainly was praiseworthy, even if the manner in which the well-being of the group was pursued makes no contribution to our purposes. Thus, what socialist thought in Africa must recapture is not the structure of the 'traditional African society' but its spirit, for the spirit of communalism is crystallized in its humanism and in its reconciliation of individual advancement with group welfare. Even if there is incomplete anthropological evidence to reconstruct the 'traditional African society' with accuracy, we can still recapture the rich human values of that society. In short, an anthropological approach to the 'traditional African society' is too much unproven; but a philosophical approach stands on much firmer ground and makes generalization feasible.

One predicament in the anthropological approach is that there is some disparity of view concerning the manifestations of the 'classlessness' of the 'traditional African society'. While some hold that the society was based on the equality of its members, others hold that it contained a hierarchy and division of labour in which the hierarchy and therefore power – was founded on spiritual and democratic values. Of course, no society can be founded on the equality of its members, although some societies are founded on egalitarianism which is something quite different. Similarly, a classless society that at the same time rejoices in a hierarchy of power (as distinct from authority) must be accounted a marvel of socio-political finesse.

We know that the 'traditional African society' was founded on principles of egalitarianism. In its actual workings, however, it had various shortcomings. Its humanist impulse, nevertheless, is something that continues to urge us towards our all-African socialist reconstruction. We postulate each man to be an end in himself, not merely a means; and we accept the necessity of guaranteeing each man equal opportunities for his development. The implications of this socio-political practice have to be worked our scientifically, and the necessary social and economic policies pursued with resolution.

Any meaningful humanism must begin from egalitarianism and must lead to objectively chosen policies for safe-guarding and sustaining egalitarianism. Hence, socialism. Hence, also, scientific socialism.

A further difficulty that arises from the anthropological approach to socialism, or 'African socialism' is the glaring division beween existing African societies and the communalistic society that was. I warned in my book 'Consciencism' that 'our society is not the old society, but a new society enlarged by Islamic and Euro-Christian influences'. This is a fact that any socio-economic policies must recognize and take into account. Yet the literature of 'African socialism' comes close to suggesting that today's African societies are communalistic. The two societies are not co-terminous, and such an equation cannot be supported by any attentive observation. It is true that this disparity is acknowledged in some of the literature of 'African socialism'; thus, my friend and colleague Julius Nyerere, in acknowledging the disequilibrium between what was and what is in terms of African societies, attributes the differences to the importations of European colonialism.

We know, of course, that the defeat of colonialism and even neo-colonialism will not result in the automatic disappearance of the imported patterns of thought and social organization. For those patterns have taken root, and are in varying degrees sociological features of our contemporary society. Nor will a simple return to the communalistic society of ancient Africa offer a solution either. To advocate a return, as it were, to the rock from which we were hewn is a charming thought, but we are faced with contemporary problems, which have arisen from political subjugation, economic exploitation, educational and social backwardness, increases in population, familiarity with the methods and products of industrialization, modern agricultural techniques. These – as well as a host of other complexities – can be resolved by no mere communalistic society, however sophisticated, and anyone who so advocates must be caught in insoluble dilemmas of the most excruciating kind. All available evidence from socio-political history discloses that such a return to a *status quo ante* is quite unexampled in the evolution of societies. There is, indeed, no theoretical or historical reason to indicate that it is at all possible.

When one society meets another, the observed historical trend is that acculturation results in a balance of forward movement, a movement in which each society assimilates certain useful attributes of the other. Social evolution is a dialectical process; it has ups and downs, but, on balance, it always represents an upward trend.

Islamic civilization and European colonialism are both historical experiences of the traditional African society, profound experiences that have permanently changed the complexion of the traditional African society. They have introduced new values and a social, cultural, and economic organization into African life. African societies are not traditional, even if backward, and they are clearly in a state of socio-economic disequilibrium. They are in this state because they are not anchored to a steadying ideology.

The way out is certainly not to regurgitate all Islamic or Euro-colonial influences in a futile attempt to recreate a past that cannot be resurrected. The way out is only forward, forward to a higher reconciled form of society, in which the quintessence of the human purposes of traditional African society reasserts itself in a modern context – forward, in short, to socialism, through policies that are scientifically devised and correctly applied. The inevitability of a forward way out is felt by all; thus, Leopold Sedor Senghor, although favouring some kind of return to African communalism, insists that the refashioned African society must accommodate the 'positive contribution' of colonial rule, 'such as the economic and technical infrastructure and the French education system'. The economic and technical infrastructure of even French colonialism and the French educational system must be assumed, though this can be shown to be imbued with a particular socio-political philosophy. This philosophy, as should be known, is not compatible with the philosophy underlying communalism, and the desired accommodation would prove only a socio-political mirage.

Senghor has, indeed, given an account of the nature of the return to Africa. His account is highlighted by statements using some of his own words: that the African is 'a field of pure sensation'; that he does not measure or observe, but 'lives' a situation; and that this way of acquiring 'knowledge' by confrontation and intuition is 'Negro African', the acquisition of knowledge by reason, 'Hellenic'. In 'African Socialism' (London and New York, 1964, pp. 72–73), he proposes that we

'consider the Negro-African as he faces the Other: God, man, animal, tree or pebble, natural or social phenomenon. In contrast to the classic European, the Negro-African does not draw a line between himself and the object, he does not hold it at a distance, nor does he merely look at it and analyse it. After holding it at a distance, after scanning it without analysing it, he takes it vibrant in his hands, careful not to kill or fix it. He touches it, feels it, smells

443

it. The Negro-African is like one of those Third Day Worms, a pure field of sensations ... Thus the Negro-African sympathises, abandons his personality to become identified with the Other, dies to be reborn in the Other. He does not assimilate; he is assimilated. He lives a common life with the Other; he lives in a symbiosis.'

It is clear that socialism cannot be founded on this kind of metaphysics of knowledge.

To be sure, there is a connection between communalism and socialism. Socialism stands to communalism as capitalism stands to slavery. In socialism, the principles underlying communalism are given expression in modern circumstances. Thus, whereas communalism in a non-technical society can be laissez-faire, in a technical society where sophisticated means of production are at hand, the situation is different; for if the underlying principles of communalism are not given correlated expression, class cleavages will arise, which are connected with economic disparities and thereby with political inequalities. Socialism, therefore, can be, and is, the defence of the principles of communalism in a modern setting; it is a form of social organization that, guided by the principles underlying communism, adopts procedures and measures made necessary by demographic and technological developments. Only under socialism can we reliably accumulate the capital we need for our development and also ensure that the gains of investment are applied for the general welfare.

Socialism is not spontaneous. It does not arise by itself. It has abiding principles according to which the major means of production and distribution ought to be socialized if exploitation of the many by the few is to be prevented; if, that is to say, egalitarianism in the economy is to be protected. Socialist countries in Africa may differ in this or that detail of their policies, but such differences themselves ought not to be arbitrary or subject to vagaries of taste. They must be scientifically explained, as necessities arising from differences in the particular circumstances of the countries themselves.

There is only one way of achieving socialism: by the devising of policies aimed at the general socialist goals, each of which takes its particular form from the specific circumstances of a particular state at a definite historical period. Socialism depends on dialectical and historical materialism, upon the view that there is only one nature subject in all its manifestations to natural laws and that human society is, in this sense, part of nature and subject to its own laws of development.

It is the elimination of fancifulness from socialist action that makes socialism scientific. To suppose that there are tribal, national or racial socialisms is to abandon objectivity in favour of chauvinism.

32

EXTRACTS FROM BOOKS ONE AND TWO OF THE HANDBOOK OF REVOLUTIONARY WARFARE

AUTHOR'S NOTE

This book has been written during my stay in Conakry. Previous notes I made for a manual of guerrilla warfare for African freedom fighters were left behind in Ghana when I departed for Hanoi on 21st February 1966. The manuscript was handed over to imperialist and neo-colonialist intelligence organizations by the military and police traitors.

This HANDBOOK, presenting a completely new approach will, I hope, help to make possible the successful completion of the armed phase of the African revolutionary struggle for total emancipation and an All-African Union Government.

The Black Power movement in the U.S.A., and the struggles of peoples of African descent in the Caribbean, South American and elsewhere, form an integral part of the African politico-military revolutionary struggle. Our victory will be their victory also, and the victory of all the revolutionary, oppressed and exploited masses of the world who are challenging the capitalist, imperialist and neo-colonialist power structure of reaction and counter-revolution.

Conakry, Guinea.
30th July 1968.

446

BOOK ONE

KNOW THE ENEMY

PREFACE

The new phase of the armed revolutionary struggle in Africa embraces the entire continent. It is essential that we know what we fight, and why we fight. Imperialism and neo-colonialism must be broken down into their component parts so that we can clearly see them. We must know their world strategy.

In this book I have attempted to show the nature and extent of imperialist and neo-colonialist aggression, and our objectives in the struggle for the freedom and the political unification of Africa.

CHAPTER ONE

THE WORLD STRATEGY OF IMPERIALISM

Know the enemy

A number of external factors affect the African situation, and if our liberation struggle is to be placed in correct perspective and we are to KNOW THE ENEMY, the impact of these factors must be fully grasped. First among them is imperialism, for it is mainly against exploitation and poverty that our peoples revolt. It is therefore of paramount importance to set out the strategy of imperialism in clear terms:

1. The means used by the enemy to ensure the continued economic exploitation of our territories.
2. The nature of the attempts made to destroy the liberation movement.

Once the components of the enemy's strategy are determined, we will be in a position to outline the correct strategy for our own struggle in terms of our actual situation and in accordance with our objectives.

Before the Second World War, the world (excluding the USSR, China, etc.) was divided into:

(a) Capitalist states practising orthodox imperialism under the generally known form of imperialism.
(b) Colonial territories which fed the economies of the capitalist imperialist states. (The Latin American territories had already passed from the status of 'Spanish' and 'Portuguese' colonies to that of neo-colonies.)

447

However, after the Second World War, serious economic, social and political tensions arose in both spheres.

(a) Inside the capitalist-imperialist states, workers' organizations had become comparatively strong and experienced, and the claims of the working class for a more substantial share of the wealth produced by the capitalist economy could no longer be ignored. The necessity to concede had become all the more imperative since the European capitalist system had been seriously shaken up by the near-holocaust which marked the experience of imperialist wars.

(b) While the capitalist system of exploitation was coming to grips with its internal crises, the world's colonized areas were astir with the upsurge of strong liberation movements. Here again, demands could no longer be cast aside or ignored especially when they were channelled through irresistible mass movements, like the Rassemblement Démocratique Africain (RDA), the Parti Démocratique de Guineé (PDG) and the Convention People's Party (CPP) in Ghana. In certain areas, for example in Vietnam, Kenya and Algeria, direct confrontation demonstrated the readiness of the oppressed peoples to implement their claims with blood and fire.

Both in the colonial territories and in the metropolitan states, the struggle was being waged against the same enemy: international finance capital under its external and internal forms of exploitation, imperialism and capitalism.

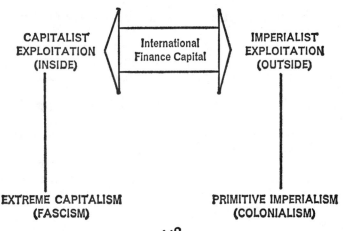

CAPITALIST EXPLOITATION (INSIDE) — International Finance Capital — IMPERIALIST EXPLOITATION (OUTSIDE)

EXTREME CAPITALISM (FASCISM)   PRIMITIVE IMPERIALISM (COLONIALISM)

Threatened with disintegration by the double-fisted attack of the working class movement and the liberation movement, capitalism had to launch a series of reforms in order to build a protective armour around the inner workings of its system.

To avoid an internal breakdown of the system under the pressure of the workers' protest movement, the governments of capitalist countries granted their workers certain concessions which did not endanger the basic nature of the capitalist system of exploitation. They gave them social security; higher wages, better working conditions, professional training facilities, and other improvements.

These reforms helped to blur fundamental contradictions, and to remove some of the more glaring injustices while at the same time ensuring the continued exploitation of the workers. The myth was established of an affluent capitalist society promising abundance and a better life for all. The basic aim, however, was the establishment of a 'welfare state' as the only safeguard against the threat of fascism or communism.

However, the problem was to find a way to avoid sacrificing the all-important principle of ever-increasing profits for the owning

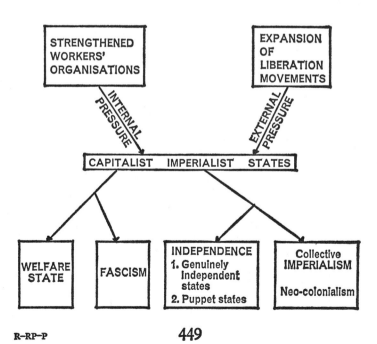

minority, and also to find the money needed to finance the welfare state.

By way of a solution, capitalism proceeded to introduce not only internal reforms, but external reforms designed to raise the extra money needed for the establishment and the maintenance of the welfare state at home. In other words, modern capitalism had come to depend more heavily than before on the exploitation of the material and human resources of the colonial territories. On the external front, therefore, it became necessary for international finance capital to carry out reforms in order to eliminate the deadly threat to its supremacy of the liberation movement.

The urgent need for such reforms was made clear by the powerful growth and expansion of the liberation forces in Africa, Asia and Latin America, where revolutionary movements had not only seized power but were actually consolidating their gains. Developments in the USSR, China, Cuba, North Vietnam, North Korea, and in Egypt, Ghana, Guinea, Mali, Algeria and other parts of Africa, showed that not only was the world balance of forces shifting, but that the capitalist-imperialist states were confronted with a real danger of encirclement.

Collective imperialism
The modifications introduced by imperialism in its strategy were expressed:

(a) through the disappearance of the numerous old-fashioned 'colonies' owing exclusive allegiance to a single metropolitan country.
(b) through the replacement of 'national' imperialisms by a 'collective' imperialism in which the USA occupies a leading position.

The roots of this process may be traced back to the period of the Second World War, when the socialist camp was still too small and weak to give decisive assistance to the European working class movement. The workers were therefore all the more easily deflected from the objectives of their struggle, and allowed themselves to be dragged into a bloody war of imperialism.

The Second World War seriously strained the political and economic strength of Europe, although capitalism as a system emerged relatively intact. However, the true winner of the whole contest turned out to be the United States of America. Having helped the allies to win the war, the USA was from then on able to retain its pre-eminent position, and to acquire increasing influence in the economic life of the exhausted European states.

This 'internationalization' or 'syndicalization' enabled US imperialism to forestall temporarily an incipient crisis by fulfilling two *sine qua non* conditions:

1. **The need to expand**

   The US–European post-war alliance not only enabled the USA to benefit from the advantages of the European market, which had hitherto been largely closed to its penetration; but also opened up new horizons in Asia, Africa, and Latin America where the USA had already superseded European supremacy and established neo-colonialist domination.

2. **The need to militarize**

   The militarization of the US economy, based on the political pretext of the threatening rise of the USSR and later of the People's Republic of China as socialist powers, enabled the USA to postpone its internal crises, first during the 'hot' war (1939–1945) and then during the 'cold' war (since 1945).

Militarization served two main purposes:

1. It absorbed, and continues to absorb, an excess of unorganized energy into the intense armaments drive which supports imperialist aggression and many blocs and alliances formed by imperialist powers over the last twenty years.

2. It made possible an expensive policy of paternalist corruption of the poor and oppressed people of the world.

The principle of mutual inter-imperialist assistance whereby American, British, French and West German monopoly capital extends joint control over the wealth of the non-liberated zones of Africa, Latin America and Asia, finds concrete expression in the formation of interlocked international financial institutions and bodies of credit:

International Monetary Fund (IMF), USA 25% of the votes.

International Bank for Reconstruction and Development (IBRD), USA 34% of the votes.

International Development Association (IDA), USA 41% of the votes.

On a lesser scale, Europe as a whole, and West Germany in particular, find profitable outlets for big business in Africa through the agencies of such organizations as the European Common Market (EEC).

The imperialists even make use of the United Nations Organization in order to camouflage their neo-colonialist objectives. This can be seen, for example in US policy in South Korea and the Congo.

Sham independence

But as far as the imperialists are concerned the real solution to the problem of continued exploitation through concessions and reform lies in the concept of 'sham-independence'. **A state can be said to be a neo-colonialist or client state if it is independent de jure and dependent de facto. It is a state where political power lies in the conservative forces of the former colony and where economic power remains under the control of international finance capital.**

In other words, the country continues to be economically exploited by interests which are alien to the majority of the ex-colonized population but are intrinsic to the world capitalist sector. Such a state is in the grip of neo-colonialism. It has become a client state.

Neo-colonialism

The pre-requisite of a correct and global strategy to defeat neo-colonialism is the ability to discover and expose the way in which a state becomes neo-colonialist. For although a neo-colonialist state enjoys only sham independence it is to all outward appearances independent, and therefore the very roots of neo-colonialism must be traced back to the struggle for independence in a colonial territory.

If the liberation movement is firmly established, the colonial power invariably resorts to a 'containment' policy, in order to stop any further progress, and to deaden its impact. To achieve this objective, the colonial power uses its arsenal of alliances, its network of military bases, economic devices such as corruption, sabotage and blackmail, and equally insidious, the psychological weapon of propaganda with a view to impressing on the masses a number of imperialist dogmas:

1. That western democracy and the parliamentary system are the only valid ways of governing; that they constitute the only worth-while model for the training of an indigenous élite by the colonial power.
2. That capitalism, free enterprise, free competition, etc., are the only economic systems capable of promoting development; that the western powers have mastered the liberal-capitalist technique perfectly; that the colonial territory should become an economic satellite in its own interest; that there is no

reason to put an end to the policy of 'co-operation' pursued during the colonial regime; and that any attempt to break away would be dangerous, since the colonial power is always ready to give 'aid'.

3. That the slightest 'lapse' on the part of the leaders of the liberation movement could push the country into the grip of 'communism' and of 'totalitarian dictatorship'.

4. That the carve-up agreed upon by the imperialists during the colonial period is fair and sacred; that it would be unthinkable even to attempt to liberate areas in terms of their common cultural and historical links; that the only acceptable version of 'liberation' must apply to the artificial units designed by the imperialists, and hurriedly labelled 'nations' in spite of the fact that they are neither culturally unified, nor economically self-sufficient.

As a further justification of its policy, **imperialism usually resorts to all types of propaganda in order to highlight and exploit differences of religion, culture, race, outlook, and of political ideology among the oppressed masses, or between regions which share a long history of mutual commercial and cultural exchange.**

Such methods aim to orientate the leaders of the liberation movements towards a brand of nationalism based on petty-minded and aggressive chauvinism, as well as to steer the liberation movement along a reformist path. The problem of 'liberation' is therefore usually raised in terms of a participation of 'good' indigenous elements in the administration of the colonized territory, for instance through a policy of 'africanization' devoid of any fundamental changes in the political, economic and administrative structure of the territory.

The transition to neo-colonialism is marked by a succession of more or less important measures which culminate into a ritual of so-called free elections, most organized through methods of intimidation. Local agents, selected by the colonial power as 'worthy representatives' are then presented to the people as the champions of national independence, and are immediately given all the superficial attributes of power: a puppet government has been formed.

By the very nature of its essential objective, which is exploitation, neo-colonialism can only flourish in a client state.

When the farce of sham elections to form a puppet government proves too difficult to enact, the colonial power tries to divide the liberation movement into a 'moderate' wing with which it seeks accommodation, and a militant wing which it endeavours to isolate and to suppress by force.

In the last resort, neo-colonialists can even set up a bogus 'progressive' party or organization using local agents and maintain an artificial liberation movement which serves both as a worthy partner for negotiations and as an intelligence and/or repression agency against the genuine liberation movement supported by the oppressed masses. Such is the role played by FLING in regard to Guinea-Bissau, and UPA in regard to Angola. And so once more the stage is set for negotiations, autonomy and the formation of a puppet government.

However, the machinations of the colonial power will fail wherever the leaders of the struggle for independence maintain a clear spirit of vigilance, and cultivate genuinely revolutionary qualities.

Then, and only then, does a truly independent government emerge, dedicated to national reconstruction in the liberated territory, and determined to assist all those engaged in anti-imperialist struggle.

Such a government is an obstacle barring the advance of neo-colonialism, and such obstacles must be increased because the example of genuine independence is contagious and will help to fortify extensive zones against imperialist aggression.

Faced with genuine independence, imperialism is increasingly compelled to resort to encirclement and subversion in order to overthrow these popular governments, using such weapons as *coups d'état*, assassination, mutiny within the party, tribal revolt, palace revolutions, and so on, while at the same time strengthening neighbouring puppet regimes to form a political safety belt, a *cordon sanitaire*.

Therefore, the main sphere in which we must strive to defeat neocolonialist intrigues is within the movement for true independence; that is, within the progressive political party which forms the government. This is particularly true in the one party state which can only function successfully under socialism. Usually, this ruling party is made up of several groups each with its distinct economic and political interests. The relative importance of each group in the party and state machinery will determine the course of development. Imperialist strategy is therefore directed towards bringing into a position of pre-eminence

454

that group which most nearly shares its economic and political views.

If a member of a group which is absolutely opposed to imperialism is in control of the state and party, attempts are made to organize: Either

1. Assassination or a coup d'état or 'palace revolution' which will permit political power to fall into the lap of the rival but pro-imperialist group.

Or

2. A decentralization of political power within the ruling party, one group being strong in the state machinery, the other strong in the party machine. Even in the state machine, the vital organs are artfully put into the hands of forces ready to parley with imperialists. The nursing of discontent and confusion within the party and among the people, through the spread of conflicting ideologies, rumours of economic run-down, maladministration and corruption, will permit the creation of an atmosphere of dissatisfaction favourable to a change in the personnel of government. Ostensibly the same party is in power. In truth, a qualitative change in the nature of political power has taken place.

Since the conglomerate nature of the ruling party is the basic fact on which neo-colonialist strategy depends, the main remedial measures must be directed to this sphere, and this problem must be

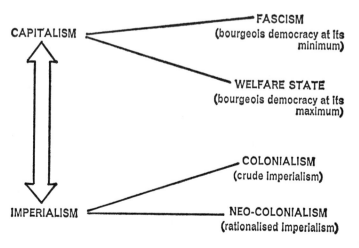

borne in mind even before the achievement of independence. It is essential that positive action should in its dialectical evolution anticipate the seminal disintegration and discover a way of containing the future schismatic tendencies.

Neo-colonialism constitutes the necessary condition for the establishment of welfare states by the imperialist nations. **Just as the welfare state is the internal condition, neo-colonialism is the external condition, for the continued hegemony of international finance capital.**

It is precisely the increasing dependence of the imperialist system on neo-colonialist exploitation on an international scale which renders its existence so precarious, and its future so uncertain.

Significantly, the neo-colonialist system costs the capitalist powers comparatively little, while enormous and increasing profits are made. This is shown by the ever-rising graphs representing the turn-over figures of the big capitalist business concerns implanted in the neo-colonialist areas of the world, and by the ever-widening gap between the wealthy and the poor peoples of the world.

In the final analysis, the neo-colonialist system of exploitation, which is the external condition for the maintenance of the capitalist welfare state, remains essentially dependent on the production of the neo-colonized workers, who must not only continue to produce under stagnant and continually worsening living conditions, but must

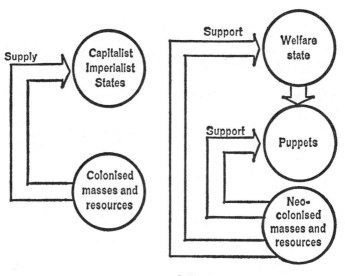

produce substantially more than they did in the colonial days. They must do more than satisfy the needs of the metropolitan state. They must cater for the insatiable demands of the client government.

The explosive character of this situation cannot be denied. The neo-colonialist government is virtually in a state of permanent conflict with its own masses, whilst the gap between the puppet administration and neo-colonized workers widens every day.

It is therefore clear that a puppet regime cannot draw its strength from the support of the broad masses. It can only stay in power as long as it manages to subsist in the teeth of popular opposition and revolt. Hence, the imperative need to depend on a foreign power for military assistance merely to keep the neo-colonized government physically in power.

Thus, the three essential components of neo-colonialism are:

1. Economic exploitation
2. Puppet governments and client states
3. Military assistance
4. Economic 'aid'

The vital necessity of 'military aid' is fulfilled through various channels: foreign technical assistance to the armed forces, control of the armed forces by officers and western military cadres, secret military agreements, the formation of special units for the repression of popular insurrection, and so on. The important thing is to know how to recognize this type of 'aid', in whatever guise it appears, for it is the most blatant proof of the anti-popular, aggressive and basically violent character of all neo-colonialist regimes. Its escalation and impact increase proportionately to the widening gap between the puppets and the oppressed masses, and it is directly related to the development of organized, popular resistance.

It is also to be noted that US policy found its most complete expression, after the murder of President Kennedy, in the Johnson doctrine whereby military aggression, under the name of 'preventive measures', became an integral part of neo-colonialist practice.

The struggle against neo-colonialism

Military strategy presupposes political aims. All military problems are political, and all political problems are economic.

Both the basic nature of neo-colonialism and the accumulated experience of liberation movements in Africa, Asia and Latin America indicate clearly that the only way for the broad masses to eradicate neo-colonialism is through a revolutionary movement

457

springing from a direct confrontation with the imperialists, and drawing its strength from the exploited and disinherited masses. The struggle against puppet governments, and against all forms of exploitation, is the basic condition for the survival and development of a genuine liberation movement in Africa. We must accept the challenge and fight to destroy this threat to our future as a free and united continent.

Independence must never be considered as an end in itself but as a stage, the very first stage of the people's revolutionary struggle.

Propaganda and psychological warfare

Throughout the struggle we must recognize and combat enemy attempts to demoralize us. For, in the face of the failure to achieve military solutions against well-organized, broadly-based guerrilla forces, as for example in Vietnam, the enemy has stepped up its efforts in the propaganda war. The aim is:

1. To prevent a liberation movement from getting under way, by destroying it at its source, i.e. by undermining the will to fight.
2. Where revolutionary warfare has actually begun, to conquer it by political means, i.e. by granting just sufficient political, economic and social 'reform' to encourage all but the so-called 'extremists' to abandon the struggle.

Psychological attacks are made through the agency of broadcasting stations like the BBC, Voice of Germany, and above all, Voice of America, which pursues its brainwashing mission through newsreels, interviews and other 'informative' programmes at all hours of the day and night, on all wavelengths and in many languages, including 'special English'. The war of words is supplemented by written propaganda using a wide range of political devices such as embassy bulletins, pseudo 'revolutionary' publications, studies on 'nationalism' and on 'African socialism', the literature spread by the so-called independent and liberal publishers, 'cultural' and 'civic education' centres, and other imperialist subversive organizations.

The paper war penetrates into every town and village, and into the remotest parts of the 'bush'. It spreads in the form of free distributions of propaganda films praising the qualities of western civilization and culture. These are some of the ways in which the psychological terrain is prepared.

When the target, a certain country or continent, is sufficiently 'softened', then the invasion of evangelist brigades begins, thus perpetuating the centuries old tactics whereby missionaries prepare the way for guns. Peace Corps divisions stream in, and Moral Rearmament units, Jehovah's Witnesses, information agencies and international financial 'aid' organizations.

In this way, a territory or even an entire continent is besieged without a single marine in sight. A sprinkling of political and little publicized murders, like that of Pio Pinto in Kenya, and Moumié in Geneva, are used to assist the process.

A recent development in the psychological war is the campaign to convince us that we cannot govern ourselves, that we are unworthy of genuine independence, and that foreign tutelage is the only remedy for our wild, warlike and primitive ways.

Imperialism has done its utmost to brainwash Africans into thinking that they need the strait-jackets of colonialism and neo-colonialism if they are to be saved from their retrogressive instincts. Such is the age-old racialist justification for the economic exploitation of our continent. And now, the recent military coups engineered throughout Africa by foreign reactionaries are also being used to corroborate imperialism's pet theory that the Africans have shamelessly squandered the 'golden opportunities' of independence, and that they have plunged their political kingdoms into blood and barbarism.

Therefore, the imperialist mission: we must save them anew; and they hail the western-trained and western-bought army puppets as saviours. The press, films and radio are fast spreading the myth of post-independence violence and chaos. Everywhere, the more or less covert implication is: Africa needs to be colonized.

The fact that Africa has advanced politically more quickly than any other continent in the world is ignored. In 1957 when Ghana became independent and the political renaissance began in Africa, there were only eight independent states. Now, in just over ten years, there are over forty and the final liberation of the continent is in sight.

Imperialists are not content with trying to convince us that we are politically immature. They are telling us, now that we are realizing that armed revolution is the only way to defeat neo-colonialism, that we are inherently incapable of fighting a successful revolutionary war.

This new psychological propaganda campaign is being waged in various subtle ways. First, there is what may be called the 'moral' argument: Africans are constantly being reminded that they are a peace-loving, tolerant and communalist-minded people. The African is projected as an individual who has always been loath to shed blood. The corollary of this argument is that it would be immoral and against our nature to engage in revolutionary warfare.

The moral argument is easily destroyed. Centuries of liberation wars, wars of conquest, revolution and counter-revolution in the west were not considered to be moral or immoral. They were simply part of western historical development. **Our armed struggle for freedom is neither moral nor immoral, it is a scientific historically-determined necessity.**

The second argument used to deflect us from the inevitability of armed struggle is the so-called 'economy' argument. It runs something like this: modern neo-colonialism does not constitute a danger to young, revolutionary African states, and therefore the military training and arming of the broad masses is an expensive and frivolous enterprise. The corollary of this reactionary argument is: since you cannot, in the present under-developed state of your economy, afford the 'luxury' of your own defence, let us take care of it for you. And the trap is set.

Last but not least, is a third series of racialist and defeatist arguments designed to spread the myth that no African revolutionary is capable of carrying an armed struggle through to the end. It condemns a-priori all African revolutionary activities to failure. It wraps revolutionary warfare on our continent in an aura of disparagement, and tries to cripple us with a sense of inadequacy as freedom fighters.

By means of press and radio, accounts are given of the capture of 'terrorists' being usually described as poorly-trained, ill-equipped, demoralized and uncertain of the cause for which they are fighting. Where arms and military equipment are seized, it is always labelled 'Russian' or 'Chinese', to suggest that the freedom fighters who use them are not African nationalists, but the dupes and tools of foreign governments.

When freedom fighters are captured and tried in courts of law, they are treated as criminals, not as prisoners of war, and are imprisoned, shot or hanged, usually after so-called confessions have been extorted. This refusal to recognize freedom fighters as soldiers is again part of imperialist strategy designed to pour scorn on the armed revolutionary movement, and at the same time to discourage further recruits.

The campaign is based on the counter-insurgency law whereby 'it is necessary to attack the revolution during the initial stages of the movement when it is still weak, when it has not yet fulfilled that which should be its main aspiration, – a total integration with the people'. (Ché Guevara.) This is why we are being told that Africans are incapable of sustaining revolutionary warfare:—

(a) racially

(b) because of our historical background

(c) for lack of cadres, ideology and leadership.

In one breath, we are accused of being too primitive to govern ourselves, and in the next we are accused of not being primitive enough to wage guerrilla warfare!

The problem is not whether one is born or is not born a natural revolutionary fighter. The problem is not whether revolutionaries are naturally suited to Africa, or Africa to revolutionary warfare. Predestination of this sort never exists. The fact is that revolutionary warfare is the key to African freedom and is the only way in which the total liberation and unity of the African continent can be achieved.

Foreign military preparedness

In pursuing their aggressive aims and fulfilling the requirements of military strategy, the imperialists have built up a system of military blocs and alliances which provide the framework for a pattern of military bases in strategically important positions all over the world. The African freedom fighters, while mainly concerned with enemy strength in Africa, must nevertheless study this world pattern if they are to assess correctly the true dimensions of their struggle. The anti-imperialist and neo-colonialist struggle will, in fact, be world-wide, since revolutionary warfare will occur wherever the enemy operates.

A substantial part of the military, anti-revolutionary effort is channelled into four organizations:

NATO – North Atlantic Treaty Organization (1949)

USA, Britain, France, Italy, Belgium, Holland, Luxembourg, Canada, Iceland, Norway, Denmark, Portugal. Since October 1951 Greece and Turkey, and since 1954 West Germany.

SEATO – South East Asia Treaty Organization (1954)

USA, Britain, France, New Zealand, Australia, Philippines, Thailand and Pakistan.

ANZUS – Australia, New Zealand, United States Treaty (1951). The Pacific Pact.

CENTO – Central Treaty Organization (1959)

Britain, Turkey, Pakistan and Iran. Emerged from the 1955

461

Baghdad Pact. USA in 1959 entered into bilateral defence agreements with Turkey, Iran and Pakistan.

In effect, this system of military blocs and alliances enables US imperialism to exert de facto leadership not only over the entire 'western' world, but over extensive zones in Latin America and Asia. This is achieved through an external network of some 2,200 bases and installations manned by approximately a million troops in readiness for war.

The US external forces of intervention may be grouped as follows.

Group One: Against the USSR with bases in Western Europe North Africa and the Middle East.

Group Two: Against China with bases in Pakistan, South East Asia and the Pacific Ocean.

Group Three: Against revolutionary movements in Latin America – the Organization of American States (OAS) group with bases in Panama, the Bermudas and Porto Rico.

In Africa, there are at present seventeen air bases owned and operated by members of NATO. There are nine foreign naval bases. Foreign military missions exist for example in Kenya, Morocco, Liberia, Libya, South Africa, Senegal, Niger, Cameroon, Chad, Gabon and Ivory Coast. In addition, there are three rocket sites and an atomic testing range in North Africa.

The armed forces of foreign powers in various strategically-important parts of our continent present a serious threat but not an insurmountable obstacle in the African revolutionary struggle. For they must be assessed in conjunction with the forces of settler, minority governments in Rhodesia and South Africa, and with imperialist forces in the few remaining colonial territories.

The formation of NATO led to the signing of the Warsaw Treaty in 1954, by which the Soviet Union, Bulgaria, Hungary, German Democratic Republic, Poland, Rumania, Czechoslavakia and Albania made arrangements to protect themselves against imperialist aggression. An attack on any one member would be regarded as an attack on all. Provision was made for:

1. A political consultative body to take political decisions and to exchange information.
2. A united military command with headquarters in Warsaw.

The need for Pan-African organization

In comparison, the Independent States of Africa are at present militarily weak. Unlike the imperialists and neo-colonialists they have no mutual defence system and no unified command to plan and direct joint action. But this will be remedied with the formation of the All-African People's Revolutionary Army and the setting up of organizations to extend and plan effective revolutionary warfare on a continental scale.

We possess the vital ingredient necessary to win, – the full and enthusiastic support of the broad masses of the African people who are determined once and for all to end all forms of foreign exploitation, to manage their own affairs, and to determine their own future. Against such overwhelming strength organized on a Pan-African basis, no amount of enemy forces can hope to succeed.

Chapter Two

OUR OBJECTIVES

Our objectives are defined by the three political components of our liberation movement:
1. Nationalism
2. Pan-Africanism
3. Socialism
The three objectives of our struggle stem from our position as peoples in revolt against exploitation in Africa. These objectives are closely inter-related and one cannot be achieved fully without the other. If one of the three components is missing, no territory on our continent can secure genuine freedom or maintain a stable government.

Nationalism
Nationalism is the ideological channel of the anti-colonialist struggle and represents the demand for national independence of colonized peoples. It is a concept most easily grasped by the population of territories where the low level of development of productive forces (and therefore of capitalist implantation), and the absence of indigenous elements in the spheres of political power, are factors that facilitate the formation of a united militant front, one of the primary conditions for a successful liberation movement.

Colonized peoples are not highly differentiated from a social point of view, and are exploited practically without discrimination by the colonial power. Hence the slogan: 'the nation must be freed from colonialism' is a universally accepted rallying cry whose influence is heightened by the fact that the agents of colonialism, exploiting the territory from within, are there for everybody to see. It is therefore the people as a whole who revolt and struggle as a 'nation-class' against colonial oppression, and who win independence.

The nationalist phase is a necessary step in the liberation struggle, but must never be regarded as the final solution to the problem raised by the economic and political exploitation of our peoples. For nationalism is narrow in its application. It works within the geopolitical framework produced by the colonial powers which culminated in the carve-up agreed upon in 1884 at the Berlin Conference, where today's political maps of Africa were drawn.

The various peoples of Africa cannot be, and historically never have been, confined behind rigid frontiers sealing off territories labelled 'Nigeria', 'Togo', 'Senegal', and so on. The natural movements of the African peoples and of their societies have from time immemorial swept along extensive axes as for example from the Nile to the Congo, from Senegal to the Niger, and from the Congo to the Zambesi.

The African 'nations' of today, created artificially by foreigners for their own purposes, neither originate from ancient African civilization, nor do they fit in with our African way of life or habits of exchange. They are not even, for the most part, economically viable. Yet they continue to struggle on, each one separately, in a pathetic and hopeless attempt to make progress, while the real obstacle to their development, imperialism, mainly in its neo-colonialist stage, is operating on a Pan-African scale. Already, huge zones of Africa have been integrated economically in the exclusive interest of international finance capital. A study of the organization and workings of most of the large trading firms, mining trusts and industrial cartels operating in Africa shows that they all function directly or indirectly on a continental scale. Many of them form part of a general network spreading over several continents.

This monopolistic system of exploitation is the direct outcome of prolonged capitalist practice, the experience being that extended and unified industrial, commercial or mining units are less costly to maintain, are more efficient, and produce higher profits.

It is time that we also planned our economic and political development on a continental scale. The concept of African unity embraces the fundamental need and characteristics of African civilization and ideology, and at the same time satisfies all the

464

conditions necessary for an accelerated economic and technological advance. Such maximum development would ensure a rational utilization of the material resources and human potential of our continent along the lines of an integrated economy, and within complementary sectors of production, eliminating all unnecessary forms of competition, economic alienation and duplication. The idea is not to destroy or dismantle the network of foreign mining complexes and industrial companies throughout Africa, but to take them over and operate them in the sole interest of the African peoples.

Finally, the limitations of 'nationalism' may be seen in the experience of countries which have succeeded in casting off one imperialism only to be oppressed by another, or by a syndicate of imperialisms, as in Latin America. Merely to change masters is no solution to colonial poverty or neo-colonialist strangulation, even if exploitation is subsequently practised in a more subtle way.

African unity gives an indispensable continental dimension to the concept of the African nation.

Pan-Africanism

The limitations of nationalism have already been acknowledged by the most mature leaders of the liberation movement; but wherever the conditions for the transition to a higher ideological level and a wider form of struggle were lacking, the necessary leap could not be made, and nationalism was never transcended.

The true dimensions of our struggle were outlined at the Fifth Pan-African Congress held in Manchester, England in 1945, when resolutions were passed specifying that the supreme objective of the national liberation movement was to pave the way to national reconstruction and to promote democracy and prosperity for the broad masses through an All-African struggle against colonialism and all the new manifestations of imperialism. No reference was made to neo-colonialism as such, because this only developed on a massive scale in Africa after 1957. But the Pan-Africanism which found expression at the Manchester Congress (1945), and the All-African People's Conference (1958) was based on the age-old aspiration towards unity of all peoples of African origin exploited as workers and as a race.

African unity therefore implies:

1. **That imperialism and foreign oppression should be eradicated in all their forms.**
2. **That neo-colonialism should be recognized and eliminated.**

3. That the new African nation must develop within a continental framework.

However, the specific content of the new social order within the developing African nation remains to be defined.

Socialism

At the core of the concept of African unity lies socialism and the socialist definition of the new African society.

Socialism and African unity are organically complementary.

Socialism implies:

1. Common ownership of the means of production, distribution and exchange. Production is for use, and not for profit.
2. Planned methods of production by the state, based on modern industry and agriculture.
3. Political power in the hands of the people, with the entire body of workers possessing the necessary governmental machinery through which to express their needs and aspirations. It is a concept in keeping with the humanist and egalitarian spirit which characterized traditional African society, though it must be applied in a modern context. All are workers; and no person exploits another.
4. Application of scientific methods in all spheres of thought and production.

Socialism must provide a new social synthesis in which the advanced technical society is achieved without the appalling evils and deep cleavages of capitalist industrial society.

Socialism has become a necessity in the platform diction of African political leaders, though not all pursue really socialist policies. We must therefore be on our guard against measures which are declared to be 'socialist' but which do not in fact promote economic and social development. An example of muddled thinking about socialism is the attempt made in recent years to suggest the existence of an 'African Socialism' peculiar to our continent.

There is only one true socialism and that is scientific socialism, the principles of which are abiding and universal. The only way to achieve it is to devise policies aimed at general socialist goals, which take their form from the concrete, specific circumstances and conditions of a particular country at a definite historical period.

The socialist countries of Africa may differ in the details of their policies. There are different paths to socialism, and adjustments

466

have to be made to suit particular circumstances. But they should not be arbitrarily decided, or subject to vagaries of taste. They must be scientifically explained.

Only under socialism can we reliably accumulate the capital we need for our development, ensure that the gains of investment are applied to the general welfare, and achieve our goal of a free and united continent.

The present stage of the liberation struggle

An objective appraisal of the degree of success so far attained in our struggle leads to the consideration of three theses of major importance:

1. The achievement of genuine independence by an African state is but a part of the over-all process of continental decolonization.
2. No independent state is immune to imperialist intrigue, pressure and subversion as long as imperialism under any guise is left free to operate on the African continent.
3. The degree of completeness of our victory over imperialism has a determining influence on how far post-independence reconstruction can go. In other words, **the people will have no equitable share in national reconstruction and its benefits unless the victory over imperialism in its colonialist and neo-colonialist stages is complete.**

It therefore follows that the unity of the African people expressed in a Union Government is necessary:

(a) to accelerate the liberation struggle in territories still under colonial domination.
(b) for the security of already independent states, and particularly for those which have chosen to follow a line of total opposition to imperialism.
(c) to protect the flanks of our drive towards socialist, domestic reconstruction.

These considerations should be able to serve as:

1. A basic formula to link up with all aspects of the anti-imperialist struggle in Africa.
2. A blue-print for the people's action.
3. A yardstick for the evaluation of political development and phases in the history of Africa.

Accumulated experience of the African People's unity movement

Equipped with a clear knowledge of our objectives, we are in a

467

position to undertake a critical appraisal of recent developments in African history. This is necessary if we are to draw positive lessons from past experience, to determine both the area of deviation and the need for correction, and to devise a more effective strategy for the future.

Shortly after Ghana achieved independence in 1957 there began a rapid succession of events caused by a great upsurge of interest in the African people's movement towards emancipation and unity. The three most significant events which sparked off the process were:

1. The first Conference of Independent African States held in Accra in April 1958. At that time there were only eight independent states: Ethiopia, Ghana, Liberia, Libya, Morocco, Tunisia and Egypt. The purpose was to:
   (a) discuss questions of mutual interest
   (b) explore ways and means of consolidating and safeguarding independence
   (c) strengthen the economic and cultural ties between the independent states
   (d) find ways of helping Africans still oppressed under colonial rule.
   The African leaders in attendance were resolutely and unanimously anti-imperialist, and agreed to co-ordinate diplomacy, mainly at UN level.
   Pan-African conferences had hitherto been held overseas. In 1958, Pan-Africanism had moved to the African continent, where it really belonged.

2. The All-African People's Conference held in Accra in December 1958. Representatives of sixty-two African nationalist organizations attended and discussed the various aspects of the liberation movement. The organization of unitary action between African political movements was then launched.

3. The third All-African People's Conference held in Cairo in March 1961, when the whole question of neo-colonialism was brought to the forefront in discussions on the African revolutionary struggle.

The development of unitary, anti-imperialist action between struggling peoples, and at the level of the governments of independent states, constituted a two-pronged attack against imperialism.

The imperialists acted accordingly:
(a) through diplomatic pressure
(b) by granting sham independence to a number of states.

468

The trick worked well. However, a clear prefiguration of later events was to be enacted at the Sanniquellie Conference held in Liberia in July 1959. Two views were expressed on the question of African unity. The first advocated the tightest 'binding together of our forces in political unity', while the second was in favour of a 'formula flexible enough to enable each state to safeguard its national sovereignty and personal identity'.

The latter views fitted in only too well with the objectives of the imperialists who had already recognized the need to adapt their policies to the changing colonial situation. Hard pressed by the armed struggle of the FLN in Algeria and to avoid any further crystallization of revolutionary awareness amongst 'extremist' African leaders, they decided to play their own version of nationalism.

Accordingly, between 1959 and 1960, thirteen independent states emerged: eleven former French colonies, and Congo-Leopoldville and Nigeria. A close analysis of the specific conditions under which each of the thirteen states became independent reveals that neo-colonialism was incipient during the movement for independence, and emerged fully once independence was acquired.

Sham independence and the unity movement

Few were deceived by such a deliberate and obvious stratagem. Imperialism was merely using the device of sham independence to prepare the African terrain to suit its own convenience, and to avoid a direct and costly confrontation with the liberation movements.

It was therefore not surprising that the divisions of opinion on the question of unity expressed at Sanniquellie, were much more in evidence during the Second Conference of Independent African States held in Addis Ababa in 1960. At this Conference:

1. The pivot of African unity was seen no longer as a firm political union, but merely as a loose policy of co-operation between African states. Moreover, the concept of regional groupings between states was endorsed.

2. The principle of a collective foreign policy as agreed upon in Accra in 1958 gave way to the principle of a separate foreign policy for each state. In this way, imperialists gained more room for manoeuvre, for infiltration and for stirring up difficulties between African states.

3. It was agreed that assistance to the Algerian liberation struggle was to take the form of diplomatic pressure on France, but

469

was to by-pass official recognition of the GPRA.* In plain words, diplomatic shilly-shallying was to take the place of a genuine anti-imperialist confrontation.

Therefore, as early as 1960, a wide gulf developed between those independent states which favoured co-operation with imperialism, and those which proclaimed an unflinching offensive against it.

The emergence of conflicting trends was not fortuitous but a logical consequence of the state of tension between qualitatively different situations:

1. **Genuine independence,** the product of a mass political movement or an armed liberation struggle.
2. **Sham independence,** established by imperialists in an attempt to arrest the progress of the people's movement through a betrayal of its essential objectives.

It is important to note that it was not the moderate policy of co-operation with imperialism which created the 'moderate' African states. On the contrary, it was the deliberate creation of such states by imperialism which gave rise to moderation and co-operation. The will to compromise is but a reflection, at diplomatic level of the neo-colonialist character of certain African states; it is the external manifestation of the inner characteristics of neo-colonial regimes.

African people's wars and imperialist escalation

However, far from weakening the anti-imperialist struggle and the vanguard revolutionary states, such measures can only strengthen their vigilance and revolutionary determination.

Since 1960, the struggle of the African people and the more or less latent state of crisis inside many African territories have reached maturity. To counter-balance the growing revolutionary character of the African situation, the enemy's reaction has become more open and direct. Both the Algerian and the Congolese wars were born of the people's determination to free themselves at whatever cost, the only difference being that the Algerian revolt developed in an essentially colonial context, whereas the Congolese struggle is being waged in a neo-colonialist setting, marked by major imperialist aggression throughout the African continent.

From a practical point of view, the differences between the various segments of the liberation struggle in time and space are minimal. The only factors which render the Congolese, Angolese or Rhodesian struggles (to take these examples only) more violent than

* Algerian Provisional Government.

others are, first, the escalation of imperialist action; and secondly, the more advanced nature of the people's organization, though the actual level of readiness to revolt may be just as high elsewhere.

Significantly, it was the frenzy of imperialist repression against the Algerian and Congolese liberation struggles which led to the calling of the Casablanca Conference in 1961, to which the GPRA was invited. The 'Casablanca' states, as they were subsequently named (i.e. Ghana, Guinea, Mali, Libya, Egypt, Morocco), and the Algerian FLN called for decisive action on the part of the independent states to support the anti-imperialist struggle in Africa. Further, a strong appeal for unity was made. For **'in unity lies strength. African states must unite or sell themselves out to imperialist and colonialist exploiters for a mess of pottage, or disintegrate individually.'**

Meantime, two new groupings, alike in content and with similar policies, were being formed:

1. The Monrovia group which met in Monrovia in May 1961 consisting mainly of English-speaking states whose loyalties were basically Anglo-American.
2. The Brazzaville group made up of French-speaking states mostly aligned to France.

Both these groups adopted a 'go slow' attitude towards African emancipation and unity, and pursued a policy of conciliation with imperialism. Their views were expressed at the Lagos Conference (January 1962) when twenty of Africa's twenty-eight independent states met to discuss ways in which co-operation could be achieved. They agreed that:

(a) The absolute sovereignty and legality of each African state must be respected.
(b) The union of one state with another should be effected on a voluntary basis.
(c) There should be non-interference in each other's affairs.
(d) Political refugees from one state should not be given asylum in another state.

North Africa was unrepresented at the Lagos Conference because the Algerian Provisional Government was not invited. The Casablanca powers and the Sudan also declined to go for the same reason.

Imperialist diplomacy appeared to have achieved its purpose admirably, in splitting up the independent states of Africa into separate and conflicting groups. The efforts of the militant Casablanca group were checked by a pro-imperialist bloc, which was in its turn sub-divided into pro-French and pro-English branches.

The Organization of African Unity (OAU)

The militant African forces did achieve a certain amount of success when all blocs and groups joined together to form the OAU at Addis Ababa in 1963. However, appearances are sometimes deceptive: the dissolution of pro-imperialist groups did not mean that the interests they represented had also vanished.

On the contrary, an examination of recent events exposes serious weaknesses within the OAU. The Organization failed to solve the crises in the Congo and Rhodesia: both of them test cases, – the former involving a direct challenge to neo-colonialism, and the latter open confrontation with a minority, settler government, In fact, the OAU is in danger of developing into a useful cover for the continued, sterile action of conflicting interests, the only difference being, that in the context of one big 'brotherly' organization reactionary tactics are camouflaged and applied through the subtleties of negotiations.

This change of tactics works as strongly as ever against the fundamental interests of progressive forces in Africa, since it hides concessions to imperialism.

Negotiations are conducted behind closed doors and surrounded by a mysterious cloak of diplomatic protocol, making knowledge of the proceedings inaccessible to the general public.

However, four explosive issues discussed at the OAU Conference in Accra in 1965, alerted progressive opinion to the dangers of continued compromise:

1. The crisis in Rhodesia.
2. The struggle in the Congo.
3. The treatment of African political refugees.
4. The problem of South West Africa.

In the first case, the African heads of state failed to agree on a practical way of checking Ian Smith's rebellion, and instead fell back on the futile policy of negotiations with Britain combined with diplomatic pressure at international and UN level.

Similarly, in the Congo, the fundamental issue of the crisis was avoided in spite of the tense situation resulting from the gallant stand of the freedom fighters carrying on the struggle in the spirit of Lumumba.

On the question of the status and treatment of African political refugees the OAU again failed to find a solution, and heads of state continued to regard them merely as outlaws or barter-goods.

472

The radical African states in the OAU were confronted with the difficulty of finding effective expression for the aspirations of the broad masses of the people. The struggle seemed to unfold in two different spheres: the one in the streets, villages, workshops and factories; and the other in the hushed and closed atmosphere of air-conditioned houses and offices. In this situation the genuine threat of imperialism and its neo-colonialist agents tended to be under-estimated, and the progressive states placed too much reliance on the OAU.

In the meantime, the pro-imperialist states, although pretending to rally to the revolutionary elements within the OAU in order to avoid a direct confrontation, had been creating and expanding an organization after their own heart: the Organization Commune Africaine et Malagache (OCAM), into a larger unit to include all French-speaking African states under the name 'Francophonie'. As a result, the progressive states, failing to close their ranks, were left to fight inadequately and alone against the massive escalation of imperialism, and the active consolidation of its position through plots and a series of coups d'etat.

Some essential features of the enemy's offensive
1. Externally
Mounting imperialist aggression in Africa foreshadows a decline in the strength of imperialism since the use of violence to maintain imperialist rule invariably sparks off a stronger explosion of revolutionary activity among oppressed peoples, and experience has shown that such movements can be neither destroyed nor contained. The American fiascos in Vietnam, Santo Domingo and Cuba illustrate the point. So, also do the resolutions condemning US imperialism passed by representatives from three continents (Africa, Asia and Latin America) when they met in conference at Havana in 1966. Taken aback by the compelling reality of tri-continental solidarity, the US imperialists hastened to condemn the Havana resolutions as 'subversive' and resolved to take 'appropriate preventive measures, including military action' against any popular movement considered to be a danger to the 'free world' under US leadership. At the same time, they predicted other coups in Africa during the ensuing year, and immediately set to work, with or without the collaboration of European accomplices, to help this prediction to come true.

It was evidently felt that the resort to quick action was necessary because of the uncompromising stand against imperialist action in the 'hot' zones of the world, taken by progressive governments. The latter were succeeding in arousing world opinion against imperialist atrocities in Vietnam, and in drawing attention to the worsening crises in Rhodesia and the Congo, the South African military build-up, NATO's assistance to Portugal in her colonial wars, and 'interventions' in Latin America and the Caribbean.

2. Internally

The capitalist imperialist states face serious economic and social difficulties. Rising prices, balance of payments problems, widespread and repeated strikes are only a few of the symptoms of the general malaise. In the United States, the grave domestic situation is aggravated by the massive counter-attacks of the African-American revolutionaries.

Almost everywhere, behind the smoke screens, the social and economic situation is unhealthy, and particularly in the second class capitalist states. And these mounting economic crises mean heavier dependence on the exploitation of the peoples of Africa, Asia and Latin America.

The need for self-critical objective diagnosis

If imperialists are faced with so many external and domestic difficulties, how then can they afford to step up their aggression in Africa? To answer this question, it is necessary to examine the internal factors which make our continent so vulnerable to attack, and particularly to look closely at the whole question of African unity. For this lies at the core of our problem.

There are three conflicting conceptions of African unity which explain to a large extent, the present critical situation in Africa:

1. **The mutual protection theory:** that the OAU serves as a kind of insurance against any change in the status quo, membership providing a protection for heads of state and government against all forms of political action aimed at their overthrow. Since most of the leaders who adhere to this idea owe their position to imperialists and their agents, it is not surprising that this is the viewpoint which really serves the interests of imperialism. For the puppet states are being used both for short-term purposes of exploitation and as springboards of subversion against progressive African states.

2. **The functional conception:** that African unity should be purely a matter of economic co-operation. Those who hold this view overlook the vital fact that African regional economic

474

organizations will remain weak and subject to the same neo-colonialist pressures and domination, as long as they lack overall political cohesion. Without political unity, African states can never commit themselves to **full** economic integration, which is the only productive form of integration able to develop our great resources fully for the well-being of the African people as a whole.

Furthermore, the lack of political unity places inter-African economic institutions at the mercy of powerful, foreign commercial interests, and sooner or later these will use such institutions as funnels through which to pour money for the continued exploitation of Africa.

3. **The political union conception:** that a union government should be in charge of economic development, defence and foreign policy, while other government functions would continue to be discharged by the existing states grouped, in federal fashion, within a gigantic central political organization. Clearly, this is the strongest position Africa could adopt in its struggle against modern imperialism.

However, any sincere critical appraisal of past activities and achievements of the OAU would tend to show that, as it is now constituted, the OAU is not likely to be able to achieve the political unification of Africa.

This is obviously why imperialists, although against the idea of political union, will do nothing to break the OAU. It serves their purpose in slowing down revolutionary progress in Africa. This state of affairs is mirrored both in the discouragement of freedom fighters in the remaining colonial territories and South Africa, and in the growing perplexity amongst freedom fighters from neo-colonized territories.

The struggle for African continental union and socialism may be hampered by the enemy within, – those who declare their support for the revolution and at the same time, by devious means, serve and promote the interests of imperialists and neo-colonialists.

Examination of recent events in our history, and of our present condition, reveals the urgent need for a new strategy to combat imperialist aggression, and this must be devised on a continental scale.

Either we concentrate our forces for a decisive armed struggle to achieve our objectives, or we will each fall one by one to the blows of imperialism in its present stage of open and desperate offensive.

BOOK TWO

STRATEGY, TACTICS AND TECHNIQUES

PREFACE

Revolutionary warfare is the logical, inevitable answer to the political, economic and social situation in Africa today. We do not have the luxury of an alternative. We are faced with a necessity.

Throughout the world, the escalation of imperialist aggression is making the issues clear, and exploitation can no longer be disguised. In Africa, a point of explosion against imperialism has been reached. But only a massive and organized will to fight can spark it off.

Time is running out. We must act now. The freedom fighters already operating in many parts of Africa must no longer be allowed to bear the full brunt of a continental struggle against a continental enemy. The collective and continental nature of our will and our space, the urgency of conquering the initiative and the protracted nature of a revolutionary war calls for a united All-African organization of all freedom fighters on the African continent.

We must co-ordinate strategy and tactics, and combine experience. Co-ordination requires organization, and organization can only be effective if each fighting unit is a disciplined part of the whole. Attack must be planned with diversion, retreat with consolidation, losses in one zone compensated for by gains in another, until the liberation movement is finally victorious, and the whole of Africa is free and united.

As a continental nation we are young, strong and resilient. The cohesive planning of our struggle and the combined strength of our will to win will do the rest.

Africa is one; and this battle must be fought and won continentally.

Chapter One

ORGANIZATION FOR REVOLUTIONARY WARFARE

A. THE MILITARY BALANCE

The dimension of our struggle is equal to the size of the African continent itself. It is in no way confined within any of the absurd limits of the micro-states created by the colonial powers, and jealously guarded by imperialist puppets during the neo-colonialist period.

For although the African nation is at present split up among many separate states, it is in reality simply divided into two: our enemy and ourselves. The strategy of our struggle must be determined accordingly, and our continental territory considered as consisting of three categories of territories which correspond to the varying levels of popular organization and to the precise measure of victory attained by the people's forces over the enemy:

1. Liberated areas
2. Zones under enemy control
3. Contested zones (i.e. hot points).

Liberated Areas

These areas may present minimal differences due to the varying ways in which independence was obtained. However, they can be collectively defined as territories where:

(a) Independence was secured through an armed struggle, or through a positive action movement representing the majority of the population under the leadership of an anti-imperialist and well-organized mass party.

(b) A puppet regime was overthrown by a people's movement (Zanzibar, Congo-Brazzaville, Egypt).

(c) A social revolution is taking place to consolidate political independence by:

1. promoting accelerated economic development
2. improving working conditions
3. establishing complete freedom from dependence on foreign economic interests.

It therefore follows that a liberated zone can only be organized by a radically anti-imperialist party whose duty it is:

(a) to decolonize, and
(b) to teach the theory and practice of socialism as applied to the African social milieu, and adapted to local circumstances.

The people's socialist parties take the necessary steps to transform the united but heterogeneous front which fought for independence into an ideological monolithic party of cadres.

Thus, in a truly liberated territory, one can observe:

1. Political growth achieved as a result of discussions and agreements concluded within the party.
2. Steady progress to transform theory into practice along the ideological lines drawn by the party.

477

3. Constant improvement, checking and re-checking of the development plans to be carried out by the party and at state level.
4. Political maturity among party members, who are no longer content to follow a vague and general line of action. Revolutionary political maturity is the prelude to the re-organization of the party structure along more radical lines.

However, no territory may be said to be truly liberated if the party leadership, apart from consolidating the gains of national independence does not also undertake to:

(a) Support actively the detachments of revolutionary liberation movements in the contested zones of Africa.
(b) Contribute to the organization and revolutionary practice of the people's forces in neo-colonialist states, i.e. in zones under enemy control or in contested areas.
(c) Effect an organic liaison of its political and economic life with the other liberated zones of the African nation.

This implies a system of mutual servicing and aid between the various detachments of the liberation movements and the liberated zones, so that a continuous exchange of experience, advice and ideas will link the progressive parties in power with the parties struggling in the contested zones.

Each liberated zone should be ready to offer the use of its territory to detachments of the liberation movements so that the latter may establish their rear bases on friendly soil, and benefit from the provision of communications, hospitals, schools, factories, workshops, etc.

It is important to bear in mind that a liberated area is constantly exposed to the many forms of enemy action and attack. It is the duty of both the liberation movements and the liberated zones:

1. To make objective and up-to-date analyses of the enemy's aggression.
2. To take action to recapture any base lost to the enemy, and to help correct the mistakes which enabled the enemy to gain temporary victory.

In fact, the liberated areas of Africa do not yet come fully up to all the standards required of them. For example, in certain liberated zones, the level of economic liberation is clearly inferior to the high level of revolutionary awareness. But the main criterion for judging them to be liberated is the actual direction in which they are moving, since our assessment is of changing, not static phenomena.

478

Zones under enemy control
The imperialists control such zones:
  (a) through an administration manned by foreigners. The territory is then externally subjected.
  (b) through a puppet government made up of local elements. The territory is then both internally and externally subjected.
  (c) through a settler, minority government. In this territory, settlers have established the rule of a majority by a minority. There is no logic except the right of might that can accept such a situation. **The predominant racial group must, and will, provide the government of a country. Settlers, provided they accept the principle of one man one vote, and majority rule, may be tolerated; but settler minority governments, never. They are a dangerous anachronism, and must be swept away completely and for ever.**

A territory under enemy control therefore is governed against the interests of the majority. Such zones are economically, militarily and politically alienated. It is precisely in these territories that the enemy has its military camps, aerodromes, naval establishments and broadcasting stations, and where foreign banks, insurance firms, mining, industrial and trading companies have their headquarters. In other words, these zones are enemy nerve centres.

Clear proof of the neo-colonialist and neo-liberated character of these states is seen in the refusal of their governments to allow liberation movements to open offices, establish bases or enjoy freedom of transit for troops and equipment on their way to the front.

The strength of a territory under enemy control may be assessed by taking into account the following factors:

  (i) the level of organization attained by the reactionary forces in control there
  (ii) the type and degree of repression exerted against the people's liberation movement
  (iii) the degree and modes of exploitation exerted upon the toiling masses
  (iv) the military means available to the reactionaries in power
  (v) the nature of the economic interests imperialism is out to promote in that territory and in neighbouring areas (for example, strategic materials, important commercial and industrial complexes, etc.).
  (vi) the over-all strategic advantages which imperialism hopes to

gain from the subjugation of the territory. Such gains may be exclusively political.

As far as our struggle is concerned, our most vital asset is the degree of revolutionary awareness attained by the workers and the masses in the zone under enemy control.

The political maturity or immaturity of the masses constitutes the main difference between an enemy-held zone and a contested zone.

The revolutionary awareness of the broad masses in an enemy-held zone, must express itself in national boycotts, strikes, sabotage and insurrection.

It would be a mistake to maintain that the total of areas under enemy control is exactly equal to the sum of neo-colonialist and colonialist governments. Socio-political phenomena are less mechanical than that. In each case it is the level of the people's awareness and participation that counts.

Contested Zones

A zone under enemy control can at any time become a contested area if the revolutionary forces in activity there are either on the verge of armed struggle or have reached an advanced stage of revolutionary organization. In some cases, a spark is enough to determine the turning point from preparation to action. In other circumstances, the embers can smoulder underground for a much longer period.

'Sham independence' zones, where the awakened masses have placed the enemy in such a precarious position that a 'single spark can start a prairie fire', can no longer be said to be 'under enemy control'. In such a situation, the enemy is only superficially in command, and relies exclusively on support in the police, civil service and the army, where it retains control only as long as the force of habit remains unchallenged. It is to be noted that the army and police are never homogeneous forces in Africa, and that this factor is of obvious tactical interest in a revolutionary struggle primarily based on the workers and peasants, but also aiming to obtain the support of all other possible elements.

In these zones of revolutionary transition, the population feels deeply in sympathy with the revolutionary forces in neighbouring areas, and often gives them invaluable assistance.

These transitional zones may:
1. Either be used to organize the liberation of another neighbouring territory which is economically more important and politically more mature, (for instance, where a party of revolutionary opposition is already operating against the government).

480

2. Or, in case of strategic necessity, be directly seized from the enemy through the organization and armed action of the dissatisfied masses.

A careful study should be made of the range of possibilities offered by a territory under puppet, neo-colonialist control. Full investigation will disclose that the puppet government is not homogeneous, and that it is therefore vulnerable. It will also be found that the people are often virtually liberated but that they are not aware of it because no one has organized them to act purposefully to seize what is their due (i.e. political control and the control of economic wealth).

Between a zone under enemy control where the masses are awakening and a hotly-contested zone, there is only one missing link: a handful of genuine revolutionaries prepared to organize and act.

There are many more contested zones than liberated ones. In fact, the total area of contested zones covers most of the African continent. All the more reason why we should take vigilant care of our liberated territories.

A contested zone is not only a zone of revolutionary activity, but it is also an area in which a people's party works underground or semi-clandestinely to organize the overthrow of a puppet government. For there is no fundamental difference between armed struggle as such and organized revolutionary action of a civil type. The various methods of our struggle, and the changing from one method to another should be determined mainly by the circumstances and the set of conditions prevailing in a given territory.

The forces struggling in the contested zones are in the front line of the revolutionary liberation movement. They must receive material support from the liberated zones in order to carry their mission through to a successful end. This involves a development of the struggle until a people's insurrectionary movement is able to assume power.

A political party operating in a contested zone may be said to be truly revolutionary if:

1. It is actively organizing the people, training cadres, etc.
2. Its essential objective is the total destruction of the puppet government or the colonial power, in order to build in its place the organs of the people's political power based on mass organization and mass education.

The latter objective can only be achieved through a policy of direct confrontation with the enemy, and not through devious negotiations and compromise. This is the only correct approach to the African situation if the problem of the revolution is to be studied in depth and from the people's point of view.

Retarding Factors

However, certain factors have retarded the final unleashing of anti-imperialist action and the unfolding of a people's revolution throughout the African nation:

1. The readiness of imperialists to exploit any cracks in our armour.
2. The undue emphasis placed on diplomatic procedure and negotiations to provide solutions.
3. The varying degrees of isolationism practised by the cadres of ruling parties in spite of their recognition, on a theoretical level, of the necessity for a continental, anti-imperialist struggle and reconstruction.
4. The tendency manifested by certain ruling parties in the liberated zones to indulge in a slack, wait-and-see policy, merely toying with progressive ideas, and neglecting to analyse and resolve national problems in a positive way. This has created a dangerous climate of uneasiness, confusion and discouragement for African revolutionaries, and fertile ground for neo-colonialist intrigue and attacks.
5. The existence of a more or less conscious opportunism amongst some leaders of the liberation movement both in the liberated and contested territories, which is symptomatic of a low level of ideological conviction.

High Command

Africa will be liberated sooner or later against all odds. But if it is to be soon, by an accelerated revolution of the people, and a total war against imperialism, then we must establish a unified continental high command here and now, to plan revolutionary war, and to initiate action.

If we fail to do this, and to lead the people's revolution, we are likely to be swept away one by one by imperialism and neo-colonialism. It is no longer feasible to take a middle course. The time for reform, however progressive, is past. For reforms cannot hold the enemy at bay, nor can they convince the silent, internal agents of neo-colonialism, eliminate the puppets, or even destroy the capitalist structure and mentality inherited from colonialism. The cancerous growths are proliferating at the very heart of our parties and territories whether they emerge under the cloak of constitutionalism, parliamentarianism, bureaucratic etiquette, an imposing civil service, officers trained in western 'a-political' tradition to maintain the bourgeois-capitalist status quo by means of military coups, or if they appear in the more obvious guise of corruption and nepotism.

The people's armed struggle, the highest form of political action, is a revolutionary catalyst in the neo-colonialist situation.

Peaceful political action to achieve liberation has been proved ineffective

(a) with the accession of the majority of African states to independence and the advent of neo-colonialism on a massive scale

(b) with the increasingly continental dimension of our struggle.

Pacific political action was, in general, potent during the national phase of the liberation movement, and mainly in sub-Saharan Africa, where independence often developed in a chain reaction. However, even then there were significant exceptions. In Kenya for example, where recourse to peaceful political action was denied to the masses, the people's movement resorted to more direct and concentrated action in the form of Mau Mau. In Algeria, a seven year armed liberation struggle was needed. Elsewhere, the independence movement pushed beyond the fringe of pacificism, as in Ghana and Guinea where 'positive action' was employed.

The crystallization of a more concentrated form of political action is in fact to be found in the development of almost all African independence movements. The reason for this was the need to establish a new social order after nominal independence has been achieved, and the escalation of imperialist action. The latter appeared in:

(i) the corruption of independence through neo-colonialism and puppet regimes.

(ii) direct imperialist aggression against liberation forces, for example in the Congo.

(iii) increased multilateral and bilateral imperialist support to:

(a) remaining colonial powers (Portugal, Spain)

(b) fascist-racist regimes (Rhodesia, South Africa)

(c) puppet regimes and local reactionaries to assist their infiltration and attempts to suppress progressive and revolutionary forces throughout the continent.

In less than three years, from 1960, the armed form of struggle became a necessity of the African anti-colonial liberation movement, and the same process may be observed in most neo-colonialist situations.

From 1961 onwards, the armed form of political action reached another turning point with the creation of a united front co-ordinating the struggle of freedom fighters in all the 'Portuguese' colonies. This organization (CONCP) links up the politico-military struggle of 12,400,000 inhabitants over an area of some 2 million square kilometres.

In effect, then, anti-imperialist pacifism is dying, and on a continental scale, because:

1. The political action which led to independence deviated to become the sole monopoly and privilege of a reactionary 'élite' which deprives the masses of the right to political action, even in its pacific and constitutional form.
2. Neo-colonialism has created a situation whereby the masses are exploited beyond the 'safe' limits of exploitation.
   The ensuing massive explosion of pent-up discontent can be nothing but violent. The masses seize back their right to political action and make maximum use of it.
3. Imperialist action is escalating
   (a) to consolidate its position (military coups d'état in neo-colonialist states).
   (b) to gain ground and recapture lost initiative (reactionary coups d'état in progressive states).
4. Imperialism constantly infiltrates revolutionary opposition groups with agents, 'special police', and others, compelling such groups to arm even before they have attained the organizational stage of armed struggle.
5. Whenever the pseudo-democratic institutions inherited from colonial rule are not used by its inheritors to build capitalism but are gradually remodelled or suddenly re-structured towards a socialist line of development, imperialists intervene violently.
6. Violence clears the 'neo-colonialist fog' and reveals the invisible enemy and the subtle methods of camouflage employed by neo-colonialists. The issues are made clear.

As soon as the initial revolutionary units emerge, the puppet regime is doomed. A chain reaction begins. The puppets are compelled to break the promises they have made. They had survived in the teeth of opposition only because they uneasily preserved an outward appearance of progressive action. Now, they have to suppress and kill openly in order to survive. Once the first drop of patriotic blood is shed in the fight the puppet regime is irrevocably condemned. Guerrilla points spread like oil stains. Not only have the internal contradictions of neo-colonialism fully ripened but the African masses have attained such a degree of political awareness that they literally force the struggle to break out into the open.

The Need for Co-ordinated Revolutionary Action

The international balance of forces, and more particularly the existence of powerful socialist states, gave rise to the theory that in certain territories dominated by imperialism on our continent it was possible to take a pacific road to socialism. But such reasoning is based on the false premise that the question of co-ordinating revolutionary action in Africa and the world has already been solved and that therefore imperialism is no longer able to concentrate its forces to act decisively against the most threatening parts of the popular liberation front.

In reality, the situation is quite different:

1. Imperialists are waging an all-out struggle against the socialist states, and the revolutionary liberation movements through military means, and through insidious but powerful methods of psychological warfare (propaganda).
2. Imperialists have formed an international syndicate of military and economic forces to achieve its aggressive aims.
3. Imperialists have, in recent years, assisted in the establishment of numerous puppet governments in Africa.

The historical experience of the people of Asia, Latin America and of Africa has shown that imperialism has often forcefully intervened to prevent the peaceful achievement of socialism. In the case of Ghana a coup occurred at the very time a decisive turning point in socialist development was about to be reached.

The continental scope now attained by popular insurrection in Africa is a reality. It remains for us to devise effective co-ordinating machinery.

Our accumulated experience has shown that only practical and planned co-ordination on a continental scale will prevent the enemy from concentrating its forces on isolated and therefore more vulnerable targets. In our war, isolation is one of the greatest dangers.

We have already been able to outpace the enemy in certain ways by:

(i) increasing our means of production
(ii) bringing a higher level of organization to the people

485

(iii) spreading the essential features of the African people's revolution

(iv) unmasking neo-colonialism and its puppets.

We have succeeded in accumulating energy and will-power. But it is also true that we have not yet defeated either the external, or the internal enemy. For victory, a politico-military organization must be established to provide the machinery for a qualitative conversion of revolutionary action in Africa.

B. POLITICO-MILITARY ORGANIZATION

The following measures should be taken:

1. The formation of the All-African People's Revolutionary Party (AAPRP) to co-ordinate policies and to direct action.

2. The creation of an All-African People's Revolutionary Army (AAPRA) to unify our liberation forces and to carry the armed struggle through to final victory.

AAPRP and the All-African Committee for Political Co-ordination (AACPC)

The formation of a political party linking all liberated territories and struggling parties under a common ideology will smooth the way for eventual continental unity, and will at the same time greatly assist the prosecution of the All-African people's war. To assist the process of its formation, an All-African Committee for Political Co-ordination (AACPC) should be established to act as a liaison between all parties which recognize the urgent necessity of conducting an organized and unified struggle against colonialism and neo-colonialism. This Committee would be created at the level of the central committees of the ruling parties and struggling parties, and would constitute their integrated political consciousness.

The AACPC as the political arm of AAPRA would fulfil the following functions:

1. Ensure co-operation between the ruling parties of the liberated territories building socialism, and enable them to support each other in the fight against the internal enemy.

2. Promote widespread and collective ideological training for the cadres of parties teaching the theory of anti-colonialist and anti-neo-colonialist struggle, the case for African unity and for the building of socialism.

This would be done in AACPC schools or in political training camps throughout the liberated territories.

3. Co-ordinate and harmonize all political effort and assistance

486

given to the revolutionary movements in colonized or apartheid areas, and to the progressive forces in all the neo-colonized areas.

4. Provide an organic link with the peoples of Africa, Asia and Latin America who are struggling against imperialism (Organization of Solidarity with the Peoples of Africa, Asia and Latin America (OSPAAAL)).

5. Ensure permanent relations with the socialist states of the world.

6. Maintain and create links with all workers' movements in the capitalist-imperialist states.

Thus the AACPC would emerge as the organizational instrument of a united struggle, and a centralizing and disciplinary organ providing permanent contact with the masses and with the scattered centres of their revolutionary activities. Such co-ordination would unify revolutionary action of the vanguard African territories and would enable them to exert decisive influence on the revolutionary liberation movement by allowing them to participate actively in it.

The All-African People's Revolutionary Army (AAPRA)
Members of AAPRA will be the armed representatives of the African people's socialist parties struggling against colonialism and neo-colonialism. They will be the direct product of the African revolutionary, liberation movement, and will be organized as in Chart 5 (Page 64).

These revolutionary armed forces will be under the direction of a high command made up of the military leaders (AAPRA) of the various revolutionary movements in Africa. This in its turn will come under the All-African Committee for Political Co-ordination (AACPC) which represents the political leadership of the entire revolutionary movement. Thus the military, i.e. the armed forces, will always be subordinate to, and under the control of, the political leadership.

* *Handbook of Revolutionary Warfare* (Panaf, 1967).

33

EXTRACTS FROM *CLASS STRUGGLE IN AFRICA*

INTRODUCTION

In Africa where so many different kinds of political, social and economic conditions exist it is not an easy task to generalize on political and socio-economic patterns. Remnants of communalism and feudalism still remain and in parts of the continent ways of life have changed very little from traditional times. In other areas a high level of industrialization and urbanization has been achieved. Yet in spite of Africa's socio-economic and political diversity it is possible to discern certain common political, social and economic conditions and problems. These derive from traditional past, common aspirations, and from shared experience under imperialism, colonialism and neo-colonialism. There is no part of the continent which has not known oppression and exploitation, and no part which remains outside the processes of the African Revolution. Everywhere, the underlying unity of purpose of the peoples of Africa is becoming increasingly evident, and no African leader can survive who does not pay at least lip service to the African revolutionary objectives of total liberation, unification and socialism.

In this situation, the ground is well prepared for the next crucial phase of the Revolution, when the armed struggle which has now emerged must be intensified, expanded and effectively co-ordinated at strategic and tactical levels; and at the same time, a determined attack must be made on the entrenched position of the minority reactionary elements amongst our own peoples. For the dramatic exposure in recent years of the nature and extent of the class struggle in Africa, through the succession of reactionary military coups and the outbreak of civil wars, particularly in West and Central Africa, has demonstrated the unity between the interests of neo-colonialism and the indigenous bourgeoisie.

At the core of the problem is the class struggle. For too long, social and political commentators have talked and written as though Africa lies outside the main stream of world historical development – a separate entity to which the social, economic and political patterns of the world do not apply. Myths such as 'African socialism' and 'pragmatic socialism', implying the existence of a brand or brands of socialism applicable to Africa alone, have been propagated; and much of our history has been written in terms of socio-anthropological and historical theories as though Africa had no history prior to the colonial period. One of these distortions has been the suggestion that the class structures which exist in other parts of the world do not exist in Africa.

Nothing is further from the truth. A fierce class struggle has been raging in Africa. The evidence is all around us. In essence it is, as in the rest of the world, a struggle between the oppressors and the oppressed.

The African Revolution is an integral part of the world socialist revolution, and just as the class struggle is basic to world revolutionary processes, so also is it fundamental to the struggle of the workers and peasants of Africa.

Class divisions in modern African society became blurred to some extent during the pre-independence period, when it seemed there was national unity and all classes joined forces to eject the colonial power. This led some to proclaim that there were no class divisions in Africa, and that the communalism and egalitarianism of traditional African society made any notion of a class struggle out of the question. But the exposure of this fallacy followed quickly after independence, when class cleavages which had been temporarily submerged in the struggle to win political freedom reappeared, often with increased intensity, particularly in those states where the newly independent government embarked on socialist policies.

For the African bourgeoisie, the class which thrived under colonialism, is the same class which is benefiting under the post-independence, neo-colonial period. Its basic interest lies in preserving capitalist social and economic structures. It is therefore, in alliance with international monopoly finance capital and neo-colonialism, and in direct conflict with the African masses, whose aspirations can only be fulfilled through scientific socialism.

Although the African bourgeoisie is small numerically, and lacks the financial and political strength of its counterparts in the highly industrialized countries, it gives the illusion of being economically strong because of its close tie-up with foreign finance capital and business interests. Many members of the African bourgeoisie are employed by foreign firms and have, therefore, a direct financial stake in the continuance of the foreign economic exploitation of Africa. Others, notably in the civil service, trading and mining firms, the armed forces, the police and in the professions, are committed to capitalism because of their background, their western education, and their shared experience and enjoyment of positions of privilege. They are mesmerized by capitalist institutions and organizations. They ape the way of life of their old colonial masters, and are determined to preserve the status and power inherited from them.

Africa has in fact in its midst a hard core of bourgeoisie who are analogous to colonists and settlers in that they live in positions of privilege – a small, selfish, money-minded, reactionary minority among vast masses of exploited and oppressed people. Although apparently strong because of their support from neo-colonialists and imperialists, they are extremely vulnerable. Their survival depends on foreign support. Once this vital link is broken, they become powerless to maintain their positions and privileges. They and the 'hidden hand' of neo-colonialism and imperialism which supports and abets reaction and exploitation now tremble before the rising tide of worker and peasant awareness of the class struggle in Africa.

BOURGEOISIE

Colonialism, imperialism and neo-colonialism are expressions of capitalism and of bourgeois economic and political aspirations. In Africa, under colonialism, capitalist development led to the decline of feudalism and to the emergence of new class structures.

Before the colonial period, the power of the chiefs – which was generally not based on land ownership – was strictly limited and controlled. The 'stool' and not the chief was sacred. Control was exercised by a council of elders. Colonialism reinforced the power of chiefs through the system of 'Indirect Rule'. They were given new powers, were sometimes paid, and became for the most part the

490

local agents of colonialism. In some colonized areas new chiefs were appointed by the colonial power. These became known as 'warrant chiefs'.

Imperialists utilized the feudal and tribal nobility to support their exploitation; and this resulted in a blunting of social contradictions, since the feudal and semi-feudal strata maintained a strong hold over the peasant masses and inhibited the growth of revolutionary organizations.

Relics of feudalism still exist in many parts of Africa. For example, in Northern Nigeria and in North and West Cameroun, tribal chiefs live on the exploitation of peasants who not only have to pay them tributes and taxes, but who often have to do forced labour.

But although feudal relics remain, the colonial period ushered in capitalist social structures. The period was characterized by the rise of the petty bourgeoisie, and of a small but influential national bourgeoisie consisting in the main of intellectuals, civil servants, members of the professions, and of officers in the armed forces and police. There was a marked absence of capitalists among the bourgeoisie, since local business enterprise was on the whole discouraged by the colonial power. Anyone wishing to achieve wealth and status under colonialism was therefore likely to choose a career in the professions, the civil service or the armed forces, because there were so few business opportunities. Foreigners controlled mining, industrial enterprises, banks, wholesale trade and large-scale farming. In most of Africa, the bourgeoisie was, in fact, for the most part petty bourgeoisie.

It was partly the restrictions placed on the business outlets of the African bourgeoisie which led it to oppose imperialist rule. After the end of the Second World War, when the pressure for national liberation was increased, imperialists were compelled to admit part of the African bourgeoisie to spheres from which it had previously been excluded. More Africans were allowed into the state machinery and into foreign companies. Thus, a new African élite, closely linked with foreign capital, was created. At the same time, repressive measures were taken against progressive parties and trade unions. Several colonialist wars were fought, as for example, the wars against the peoples of Madagascar, Cameroun and Algeria. It was during this period that the foundations of neo-colonialism were laid.

During the national liberation struggle, the petty bourgeoisie tends to divide into three main categories. Firstly, there are those who are heavily committed to colonialism and to capitalist economic and social development. These are in the main the 'officials' and

491

professional men, and agents of foreign firms and companies. Secondly, there are the 'revolutionary' petty bourgeoisie – the nationalists – who want to end colonial rule but who do not wish to see a transformation of society. They form part of the national bourgeoisie. Thirdly, there are those who 'sit on the fence', and are prepared to be passive onlookers.

In general, few members of the African bourgeoisie amassed sufficient capital to become significant in the business sector. The African bourgeoisie remains therefore largely a comprador class, sharing in some of the profits which imperialism drains from Africa. Under conditions of colonialism and neo-colonialism, it will never be encouraged sufficiently to become strong in the economic sphere since this would mean creating business competitors. The local bourgeoisie must always be subordinate partners to foreign capitalism. For this reason, it cannot achieve power as a class or govern without the close support of reactionary feudal elements within the country, or without the political, economic and military support of international capitalism.

Imperialism may foster liberation movements in colonial areas when capitalist exploitation has reached the stage of giving rise to a labour movement which seriously threatens the interests of international capitalism. By the granting of political independence to bourgeois Parties, reactionary indigenous forces can thereby be put into positions of power which enable them to cement their alliance with the international bourgeoisie. In practically every national liberation struggle, there emerge two liberation Parties. One of them is the genuine people's Party, committed not only to national liberation but to socialism. The other aims at political independence, but intends to preserve capitalist structures, and is supported by imperialism.

In the majority of the independent African states there exist embryonic elements of a rural bourgeoisie. In Ghana, large farmers and cocoa brokers come into this category. According to the 1960 census, the rural bourgeoisie number 1.4 million, while the urban middle class was estimated at 300,000. This was in a population 24 per cent of which was defined as urban. In most cases, both urban and rural bourgeoisie are not conscious of themselves as a class, though they are very much aware of their strength and importance, and conscious of the threat to their privileged positions in society by the increasing pressure of worker-peasant resistance.

In the struggle for political independence, urban workers, peasants and the national bourgeoisie, ally together to eject the colonial power. Class cleavages are temporarily blurred. But once independence is achieved, class conflicts come to the fore over the social and economic policies of the new government.

It is possible for classes to combine in the post-colonial situation, and the nature of the government is assessed by which particular class interests are dominant. Theorists arguing that proletariat and petty bourgeoisie should join together to win the peasantry, in order to attack the bourgeoisie, ignore the fact that the petty bourgeoisie will always, when it comes to the pinch, side with the bourgeoisie to preserve capitalism. It is only peasantry and proletariat working together who are wholly able to subscribe to policies of all-out socialism. Where conflict involves both political and economic interests, the economic always prevails.

The African bourgeoisie, in common with their counterpart in other parts of the world, hold the view that governments exist to protect private property, and that success is measured by wealth, the acquisition of property and social status. They set up bourgeois organizations such as clubs and professional associations on the model of those existing in the bourgeois societies of Europe and the Americas. They want politics to be confined to the struggles between various propertied groups. It is common in Africa, and in other coup areas of the world – notably Asia and Latin America – for there to be a succession of bourgeois coups d'état in a single state. The propertied fight the propertied for political supremacy. For the independent states of Africa, Asia and Latin America have a similar historical past in that they have suffered from imperialism and colonialism; and after political independence have in almost every case, been swept into the orbit of neo-colonialism. In this situation, the majority are governed by bourgeois elements who compete among themselves for political domination. For whichever group succeeds in dominating the political scene is in a position to enhance its property and status. Other factors such as regionalism and tribalism obviously enter into the struggle for power among the indigenous bourgeoisie, but the essential point remains, that these struggles take place among the propertied class, and are not struggles between classes.

The tribal formula is frequently used to obscure the class forces created in African society by colonialism. In many areas, uneven economic development under colonial rule led to a differentiation of economic functions along ethnic lines. This tendency is exploited in the interests of international capitalism.

A distinction must be made between tribes and tribalism. The clan is the extended family, and the tribe is the extended clan with the same ethnic language within a territory. There were tribes in Africa before imperialist penetration, but no 'tribalism' in the modern sense. Tribalism arose from colonialism, which exploited feudal and tribal survivals to combat the growth of national liberation movements.

The formation of nationalities was retarded as a result of colonial conquest, when the imperialists carved up Africa among themselves, disregarding geographical, linguistic and ethnic realities. The normal growth of the economy and of the class structure of African society was hindered and distorted. Patriarchal and feudal structures were artificially preserved, and all possible obstacles erected to prevent the emergence of a class-conscious proletariat.

Capitalist methods of exploitation inevitably gave birth to a proletariat, particularly in areas where mines and plantations were highly developed, as in South and East Africa, and in Congo Kinshasa. Here, workers were kept in tribal or traditional structures, and in reservations, in an attempt to prevent the growth of class consciousness.

At Independence, the colonial powers again fostered separatism and tribal differences through the encouragement of federal constitutions. Genuine independence was prevented through the operation of diverse forms of neo-colonialism.

In the era of neo-colonialism, tribalism is exploited by the bourgeois ruling classes as an instrument of power politics, and as a useful outlet for the discontent of the masses. Many of the so-called tribal conflicts in modern Africa are in reality class forces brought into conflict by the transition from colonialism to neo-colonialism. Tribalism is the result, not the cause, of underdevelopment. In the majority of 'tribal' conflicts, the source is the exploiting bourgeois or feudal minority in co-operation with imperialists and neo-colonialists seeking to promote their joint class interests. Support has tended to be withdrawn from traditional rulers and transferred to the rising urban bourgeoisie who are, under neo-colonialism, in a better position to maintain and promote the interests of international capitalism. The process assumes the appearance of a tribal confrontation, but in reality is part of the class struggle.

The emergence of tribes in any country is natural, or due to historical development. Tribes, like nationalities may always remain in a country, but it is tribalism – tribal politics – that should be fought and destroyed. Under a socialist Union Government of Africa, tribalism, not tribes, will disappear.

Certain elements among the African bourgeoisie and traditional rulers – for example, revolutionary intellectuals – may dissociate themselves from their class origin and the ideology connected with it. These are 'revolutionary outsiders', who can be absorbed into the ranks of the socialist revolution.

For the most part, however, in areas of the world where capitalist development is in its infancy, the bourgeoisie – heavily outnumbered by peasantry and proletariat – feel threatened by the rising tide of socialism. As a result, there is a close drawing together of bourgeois elite groupings, and special reliance is placed on the military. Neo-colonialist, bourgeois military coups take place to forestall or to

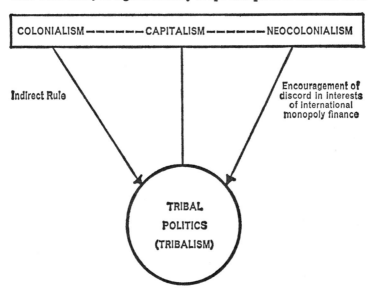

destroy the power of workers and peasants, and of socialist-oriented governments.

Such coups are strongly supported by the machinery of neo-colonialism. For imperialists and neo-colonialists seek, in their own interests, to support the privileged class which emerged under colonialism. Both indigenous bourgeoisie and neo-colonialists have common interests in prolonging their dominance by preserving the fundamental features of the colonial state apparatus. The bureaucratic bourgeoisie, in particular, is the spoilt child of neo-colonialist governments. Many African states spend ridiculously large sums of money on their bureaucrats. For example, Gabon, with a population of less than half a million has a Parliament of 65 members, each earning 165,000 francs a year. Yet the average worker in Gabon earns only 700 francs annually. In Dahomey, 60 per cent of the national income is spent on paying the salaries of government officials.

The bureaucratic bourgeoisie, the inheritors of the functions of earlier ruling classes, are closely connected with foreign firms, with the diplomats of imperialist countries, and with the African exploiting classes. Although not a cohesive elite, they are in general dedicated to the capitalist path of development, and are among the most devoted of indigenous agents of neo-colonialism. Their education and class position largely isolate them from the masses.

At Independence, their position is strengthened immeasurably by the Africanization policies of the newly-independent government, and by the tremendous increase of work entailed in the large scale economic and social planning undertaken by the new government. They provide the administrative and technical expertise required. Further, they are able to select and organize the information to be laid before ministers responsible for the formulation of policy. In this way, they play a considerable part in actual decision-making. Many top bureaucrats assume responsibilities and powers for which they are not equipped. They tend to become arrogant and isolated from the lower strata of civil servants and clerks, and submissive to foreign, neo-colonialist bureaucrats. When they exert influence on policy it is likely to be along class lines. Their education and class position make them separate from the masses, and they become the willing accomplices of local capitalists, dishonest intellectuals, ambitious army and police officers, and of neo-colonialists. Although subject always to the control of a political and military authority, they occupy an extremely strong position in the neo-colonialist state apparatus, and exert their influence in support of the ruling classes. They become in some cases, particularly under military-police dictatorships, the de facto policy makers, without being answerable to the public. This becomes particularly apparent when they act in league with foreign bureaucrats.

When reactionary military coups take place, whether or not they have been involved in planning them, they readily support the bourgeois coup-makers by carrying on the day to day work of administration, and by assisting in the drawing up and carrying out of decrees and regulations. Top bureaucrats sit on the innumerable councils, commissions of inquiry and so on which proliferate after a coup. In effect, the establishment of arbitrary military-police rule enhances their position since the reactionary new rulers are utterly dependent on them. Unlike 'civilian governments', military regimes are in a position to impose policies without having to obtain the consent of the people's representatives. They can, therefore, allow bureaucrats much greater freedom of action.

Top civil servants assist in policy making in most countries. In the USA, they change with a change of government and are very much a part of the decision-making power elite. In Britain, they are supposed to be apolitical and to serve whichever government is in power.

But in Africa, the bourgeoisie as a whole cannot be seen in isolation from imperialism, colonialism and neo-colonialism. While representing only a very small fraction of the population it is nevertheless a great danger to the African masses because of the strength it derives from its dependence on foreign bourgeois capitalism which seeks to keep the peasants and workers of Africa in a condition of perpetual subjection.

It is, in fact, impossible to separate the interests of the African bourgeoisie and those of international monopoly finance capital. The weakening of either one of them inevitably results in the weakening of the other.

The alliance between the indigenous bourgeoisie and international monopoly finance capital is being further cemented by the growing trend towards partnership between individual African governments, or regional economic organizations, and giant, imperialist, multi-national corporations. African governments, some of which claim to be pursuing a socialist path of development and 'nationalizing' key industries, are in fact merely 'participating' in them. They are combining with collective imperialism in the continuing exploitation of African workers and rural proletariat. The African government shields the corporations from the resistance of the working class, and bans strikes or becomes the strike-breaker; while the corporations strengthen their stranglehold of the African economy, secure in the knowledge that they have government protection. In fact, the African governments become the policemen of imperialist, multi-national corporations. There thus develops a common front to halt socialist advance.

It is the indigenous bourgeoisie who provide the main means by which international monopoly finance continues to plunder Africa and to frustrate the purposes of the African Revolution. The exposure and the defeat of the African bourgeoisie, therefore, provides the key to the successful accomplishment of the worker-peasant struggle to achieve total liberation and socialism, and to advance the cause of the entire world socialist revolution.

PROLETARIAT

A modern proletariat already exists in Africa, though it is relatively small in size. This is the class base for the building of socialism, and must be seen in the context of the international working class movement from which it derives much of its strength.

The emergence of the working class in Africa is associated with colonialism and with foreign capital. In most areas, the size of the proletariat remained small because of the lack of large scale industrialization. However, in countries with most developed economies, such as Egypt and South Africa, a strong working class emerged. It was in these countries, in the 1920s, where Africa's first communist parties, consisting of workers, peasants and intellectuals were formed. At about the same time, communist parties linked with the French Communist Party, were founded in Algeria, Morocco and Tunisia.

By the mid-1950s, Africa had more than ten million wage workers. Some 50 per cent of all persons in paid employment were engaged in agriculture; 40 per cent in industry and transport; and 10 per cent in civil service and in trading establishments. By 1962, it is estimated that there were 15 million workers in Africa, representing about 6 to 7 per cent of the whole population. While this percentage may appear very small, for example compared with Asia where workers are said to number approximately 100 million, it must be assessed by its performance and its potential, and in solidarity with world proletarian movements.

African workers played an important role in national liberation struggles. By strike action they succeeded in disrupting economic life and caused great embarrassment to the colonial administration. There were general strikes in Kenya, Nigeria, Ghana and Guinea in the years leading up to independence. In addition, there were throughout colonial Africa innumerable strikes which affected particular sectors of the economy. The Rand miners' strike of 1946, and the strikes in the Tanganyika sisal industry between 1957–9 are typical examples. During these strikes, and others equally effective but far too numerous to list, mass feeling was awakened, and workers became to some extent conscious of themselves as a class.

South Africa is probably the most urbanized part of Africa. In 1966 it is estimated that there were about seven million African workers living in the towns. It is because of this that some theorists argue it is possible to by-pass the stage of bourgeois democracy in South Africa and to proceed straight to socialism. An interesting consideration in this respect, is the fact that in China, the industrial working class was only one per cent of the population before the Communist Revolution. Liberation armies were based largely on the peasantry. At present, the industrial working class of China is only about 3 per cent of the total population.

It is the task of the African urban proletariat to win the peasantry to revolution by taking the revolution to the countryside. For the most part, the peasantry are as yet unorganized, and unrevolutionary. Large numbers are illiterate. But once both urban proletariat and peasants join forces in the struggle to achieve socialism, the African Revolution has in effect been won. For the African bourgeoisie and their imperialist and neo-colonialist masters cannot successfully resist their overwhelming combined strength.

In many of the African independent states, the absence of large-scale industry, and the relatively low skill and educational standards of the workers retards class consciousness. They are often non-revolutionary, and have a petty bourgeois mentality. Yet in Senegal, for example, where the working class is larger than in many other African states, and where there is 95 per cent illiteracy among male workers, and 99 per cent among women, there is a vigorous working class movement.

Under colonialism, the workers' struggle was largely directed against the foreign exploiter. It was in this sense more an anti-colonial, than a class struggle. It has, furthermore, strong racial undertones. This class-race aspect of the African workers' struggle remains under conditions of neo-colonialism, and tends to blunt the awareness of the workers to the existence of indigenous bourgeois exploitation. The workers' attack is directed against Europeans, Lebanese, Indians and others, while the indigenous reactionary exploiter is overlooked.

In neo-colonialist states where there are immigrant workers, and where unemployment is rife, a similar situation develops. The anger of workers is surreptitiously fomented and directed by the neo-colonialist puppet regime not so much against its own reactionary policies as against the 'alien' workers. It is they who are blamed for the scarcity of jobs, the shortage of houses, rising prices and so on. The result is that the African immigrant worker is victimized both by the government and by his own fellow workers. The government brings in measures to restrict immigration, to limit the opportunities of existing immigrants, and to expel certain categories. The indigenous workers, for their part, are led to believe by the government's action, that the cause of unemployment and bad living conditions is attributable in large measure to the presence of immigrant workers. Mass feeling against them is aroused, and helps to increase any already existing national and ethnic animosities. Instead of joining with immigrant workers to bring pressure on the government, many of them strongly support measures taken against them. In this they show lack of awareness of the class nature of the struggle; and the bourgeoisie benefit from the split among the ranks of the working class.

Workers are workers, and nationality, race, tribe and religion are irrelevancies in the struggle to achieve socialism.

In the context of the African socialist revolution there is no justification for regarding non-African workers as a hindrance to economic progress, and there is similarly no justification for the victimization and the expulsion of migrant African labour from one territory to another. In Africa there should be no African 'alien'. All are Africans. The enemy wall to be brought down and crushed is not the African 'alien' worker but Balkanization and the artificial territorial boundaries created by imperialism.

The migrant urban population can be a very powerful force for the spread of revolutionary socialism. The many workers who go to the cities and to other African countries to work for a period of time and then return to their homes, link the revolutionary movements of the proletariat with the countryside and with the labour movements of other states. They are an indispensable part of the revolutionary process, and the permanent mobility of the African labour force must be encouraged and organized.

Large scale migrations of people is a feature of Africa. There is on the one hand, the migration of country folk to the towns, and on the other hand, the migration of labour from one country to another. Towns are largely the product of external forces. They developed, in the main, as a result of the market economy introduced by European colonialism. Among the reasons for the migration from the countryside to the towns, are the search for employment; the desire for cash to buy manufactured goods, and to pay for the education of children; and the wish to enjoy the many amenities of town life.

There has in recent years been a great increase in the urban population of Africa. For example, the figures below show the rate of growth in three of Ghana's main cities:

	Year	Population
		(figures are approximate)
Accra	1936	38,000
	1960	338,000
Kumasi	1921	24,000
	1966	190,000
Tamale	1921	4,000
	1960	40,000

Broadly, the class structure of African towns may be said to include, the bourgeois class of professional, intellectual, bureaucratic, military, business, political and managerial elites; the schoolteachers, clergy, small business men, executives in government departments, shopkeepers; and the lower middle class strata of junior clerks, artisans, tradesmen and semi-skilled workers. Secondly, there is the working class, comprising the broad mass of petty traders, manual workers, market women, and migrant labourers. Finally, there are what may be described as the 'déclassés'. These are the beggars, prostitutes and general layabouts who form the lumpen-proletariat; and those – mostly young people – connected with petty bourgeois or workers' families, who go to the towns from the rural areas, and who usually do no work but live at the expense of their families. These young people may play an important part in the liberation struggle. They are in touch with both town and countryside, and may become effective revolutionary cadres.

Members of the bourgeois elites mix freely in clubs and societies, which cut across race and emphasize social class. The existence of class feeling is shown in the desire of many to join associations which will enhance status. The higher the educational qualifications, the higher the status and opportunities for top level employment, an overseas education being rated the highest qualification of all.

The migrant labourers bring with them their own social strata, ideologies, religions and customs. Some of them become completely submerged and absorbed within the local population. But relatively few settle permanently. The vast majority work for a few years and then return to their native home. According to the 1960 census in Ghana, only 25 per cent of the population of Takoradi were of local origin. In Kumasi the figure was 37 per cent. In Sekondi, 40 per cent only were of local origin. In 1948, over half the population of Takoradi, and 36 per cent in the case of Accra, had lived in those towns for less than five years. It is estimated that some 40 per cent of wage earners in Ghana are migrants.

Though the percentage of migrant labour among urban population elsewhere in Africa may differ substantially, wherever immigrant labourers exist they represent a vast mobile force which can become a vital factor in the African socialist revolution. They can assist the integration of workers in the revolutionary struggle and infiltrate every sector of the neo-colonialist and bourgeois economy.

Under conditions of neo-colonialism, migrant labour tends to retard the development of class consciousness and to hinder the growth of workers' organizations. Migrant labourers form their own tribal associations, which are mainly benefit societies.

Yet there was a big expansion of trade unionism in Africa after the Second World War. In many countries, trade unions participated actively in the liberation struggle, organizing strikes, boycotts and other industrial action. The development of trade union militancy was vigorously opposed by the colonial powers who tried, and sometimes succeeded in eroding the leadership by reformism, and the infiltration of Right-wing socialist ideas.

In May 1961, on the initiative of trade unions in Ghana, Guinea and Mali, the All-African Trade Union Congress was held in Casablanca, at which 45 trade union organizations and 38 countries were represented. The All-African Trade Union Federation (AATUF) was set up, founded on the principles of proletariat solidarity and internationalism. A rival trade union organization, the African Trade Union Congress (ATUC), was founded in January 1962, as the result of a conference held in Dakar attended by delegates from African organizations affiliated with the International Confederation of Free Trade Unions, and eight independent trade union organizations. No mention was made in the Charter of the Confederation of African Trade Unions of either foreign monopolies or proletariat internationalism.

The African trade union movement must be organized on a pan-African scale, be genuinely socialist oriented, and developed as an integral part of the African workers' class struggle. For this purpose, an All-African Trade Union Congress must be established to co-ordinate and direct trade union activity throughout the entire African continent. It must be quite separate from the trade union organizations of other countries, though work at the international level in close association with them.

Urbanization is at the core of social change. Therefore, industrialization, which is the main cause of urban growth, determines the social pattern. With growing industrialization, the African proletariat will increase in numbers and become more class conscious.

At present, Africa is industrially one of the least developed continents in the world. It produces one-seventh of the world's raw materials, but only one-fiftieth of the world's manufactures. The share of industry in Africa's total income is less than 14 per cent. This situation is a legacy of imperialism and colonialism, and the exploitation of Africa to serve the interests of international monopoly finance capital. But it is also a result of the continuing imperialist and capitalist exploitation of Africa through neo-colonialism.

Western monopolies still dominate about 80 per cent of the volume of African trade. A significant factor in recent times has been the rapid development of US penetration:

	1950	*1960*	*1964*
Investments:	$287 million	$925 million	$1,700 million
Exports from *USA to Africa:*	$494 million		$916 million
Imports from *Africa:*	$362 million		$1,211 million

Between 1951–55, direct US investments in Africa increased more than 2·5 times – from $313 million to $793 million. Particularly deep penetration was made into South Africa, Rhodesia and Congo Kinshasa.

The methods of neo-colonialism are economic control, in the form of 'aid', 'loans', trade and banking; the stranglehold of indigenous economies through vast international interlocking corporations; political direction through puppet governments; social penetration through the cultivation of an indigenous bourgeoisie, the imposition of 'defence' agreements, and the setting up of military and air bases; ideological expansion through the mass communications media of press, radio and television – the emphasis being on anti-Communism; the fomenting of discord between countries and tribes; and through collective imperialism – notably the politico-economic and military co-operation of Rhodesia, South Africa and Portugal.

Neo-colonialism, by its very nature, cannot overcome its own problems and contradictions. Imperialism is moribund capitalism;

neo-colonialism is moribund colonialism. Both sharpen the contradictions in their nature, which eventually lead to their destruction. Neo-colonialism cannot prop up the governments of the 'new bourgeoisie', and promote stable economic development when the objective is profit for the foreign investor. Therefore, the indigenous bourgeoisie can never become a really safe governing class, and the need arises for more and more forceful intervention from external interests, and repression from within. This state of affairs accelerates the emergence of a really revolutionary class struggle.

The granting of economic 'aid' from capitalist countries is one of the most insidious ways in which neo-colonialism hinders economic progress in the developing world, retarding industrialization and delaying the development of a large proletariat. Only 10 per cent of US 'aid' to Africa is spent on industrialization, and most of this is in those areas regarded as 'safe' for capitalism. In contrast, 70 per cent of aid from socialist countries is spent on industrialization and the organization of profitable production. Interest rates on loans from capitalist countries vary from between $6\frac{1}{2}$ to 8 per cent, whereas socialist creditors charge only $2\frac{1}{2}$ per cent. Aid from socialist countries is used mainly for state projects. This again is in striking contrast to 'aid' from the West, which is almost entirely in the private sector.

France spends something like two thousand million francs on 'aid' to the francophone countries in Africa. These two thousand million are the means by which France maintains very close cultural, political and economic ties with them, for they are large markets for French exports. In fact, the 'aid' is considered by French governments to be 'good investment'.

A considerable proportion of money disbursed as bilateral 'aid' from the West either does not leave the donor country at all, the 'aid' being provided in the form of goods, or returns in a relatively short period as payment for additional exports, or in other ways. Of every £100 of bilateral 'aid' disbursed by the UK in the period 1964–66, £72·5 was 'aid' tied to the supply of British goods, or resulted in direct spending on British goods and services.

Multilateral 'aid' similarly serves mainly to improve the economic position of the donor countries. It has been estimated that the UK has secured export orders of over £116 for every £100 of its multilateral 'aid', due largely to the operations of the International Development Agency (IDA). For example, a recent Whitehall study on the subject has calculated that for every £100 contributed to IDA by the UK in 1964–66, IDA spent about £150 on UK goods.

Indeed, many projects accomplished through foreign 'aid' are designed to help the donor's balance of payments rather than the recipient's economic development. The recipient is burdened not only with a costly loan to repay, but also sometimes with uneconomic projects, and with political and economic strings which hamper independent development, and positively retard economic growth.

Credits are granted by capitalist states to countries of Africa, Asia and Latin America, so that they can be equipped with the infrastructure necessary for their further exploitation by private monopolists. The aim is political as well as economic. It seeks to block socialist advance by winning over the indigenous bourgeoisie, by giving them an interest in the business; and at the same time to extend the stranglehold of international monopoly finance on the economies of the developing world.

The rural proletariat – small farmers and plantation workers producing cotton, sisal, cocoa, coffee, rubber, citrus fruits and other crops, which bring them within the orbit of international trade and industry, are strategic links in the chain of African proletariat struggle. Imperialism in its neo-colonialist phase, however, draws the bulk of its profits from its grip over the advanced sectors of production such as mining, manufacturing, commerce, retail trade, fisheries, and transport. About 90 per cent of all western capital invested in Africa is sunk into enterprises connected with these sectors, and it is in these key sectors where the industrial proletariat – the indispensable labour force for the continued existence of neo-colonialism – is in a position to spearhead the socialist revolution.

Attempts have been made to deny the existence of a working class in Africa. In areas where it has been impossible to ignore its existence – such as the mining areas of South Africa, Congo Kinshasa and Zambia – strenuous efforts have been made to integrate it within the neo-colonialist, capitalist system of exploitation. This is done by fostering the growth of trade unions under reformist leadership, and by granting a certain measure of 'welfare' benefits. In some parts of Africa, specially in the highly developed mining areas, Africanization policies are pursued to placate workers, and wages and salaries of Africans are brought closer to expatriate levels. This has had the effect in some cases of making the workers less likely to indulge in revolutionary activities.

The tendency in the transitional period between capitalism and socialism is embourgeoisement. The working class vision of socialism during this period may be blurred by the corruption of the 'welfare state'. In these conditions, the worker becomes a well fed Philistine and turns towards reaction and conservatism. Socialist revolution then becomes a minor issue.

Economically and industrially, Europe and the USA are ready and poised for socialism. There are the necessary material ingredients which could make socialism possible overnight. In the USA when automation and cybernation aided by nuclear energy reach their highest form of development, the forces of production will have been developed to a point at which there could be the classless society which Marx predicted could come only under communism. But although the USA is at present one of the most affluent and industrialized countries in the world, it is at the same time one of the most socially and politically backward.

A part of the working class of Europe and the USA had identified itself with capitalism. Strata of workers have become embourgeoised, and have thus weakened the working class forces for socialist revolution. In 1968, some ten million French workers went on strike and practically paralysed the government, and yet, they were unable to achieve revolutionary change.

Throughout the world, student protest has become an increasingly prominent feature of contemporary times. But students suffer a double alienation. They are alienated from the Establishment, and in many cases from their own families; but more important, they are alienated from the working class which should make use of their efforts in the revolutionary struggle.

In Britain, English manual workers who vote Conservative provide the Party with nearly half its electoral strength. Economic affluence, or status aspirations induce many members of the working class to claim middle class membership. In the so-called 'welfare state', many working class live like the lower middle class. Economic satisfaction leads to middle class identification, which in its turn results in conservative voting.

In this situation, extension of voting rights to the mass of the population has not so much reduced the power of the ruling class, as caused the radicalism of the working class to decline. The tendency for some working class movements in capitalist societies to confine their activities only to trade unionism is a danger to socialist advance.

While conditions of embourgeoisement exist among the working class of capitalist countries an added responsibility rests on the exploited peoples of Africa, Asia and Latin America to promote the world's socialist revolution. In this process, the African proletariat has a vital and strategic part to play as the African Revolution gains momentum.

In Africa, the peasantry is by far the largest contingent of the
working class, and potentially the main force for socialist revolution.
But it is dispersed, unorganized, and for the most part unrevolutionary. It must be awakened and it must be led by its natural class allies
– the proletariat and the revolutionary intelligentsia.

At the top of the class structure in rural areas are the traditional
feudal landlords who live on the exploitation of the peasants; and
the capitalist landlords – many of whom are absentee – who are
dependent on the exploitation of wage labour. Among the latter –
who form part of the rural bourgeoisie – are the clergy of various
sects and religions who live on the feudal and capitalist exploitation
of peasants. The rural bourgeoisie own relatively large farms. They
own capital, exploit wage labour, and for the most part specialize in
export or 'cash' crops. The small farmers, who may be classed as
petty rural bourgeoisie, possess little capital and cultivate land which
they either own or rent. They employ members of their family or
clan and/or wage labour. If the land is rented, the normal practice
is for the petty farmer to retain about two-thirds of the proceeds of
the farm for himself, and to pay one-third to the owner of the land.
Below the petty rural bourgeoisie in the rural strata, are the peasants,
those who cultivate negligible areas of land, and are often forced to
sell their labour power to become seasonal workers. Finally, there
are the agricultural labourers, the rural proletariat, who own nothing
but their labour.

Thus the composition of the agrarian social strata consists of two
major groups – the exploiting group and the exploited. These
groups can each be sub-divided into smaller groups:

The *exploiting* classes consist of
    (1) plantation owners
    (2) 'absentee' landlords
    (3) farmers (comparatively large property owners)
    (4) petty farmers.

The *exploited* classes are:
    (1) peasants
    (2) rural proletariat.

The plantation owners are for the most part aliens (e.g. UAC in
Nigeria, Cameroun and Congo Kinshasa and white minority settlers
in South Africa and Rhodesia). These plantations are extensions of

monopolies in Africa. The system of exploitation here conforms to the basic law of capitalism. The farm or plantation labourers are exploited. This exploitation of African workers is made possible by the low level of the standard of living of the workers which enables the monopolies to pay low nominal wages. But due to the ever rising prices of consumer goods, the real wages of these labourers are always declining. Hence the conflict between labour and capital is always grave. The foreign monopolies are alien absentee owners. But there also exist local absentee owners.

The local 'absentee' landlords are mainly African land proprietors who live in the urban areas in luxury, while with the aid of capital, they control vast stretches of land in the rural areas. They live by exploiting the farm worker. The special peculiarity of exploitation applied here is that of payment in kind. Thus the farm labourer does not get guaranteed wages. He almost lives from hand to mouth. Hence the struggle between capital and labour here is as intense as that on the plantations. In many cases the absentee landlord also exploits the worker in the city through exorbitant house rents.

Another class in this sector of exploiters is the farmer. The farmer is normally an indigenous landowner, sometimes as large or larger than the 'absentee' owner. Unlike the absentee owner he stays on the farm with his family. He is prosperous due to the fact that he owns fertile land, more farm implements and is therefore in a position to hire the labour of others. Farmers are always outstanding personalities in their respective areas, and usually have large families. Mostly, they are semi-feudal in methods of production, and sometimes also practise the system of payment in kind. They often owe allegiance to another big village chief or elder. The cultivation of export crops preoccupies them.

Just below the farmers in the rural social strata is the class of petty farmers. The petty farmer is a small property owner. He also owns a few implements and livestock. He is in the Marxist sense of revolutionary behaviour, unstable and vacillating. He mostly uses the labour of his family, and hires seasonal labour during times of tilling and harvest. He also aspires to become a prosperous farmer, to be able to maintain regular labourers and to own large property. Mostly he is preoccupied with the production of local products for home consumption.

The neighbour of the petty farmer is the peasant. The peasant is the smallest property owner. His life is governed by insecurity. He works a little land with or without livestock. He is largely dependent on natural forces; good weather brings him a favourable harvest;

bad weather may ruin him and force him to become a paid agri-cultural labourer working on a large plantation or farm. Due to the ever rising cost of living, for example, soaring prices of manufactured goods, the difficulties of the peasant grow. He produces practically all he requires at home, and seldom requires exchange. The peasantry can be a revolutionary class if led by the urban and rural proletariat.

The rural proletariat are workers in the Marxist sense of the word. They are part of the working class and the most revolutionary of the African rural strata.

It is the revolutionary potential of the rural strata of peasants and agricultural labourers which must be developed for it is they who will provide the revolution with its main strength. It is the task of revolutionary cadres in the first place to awaken them to the realities of their economic potential, and to win them and the petty farmers over to socialist forms of organization of agricultural production and distribution. This may be done through the development of various types of agricultural co-operatives, which are essential if the transition from private agriculture based on small-scale production to modern, mechanized, socialist agriculture is to be accomplished. Market co-operatives already operate in many African countries with great success; though credit co-operatives are less general, due to the shortage of funds. But by far the highest form of co-operation in agriculture is the production co-operative, which organizes the administration and mechanism of agricultural production. This kind of co-operative is in its infancy, largely because of a lack of skilled personnel to operate it, and the scarcity of agricultural machinery. It can be abused if not supervised by a progressive government. Already, in neo-colonialist states, the co-operative movement largely serves the interests of the rural bourgeoisie and the monopoly capitalists. The neo-colonialist elites exploit the relative isolation and cultural backwardness of the peasantry, and so induces it to accept their political dominance.

It is in the countryside where those feudal relics which still exist, are mainly to be found. In parts, the peasantry lives under conditions little different from pre-colonial and colonial periods. They bear heavy tax burdens, and in some areas are compelled to do forced labour. If they migrate to the towns they usually fall victim to colonial and neo-colonial exploitation.

The African peasantry, like the peasantry of Asia and Latin America, has for a long time suffered from feudalism and from imperialist-capitalist exploitation. From Cairo to Cape Town and from the Cape Verde Islands to Kenya and Zanzibar the African peasant's situation and problems are practically the same. The peasantry must be liberated from semi-feudal and capitalist relationships. Agriculture must be developed from small-scale production to a modern agriculture based on production co-operatives able to utilize the latest machinery and techniques.

At present, the African peasantry is, in general, based on the petty ownership of the means of production, except in those parts where there is subsistence farming and a system of communal land ownership. In West Africa, the prevalence of small-scale commodity production is the core of the agrarian problem. In Ghana, 97 per cent of farms have a surface area of less than four hectares; and 60 per cent of them have less than two hectares. Small scale private farming is an obstacle to the spread of socialist ideas. It makes for conservatism and acquisitiveness and the development of a bourgeois mentality.

Under colonialism, and also in neo-colonialist states, the government makes great use of the peasantry to form the rank and file of army and police. They are said to be 'more loyal'. In this, they exploit the illiteracy and qualities of submissiveness and conservatism characteristic of unawakened peasantry throughout the world.

During the national liberation struggle, the peasantry are pro-independence and against feudalism when they are led by political movements created in the towns by trade union leaders, workers and revolutionary intellectuals. For the peasantry, if it is to succeed in socialist revolutionary struggle, needs a class ally. In areas of the world where socialist revolutionary struggles have resulted in the successful overthrow of bourgeois governments – in China, Cuba, Vietnam, Korea – the peasantry, in alliance with other class forces, have been led by Marxist Parties. The close links between the proletariat and peasantry are analagous to the links between the urban and the rural guerrilla. Each is an integral part of the socialist revolutionary struggle, and one cannot achieve final victory without the other.

In Africa, the socialist revolutionary struggle must be based on the peasantry and rural proletariat. They form the overwhelming majority of the population and their future lies with socialism. Freedom fighters operate in their midst, and are dependent on them for recruits and for supplies.

The countryside is the bastion of the revolution. It is the revolutionary battlefield in which the peasantry in alliance with their natural class allies – proletariat and revolutionary intelligentsia – are the driving force for socialist construction and transformation.

The highest point of political action, when a revolution attains its excellence, is when the proletariat – comprising workers and peasants – under the leadership of a vanguard party the principles and motivations of which are based on scientific socialism, succeeds in overthrowing all other classes.

The basis of a revolution is created when the organic structure and conditions within a given society have aroused mass consent and mass desire for positive action to change or transform that society. While there is no hard and fast dogma for socialist revolution, because no two sets of historical conditions and circumstances are exactly alike, experience has shown that under conditions of class struggle, socialist revolution is impossible without the use of force. Revolutionary violence is a fundamental law in revolutionary struggles. The privileged will not, unless compelled, surrender power. They may grant reforms, but will not yield an inch when basic pillars of their entrenched positions are threatened. They can only be overthrown by violent revolutionary action.

Great historical advance is seldom, if ever, achieved without high cost in effort and lives; and those who argue that the transition from capitalism to socialism can be accomplished without the use of force are under a delusion. The qualitative change implicit in the socialist revolution is far more profound than that which was involved in the transition from feudalism to capitalism. Socialist revolutionaries seek a complete and fundamental transformation of society, and the total abolition of privileged classes; whereas the decline of feudalism merely ushered in a new stratification of society in which money, and not titles and land, became the basis of power and privilege. Socialist revolution opposes all concepts of elitism, and ends class antagonisms and racism. The socialist revolutionaries are fighting for a type of state which really expresses the aspirations of the masses, and which ensures their participation in every aspect of government.

Under capitalism, freedom is the right to do what the law permits, in the interests of the ruling bourgeois class. The more capitalism develops, the more anarchic it becomes; and socialist revolution is the logical and inevitable result.

Where capitalist development and industrialization is in its infancy, and the bourgeoisie only represents a very small section of the population, socialist revolution can be achieved by workers and peasants seizing power by means of revolutionary action. Through socialist revolutionary leadership, Africa can proceed from bourgeois-capitalist ownership of property to arrive at socialist-communist ownership of property and the means of production and distribution. But in the revolutionary struggle, no reliance can be placed on any section of the bourgeoisie or petty bourgeoisie. Though these elements may join in revolutionary action during the struggle for national liberation, they will always, when it comes to the pinch, try to block the creation of a socialist state. They are committed to capitalism, and dependent for their very existence on the support of imperialism and neo-colonialism. It is only when the bourgeois ruling class in neo-colonialist states is overthrown by class-based socialist revolution, that fundamental changes in society can be accomplished.

Certain factors advance the process of socialist revolution. Foremost among them is capitalist development and industrialization, which leads to an increase of urban workers – the sector of the population which generates the leadership of the proletarian revolution. Among other factors, are the desertion of the ruling class by the intellectuals; inefficient governmental machinery, and a politically-inept ruling bourgeois class. The example and the help of other socialist revolutions also assist the process. Finally, bitter class antagonism, and race-class problems, have the effect of accelerating the advance to socialism.

In the twentieth century, most forcible seizures of political power have occurred in areas of the world which have a relatively low level of industrialization – namely areas which have a history of imperialism, colonialism and neo-colonialism. These violent changes in the status quo cannot be explained in terms of the power struggles of elite groups. They represent actions of whole classes. In the case of socialist revolution, the seizure of power is by the working class; but in reactionary coups d'état, the bourgeoisie is further entrenched either by the ejection of a socialist-oriented government, or by a power struggle between different sections from within the existing bourgeois framework.

The economic, political and social ferment of Africa, Asia and Latin America, must be seen in the context of the world socialist revolution. For the world revolutionary process today unites three main streams: the socialist world system, the liberation movements of the peoples of Africa, Asia and Latin America, and the working class movement in the industrialized, capitalist countries.

The peoples of the less industrialized areas of the world are in a good strategic position to advance in the direction of socialist revolution as a result of their experience of imperialism, colonialism and neo-colonialism. They see the issues clearly, since productive and distributive processes are not obscured or blurred by the trappings and diversions of the capitalist 'welfare state', and capitalist corruption.

The cause of international proletarian revolution is part and parcel of the liberation struggles of the developing world. The class antagonisms in the contemporary world are highly concentrated in these areas. They have become the storm centres of world revolution, dealing direct and deadly blows at imperialism.

The embourgeoisement of certain sections of the international working class and the economism of socialist and working class leadership in some areas, has made the socialist revolutionary struggle in the developing world of even greater importance in the world socialist revolutionary process. Thus, in some respects, the socialist revolutionary struggle has developed a class-race complexion. But while it would be harmful not to recognize the emergence of a racial factor in the revolutionary struggle, it must not be allowed to confuse or obscure the fundamental issue of socialist revolution, which is the class struggle.

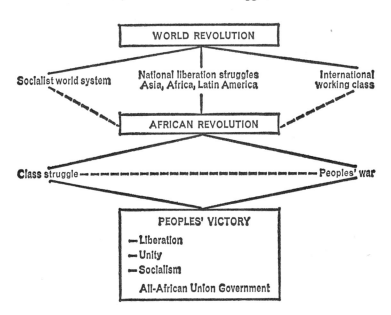

The developing world is not a homogeneous bloc opposed to imperialism. The concept of the 'Third World' is illusory. At present, parts of it lie under imperialist domination. The struggle against imperialism takes place both within and outside the imperialist world. It is a struggle between socialism and capitalism, not between a so-called 'Third World' and imperialism. Class struggle is fundamental in its analysis. Furthermore, it is not possible to build socialism in the developing world in isolation from the world socialist system.

CONCLUSION

The African Revolution, while still concentrating its main effort on the destruction of imperialism, colonialism and neo-colonialism, is aiming at the same time to bring about a radical transformation of society. It is no longer a question of whether African Independent States should pursue a capitalist or non-capitalist path of development. The choice has already been made by the workers and peasants of Africa. They have chosen liberation and unification; and this can only be achieved through armed struggle under socialist direction. For the political unification of Africa and socialism are synonymous. One cannot be achieved without the other.

'Peoples' capitalism', 'enlightened capitalism', 'class peace', 'class harmony' are all bourgeois capitalist attempts to deceive the workers and peasants, and to poison their minds. A 'non-capitalist road', pursued by a 'united front of progressive forces', as some suggest, is not even practical politics in contemporary Africa. There are only two ways of development open to an Independent African State. Either it must remain under imperialist domination via capitalism and neo-colonialism; or it must pursue a socialist path by adopting the principles of scientific socialism. It is unrealistic to assert that because industrialization is in its infancy, and a strong proletariat is only beginning to emerge, that it is not possible to establish a socialist state. History has shown how a relatively small proletariat, if it is well organized and led, can awaken the peasantry and trigger off socialist revolution. In a neo-colonialist situation, there is no half-way to socialism. Only policies of all-out socialism can end capitalist-imperialist exploitation.

Socialism can only be achieved through class struggle. In Africa, the internal enemy – the reactionary bourgeoisie – must be exposed as exploiters and parasites, and as collaborators with imperialists and neo-colonialists on whom they largely depend for the maintenance of their positions of power and privilege. The African bourgeoisie provides a bridge for continued imperialist and neo-colonialist domination and exploitation. The bridge must be destroyed. This can be done by worker-peasant solidarity organized and directed by a vanguard socialist revolutionary Party. When the indigenous bourgeoisie and imperialism and neo-colonialism are defeated, both the internal and the external enemies of the African Revolution will have been overcome, and the aspirations of the African people fulfilled.

As in other areas of the world where socialist revolution is based largely on the peasantry, African revolutionary cadres have a tremendous task ahead of them. Urban and rural proletariat must be won to the revolution, and the revolution taken to the countryside. It is only when the peasantry have been politically awakened and won to the revolution that freedom fighters – on whom the revolution largely depends in the armed phase – will be able to develop and to expand their areas of operation. At the same time, the two main internal props of bourgeois power – the bureaucracy and the police and professional armed forces must be politicized.

The ultimate victory of the revolutionary forces depends on the ability of the socialist revolutionary Party to assess the class position in society, and to see which classes and groups are for, and which against, the revolution. The Party must be able to mobilize and direct the vast forces for socialist revolution already existing, and to awaken and stimulate the immense revolutionary potential which is at present lying dormant.

But as long as violence continues to be used against the African peoples, the Party cannot achieve its objectives without the use of all forms of political struggle, including armed struggle. If armed struggle is to be waged effectively, it also, like the Party, must be centrally organized and directed. An All-African Military High Command under the political direction of the All-African working class Party would then be able to plan unified strategy and tactics, and thus deliver the final blows at imperialism, colonialism, neo-colonialism, and settler minority regimes.

Armed resistance is not a new phenomenon in Africa. For hundreds of years, Africans fought against colonialist intrusion though these heroic struggles have received scant attention in the histories of Africa compiled largely by foreign bourgeois writers. Indeed, it may be said that Africans have never ceased to resist imperialist penetration and domination, though the resistance became for the most part non-violent as imperialism intensified its suppression and exploitation. For a time, when colonialism was in its hey-day, it seemed on the surface as though African resistance had been finally overcome, and that the continent would remain indefinitely under foreign economic and political domination. But resistance was always simmering just below the surface, and after the Second World War, re-emerged in a new active form in the struggles for national liberation. Though some of the liberation struggles were accomplished successfully without resort to arms, others were achieved only after years of bitter fighting.

But political independence did not bring to an end economic oppression and exploitation. Nor did it end foreign political interference. The neo-colonialist period begins when international monopoly finance capital, working through the indigenous bourgeoisie, attempts to secure an even tighter stranglehold over the economic life of the continent than was exercised during the colonial period.

Under neo-colonialism a new form of violence is being used against the peoples of Africa. It takes the form of indirect political domination through the indigenous bourgeoisie and puppet governments teleguided and marionetted by neo-colonialists; direct

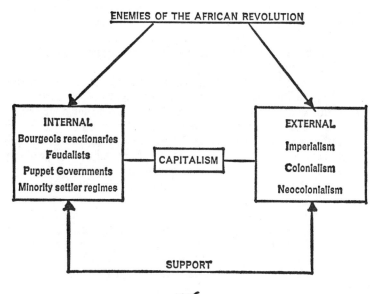

516

economic exploitation through an extension of the operations of giant interlocking corporations; and through all manner of other insidious ways such as the control of mass communications media, and ideological penetration.

In these circumstances, the need for armed struggle has arisen once more. For the liberation and unification of Africa cannot be achieved by consent, by moral precept or moral conquest. It is only through the resort to arms that Africa can rid itself once and for all of remaining vestiges of colonialism, and of imperialism and neo-colonialism; and a socialist society be established in a free and united continent. In this the African masses have the support and assistance of the socialist world.

The African revolutionary struggle is not an isolated one. It not only forms part of the world socialist revolution, but must be seen in the context of the Black Revolution as a whole. In the USA, the Caribbean, and wherever Africans* are oppressed, liberation struggles are being fought. In these areas, the Black man is in a condition of domestic colonialism, and suffers both on the grounds of class and of colour.

The core of the Black Revolution is in Africa, and until Africa is united under a socialist government, the Black man throughout the world lacks a national home. It is around the African people's struggles for liberation and unification that African or Black culture will take shape and substance. Africa is *one* continent, *one* people, and *one* nation. The notion that in order to have a nation it is necessary for there to be a common language, a common territory and a common culture, has failed to stand the test of time or the scrutiny of scientific definition of objective reality. Common territory, language and culture may in fact be present in a nation, but the existence of a nation does not necessarily imply the presence of all three. Common territory and language alone may form the basis of a nation. Similarly, common territory plus common culture may be the basis. In some cases, only one of the three applies. A state may exist on a multi-national basis. The community of economic life is the major feature within a nation, and it is the economy which holds together the people living in a territory. It is on this basis that the new Africans recognize themselves as potentially one nation, whose dominion is the entire African continent.

The total liberation and the unification of Africa under an

* All peoples of African descent, whether they live in North or South America, the Caribbean, or in any other part of the world are Africans and belong to the African nation.

All-African socialist government must be the primary objective of all Black revolutionaries throughout the world. It is an objective which, when achieved, will bring about the fulfilment of the aspirations of Africans and people of African descent everywhere. It will at the same time advance the triumph of the international socialist revolution, and the onward progress towards world communism, under which, every society is ordered on the principle of – from each according to his ability, to each according to his needs.

CONCLUSION

The immense resources of Africa can only be fully utilized to raise the standard of living of the masses if our continent is totally liberated from all forms of oppression and exploitation, and if our economy is developed on a continental basis. The essential pre-requisite is socialist planning within the framework of political unification.

If the independent African states cannot come together peacefully into such a union, then armed force must be used to achieve our socialist revolutionary objectives. It must be directed against those states and elites which still resist the processes of the African Revolution. Colonialist and neo-colonialist governments, racist settler regimes, and privileged groups in our society, can be tolerated no longer. The neo-colonialist puppet governments are even more insufferable than the governments of territories still under direct colonial rule, since they represent the exploitation and oppression of African by African, and the interests of international monopoly finance working through the indigenous bourgeoisie.

The African Revolution has already entered the armed phase, but the struggle lacks a securely liberated and sufficiently strong territorial base, adequate political and military cohesion, and ideological clarity. Unified action requires an ideology based on a correct analysis of the

519

revolutionary situation. Top priority throughout the struggle must therefore be given to mass ideological education and training.

Just as national liberation can never be considered as an end in itself, so also must the struggle for the total liberation and unification of Africa never become merely an expression of bourgeois nationalism. Attempts by reactionaries, indigenous and foreign, who appear to encourage liberation and unification movements in order to gain control of them to perpetuate capitalism and to block the socialist transformation of our society, must be exposed and defeated.

The formation of an All-African High Command, an All-African political vanguard party, and an All-African Executive Council as a first step in the establishment of a socialist All-African Union Government, is more urgent than ever before to give unified political and military direction to our struggle, and to combat increasing imperialist and neo-colonialist aggression. At the same time, and as an integral part of our Pan-African planning, the strategy and tactics of freedom fighter movements and organizations must be co-ordinated and combined, and their operations extended. Through the guerrilla camps, deep in the forests, may well emerge some of the new leadership which Africa so badly needs.

The African people, in solidarity with comrades in every part of the world, have the means, the ability and the determination to banish once and for all, imperialism, neocolonialism, settler minority rule, and all forms of oppression from our continent. A unified and socialist society in which the African Personality will find full expression can and must be constructed. There is victory for us.

Bucarest
15 October 1971

INDEX

Entente States, 298–9

Eritrea, 332

Ethiopia (Abyssinia), 21, 35, 126–7, 210, 213, 215, 220, 230, 234, 245, 248, 251, 257–60, 263, 272, 276, 282, 284–5, 290, 468

Europe, Europeans, 19, 22, 28, 30, 34, 36–8, 54, 76, 82, 205, 208–14 passim, 223–6 passim, 231, 240, 263, 267, 273–4, 282, 287–8, 321, 324, 328, 333, 342, 346, 351–5 passim, 358–9, 365, 399, 440, 442–3, 448, 450–1, 462, 473, 493, 499–500, 506; East European countries, 327, 333

European Economic Community (EEC), 219–21, 223, 225, 231, 307, 406, 451

Evening News (see *Accra Evening News*)

Ex-Servicemen's Union (Accra), 55, 60, 90, 121

Fanon, Franz, 435

Fanti Confederation (1868), 109

FAO (UN Food and Agricultural Organization), 412

Far East(ern), 318, 320

Fashoda, 20

Federal Bureau of Investigation (FBI), 332

Ferry, Jules, 19

Finland, 321

Firestone Rubber Company, 414

First Africanist Conference (1962), 206–17

First Five Year Development Plan, 181, 395, 406

First World War, 21, 31

Flagstaff House, 173–4

FLING, 454

FLN (Algerian), 138, 469, 471

Force Publique, 145

Foreign Exchange Committee, 200

Foreign Jurisdiction Act (1890), 29

Formosa, 325

Fort Knox, 237

France, French, 15–16, 18–21 passim, 32, 35, 45, 214, 218–19, 221, 223, 235, 257–8, 264, 289, 293, 303, 315, 318, 366, 416, 443, 451, 461, 469, 471–2, 498, 504, 506

Francophone (Africa), 221, 416, 473, 504

French Community, 218–9, 365, 473

French Indo-China, 16

Ga State, 54; Council, 85–6, 92

Gabon, 219, 259, 324, 462, 495–6

Gambia, 21, 215, 303

Garfield Todd, 359

Garvey, Marcus, 422

General Assembly (UN), 356

Geneva, 288, 306, 412, 459

Germany, German, 19–20, 93, 216, 223, 258; East (GDR), 325, 462; Voice of, 458; West, 324–5, 416, 451, 461

Ghana (Gold Coast), Ghanaians, 21, 30, 43, 47, 52, 54–5, 58, 70, 73, 75–8 passim, 81–4, 86, 88, 90–91, 95, 98, 100–1, 103–5, 107–8, 111, 113, 118–20, 125–7, 132, 134–5, 138, 141–6 passim, 148, 150, 153, 156–7, 159–64 passim, 166–7, 169, 174, 181–6 passim, 188–201 passim, 204, 207, 209, 211, 217, 229–30, 233–4, 242, 245, 259–60, 263, 265–6, 269, 272, 280, 290, 293–4, 298–9, 302–3, 306,